Public Relations Campaigns
An Integrated Approach

Regina M. Luttrell

Syracuse University, New York

Luke W. Capizzo

University of Maryland, College Park

$SAGE

Los Angeles | London | New Delhi
Singapore | Washington DC | Melbourne

SAGE

FOR INFORMATION:

SAGE Publications, Inc.
2455 Teller Road
Thousand Oaks, California 91320
E-mail: order@sagepub.com

SAGE Publications Ltd.
1 Oliver's Yard
55 City Road
London, EC1Y 1SP
United Kingdom

SAGE Publications India Pvt. Ltd.
B 1/I 1 Mohan Cooperative Industrial Area
Mathura Road, New Delhi 110 044
India

SAGE Publications Asia-Pacific Pte. Ltd.
3 Church Street
#10–04 Samsung Hub
Singapore 049483

Acquisitions Editor: Terri Accomazzo
Content Development Editor: Anna Villarruel
Editorial Assistant: Erik Helton & Sarah Wilson
Production Editor: Nevair Kabakian
Copy Editor: Michelle Ponce
Typesetter: Hurix Digital
Proofreader: Jeff Bryant
Indexer: Jeanne Busemeyer
Cover Designer: Michael Dubowe
Marketing Manager: Allison Henry

Copyright © 2019 by SAGE Publications, Inc.

All rights reserved. No part of this book may be reproduced or utilized in any form or by any means, electronic or mechanical, including photocopying, recording, or by any information storage and retrieval system, without permission in writing from the publisher.

Printed in the United States of America.

Library of Congress Cataloging-in-Publication Data

Names: Luttrell, Regina. | Capizzo, Luke W., author.

Title: Public relations campaigns : an integrated approach / Regina M. Luttrell, Syracuse University, New York, Luke W. Capizzo.

Description: First Edition. | Thousand Oaks : SAGE Publications, [2018] | Includes bibliographical references and index.

Identifiers: LCCN 2017048146 | ISBN 9781506332512 (pbk. : alk. paper)

Subjects: LCSH: Public relations. | Public relations–Management.

Classification: LCC HM1221 .L878 2018 | DDC 659.2–dc23 LC record available at https://lccn.loc.gov/2017048146

This book is printed on acid-free paper.

18 19 20 21 22 10 9 8 7 6 5 4 3 2 1

Public Relations Campaigns

SAGE was founded in 1965 by Sara Miller McCune to support the dissemination of usable knowledge by publishing innovative and high-quality research and teaching content. Today, we publish over 900 journals, including those of more than 400 learned societies, more than 800 new books per year, and a growing range of library products including archives, data, case studies, reports, and video. SAGE remains majority-owned by our founder, and after Sara's lifetime will become owned by a charitable trust that secures our continued independence.

Los Angeles | London | New Delhi | Singapore | Washington DC | Melbourne

Brief Contents

FOREWORD		xvii
PREFACE		xx
ACKNOWLEDGMENTS		xxvi
ABOUT THE AUTHORS		xxvii
INTRODUCTION:	Campaigns in the Professional Public Relations Context	1
CHAPTER 1	Introduction to Integrated Campaigns	14
CHAPTER 2	Strategic Communication Campaign Fundamentals	25
CHAPTER 3	Understanding PESO	40
CHAPTER 4	Research, Part 1: Diagnosis and Developmental Research	54
CHAPTER 5	Research, Part 2: Goals	77
CHAPTER 6	Objectives	92
CHAPTER 7	Strategies	110
CHAPTER 8	Tactics	131
CHAPTER 9	Implementation	149
CHAPTER 10	Reporting and Evaluation	166
CHAPTER 11	Formulating an Integrated Campaign—Case Studies	184
APPENDIX		222
GLOSSARY		246
REFERENCES		254
INDEX		267

Detailed Contents

FOREWORD	xvii
PREFACE	xx
WHY INTEGRATED CAMPAIGNS? WHY NOW?	xx
ORGANIZATION OF THE BOOK	xxi
ACKNOWLEDGMENTS	xxvi
ABOUT THE AUTHORS	xxvii

INTRODUCTION: Campaigns in the Professional Public Relations Context   1

PUBLIC RELATIONS THEORIES AND PRINCIPLES	2
Excellence Theory	2
Systems Theory	3
Diffusion Theory	4
Framing Theory	5
Agenda Setting & Agenda Building Theories	6
Situational Crisis Communication Theory	7
Two-step Flow Model	7
MODELS OF PUBLIC RELATIONS PRACTICE	9
Press Agentry	9
Public Information	9
Two-way Asymmetrical	9
Two-way Symmetrical	10
PUBLIC RELATIONS PLANNING MODELS	10
R-A-C-E, R-O-P-E, or R-O-S-I-E	10
ROSTIR: Research, Objectives, Strategies, Tactics, Implementation & Reporting	11
Communication Goals	11
PULLING IT ALL TOGETHER	12
THINK CRITICALLY	13
KEY TERMS	13
CONCEPT CASE: EQUALITY TODAY	13

CHAPTER 1   Introduction to Integrated Campaigns   14

A NEED FOR NEW PUBLIC RELATIONS PLANNING MODELS	15
Emerging Models	15
THE SIX STEPS OF ROSTIR	16
THE VALUE OF PUBLIC RELATIONS PLANNING MODELS	16
CONCLUSION	20

THINK CRITICALLY	20
KEY TERMS	20
CONCEPT CASE: INTRODUCING EQUALITY TODAY	21
CASE STUDY: "SEIZE THE HOLIDAYS" WITH KRUSTEAZ: A VIRTUAL BAKING EVENT	21
Research/Diagnosis	21
Objectives	22
Strategies	22
Tactics	22
Earned	*23*
Shared	*23*
Owned	*23*
Implementation	23
Reporting/Evaluating	23
Theories	24
Models	24

CHAPTER 2   Strategic Communication Campaign Fundamentals   25

WHY WE PLAN	26
ELEMENTS OF A STRATEGIC PLAN	28
Research, Diagnosis, and Goal Setting	29
Objectives	29
Strategies	30
Tactics	30
Implementation	32
Reporting/Evaluation	32
Budget	33
PUTTING IT ALL TOGETHER	33
CONCLUSION	34
THINK CRITICALLY	35
KEY TERMS	35
CONCEPT CASE: MISSION-DRIVEN PLANNING FOR EQUALITY TODAY	35
CASE STUDY: OSCAR MAYER'S WAKEY, WAKEY, EGGS AND BAKEY!	36
Research/Diagnosis	36
Objectives	37
Strategies	37
Target Audience	*37*
Tactics	37
Owned	*37*
Shared	*38*
Earned	*38*
Implementation	38
Reporting/Evaluation	38
Theories	39

CHAPTER 3 Understanding PESO — 40

- WHAT IS PESO? — 40
  - Paid Media — 42
  - Earned Media — 43
  - Shared Media — 43
  - Owned Media — 43
- WHEN SHOULD EACH OF THE PESO CHANNELS BE USED? — 43
  - Campaigns in Action — 44
  - Paid Media — 44
  - Earned Media — 45
  - Shared Media — 46
  - Owned Media — 47
- CONTINUOUS INTEGRATION — 49
- CONCLUSION — 50
- THINK CRITICALLY — 50
- KEY TERMS — 51
- CONCEPT CASE: EQUALITY TODAY'S CHANNEL, PARTNER, AND MEASUREMENT BRAINSTORMING — 51
- CASE STUDY: THE PROUD WHOPPER—BE YOUR WAY CAMPAIGN — 51
  - PESO Model — 51
    - *Owned* — *51*
    - *Shared* — *52*
    - *Earned* — *52*
    - *Paid* — *52*
  - Theories — 53

CHAPTER 4 Research, Part 1: Diagnosis and Developmental Research — 54

- DEVELOPMENTAL RESEARCH: DIAGNOSING THE PROBLEM AND/OR OPPORTUNITY — 55
- RESEARCHING AND MEASURING THE PROBLEM/OPPORTUNITY — 58
- RESEARCH TERMINOLOGY AND TECHNIQUES — 60
  - Data — 60
  - Qualitative and Quantitative Research — 60
  - Secondary and Primary Research — 61
  - Validity — 61
- CONDUCTING RESEARCH — 62
  - Secondary Research — 62
    - *Case Studies* — *63*
    - *Government Data* — *63*
    - *Scholarly Research* — *63*
    - *Think Tank/Nonprofit Reports* — *63*
    - *Trade Association Research* — *64*

- Primary Research — 64
  - Polling and Surveys: Opinion and Awareness — 64
  - Content Analysis — 66
  - Competitor Analysis — 68
  - Experimental Research — 69
  - Interviews — 69
  - Focus Groups — 70
- CONCLUSION — 72
- THINK CRITICALLY — 72
- KEY TERMS — 72
- CONCEPT CASE: RESEARCH FOR ISSUE PRIORITIZATION AT EQUALITY TODAY — 72
- CASE STUDY: HALLMARK ITTY BITTYS STEAL THE SPOTLIGHT — 73
  - Research/Diagnosis — 73
    - Primary Research: Getting to Know the Consumer — 73
  - Objectives — 74
  - Strategy — 74
  - Implementation — 74
  - Tactics — 74
    - Paid — 75
    - Earned — 75
    - Shared — 75
  - Reporting/Evaluation — 75
  - Theories — 76

CHAPTER 5 Research, Part 2: Goals — 77

- UNDERSTANDING YOUR ORGANIZATION AND ITS GOALS — 79
- THE GOAL-SETTING PROCESS — 80
  - Seeking the Impact Role for Communication — 80
  - Defining the Scope — 82
  - Selecting Audiences for Outreach — 82
  - Defining the Desired Change — 84
  - Prioritizing Budgets and Resources — 84
- WRITING GOALS — 85
  - Types of Goals — 85
  - Context: Mission versus Situation — 85
  - Visionary Goals, Concrete Objectives — 86
- GOAL-SETTING CHALLENGES — 87
  - Working with Organizational Decision Makers — 87
  - Prompting More Research — 88
- CONCLUSION — 88
- THINK CRITICALLY — 89
- KEY TERMS — 89
- CONCEPT CASE: EQUALITY TODAY SETS COMMUNICATION GOALS — 89

CASE STUDY: #WEIGHTTHIS—REDEFINING
SELF-WORTH FROM LEAN CUISINE					89
    Research/Diagnosis					90
    Objectives					90
    Strategy					90
    Tactics					90
        Paid					90
        Earned					91
        Shared					91
        Owned					91
    Implementation					91
    Reporting/Evaluation					91
    Theories and Models					91

## CHAPTER 6 Objectives					92

WHAT MAKES HIGH-VALUE OBJECTIVES?					93
MANAGEMENT BY OBJECTIVES					94
    Types of Objectives					95
    Writing S.M.A.R.T. Objectives					96
        Specific					97
        Measurable					97
        Attainable					98
        Relevant					99
        Time-Bound					99
    Additional Objective Frameworks					100
CONNECTING OBJECTIVES TO KEY INTERNAL
AUDIENCES					101
    Do Your Objectives Make Organizational Decision
    Makers Excited?					102
    Proving Relevance: Will Completing Your Objectives
    Drive Positive Change?					102
    Are You Connecting Short- and Long-Term Objectives?					103
CONCLUSION					105
THINK CRITICALLY					105
KEY TERMS					106
CONCEPT CASE: SETTING OBJECTIVES
FOR EQUALITY TODAY					106
CASE STUDY: COOKIE CARE DELIVERS SWEET
RESULTS FOR DOUBLETREE BY HILTON					106
    Research/Diagnosis					107
    Objectives					107
    Strategy					107
    Tactics					107
        Paid					108
        Shared					108
        Owned					108
    Reporting/Evaluation					108
    Theories					109

CHAPTER 7 Strategies — 110

- CHOOSING YOUR CHANNELS: THE PESO MODEL — 112
  - The Model — 113
    - *Paid* — *113*
    - *Earned* — *114*
    - *Shared* — *114*
    - *Owned* — *115*
  - HOW THE MODEL OVERLAPS — 115
    - How to Build an Integrated Campaign Strategy around PESO — 116
- THE RIGHT APPROACH FOR YOUR AUDIENCE(S) — 119
  - Demographics — 120
  - Geography — 120
  - Psychographics — 121
  - Activity/Interest — 121
  - Influence — 121
  - Channel Consumption — 121
- LEVERAGING YOUR ORGANIZATION'S STRENGTHS AND RESOURCES — 122
  - Subject Matter Expertise — 123
  - Imagery/Visuals — 123
  - Dynamic Presenters/Personalities — 123
  - Data — 123
  - Organizational Vision or Narrative — 123
  - History/Institutional Authority — 124
- THE COMPETITIVE LANDSCAPE — 124
  - Understand Competitors and External Challenges — 125
  - Avoid What Everyone Else Is Already Doing — 125
- CONCLUSION — 126
- THINK CRITICALLY — 126
- KEY TERMS — 126
- CONCEPT CASE: CHANNEL SELECTION FOR EQUALITY TODAY — 126
- CASE STUDY: MASTERCARD BITES INTO APPLE PAY — 127
  - Research/Diagnosis — 128
  - Objective — 128
  - Strategy — 128
  - Tactics — 128
    - *Earned & Paid* — *128*
    - *Owned* — *129*
    - *Shared & Owned* — *129*
    - *Paid, Earned, Shared & Owned* — *129*
  - Implementation — 129
  - Reporting/Evaluation — 129
    - *Cut through the Chatter* — *129*
    - *Lead the Conversation on Contactless Security* — *129*
    - *Drive MasterCard Sign-ups on Apple Pay* — *130*
  - Theories — 130

CHAPTER 8   Tactics   131

TACTICAL APPROACHES   133
Paid Media   133
- *Timing*   133
- *Budget*   134
- *Messaging*   134
- *Content Creation*   134
  - **Advertising**   134
  - **Advertorial Content**   136

Earned Media   136
- *Timing*   137
- *Budget*   137
- *Messaging*   137
- *Content Creation*   139
  - **Media Relations**   139

Shared Media   140
- *Timing*   140
- *Budget*   140
- *Messaging*   140
- *Content Creation*   141

Owned Media   141
- *Timing*   142
- *Budget*   142
- *Messaging*   142
- *Content Creation*   142
  - **Website Content Management**   142
  - **Marketing**   143
  - **Publications**   143

CONCLUSION   145
THINK CRITICALLY   145
KEY TERMS   145
CONCEPT CASE: TACTICAL CHOICES FOR EQUALITY TODAY   146
CASE STUDY: CINNAMILK BY GENERAL MILLS   146
Campaign Focus: Promotional   146
Research/Diagnosis   146
Objective   147
Strategy   147
Tactics   147
- *Paid & Owned*   147
- *Earned*   147
- *Shared*   148

Implementation   148
Reporting/Evaluation   148
Theories   148
Model   148

CHAPTER 9 Implementation — 149

- KEY SKILLS FOR IMPLEMENTING PR CAMPAIGNS — 150
  - Project Management Basics — 150
  - Budgeting — 150
  - Dividing Tasks among a Team — 152
  - Creating Timelines and Deadlines — 152
  - Setting Clear Expectations and Ensuring Clear Communication — 153
  - Working with Non-PR People — 154
  - Working with the Media — 155
  - Self-awareness and Self-evaluation — 157
  - Persistence and Perseverance — 158
- PREPARING FOR CHANGE — 161
- CONCLUSION — 162
- THINK CRITICALLY — 162
- KEY TERMS — 162
- CONCEPT CASE: EQUALITY TODAY MEETS UNEXPECTED OBSTACLES — 162
- CASE STUDY: MISSING TYPE—U.K.'S NATIONAL HEALTH SERVICE — 163
  - Research and Diagnosis — 163
  - Objectives — 163
  - Strategy — 164
  - Tactics — 164
    - *Earned* — *164*
    - *Shared* — *165*
    - *Owned* — *165*
  - Implementation — 165
  - Reporting/Evaluation — 165
  - Theories — 165
  - Model — 165

CHAPTER 10 Reporting and Evaluation — 166

- EVALUATING YOUR CAMPAIGN — 167
  - Media Evaluation — 169
  - Digital Evaluation Metrics and Approaches — 170
  - Turning Evaluation into Improvement — 172
- REPORTING ON YOUR CAMPAIGN — 172
  - Objective-driven Reporting — 173
  - Prioritization: What Information Is Most Important for the Reader? — 175
  - Format: How Should Your Information Be Best Presented to Your Audience? — 175
- PESO: SPECIAL REPORTING CONSIDERATIONS — 176
  - Paid Media — 176
  - Earned Media — 176

Shared Media	177
Owned Media	177
Integrated Reporting	178
CONCLUSION	179
THINK CRITICALLY	179
KEY TERMS	180
CONCEPT CASE: REPORTING RESULTS—EQUALITY TODAY'S ANNUAL MEETING	180
CASE STUDY: CANS GET YOU COOKING	180
Research/Diagnosis	180
Developmental Research and Insights	*180*
Objectives	181
Strategies	181
Tactics	181
Paid	*181*
Earned	*182*
Shared	*182*
Owned	*182*
Implementation	182
Reporting/Evaluation	183
Theories	183

CHAPTER 11 Formulating an Integrated Campaign—Case Studies — 184

PRODUCT MARKETING	184
Brewing Inspiration to Engage Coffee Fans	185
Research/Diagnosis	185
Objectives	186
Strategies	186
Tactics	186
Shared	*186*
Paid + Shared	*187*
Owned	*187*
Paid + Owned + Shared	*188*
Earned + Shared	*188*
Owned + Shared	*188*
Implementation	189
Reporting/Evaluation	189
Earned	*189*
Shared	*190*
Theories	190
Model	191
ACTIVISM	191
One for All: Mississippians' Fight for a New Flag	191
Research/Diagnosis	191
Objectives	192
Strategy	192
Tactics	193

Earned + Owned	*193*
Shared	*193*
Owned	*193*
Implementation	194
Reporting	194
Theories	194
Model	195

ENGAGEMENT 195

Appreciating Mom; World's Toughest Job—American Greetings	**196**
Research/Diagnosis	196
Objectives	196
Strategies	197
Tactics	197
Shared + Owned	*197*
Implementation	198
Reporting/Evaluation	198
Earned	*198*
Shared	*198*
Owned	*199*
Theories	199
Model	199

CRISIS COMMUNICATION 199

Harambe's Last Day at the Cincinnati Zoo and Botanical Garden	**200**
Research/Diagnosis	200
Objectives	200
Strategies	201
Tactics	201
Owned	*201*
Earned	*201*
Shared	*201*
Implementation	202
Reporting/Evaluation	202
Theories	203
Model	204

GLOBAL AND MULTICULTURAL 204

UNICEF: Toys in Mourning	**205**
Research/Diagnosis	205
Objectives	205
Strategies	205
Tactics	206
Earned + Shared + Owned	*206*
Implementation	207
Reporting/Evaluation	207
Theories	207
Model	207
Teens 4 Pink: Sisters Network and Eisai Inc. with Shared Voice Public Relations	**208**
Research/Diagnosis	208

Objectives	209
Strategy	209
Tactics	209
Earned	*209*
Shared	*210*
Owned	*210*
Implementation	210
Reporting/Evaluation	210
Theories	211
Model	212
INTERNAL COMMUNICATION AND EMPLOYEE RELATIONS	**212**
Responding to "Ferguson": From Tragedy to Positive Change	212
Research/Diagnosis	213
Objectives	214
Strategies	214
Tactics and Implementation	214
Earned + Shared	*214*
Owned	*215*
Reporting	216
Theories	217
Model	217
HP Global Wellness Challenge	217
Research/Diagnosis	217
Objectives	218
Strategies	218
Tactics	219
Owned & Shared	*219*
Implementation	220
Challenges during Implementation	*220*
Reporting/Evaluation	220
Theories	221
Model	221
APPENDIX	**222**
GLOSSARY	**246**
REFERENCES	**254**
INDEX	**267**

Foreword

The world of public relations has never been more exciting! When I began my career (back when we walked uphill both ways to school . . . in the snow and barefoot), there were a handful of things communicators did: media relations, events, reputation management, crisis communications, internal communications, and public affairs.

Today, nearly everything an organization does to communicate with its stakeholders is considered public relations—from Facebook ads and influencer relations to content marketing and search engine optimization. It's so prevalent, in fact, that many marketers are beginning to expand their communications skills so they can keep up. The best part about that is they have to keep up—we're already there.

There are search engine specialists learning how to pitch journalists and bloggers to *earn* the precious link back to their websites. There are product marketers learning how to write so they can create *owned* content that is interesting and valuable to an audience. And there are social media experts who have been thrown headfirst into a crisis and have had to figure out *how to communicate* their way out.

To boot, we *finally* have a way to show the effectiveness of a public relations program through data. Call it Big Data, small data, or attribution, a communicator has the tools at his or her disposal to prove we are an investment, rather than an expense—as has so long been the case.

It is our time to shine, and we have to make the most of it.

But we aren't quite there yet. I have a friend who is an executive at a Global 500 company. She recently said to me, "You know what's wrong with the PR industry? Most don't know what a strategy is or how to develop one."

That's a real challenge. As an industry, we tend to focus on the tactics and start there versus starting with the end (and the organization's goals) in mind.

I often say to our freshly graduated new hires, "Let's say you're getting married and we're at the wedding a year from now. What does it look like?" I ask them to picture everything—from flowers and invitations to dinner and the band. After they've described it to me, I explain that what they just did is create the strategy for their wedding. It's the picture of what it looks like when the day arrives. From there, I ask them to work backward and figure out what needs to be done to get there—this is where the tactics come into play.

As you begin your career—or a new campaign for a new year—think about what success looks like in the end. Picture what will have had to happen for you to reach your vision. Will you have built a community? What does that look like? Will you have everyone talking about your brand? What will that include? How many people will you have in the nurturing pipeline? What kinds of sales will you have created?

After you know *what* you want to accomplish, you can work backward to figure out *how* you'll get there.

The only way to change the perception people have of the PR industry—that we don't do only media relations, that we can develop a strategy, that we can measure our work—is to do things differently. And that begins with strategy development that has measurable goals and more than earned media—or media relations—included.

Now that you know what you want to accomplish, it's time to implement the ROSTIR and PESO models. You'll learn more about these, and how they work, in *Public Relations Campaigns: An Integrated Approach*. You'll learn how to implement them and measure both models.

What you will know how to do, by the time you finish reading, is how to do research (R) to help you develop your goals, create your objectives (O) and strategies (S), build a list of tactics (T), figure out your implementation (I) and timeline, and then design your reporting tools (R), and do your evaluation.

The tactics are where PESO comes in—paid, earned, shared, and owned media.

Paid media is advertising. Not just Super Bowl–type advertising but the kind that you can use to amplify your messages online, such as Facebook advertising or pay-per-click. E-mail marketing also falls under paid marketing because there is an expense to developing a program.

Earned media is what most people know as publicity—or media relations. You are earning the coverage or mention or interview or story with journalists, bloggers, and influencers.

Shared media is social media. It's more than just posting on your networks, though. It's being strategic about what you're sharing, engaging in conversation, and building community.

And owned media is content marketing. Though it started out as blogging, it's evolved to website content, contributed content for publications and blogs, podcasts, videos, livestreaming, and more.

I am often asked which is the most important of the four media types. While they're of equal importance, particularly in an integrated campaign, I am preferential to owned media. You cannot have P, E, or S without O. You need content to share on social media. You need content to amplify through paid media. And you need content to share with journalists and bloggers to prove you have a unique perspective and can string together some sentences intelligently. Content sits at the middle of the model. Get that right—and I mean really right—and you'll win every time.

If you start your planning process with ROSTIR and create an integrated model with PESO, you'll have better search engine optimization and first page Google results. You'll even come up in voice search. You'll build community and engage brand ambassadors and loyal customers. You'll develop mini sales teams outside of your organization—the people who cannot wait to tell others about you. And you'll work with your internal sales team to convert leads to customers.

That is the pot of gold at the end of the rainbow. If you can prove communications brought leads into the organization, and you helped to convert them, you suddenly go from a "nice to have" to a necessity.

Regina Luttrell and Luke Capizzo will help you get there. If you are a student or a seasoned professional, the case studies, tips, "Think Ahead" points, and the "Think

Critically" questions included in this book will help you make the most of your future in communications.

The world, as they say, is our oyster right now. Let's not let marketing or search engine specialists or advertisers take what belongs to us. It's time to stand up and prove we can do more than media relations. Build programs that are strategic. Measure our effectiveness (and tweak, as necessary). And take the lead with public relations. I hope you'll join Regina, Luke, and me in showing every organization in the world that public relations is where they should start and end.

— Gini Dietrich, CEO of Arment Dietrich and author of *Spin Sucks*

Preface

WHY INTEGRATED CAMPAIGNS? WHY NOW?

The U.S. Bureau of Labor Statistics predicts the employment of public relations specialists will grow by 12 percent between 2012 and 2022. Growth is being driven by the need for organizations to maintain their public image and build relationships with critical stakeholders and publics. Students are graduating and moving into a communications work environment that is fully integrated: public relations, social media, marketing, and advertising are all part of the equation at many organizations. In fact, the 2017 Global Communications Report, the second collaborative research project between The Holmes Report and the USC Annenberg Center for Public Relations, states that 47 percent of public relations professionals believe public relations will be more closely aligned with marketing over the next five years Paul Holmes, "2017 Global Communications Report Predicts Convergence of Marketing and PR." holmesreport.com. (https://www.holmesreport.com/latest/article/2017-global-communications-report-predicts-convergence-of-marketing-and-pr). What is evident is that the profession of public relations is shifting. Central to success in this changing environment is a strategic approach to strategic public relations planning that balances paid, earned, shared, and owned media.

Our book—designed for an upper-level Public Relations Campaigns class—integrates public relations strategies, marketing approaches, and new media opportunities. Readers will learn about how today's practitioners implement award-winning campaigns and the research-driven, strategic choices that underscore that success. *Public Relations Campaigns: An Integrated Approach* leads with public relations but provides broad coverage of the rapidly changing skills and tactics students and practitioners need to thrive in the field of public relations. The foundation of the book is rooted in public relations principles that emphasize a practical approach to developing successful integrated public relations campaigns. It provides students with the framework and theory-based knowledge to begin their work not just as tacticians but as counselors who provide research, perspective, and insights that help organizations communicate more effectively, understand complex environments, build relationships, and add strategic value and insights.

While practical in nature, the pedagogical approach to this textbook is student-centered, inquiry-based learning. Readers have the opportunity to first examine the essential elements of public relations planning, then analyze various public relations case studies, and also develop the skills and perspective to plan an integrated campaign of their own with the information they have learned.

A variety of features reinforce this approach, providing tips, structure, examples, and context. Each chapter is organized with clear learning objectives ("Think Ahead" points to begin each chapter) and "Think Critically" questions to reinforce and practice key elements. *Public Relations Campaigns: An Integrated Approach* is geared toward the many public relations (PR) students each year enrolling in "campaigns" classes, with the goal of providing learners with a robust and realistic framework for understanding, developing, and executing integrated public relations campaigns. We designed this book to be a guide and reference point for readers by including a series of real-world examples that give context and insight into the world of public relations today.

ORGANIZATION OF THE BOOK

Leveraging practical applications of each theory or model of interest, this book provides numerous case studies to aid in a deeper understanding of the underlying principles. **Part I** introduces readers to the theories behind public relations and the process of public relations planning, placing particular importance on the ROSTIR model for public relations planning: Research/Diagnosis, Objectives, Strategy, Tactics, Implementation, and Reporting/Evaluation as well as the PESO model—paid media, earned media, shared/social media, and owned media. For an advanced course on campaign development, this model moves beyond traditional R.O.P.E. or R.A.C.E. planning models to focus students on each step of the strategic planning process.

Part II delves deeper into each individual component of both ROSTIR and PESO so that students are exposed to a richer discussion of each step of the planning process of an integrated campaign, including how public relations practitioners are aligning strategies to achieve client objectives. Key definitions are provided to help in mastering the language of public relations professionals. A wide variety of strategies and tactics are introduced to expose students to the many paid, earned, shared, and owned media approaches available to them. It also showcases the ways in which these approaches can combine to support achieving organizational and communication goals and objectives.

Part III brings the text together by including a series of strategic public relations campaigns that give readers the opportunity to review, discuss, and critically analyze multiple public relations campaigns across a variety of disciplines. Using theories and models presented in the text, learners can evaluate the strengths and weaknesses of individual campaigns, assess how ROSTIR and PESO were critical to the planning process, and understand how multiple organizations from Fortune 500 companies to nonprofit organizations developed, implemented, and evaluated their public relations campaigns.

Introduction: Campaigns in the Professional Public Relations Context

This section provides an introduction to some of the most commonly used PR models, theories, and principles in the practice of public relations.

Part I: Strategic Public Relations Planning

Chapter 1: Introduction to Integrated Campaigns

Real-world campaigns are challenged by time, budgets, personnel, personalities, and internal barriers. But talented practitioners can use the tools of public relations and integrated communication to develop comprehensive, cohesive, results-driven strategic campaigns. Students begin to understand the impact of campaigns while learning the strategy behind integrated planning.

Chapter 2: Strategic Communication Campaign Fundamentals

This chapter hones in on why public relations practitioners plan, expands on the elements of a strategic plan, and explores the ROSTIR framework for campaign development.

Case Study: Oscar Mayer's Wakey, Wakey, Eggs and Bakey!

Chapter 3: Understanding PESO

The key to mastering integrated public relations is to recognize the importance of the PESO model and formulate strategic plans based on weaving together paid, earned, shared, and owned media. This chapter explains what PESO is and introduces how each approach can be used to form a strategic, holistic campaign.

Case Study: The Proud Whopper—Burger King's Be Your Way Campaign

PART II: Discovering ROSTIR

Chapter 4: Research, Part I: Diagnosis and Developmental Research

Research is the first step in the public relations planning process. This chapter centers on understanding your organization's industry and community environment, crafting research questions, and selecting research methods for integrated public relations campaigns.

Case Study: Hallmark Itty Bittys Steal the Spotlight

Chapter 5: Research, Part II: Goals

Understanding an organization and its goals helps public relations practitioners define key audiences, stakeholders, and publics. This chapter provides insights to help apply organizational goals to communication- and campaign-focused goals.

Case Study: #WeighThis—Redefining Self-worth from Lean Cuisine

Chapter 6: Objectives

In this chapter, readers begin to identify what constitutes high-value objectives. Readers will be able to differentiate between various types of objectives, recognize and craft S.M.A.R.T objectives, and learn to focus objectives toward key audiences.

Case Study: Cookie Care Delivers Sweet Results for Doubletree by Hilton

Chapter 7: Strategies

Choosing the right channels can be challenging. Chapter 7 summarizes how best to integrate strategies into public relations campaigns by assessing the right approach for an organization's target audience, leveraging an organization's strengths and resources, and examining the competitive landscape.

Case Study: MasterCard Bites into Apple Pay

Chapter 8: Tactics

Defining the right tools and tactics is critical for the success of any campaign. This chapter classifies the various types of paid, earned, shared, and owned tactics and illustrates how they are strategically used in public relations planning.

Case Study: Cinnamilk by General Mills

Chapter 9: Implementation

This chapter demystifies the processes behind implementation, including implications surrounding the components of the campaign such as creating timelines, dividing tasks among a team, setting deadlines, setting clear expectations, working with other people outside of the field of public relations, building relationships with the media, prioritizing, and the importance of awareness and self-evaluation.

Case Study: Missing Type—U.K.'s National Health Service

Chapter 10: Reporting and Evaluation

This chapter focuses on connecting measurement and evaluation to the overall objectives, how to tell if objectives are achievable, and the best path to prioritize information based on their value to the decision-making process.

Case Study: Cans Get You Cooking—Can Manufacturers Institute with Hunter Public Relations

Part III: Campaigns in Action

Chapter 11: Formulating an Integrated Campaign—Case Studies

This chapter includes a variety of standard campaign types with which all PR professionals should be familiar and comfortable. These archetypal campaigns include product marketing, activism, community and consumer engagement, crisis communication, global and multicultural communication, and internal relations. This chapter contains campaigns that demonstrate both the ROSTIR and PESO models combining a variety of paid, earned, shared, and owned media strategies and tactics so that students can fully understand the circumstances under which each of these channels can add value to the process.

Student Learning Resources

This book leads with public relations but offers an integrated approach that encompasses aspects of social media, marketing, advertising, and client management, for a broader view of the campaign planning process. This text is offered in 11 chapters, making the content easy to digest within a one-semester course.

Think Ahead: Learning objectives appear at the beginning of each chapter to engage students, encouraging them to think about the material before they connect with the text.

Think Critically: These end-of-chapter questions challenge students to reflect on and apply the material they have learned.

Case Studies: Numerous case studies demonstrate the proven ROSTIR (research/diagnosis, objectives, strategies, tactics, implementation, reporting/evaluation) and PESO (paid, earned, shared, owned) campaign processes from research to reporting, illustrating exactly how PR campaigns function in the professional world.

Concept Case: At the conclusion of each chapter, readers are introduced to a series of exercises where they can apply the takeaways from each topic to the operational activities of a fictitious client, Equality Today, an LGBTQ advocacy organization whose mission is to achieve equal rights for individuals across the spectrums of gender and sexual orientation in their family, professional, and civic lives.

PRo Tips: Call-out boxes highlight tips from public relations professionals and educators.

Key Terms: Highlighted vocabulary is used as a study guide with complete definitions in the glossary.

Appendix: The appendix includes additional reading material that accompanies and adds additional depth to chapters from the text, particularly in the areas of research, strategy, and tactics.

Digital Resources

Instructor Teaching Site (Password Protected)

SAGE edge for Instructors supports your teaching by making it easy to integrate quality content and create a rich learning environment for students. The site includes the following resources:

- **Test banks** provide a diverse range of pre-written options as well as the opportunity to edit any question and/or insert your own personalized questions to effectively assess students' progress and understanding.

- **Sample course syllabi** for semester and quarter courses provide suggested models for structuring your courses.

- Editable, chapter-specific **PowerPoint® slides** offer complete flexibility for creating a multimedia presentation for your course.

- EXCLUSIVE! Access to full-text **SAGE journal articles** that have been carefully selected to support and expand on the concepts presented in each chapter is included.

- Carefully selected web-based **video resources** feature relevant interviews, lectures, personal stories, inquiries, and other content for use in independent or classroom-based explorations of key topics.

- **Web resources** are included for further research and insights.

Student Study Site (Open Access)

SAGE edge for Students provides a personalized approach to help students accomplish their coursework goals in an easy-to-use learning environment. The site includes the following resources:

- Mobile-friendly **eFlashcards** strengthen understanding of key terms and concepts.

- Mobile-friendly practice **quizzes** allow for independent assessment by students of their mastery of course material.

- Carefully selected web-based **video resources** feature relevant interviews, lectures, personal stories, inquiries, and other content for use in independent or classroom-based explorations of key topics.

- **Web resources** are included for further research and insights.

- EXCLUSIVE! Access to full-text **SAGE journal articles** that have been carefully selected to support and expand on the concepts presented in each chapter is included.

The website also offers a complete planning framework with an abundance of example/template materials:

- Complete PR plan framework
- Example media alerts
- Sample press releases
- Media pitches
- Process documents
- Example project reports

Regina M. Luttrell
Syracuse University, New York

Luke W. Capizzo
University of Maryland, College Park

Acknowledgments

We would like to express our deepest appreciation to those who reviewed drafts of the manuscript and made truly insightful suggestions that we have done our best to incorporate into this book:

Jennie Donohue, *Marist College*

Chike Anyaegbunam, *University of Kentucky*

Minjeong Kang, *Indiana University*

Nicki L. Boudreaux, *Nicholls State University*

Nancy Kerr, *Champlain College*

Donna J. Downs, *Taylor University*

Robin Street, *University of Mississippi*

Shirley A. Serini, *Valdosta State University*

L. Simone Byrd, *Alabama State University*

Colleen Fitzpatrick, *Saint Mary's College*

Janis Teruggi Page, *The George Washington University*

Astrid Sheil, *California State University San Bernardino*

Maha M. Bashri, *Bradley University*

Felicia LeDuff Harry, *Nicholls State University*

Lars J. Kristiansen, *James Madison University*

Bernardo H. Motta, *University of South Florida Saint Petersburg*

John Powers, *Quinnipiac University*

We give special thanks to Terri Accomazzo and Anna Villarruel, our editors at SAGE. Your direction, guidance, thoughtfulness, and patience resulted in a book beyond our expectations. A special note of gratitude to Michelle Ponce for the superior copyediting as well as Nevair Kabakian and Erik Helton for facilitating the details.

We would be remiss if we did not thank Fred Antico, Karen McGrath, Kelly Gaggin, and Adrienne Wallace for their meticulous efforts in pulling together the ancillary materials. We appreciate your experience and wisdom.

Without the countless public relations professionals, public relations educators, case study contributors, and the Public Relations Society of America that granted permissions and shared their knowledge and resources, this book would not be possible. In particular, Gini Dietrich and her deep knowledge of and evangelism for the PESO model and integrated public relations approaches is a leader in demonstrating its power and practicality. To all, please accept our sincere gratitude.

About the Authors

Regina M. Luttrell, PhD, is currently an assistant professor of Public Relations and Social Media at the S.I. Newhouse School of Public Communications at Syracuse University. A contributor to *PR Tactics* and *PR News*, as well as peer reviewed journals, she is a noted speaker where she frequently presents at national and international conferences and business events on topics related to the current social media revolution, the ongoing public relations evolution, and Millennials within the classroom and workplace. She is the (co)author of the following books: *Social Media: How to Engage, Share, and Connect*; *The Millennial Mindset: Unraveling Fact from Fiction*; *Brew Your Business: The Ultimate Craft Beer Playbook*; *The PR Agency Handbook*; and *A Practical Guide to Ethics in Public Relations*. Prior to entering the educational field, she spent the first portion of her career in corporate public relations and marketing. Her extensive background includes strategic development and implementation of public relations and social media, advertising, marketing, and corporate communications. She has led multiple rebranding campaigns, designed numerous websites, managed high-level crisis situations, and garnered media coverage that included hits with the *New York Times*, the CBS Evening News, and the Associated Press.

Luke W. Capizzo is a PhD student and instructor in the Department of Communication at the University of Maryland, specializing in public relations. He is the coauthor (with Regina Luttrell) of *The PR Agency Handbook*. His research interests include global public relations, civil society, financial communication, and public relations education. Before coming to the University of Maryland, he practiced public relations for eight years with a focus on media relations in the financial services, commercial real estate, manufacturing, retail, and technology industries, serving in both agency and in-house roles. Working with a wide variety of clients—from the Fortune 500 to small businesses and nonprofits—he garnered media coverage in top national outlets and trade publications, secured and prepared clients for national cable news interviews, and led projects to improve agency-wide media training, staff on-boarding, and client evaluation and reporting metrics. He has earned the APR (Accreditation in Public Relations) designation through the Public Relations Society of America.

Introduction

CAMPAIGNS IN THE PROFESSIONAL PUBLIC RELATIONS CONTEXT

THINK AHEAD

0.1 Describe relevant theories of communication and explain how they relate to the practice of public relations.

0.2 Grasp different approaches to public relations campaign planning using both communication theory and public relations planning models.

0.3 Identify the five objectives a communicator employs that provide a clear set of potential outcomes for strategic campaigns.

Theories exist to provide a framework for public relations practitioners to develop their decision-making processes and for planning integrated campaigns. Numerous books are available regarding the topic of **communication theory** and how it relates to public relations. This is not one of those books. What you will find within these initial pages is an introduction to some of the most prominent theories and planning models in the practice of public relations. This introduction should be used as an overarching summary of the theories and planning models employed in public relations campaign planning.

This book is intentionally organized with the many theories and principles of public relations introduced first to provide readers with a better sense of the "why" behind the "how" of planning. **Public relations** theories, principles, and goals are

> ## *PRo Tip*
>
> ### CRITERIA FOR EVALUATING THEORY
>
> Scholars Marianne Dainton and Elaine D. Zelley developed a means by which scholarly theories of communication can be evaluated.[1] These include accuracy, practicality, succinctness, consistency, and acuity.
>
> | | |
> |---|---|
> | Accuracy | Has research supported that the theory works the way it says it does? |
> | Practicality | Have real-world applications been found for the theory? |
> | Succinctness | Has the theory been formulated with the appropriate number (fewest possible) of concepts or steps? |
> | Consistency | Does the theory demonstrate coherence within its own premises and with other theories? |
> | Acuity | To what extent does the theory make clear an otherwise complex experience? |
>
> *Source:* Dainton, Marianne, and Elaine D. Zelley. *Applying Communication Theory for Professional Life: A Practical Introduction.* Thousand Oaks, CA: SAGE, 2015.

fostered from the ideologies found within the study of communication. Therefore, it is the job of the practitioner to consider the appropriate theories and models when making decisions and building successful relationships with stakeholders. Properly understanding the theory can help explain how to best develop public relations plans that are most effective in practice for the clients that we represent.

PUBLIC RELATIONS THEORIES AND PRINCIPLES

A **theory** is an idea or set of ideas that is intended to explain related facts or events.[2] The public relations industry is built upon various theories, mainly due to the fact that there is no single theory that is able to fulfill every plan or proposal that a practitioner must organize and execute. Practitioners, therefore, must consider which theory and model is appropriate for their specific planning situations. An obvious place to begin is by examining some of the most widely used theories used in the practice and planning of public relations.

Excellence Theory

Considered a monumental study in public relations, the Excellence Study and resulting **excellence theory** can be seen as an integration of strategic management theories of public relations into a greater whole.³ Led by James E. Grunig, the excellence theory is the culmination of a fifteen-year study (1985-2000), funded by the International Association of Business Communicators (IABC), that focused on unveiling the best practices in communication management. Grunig reasoned that the ideal role for public relations is in a strategic management function. By being part of the management team, practitioners encourage leadership to share power through symmetrical two-way communication between an organization and its publics. Rather than using persuasion or one-way "press agentry" approaches, Grunig concluded that providing and receiving information is the most effective and ethical approach to achieving long-term organizational goals, improved relationships with publics, and mutual understanding.⁴ The premise behind the excellence theory expressed that the value of public relations lies in the importance of the relationship between an organization and its publics. The development of sound relationships with strategic publics is a critical component for organizations to properly define and achieve goals desired by both the organization and its publics, reduce costs of negative publicity, and increase revenue by providing products and services needed by stakeholders.⁵ It is the responsibility of public relations practitioners to identify key publics and cultivate long-term relationships with them using open two-way symmetrical communication. Grunig and his team identified three particular areas of importance to consider:⁶

- Senior management: Involvement in strategic leadership is a critical characteristic of excellent public relations. Public relations executives play a strategic managerial role by having access to key organizational decision makers.

- Organization of communication: The public relations function loses its unique role in strategic management if it is redirected through marketing or other management channels. Therefore, it is essential that the public relations department is headed not by a technician but by a manager who has the ability to conceptualize and direct public relations functions.

- Diversity in public relations: Research illustrates that organizations with excellent public relations value women as much as men within these strategic roles and develop programs to empower women throughout the organization. Today, we continue to see the value of diversity within an organization.

Systems Theory

Each organization should be considered interdependent and interact with various stakeholders to survive and thrive. **Systems theory** can help public relations practitioners recognize many of the boundaries found within organizations. This theory understands that organizations are comprised of interrelated parts, adapting and adjusting to changes in the political, economic, and social environments in which they operate.⁷ Consider the following example. Envision, for a moment, that you work for a company that makes ice cream. This organization must rely on farmers to provide milk, sugar, and other essential ingredients; customers to purchase their product; the government to set food regulations;

FIGURE 0.1
Systems Theory

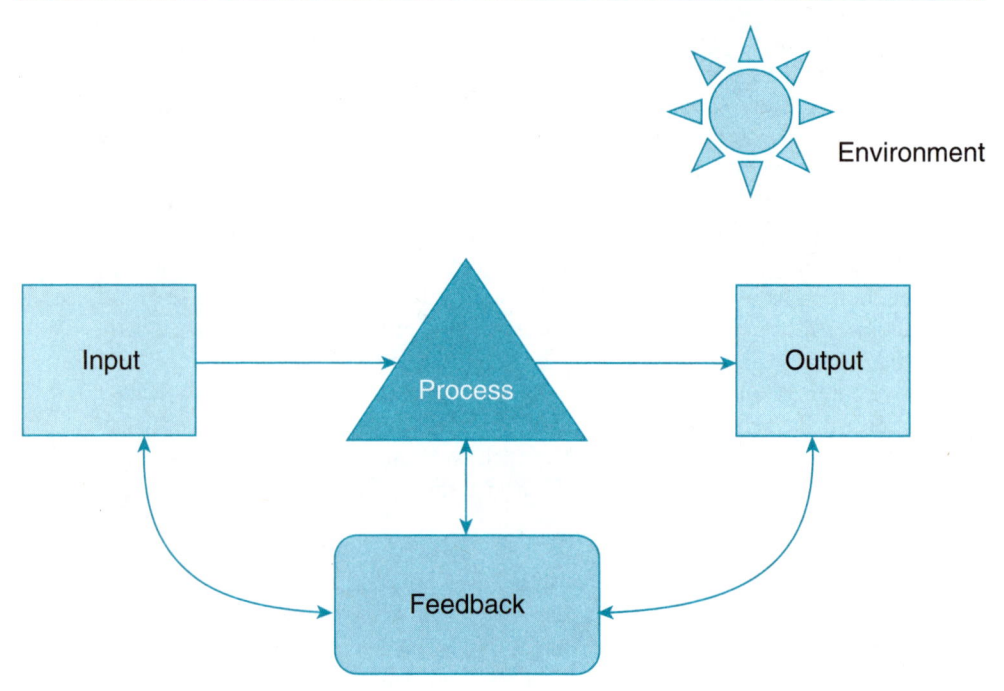

Systems theory positions organizations as part of systems, where one action or process creates feedback and impacts all actors within the environment.

the media to help spread their message; and financial institutions to keep them moving forward. As a public relations practitioner, how might you approach any disturbances/evolutions that may occur in the overall business environment? According to Cutlip, Center, and Broom, in an organization such as this, one of the essential roles of public relations is based on a systems theory approach: to help this organization adjust and adapt to changes in its environment.[8]

Diffusion Theory

Diffusion theory is a specific area of communication concerned with the spread of messages that are perceived as new ideas. This theory was developed to explain how, over time, an idea or product gains momentum and spreads through a specific population or social system.[9] Everett Rogers, communication researcher, claimed that people make decisions or accept ideas based on the following principles:

1. "Awareness: Individuals are exposed to an idea.
2. Interest: The idea stimulates the individual.

FIGURE 0.2
Diffusion Theory

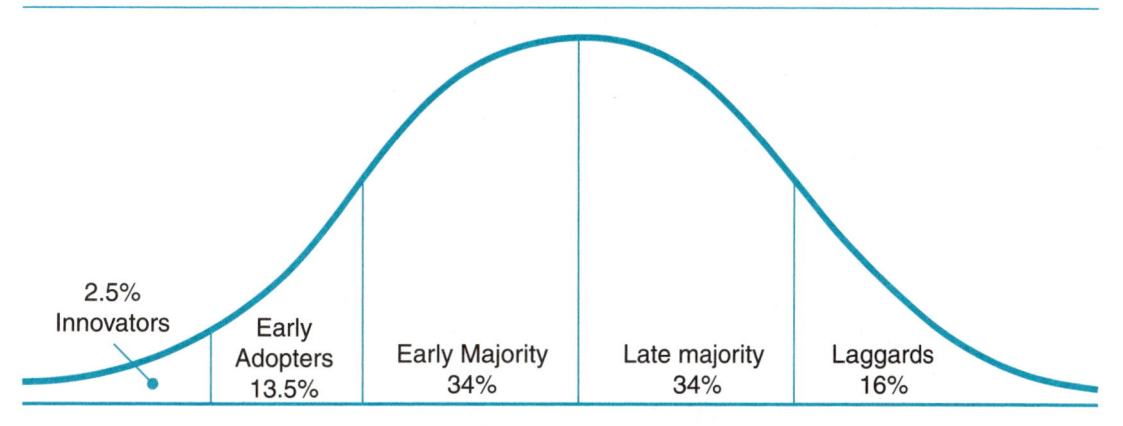

- 2.5% Innovators
- Early Adopters 13.5%
- Early Majority 34%
- Late majority 34%
- Laggards 16%

While many companies and organizations focus on the first people to try a new product or technology (innovators and early adopters), the majority of consumers wait and see rather than rushing to adopt.

3. Evaluation: The individual considers the idea as potentially useful.
4. Trial: The individual tests the idea.
5. Adoption: The individual acceptance or adoption of the idea after having successfully moved through the four earlier stages."[10]

Public relations practitioners use this approach when planning campaigns to understand how information about organizations, events, products, or issues will be received by the intended audience. It is also useful when evaluating how to appropriately segment messages and develop outreach approaches for different audience groups, as some individuals seek out new experiences, processes, and products (innovators and early adopters) while others wait until nearly everyone else around them has a new piece of technology before using it (laggards).

Framing Theory

The development of **framing theory** has been attributed to sociologist Erving Goffman and anthropologist Gregory Bateson. Framing involves the process of calling attention to a particular aspect of the reality described.[11] Essentially, Goffman and Bateson are suggesting that what is presented to the audience, often called "the frame," can influence the choices that people make about how to process the information they are receiving. For example, when journalists and editors make decisions about whom to interview, what questions are appropriate to ask, and the article content, they are "framing" the story.[12] In essence, framing is the way that a communication source defines and constructs any piece of communicated information.[13] The most common use of frames for public relations practitioners is in how they define problems, diagnose or identify the root cause of the problem, decisions on how to proceed, and developing solutions to the problem.[14] The media are often thought to influence the perception of the news because they not only tell the audience what to think about but also how to think about a particular issue simply by the way that the news is written, presented, and disseminated. Because public relations practitioners often act as sources themselves, these individuals can be seen as contributing to framing a story that is presented in the media.[15] Framing and the agenda setting theory are often connected.

Agenda Setting & Agenda Building Theories

Maxwell McCombs and Donald Shaw were the first researchers to solidify the idea of **agenda setting**. They originally proposed that the media sets the public agenda by not necessarily telling people what to think but what to think *about*.[16] McCombs and Shaw noted,

> In choosing and displaying news, editors, newsroom staff, and broadcasters play an important part in shaping political reality. Readers learn not only about a given issue, but also how much importance to attach to that issue from the amount of information in a news story and its position.[17]

While this theory was originally intended for the news media, public relations professionals can be perceived as using agenda setting when they create and disseminate messages to various audiences, as well as when they work with media as sources on news stories and articles.

Similarly, **agenda building** is the process by which active publics and organizations focused on a cause attract the attention of the news media and public officials to add their issue to the public agenda.[18] The agenda building theory is considered to be an extension of agenda setting. Examples of agenda building can include the release of a report on the effects of global warming, a speech about the movement Black Lives Matter, or even a Facebook page promoting the worldwide rallies held by The Women's March to advocate for legislation and policies regarding human rights and other

---

PRo Tip

AGENDA SETTING

"In political campaigns, the media may not be effective in swaying public support toward or against a particular issue or candidate. But by continually raising particular questions and issues, or simply by showing an interest in a particular political candidate or issue, the media can lead the discussion toward or away from issues important to the candidate and even to the public (as identified through polls)."[19]

Professor Ron Smith, The State University of New York at Buffalo.

issues, including women's rights, immigration reform, healthcare reform, reproductive rights, the natural environment, LGBTQ rights, racial equality, freedom of religion, and workers' rights.

The difference between the two theories can be understood in this way: traditional agenda setting explained the news media's influence on audiences by their choice of what stories to consider newsworthy and how much prominence and space to give them, whereas agenda building theory suggests there is an exchange between the media and sources or society broadly to build an agenda.[20]

Situational Crisis Communication Theory

One of the most widely used theories is **situational crisis communication theory**, also known as SCCT. One of the leading researchers in this area, W. Timothy Coombs, notes that SCCT attempts to predict the level of threat to an organization's reputation during a crisis situation. Crisis management is a growing area within public relations and should play a central role in public relations practitioners' planning. As described in this theory, a crisis is defined as "the negative event that leads stakeholders to assess crisis responsibility."[21] Public relations practitioners often use this theory when faced with responding to a crisis. SCCT provides a recommended framework for response strategies when facing a reputational threat by helping practitioners assess the initial crisis responsibility, crisis history, and prior relational reputation.[22]

As with any discipline based on numerous models, theories on how to properly practice public relations will continue to evolve and develop over time. The seven aforementioned theories present a solid foundation to build upon as we begin to introduce different models for public relations planning. As you will see, these models give practitioners a way to organize concepts and ideas by types of public relations practice. Theories, coupled with planning models, help public relations practitioners predict more effectively what will and will not work in the practice of public relations.

Two-step Flow Model

One of the earliest mass communication models of adoption in the field of public relations is the **two-step flow model**.[23] This model states that an organization initially targets its message to the mass media, which in turn delivers that message to the throngs of viewers, readers, and listeners. Individuals that take the time to seek out and understand information on particular societal topics are considered "opinion leaders." Opinion leaders can have substantial influence over their followers. Research indicates that opinion leaders who share the same social status as their followers are the most effective.[24] Opinion leaders consist of individuals from a large range of backgrounds, including family members, doctors, local politicians, mommy bloggers, parish leaders, or educators. Most of the time, opinion leaders are individuals who are well respected within their circle of influence. In the social media world these leaders are often referred to as "influencers."

FIGURE 0.3
Two-step Flow Model

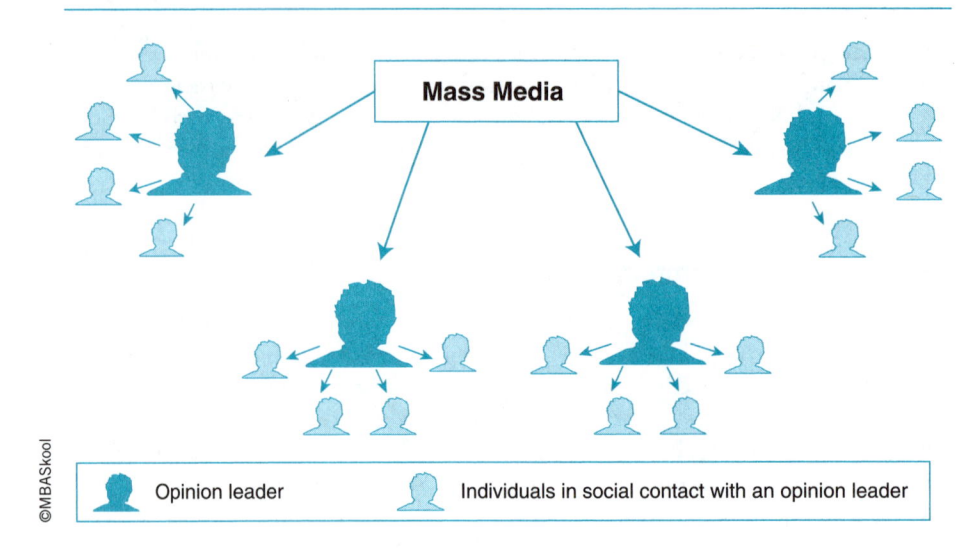

Mass Media

Opinion leader — Individuals in social contact with an opinion leader

---

PRo Tip

THEORIES IN PRACTICE—MODELING MEDIA RELATIONS

Public relations scholars Lynn Zoch and Juan-Carlos Molleda created a theoretical model for media relations by combining framing theory and agenda building with the concept of information subsidies. In this case an *information subsidy* represents the value of content within a particular pitch made by a public relations professional to a journalist. It could include access to a difficult-to-reach source, a head start on information not yet available to the public, or details about a particular situation not shared with other media outlets.

To create the theoretical model, Zoch and Molleda explain that practitioners create information subsidies for journalists that frame issues based on the way the organization would prefer to see an issue addressed publicly. Journalists can accept or reject the frame presented as part of their research and preparation in writing a story. In this way, practitioners contribute to agenda building by supporting journalistic interest and coverage of desired issues by mainstream media.

Source: Lynn M. Zoch and Juan-Carlos Molleda, "Building a Theoretical Model of Media Relations Using Framing, Information Subsidies and Agenda Building," in *Public Relations Theory II*, ed. Carl H. Botan and Vincent Hazleton (Mahwah, NJ: Lawrence Erlbaum, 2006), 279-309.

MODELS OF PUBLIC RELATIONS PRACTICE

Organizations can practice public relations from a variety of different perspectives, whether it is to get information out into public view; to serve as an objective, journalistic voice within and for an organization; to advocate on behalf of an organization in public view; or to provide perspective and eternal insights to balance the relationship between an organization and its publics. These viewpoints are captured in Grunig and Hunt's four models of public relations: press agentry, public information, one-way asymmetrical, and two-way symmetrical.[26]

Press Agentry

In the **press agentry model**, or publicity model, public information flows in one direction—from the organization to its audiences and publics. Grunig and Hunt noted that persuasion is often used to achieve organizational goals. This model is one of the oldest forms of public relations and is often synonymous with promotions and publicity. Public relations practitioners using this model are generally looking for "ink": media coverage. Essentially, these practitioners are hoping to get their organization mentioned in the media for purposes of promotion. This model can include propaganda tactics and publicity stunts such as giveaways, large events, or celebrity sponsorships.

Public Information

The purpose of the **public information model** is to provide relevant and useful information directly to the public rather than for promotional purposes or targeted publicity. This model, positioning public relations practitioners as journalists-in-residence, employs one-way communication and is widely leveraged within the areas of government relations, educational institutions, nonprofit corporations, and some corporations.[27] While this approach is neutral in its overall outreach, it is considered "craft" rather than "professional" public relations due to its nonstrategic nature. For example, many government officials leading communication efforts go by job titles such as *public information officer*, with their mandate to inform the public—using both traditional earned media and digital channels—about what is going on in their specific department or agency.

Two-way Asymmetrical

By implementing scientific persuasion methodologies, the goal of the **two-way asymmetrical model** of public relations planning is to convince others to accept an organization's message. Public relations practitioners capitalize on the use of surveys, interviews, and focus groups to measure relationships in an effort for the organization to design public relations programs that will gain the support of key, targeted publics. Information does flow between the organization and its publics; however, the organization is more interested in having their publics adjust to the organization rather than the opposite. Political campaigns as well as traditional public health initiatives are examples of the two-way asymmetrical model.

Two-way Symmetrical

The **two-way symmetrical model** presents a balanced, strategic, and informed approach to public relations. Organizations and their publics adjust to each other and attempt to achieve mutual understanding using two-way communication, not persuasion. When public relations practitioners employ the two-way symmetrical model they not only provide information to their intended publics but also listen and receive information. Some believe that the development and adoption of social media as a communication platform provides an effective and efficient avenue for conducting two-way symmetrical communication.[28]

Public relations is a strategic process established to influence public opinion, through sound ethical and accurate implementation, based on mutually satisfactory two-way communication. In practice, public relations departments use mixture of these models depending on the goal, message, or public at hand. Some of the more historically well-known models are also extremely valuable as tools in strategic planning.

PUBLIC RELATIONS PLANNING MODELS

Several useful planning models identify central ideas within public relations and inform development of campaign objectives, strategies, and tactics. Each of these models are presented below, including the R.O.P.E., R.A.C.E., and R.O.S.I.E. planning models.[29] Let us take a closer look.

R-A-C-E, R-O-P-E, or R-O-S-I-E

We've already seen that planning and processes are an integral part of the successful execution of a public relations campaign. John Marston developed the four-step management process for public relations in his 1963 book, *The Nature of Public Relations*, which he called the R-A-C-E model.[30] To this day many public relations practitioners implement and follow regularly:

Research: Practitioners must first conduct research to understand the problem or situation.

Action: Practitioners decide what actions will be taken to address the problem or situation.

Communication: Practitioners determine which channels will be used to communicate the plan of action to the public.

Evaluation: Practitioners assess whether or not the defined goals were achieved.

Shelia Clough-Crifasi expanded on the R.A.C.E. model in the year 2000 to encompass a more managerial approach when she developed the R.O.S.I.E. model: R—Research, O—Objectives, S—Strategies and planning, I—Implementation, and E—Evaluation.[31] Other iterations of the R.A.C.E. and R.O.S.I.E. model exist in public relations planning as well, including the P-A-C-E (planning, action, communication, evaluation) model, the A-C-E (assessment, communication, evaluation) model, and the S-T-A-R-E (scan, track, analyze, respond, evaluate) model.[32] Regardless of which model is subscribed to, planning is essential if practitioners want to achieve positive outcomes that enhance an organization's relationships with its public. Each of these models outlines the importance of several key factors: the role of research and planning to understand the situation at hand; the identification of clear, measurable objectives; the planning and execution of the campaign itself; and the evaluation of the campaign's success based on its achievement of those objectives.

ROSTIR: Research, Objectives, Strategies, Tactics, Implementation & Reporting

This book is organized around a new evolution of this approach, the ROSTIR model, which emphasizes the steps in this process necessary for successful campaigns in today's rapidly changing public relations landscape. ROSTIR stands for Research (including developmental research, diagnosis, and goal setting), Objectives, Strategies, Tactics, Implementation, and Reporting/Evaluation. As we'll explore in the chapters to come, this model clearly reflects the campaign planning needs of practitioners and can be understood in conjunction with the models.

Each of these models enriches our understanding of how public relations is practiced, but they can only take public relations planning so far. Every approach to campaign planning should be thought of as either circular or ongoing and including research and evaluation as a central component during every stage of the planning process. As a strategic management function, public relations adds value to organizations by continually assessing the organizational environment and adjusting communication strategies and tactics accordingly. Campaigns may end, but the planning process never does: the end of one campaign becomes the beginning of the next. That being said, any good model also relies on the development of solid strategic communication targets with appropriately defined goals, objectives, and purpose.

Communication Goals

Strategic communication can be either informational or persuasive in nature; however, its overarching purpose is to build an understanding and garner support

---

PRo Tip

STRATEGIC MESSAGING

When creating strategic messaging, Jamie Turner from the *60 Second Marketer* advises practitioners should do the following:

- Prioritize and crystallize information
- Ensure consistency, continuity, and accuracy
- Measure and track success

Source: Jaimie Turner, "Three Tips to Overcome Email Fatigue in the New Year." *60 Second Marketer*, January 20, 2015, https://60secondmarketer.com/blog/2015/01/20/three-tips-overcome-email-fatigue-new-year/.

for ideas, causes, services, and products. Given that public relations is a deliberate process, every instance of communication must contain a goal, objective, and purpose. There are four standard communication goals that are regularly referred to in the industry: to inform the recipient, persuade the recipient, motivate the recipient, and build a mutual understanding between the recipient and the originator of the message.[33] Patrick Jackson, former editor of *pr reporter*, believes that when creating a piece of communication, "the communicator should ask whether the proposed message is appropriate, meaningful, memorable, understandable, and believable to the prospective recipient."[34]

Just as the development of appropriate content is important, public relations practitioners must also pay special attention to the objectives of the messages being communicated. In addition to contributing to multiple public relations theories, James E. Grunig has also introduced five objectives for a communicator in order to provide a clear set of potential outcomes for strategic campaigns:[35]

1. **Message exposure:** Audiences are exposed to messages in various forms. From newsletters to brochures, blogs, and social media channels, public relations practitioners often provide materials to the mass media to disseminate their messages.

2. **Accurate dissemination of the message:** Information can be filtered by editors, journalists, and bloggers, but the overarching message stays intact as it is transmitted through various channels.

3. **Acceptance of the message:** The audience retains the message and can accept it as valid based on their perceptions and views.

4. **Attitude change:** The audience members will make a mental or verbal commitment to change their behavior as a result of the message.

5. **Change in behavior:** The audience genuinely changes their behavior. This could be to purchase the product and use it or vote for a different candidate in an election.

PULLING IT ALL TOGETHER

Theories and models related to practical public relations execution continue to evolve and contribute to the predicted successes in practice. Theories and models provide practitioners with guidance on how to organize concepts as warranted by the differing types of public relations practice. By progressing the mind-set of public relations beyond the early models of planning toward a more clearly defined set of measurable variables, researchers such as Grunig, Cutlip, Scott, and Allen introduced to the field a far more sophisticated way to evaluate public relations.

THINK CRITICALLY

1. Evaluate each theory presented in the chapter, and discuss the one(s) you believe are used most often in public relations planning.

2. Search the Internet to find examples of organizations using theory as the foundation for their public relations campaigns.

3. Compare and contrast the public relations planning models then discuss which planning model you perceive to be most effective and why.

4. According to AdAge, Netflix's *Gilmore Girls* revival ranked as the No. 3 most-watched original series on the platform. The four-part series "averaged 5 million viewers among 18- to 49-year-olds and pulled a 3.59 rating in the demo in the three days after it dropped on Netflix."[36] Using what you have learned in this chapter, explain what theories and public relations models were implemented that help explain the success of the revival. Critique whether or not Netflix successfully applied James E. Grunig's five objectives for communicators.

KEY TERMS

Agenda building theory 6
Agenda setting theory 6
Communication theory 1
Excellence theory 2
Framing theory 5
Press agentry model 9
Public relations 1
Public Information Model 9
Situational crisis communication theory (SCCT) 7
Systems theory 3
Theory 2
Two-step flow model 7
Two-way asymmetrical model 9
Two-way symmetrical model 10

CONCEPT CASE: EQUALITY TODAY

This textbook features a reoccurring Concept Case that takes readers through exercises based on a fictitious client, Equality Today, an LGBTQ advocacy organization whose mission is to achieve equal rights for those across the spectrums of gender and sexual orientation in their family, professional, and civic lives. As you progress through the textbook, you will consider and apply the learnings of each topic to the operational activities of Equality Today.

- Choose two theories in this chapter, and explain how Equality Today might use them when planning an advocacy campaign.
- How can strategic thinking be incorporated into the models presented in this chapter, and how can they benefit Equality Today?
- Search the Internet to find organizations similar to Equality Today. What types of activities are they implementing to get their messages out to their audiences? Identify the theories and models they used.

1 Introduction to Integrated Campaigns

THINK AHEAD

1.1 Identify the need for new models of public relations planning.

1.2 Describe the six steps of the ROSTIR public relations planning model when developing an integrated campaign.

1.3 Discuss the different ways ROSTIR contributes to an organization's overall public relations efforts.

©iStockPhotos/Leonardo Patrizi

There are moments in the life cycle of an organization when public relations (PR) efforts may signal the difference between the success and failure of a brand. Our approach to planning begins with the premise that, while there are many valid choices that public relations practitioners can make over the course of a campaign, not all are created equal. How can we craft objectives and select strategies and tactics that serve as the foundation for successful, ethical campaigns and respected organizations? Our industry has long suffered mixed perceptions regarding the role of public relations professionals. We have been called "PR flacks" and "spin doctors," and have battled mightily in defense of our expertise, budgets, and professional worth. By using a research-first approach and addressing challenges, failures, corrections, and revisions incorporating real-world, integrated campaign situations, students will be provided the necessary tools to make more thoughtful and informed choices as practitioners.

A NEED FOR NEW PUBLIC RELATIONS PLANNING MODELS

A recent study[1] by Marlene Neill and Erin Schauster highlighted that historical competencies required to be successful within public relations, including writing and presentation skills, remain a foundation within the profession; however, additional proficiencies are now necessary. Newly created roles in today's workforce including **content amplification** of earned media, **native advertising**, **online community management**, **programmatic buying**, **social listening**, and **social media analytics** are contributing to the rapidly expanding vocabulary for those teaching and learning about the profession of public relations. At present, a gap exists in public relations education as a result of the evolution that our field has experienced over the past ten years, particularly the impact of **social media** on the profession.[2] This book identifies two new models supporting successful integrated campaign planning and execution and also highlights methods that today's practitioners use to plan, execute, and measure their public relations campaigns.

Emerging Models

The process of conducting effective public relations is grounded in sound methodologies for solving problems and robust planning. The role that research plays to fully understand a situation and set communication goals; the identification of clear, measurable objectives; the execution of the campaign itself; and the evaluation and reporting of the campaign's success are all critical elements to consider as a practitioner. Within this text, we will explore a new evolution of this process using the ROSTIR (Research/Diagnosis, Objectives, Strategy, Tactics, Implementation, and Reporting/Evaluation) model. This emerging model emphasizes those steps critical to the development of successful campaigns in today's rapidly changing public relations landscape, including the incorporation of **PESO's** (paid, earned, shared, and owned media) wide variety of related tactical elements. In fact, these two models reflect work practiced on a daily basis in public relations agencies around the globe. As a result of the integration of many public relations, **marketing**, and **advertising** functions within organizations, new models need to be adopted that prepare the next generation of professionals.[3]

PRo Tip

INTEGRATING CAMPAIGNS

The most effective campaigns are integrated from the start; researched and planned so that all available strategies, channels, and tactics are considered and coordinated.

FIGURE 1.1

The ROSTIR Model

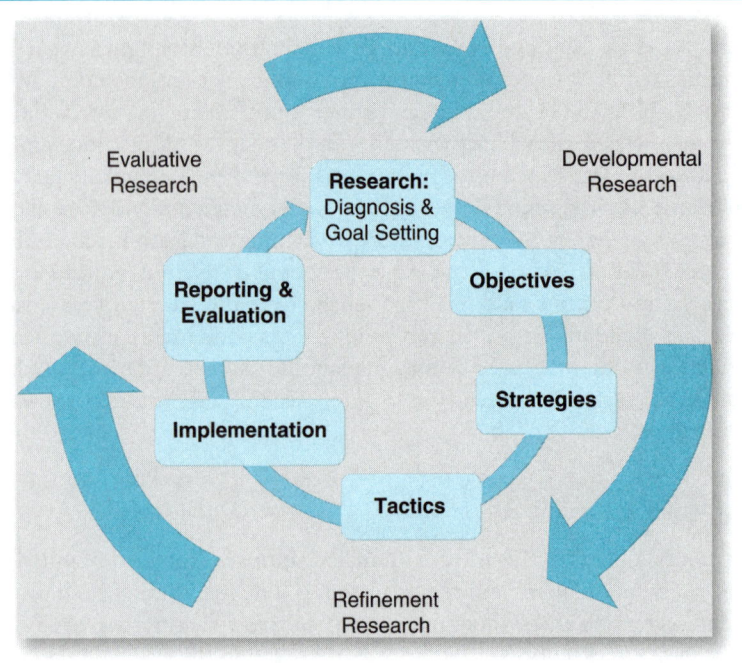

Research is critical at every stage of campaign development and execution. Insights from before (developmental research), during (refinement research), and after (evaluative research) implementation should inform public relations outreach and future campaigns.

THE SIX STEPS OF ROSTIR

ROSTIR stands for Research/Diagnosis, Objectives, Strategies, Tactics, Implementation, and Reporting/Evaluation. As we explore in subsequent chapters, this model appropriately reflects the needs of today's practitioners. While the traditional models of public relations including R.A.C.E. (Research, Action, Communication, Evaluation) and R.O.P.E. (Research, Objectives, Communication, Evaluation) certainly apply, the industry has experienced a clear shift toward approaches that not only position a company as a strategic leader in its respective industry but also as a genuine, authentic, and progressive company desiring to connect with its audience.

THE VALUE OF PUBLIC RELATIONS PLANNING MODELS

The value of any model is in its ability to help enrich our understanding of how an industry or function is practiced. In the world of public relations, traditional models can only take the task of planning so far. Plans should be reviewed and revised on a regular basis, leveraging research at every stage, not merely during the initial planning phase as depicted in R.A.C.E. and R.O.P.E.

ROSTIR PR Planning Guide

STAGE	ACTIONS
Research and Diagnosis	• *Perform Developmental Research*: Conduct secondary and primary research to better understand the organization and its environment. • *Diagnose Challenges and Opportunities*: Define the problems or possibilities for the organization. • *Set Communication Goals*: Connect organization-wide goals to communication or public relations goals to define the impact role for communication and set the scope of the campaign. • *Target Key Audiences and Stakeholders*: Research, select, and prioritize audiences, publics, and stakeholders.

Objectives	• *Set S.M.A.R.T. Communication Objectives*
	   ○ *Specific*: Focus on the situational communication problem or opportunity at hand for a particular public.
	   ○ *Measurable*: Define success through output, outtake, and (preferably) outcome metrics.
	   ○ *Attainable*: Make objectives realistically achievable within budgetary, time, and competitive constraints.
	   ○ *Relevant*: Support and prioritize an organization's mission and goals.
	   ○ *Time-Bound*: Create a clear timetable for execution and measurement.

Strategies	• *Leverage Organizational Strengths*: Strategies should reflect the unique internal and external organizational environment to place the campaign in the best-possible light. • *Complimentary Channel Selection*: Support objectives through complementary channel approaches reflecting different audiences, implementation stages, or message components.

Tactics	• *Craft Effective Messaging*: Create memorable campaign-wide and audience-specific messages supported by research.
	• *Define a Campaign's PESO Approaches*: The tactical mix should reflect audience(s)/publics, timeline, budget, messaging, and team expertise.
	   ○ *Paid Media*
	   ○ *Earned Media*
	   ○ *Shared Media*
	   ○ *Owned Media*
	   ○ *Converged Media*

Implementation	• *Project Management*: Define the budget, timelines, and workflow processes needed to execute the campaign.
	• *Implementing the Plan*: Demonstrate persistence, perseverance, and flexibility in communicating with stakeholders.
	• *Continuous Improvement*
	   ○ *Self-awareness and Self-evaluation*: Create space for reflection and to regularly adjust personal processes in outreach efforts.
	   ○ *Refinement Research*: Track metrics and responses to outreach and messages to see which strategies and tactics are most effective.
	   ○ *Embrace Change*: Rather than executing a plan exactly as written, practitioners should regularly examine the lessons learned throughout a campaign and adjust accordingly.

Reporting and Evaluation	• *Evaluative Research*: Review objective-centered metrics and examine unexpected results—both qualitatively and quantitatively—to create a holistic perspective on your campaign. • *Turning Evaluation into Improvement*: To inform future campaigns, define lessons learned for the PR team as well as for the organization itself. • *Reporting Results*: Generate easy-to-understand, scannable, and customized reporting documents for key stakeholders and organizational leaders.

PRo Tip

THE PESO MODEL

The PESO model, developed by Gini Dietrich, takes the four media types—paid, earned, shared, and owned—and merges them together.

Paid Media: Paid media for a PR program is social media advertising, sponsored content, and e-mail marketing.

Earned Media: Earned media is commonly referred to as either publicity or media relations. It is getting a company's name in print. It is having a newspaper or trade publication write about you, your company, or its offerings. Earned media is what the PR industry is typically known for, because it is one of the most tangible tactics.

Shared Media: Shared media is also known as social media. This area continues to build beyond simply marketing or customer service. Soon, organizations will share it as their main source of communications internally and externally.

Owned Media: Owned media is also known as content. It is something that you own, and it lives on your website or blog. You control the messaging and tell the story in the way that you want it told.

Source: Dietrich, Gini, "PR Pros Must Embrace the PESO Model," Spin Sucks, (March 23, 2015), http://spinsucks.com/communication/pr-pros-must-embrace-the-peso-model.

Public relations should be considered a strategic management function, adding value to organizations through the continual assessment of the organizational environment and then adjusting communication strategies and tactics accordingly. It is important to note that many of the best **public relations campaigns** are rarely ever finished. Real-world campaigns are judged on impact, actions that consumers take, and awareness with regard to a brand, product, event, or even an individual. When planning and executing a PR plan, organizational leaders are interested to see that their audience is connecting, purchasing, attending, sharing, and engaging with them. Campaigns are not only about creating a perfect plan, rather, they are also about connecting the targeted audience(s) with the correct message(s) at a specific time in order to drive action/change. In truth,

FIGURE 1.2
The PESO Model

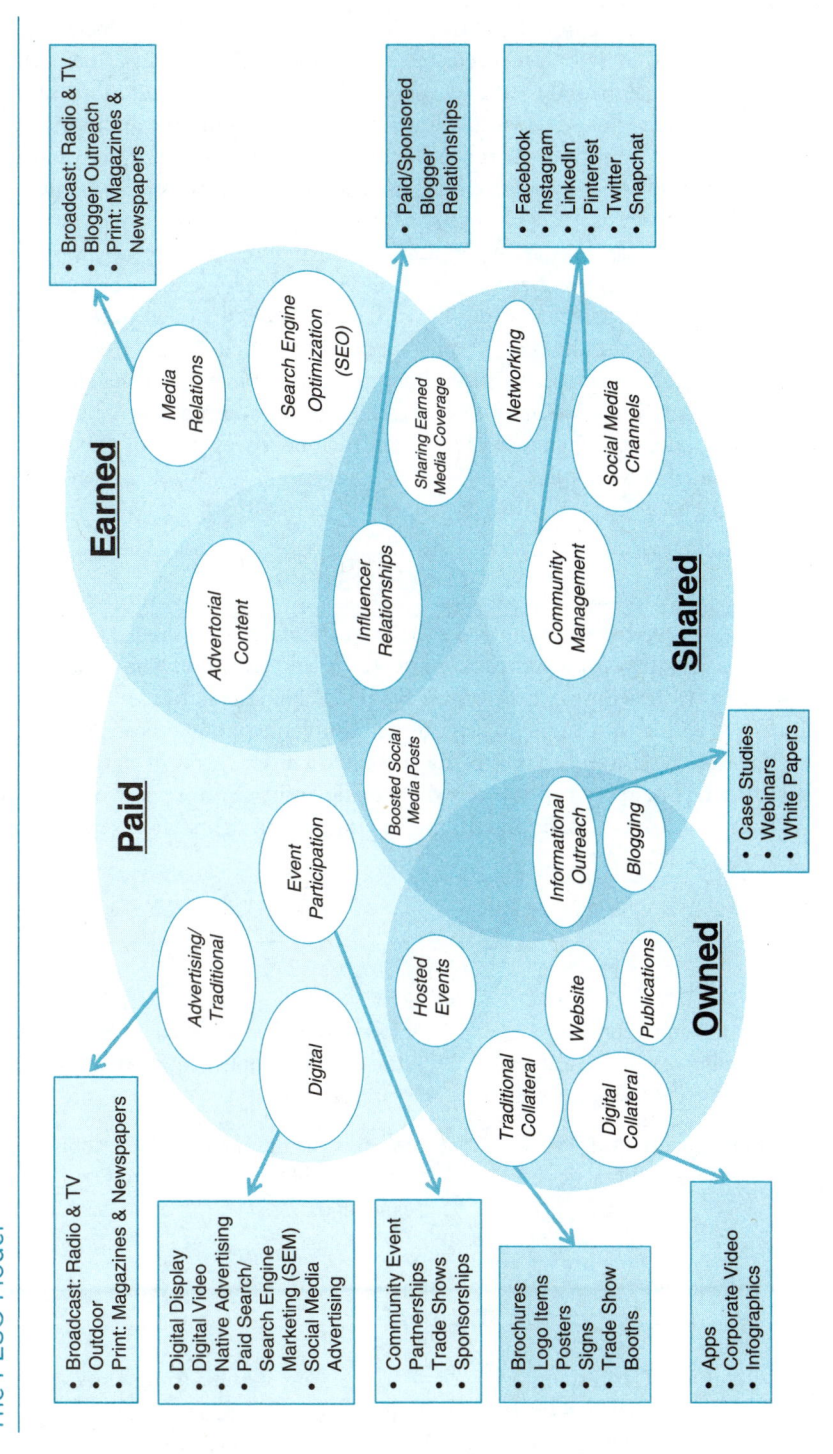

Paid
- Advertising/Traditional
  - Broadcast: Radio & TV
  - Outdoor
  - Print: Magazines & Newspapers
- Digital
  - Digital Display
  - Digital Video
  - Native Advertising
  - Paid Search/Search Engine Marketing (SEM)
  - Social Media Advertising
- Event Participation
  - Community Event Partnerships
  - Trade Shows
  - Sponsorships

Earned
- Media Relations
- Search Engine Optimization (SEO)
  - Broadcast: Radio & TV
  - Blogger Outreach
  - Print: Magazines & Newspapers
- Advertorial Content
- Influencer Relationships
  - Paid/Sponsored Blogger Relationships

Shared
- Sharing Earned Media Coverage
- Networking
- Social Media Channels
  - Facebook
  - Instagram
  - LinkedIn
  - Pinterest
  - Twitter
  - Snapchat
- Community Management
- Boosted Social Media Posts
- Informational Outreach
- Blogging
  - Case Studies
  - Webinars
  - White Papers

Owned
- Hosted Events
- Website
- Publications
- Traditional Collateral
  - Brochures
  - Logo Items
  - Posters
  - Signs
  - Trade Show Booths
- Digital Collateral
  - Apps
  - Corporate Video
  - Infographics

C-suite (Chief Executive Officer, Chief Marketing Officer, Chief Operating Officer, etc.) leaders are generally less interested in the approach or tactics (media relations, marketing, or social media) used in developing a successful plan and more interested in the results. This is why it is critically important to understand the appropriate tools to implement at the right time. At the end of the day, good public relations models incorporate the development of solid **strategic communication** targets with aptly defined goals and objectives, tied to a clear organizational purpose.

The process of appropriately planning a campaign requires a practitioner to anticipate challenges, ensure that audiences are clearly defined, identify objectives, and prioritize resources efficiently in order to work best with each **stakeholder**. The practice of public relations should take on an integrated approach. When we commit to our audience, mission, and goals, we ensure that the best resources are being allocated to our campaign efforts. Let's face it, not every challenge or opportunity will be solved in the same way. Tactics may change over time, but the underlying rules of effective communication will remain the same.

CONCLUSION

When considered together, the ROSTIR and PESO models create a framework for public relations practitioners to plan effectively and use all of the resources at their disposal to create winning campaigns. ROSTIR helps practitioners to execute each critical step within the campaign planning and implementation process. PESO reminds us of the wide variety and complimentary value in a diverse array of channels and tactics for outreach. The rest of this book will provide an in-depth review of both of these frameworks and the tools for practitioners to implement them with organizations large and small.

THINK CRITICALLY

1. Can you identify which communication and media trends are transforming the public relations industry? In which ways are they most impactful?

2. In what ways has PESO influenced the way in which public relations strategies and tactics are formed?

3. How does ROSTIR build an organization's strategic plan implementation? Give specific examples.

4. What is the importance of developing a clear set of outcomes for strategic campaigns?

KEY TERMS

Advertising 15
C-Suite 20
Content amplification 15
Diffusion theory 24
Marketing 15
Native advertising 15
Online community management 15
PESO 15

Programmatic buying 15
Public relations campaign 18
Social listening 15
Social media 15
Social media analytics 15
Stakeholder 20
Strategic communication 20

CONCEPT CASE: INTRODUCING EQUALITY TODAY

As discussed in this chapter, effective integrated public relations and marketing campaigns take considerable planning. Equality Today has just received its most momentous victory to date. Let's decide what to do next.

It is June 26, 2015. The Supreme Court has just announced its decision in *Obergefell v. Hodges*, legalizing same-sex marriage across the United States. The decision is felt deeply nationwide, but you have a particularly important connection: You're the public relations manager for Equality Today, an LGBTQ advocacy organization whose mission is to achieve equal rights for those across the spectrums of gender and sexual orientation in their family, professional, and civic lives.

The five-year-old organization is funded by a variety of foundations and individual donors, its advocacy efforts focus on mobilizing college students and recent graduates to take action supporting causes they believe in. It is a day of celebration for your organization, but also a clear moment of decision. The greatest victory in the movement's history has just been won, but it is unclear what comes next. For an organization supporting advocacy and seeking concrete public policy victories, respond to the following:

- Describe the role public relations should play in the organizational decision-making process.
- Consider how the ROSTIR planning model informs the creation of a strategic public relations campaign.
- Identify the goals that are most feasible and the strategies that best support such efforts.
- Construct action items using the PESO framework: What channels should this type of organization be using?
- Assess the role of leadership, internal stakeholders (such as employees and donors), and external stakeholders (such as community members and funders) in developing and executing these priorities.
- What external obstacles might stand in the way of Equality Today achieving its communication goals?

CASE STUDY: "SEIZE THE HOLIDAYS" WITH KRUSTEAZ: A VIRTUAL BAKING EVENT

From Continental Mills with 360 Public Relations
Campaign Focus: Consumer Engagement

The winter holidays are prime baking season, but, let's face it, they're also the most hectic time of year. Enter Krusteaz, a family-owned baking brand, best known for its pancake mixes and, prior to this campaign, less known for the brand's broader line of cookie, bread, and muffin mixes. Krusteaz's speed-scratch mixes make it easy to bake holiday treats. So, on December 14, 2013, the busiest baking Saturday of the entire year, Krusteaz helped consumers across the country "Seize the Holidays with Krusteaz!"

Research/Diagnosis

Research conducted by the brand defined its target consumer as "Kim," a woman who is "creative" with a lower-case c: while baking is very enjoyable, she's busy and needs convenient ways to put her own creative stamp on the food that she makes for her friends and family.

This audience insight was the basis for a communications strategy that highlighted how easy Krusteaz makes it to bake holiday foods and treats. Krusteaz mixes offered consumers like Kim infinite possibilities to create unique treats by simply adding a few extra ingredients like nuts and shredded coconut. Call it "speed-scratch."

Continental Mills, the parent company for Krusteaz, along with 360 Public Relations, turned to online video for their delivery mechanisms. As of 2017, more than 1 billion hours of YouTube are viewed each day, and consumers' hunger for how-to videos was cited as a key driver of online video viewing.[4] They also tapped into the do-it-yourself (DIY) trend of homemade food gifts. A review of traditional media, social searches, and Google Trends data showed that DIY gifts, and especially food gifts, had been growing in popularity.

Finally, Continental Mills and 360 Public Relations identified the second Saturday of December as the busiest of holiday baking days, according to research from Allrecipes.com.

Objectives

The "Seize the Holidays with Krusteaz" webcast baked a tasty brand story and delicious results during the brand's most important sales season of the year. Campaign objectives included the following:

- Drive traffic to Krusteaz.com so consumers could learn about the range of Krusteaz mixes and where to buy them.

- Increase brand conversation that establishes Krusteaz as a holiday baking resource.

- Acquire new fans, and increase engagement on the brand's social channels with emphasis on Twitter, Facebook, and Pinterest.

Strategies

Based on the brand objectives and insights from brand and agency research, 360 Public Relations devised a strategy to host a live Krusteaz holiday baking webcast that would, in turn, generate earned media attention, influencer engagement, and consumer engagement.

The recipe for success was one-part video and one-part speed-scratch recipes, specifically timed to reach consumers surrounding the busiest baking day of the year. The firm, 360 Public Relations, identified popular cookbook author, Weelicious blog founder, and mom of two, Catherine McCord, to host the Krusteaz holiday baking webcast. Catherine's passion for baking and strong social media presence helped bring the Krusteaz brand to the forefront. Catherine's pre-event social media and online activities included a cocurated holiday board with Krusteaz on Pinterest and tweets and Facebook posts about the baking webcast that were instrumental in driving other influential food bloggers to participate in and share the webcast.

Tactics

- Two-hour webcast with baking tips, recipes, and gift giving ideas

- Video vignettes available through Krusteaz.com
  - Cross promotion on Catherine's YouTube channel Weelicious

- Bloggers invited to cover the virtual event

- Seize the Holidays Baking Kit sent to 50 top-tier bloggers

Earned

The Seize the Holidays campaign exemplified earned media through the bloggers who were involved with the campaign. The support and engagement that this campaign received from the hundreds of bloggers, including fifty who were sent supplies for the baking day, demonstrated earned media through their interactions with the campaign and during the virtual event.[5,6]

Shared

Social media played a large role in this campaign as well, highlighting the impact of shared media on the campaign. With one of the objectives being to increase the interactions and engagements on Twitter, Facebook, and Pinterest, many of the tactics used drove consumers and the target audience to these platforms. As recipes were posted, audience members were able to interact with the brand and with like-minded individuals supporting the Krusteaz campaign through various social media platforms. These interactions played a crucial role in meeting the objectives presented at the beginning of the campaign.[7] For example, Catherine McCord, the host of the online baking event, posted a video to her personal YouTube page that showed her participating in the campaign. This video ultimately ended up gaining more than 10,000 views, providing the campaign with a valuable earned media opportunity to reach more consumers.[8]

Owned

Owned media was the foundation for the virtual baking event during the Seize the Holidays campaign. Audience members created their own recipes and shared them on numerous social media platforms, using the event-related hashtags. This created a great deal of user-generated content, helping drive the overall success of the campaign.[9]

Implementation

Catherine's kitchen provided an authentic, relatable backdrop for the two-hour webcast, which incorporated baking tips, demos of five recipes using Krusteaz mixes, holiday gifting ideas made from homemade goods, and tips for getting kids involved in the kitchen. The topics resonated with the engaged viewers, who especially enjoyed being able to ask their baking, gifting, and entertaining questions in real time.

After the event, the entire webcast was edited into several video vignettes and made available to consumers visiting Krusteaz.com. Additionally, Catherine posted an excerpt of the video to her Weelicious YouTube page, which received more than ten thousand views in less than 48 hours.

Reporting/Evaluation

Staff members from 360PR vetted and invited several hundred bloggers to attend the virtual event, and over 200 influencers tuned in to the December 14 webcast, not only watching from home but also sharing the information with their social media friends. Representatives from 360PR staffed the Krusteaz Facebook and Twitter sites to further engage the web-based audience and spread the message via photos, webcast commentary, and Krusteaz giveaways. The fifty blogger hosts also helped drive the online conversation.

The "Seize the Holidays with Krusteaz" Virtual Baking event gave the brand reason to celebrate, serving up sweet results:

- Drive traffic to Krusteaz.com: The webcast drove a 60 percent year-over-year increase in visits to Krusteaz.com, with one in ten website visitors clicking through to the Krusteaz retail locator showing intent to purchase and learning where to buy Krusteaz mixes. In December, thirty-six earned media and blog placements were among the top-fifty referrers to Krusteaz.com; 96 percent of participating bloggers linked to Krusteaz.com or Krusteaz.com/Holidays; the spokesperson's blog, Weelicious, was a top-five referrer to Krusteaz.com in December. (Source: Google Analytics)

- Use the webcast as a news-making and conversation-driving event that establishes Krusteaz as a holiday baking resource: The webcast drove a 320 percent increase in online brand conversation compared to the previous month; conversation was centered on the December 14 baking event and the content that showcased Krusteaz as a resource to home bakers. #KrusteazHolidays became a trending topic on Twitter. The webcast also drove more than seventy-five pieces of earned media coverage and 200 million earned and social media impressions. (Sources: Radian6, Compete, and Cision)

- Acquire new fans and increase engagement on the brand's social media channels (Facebook, Twitter, and Pinterest): Fan acquisition on the Krusteaz Pinterest account increased 71 percent and 55 percent on Twitter. On Facebook, traffic on the day of the webcast rose by 98 percent compared to the previous Saturday. Influence from the group of bloggers spanned further than just their blogs with more than 450 posts on Twitter for 14 million impressions (#KrusteazHolidays was a "trending topic") and more than half sharing on Facebook (over 300 thousand impressions). (Sources: Facebook Insights, Sprout Social, and analysis by 360PR's Research & Analytics Specialists)

Theories

Diffusion theory is typically concerned with the spread of messages that are perceived as new ideas. By creating a virtual baking event, Krusteaz and 360PR gained enough momentum to increase traffic to the Krusteaz website and make consumers more aware of the multitude of options of baking mixes available from Krusteaz and to establish Krusteaz as a baking resource to consumers, specifically during the holiday season.

Models

Additionally, a **two-way symmetrical model** of communication was also used in this campaign. This model presents a balanced, strategic, and informed approach to public relations. Organizations and their publics adjust to each other and attempt to achieve mutual understanding using direct, two-way communication, not persuasion. The use of social media channels, specifically Twitter, Facebook, and Pinterest, increased engagement with the Krusteaz target audiences.

Strategic Communication Campaign Fundamentals

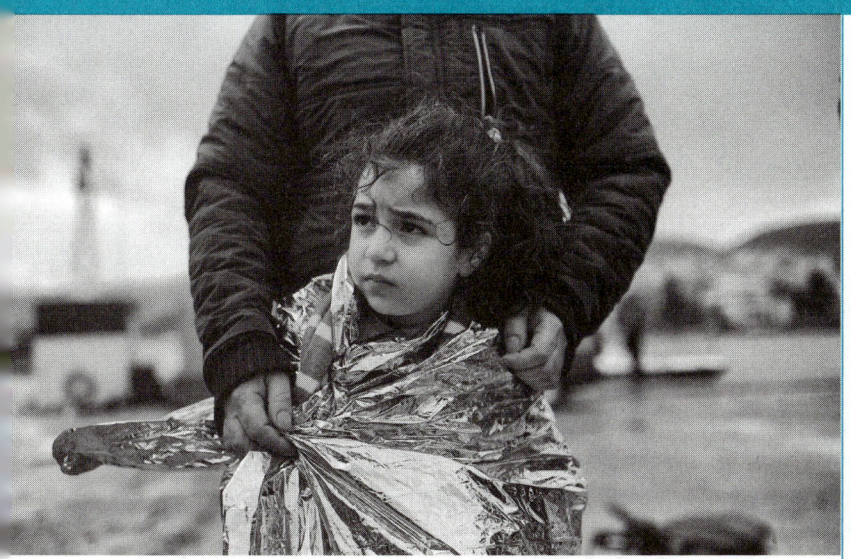

2

THINK AHEAD

2.1 Understand that communication campaigns are part of broader, ongoing public relations strategies.

2.2 Explain the importance of each step in the planning process beginning with research and ending with evaluation.

2.3 Recognize that campaign planning should be built around stakeholder needs.

As Syrian refugees fled their homeland due to a violent war, people across the world watched, commented, shared, raised funds, protested in outrage, and opened their boarders to migrants who were suffering. The BBC reported that more than 33,000 tweets were sent using the Arabic **hashtag** #Welcoming_Syria's_refugees_is_a_Gulf_duty to highlight the humanitarian challenge at hand.[1] Many of these tweets illustrated the seemingly hypocritical nature of Arab leaders asking Europe to do more for refugees, when these countries, who all share similar languages, heritage, and religion stood by and watched the crisis unfold. Although these events happened in what may have seemed like a world away, they were brought to life on the **social sphere** with photographs, tweets, articles, and breaking news videos. This is communication today. The transmission of oral and written word has never been a more important tool than in our always-on, 24/7, minute-to-minute information cycle.

So, you may be wondering, what does this have to do with public relations and campaign planning? Well, in a word, everything.

As public relations (PR) practitioners, we are professional communicators. Management relies upon this role to be better than most at communicating an organization's messaging. All too often, public relations practitioners are pigeonholed into being labeled media liaisons or relationship managers; however, this role is more than that; PR practitioners are strategic market counselors. In order to successfully execute strategic integrated campaigns, we must be able to see the big picture and the minute details. It is impossible for organizations to disconnect from the world around them and to operate in a vacuum.

WHY WE PLAN

The foundation of a well-developed public relations plan is an effective approach devised from a robust communication blueprint. Using a strategic approach has everything to do with identifying key stakeholder outcomes, targeting the right audience, formulating the most impactful objectives and message, and incorporating the most effective tactics to accomplish the necessary goals. A plan is an avenue that is used to propose and obtain approvals, as well as a mechanism for monitoring and evaluating a product that distinguishes true public relations professionals.[2]

The goal of strategic public relations is to contribute to the overarching mission of an organization by supporting its defined goals. In order for the strategies to be successful, it is imperative that public relations practitioners obtain accurate information about the challenges at hand, the publics with which they communicate, the effectiveness of each communication initiative, and the relational impacts that each program has with critical stakeholders.

PRo Tip

LISTEN FIRST, PLAN SECOND

Before you begin planning, listen. The strongest and most strategic campaigns are informed by what customers, prospects, and stakeholders are sharing and posting in the public and social spheres, so listen to what they are saying or, for that matter, *not* saying. Listening is one of the most important but underused tools of the public relations practitioner.[3]

Source: James Macnamara, "Organizational Listening: Addressing a Major Gap in Public Relations Theory and Practice," Journal of Public Relations Research 28 (2016): 146–169.

Shayna Englin, who teaches graduate courses in strategic communication at Georgetown University and George Washington University, notes that **strategic communication** "means communicating the best message, through the right channels, measured against well-considered organizational and communications-specific goals."[4] Understanding the specific executable tasks and their impacts can ensure that programs are delivered more effectively and highlights the value that the public relations function brings to the organization.

One approach to planning is a process called **management by objectives**, commonly referred to as MBO. Organizations have missions and goals, which can be broken down into measurable objectives. Responsibility for execution and completion of goals is held by different parts of the organization. Public relations professionals often use communication objectives to provide focus and define direction when formulating a strategy targeting or supporting specific organizational objectives.[5] Norman Nager and T. Harrell Allen outline several steps of MBO that assist practitioners in building a plan that includes examining client and employer objectives; audience analysis; media channels; primary and secondary sources; communication strategies; message sentiment; and visually appealing artifacts such as photos, infographics, artwork, or videos.[6] These steps can be used to form a checklist to spur public relations practitioners in formulating a comprehensive plan and a sound foundation for strategic development.

As presented in the Introduction, a simplified approach to planning is typically composed of four steps. First, practitioners use research to define the problem or situation; then they develop objectives and strategies that address the situation; once complete, they implement the strategies; and finally measure the results of the public relations efforts. John Marston's **R.A.C.E.**[7] model—Research, Action planning, Communication, Evaluation—or Jerry Hendrix's **R.O.P.E.**[8] model—Research, Objectives, Programming, Evaluation—are commonly used to describe the process.

Both planning models begin with research and end with evaluation. The four steps encompass the following:

1. Conduct research to analyze the situation facing the organization and to accurately define the problem or opportunity in such a way that the public relations efforts can successfully address the cause of the issue and not just its symptoms.

2. Develop a strategic action plan that addresses the issue that was assessed in the first step. This includes having an overall goal, measurable objectives, clearly identified publics, targeted strategies, and effective tactics.

3. Execute the plan with communication tools and tasks that contribute to reaching the overarching objectives.

4. Measure whether the campaign was successful in meeting the goals using a variety of evaluation tools.

All planning models have varying strengths and weaknesses. In this book, we expand our focus on the planning stage using the ROSTIR model to emphasize the importance

Secondary and primary research, diagnosing the organizational problem or opportunity, and setting communication-specific goals are critical first steps to a successful campaign.

of understanding and diagnosing the problem, challenge, or opportunity at hand; setting communication goals and objectives; and building strategies and tactics from them.

ELEMENTS OF A STRATEGIC PLAN

It may seem proper to begin the process of planning with tactics including brochures, press releases, an event, or even a blog post; however, an appropriate plan should even precede the selection of tactics. By first conducting research, practitioners are able to define the overall goals, objectives, and strategies of the plan, otherwise efforts may be wasted from the outset. Some practitioners create a brief outline, while others develop an expansive document that includes a substantial amount of detail. Another model for the planning process, the ROSTIR strategic planning model, includes six key elements, all of which will be expanded upon in upcoming chapters. The following is a brief summary of each element:

- Research: diagnosis/goal setting
- Objectives
- Strategies
- Tactics
- Implementation
- Reporting/evaluation

Research, Diagnosis, and Goal Setting

The term *diagnose* means to ascertain the cause or nature of something, usually an issue or problem that must be solved.[9] In this initial stage of planning, practitioners ask themselves the following question: Why is a PR plan necessary? There are many situations that prompt the need for strategic public relations planning. Some include

- overcoming a problem or negative situation;
- conducting a specific, one-time project supporting the launch of a new product or service;
- reinforcing an ongoing effort to preserve a reputation or public support;
- expanding your organization's outreach to a new audience;
- creating and reinforcing a brand and professional corporate image;
- mitigating the impact of negative publicity and/or corporate crisis; or
- establishing expertise among your peers, the press, or your potential clients or customers.

Once the decision to create the plan has been made, regardless of the rationale, the foundation for the overarching strategy has to be defined. Research accompanies this stage of development. **Research** is the methodical collection and explanation of information used to increase understanding of needs, audiences, channels, and communication baselines.[10] Strategic planning cannot work without intimate knowledge of the intended audience. Research is key to understanding the target audience and the needs of the plan. This initial, developmental research provides practitioners with the insights to diagnose challenges and opportunities, before prioritizing and reframing them as communication goals.

Objectives

After research is conducted, a clear diagnosis is realized, and broad communication goals are set, the next step of the process is to establish appropriate **objectives** for the plan. Objectives must be measurable. At the end of the day, the C-suite executives place emphasis on the bottom line. Executive management is looking to see data, analysis, measurement, and how each relate back to public relations efforts. Statistics and data are often necessary to show that efforts put forth by a public relations department are contributing to the overarching goals of the company. Outcomes can evaluate whether or not a change in behavior or relationships is influenced by the public relations strategy. Examples of high quality outcomes might include an increase in the sale of a product or an uptick in donations due to an executed public relations campaign. As organizational resources are precious and companies are becoming increasingly frugal, executives are often unwilling to spend money unless an outcome contributes to a business objective.[11]

Objectives should connect four key elements: the target audience or public, the specific outcome, the measurement or magnitude of the change required to reach this outcome, and the target date.[12] Campaign objectives should contain an impact factor, such as a knowledge outcome, a change of opinion, or a change of behavior.[13] Strategies and tactics should be designed to support the achievement of the objective.

- **Example:** Focused on bottom line metrics, objectives are outcomes that can be quantified. Armed with $2.75 million in grant funding, the Texas Council on Family Violence launched two public awareness campaigns, "There is Help, There is Hope" and "Family and Friends." The goals for both campaigns were measurable.[14]
    - **Objective:** Achieve 20 percent increase in Texas-based calls to the national family violence hotline during paid media flights.
    - **Strategy:** Connect with families directly by creating an informational brochure to increase awareness for the program.
    - **Tactic:** Distribute one million educational campaign brochures over the duration of the campaign.

It can be difficult to measure how well a particular informational objective has been achieved. Objectives should have clear metrics that can be tracked and quantified. The public relations practitioner, along with management, must set the objectives together. As noted earlier, objectives must be realistic, achievable, and measurable in order to illustrate success. To simply state "increase awareness by 25 percent" is not enough. A solid baseline is needed to indicate whether or not the target audience increased awareness by 25 percent. Therefore, developmental research must provide an initial baseline (e.g., Initial awareness may be at 40 percent among the public in question, therefore 65 percent would be the target). Measurement before, during, and after the campaign is critical to understand whether the objective has been achieved.

Strategies

Strategies are the choices made to select specific channels and approaches, focusing efforts toward achieving the objectives. For each objective, there may be a single overall strategy, or there may be multiple strategies depending on the public relations plan. Some strategies may also support multiple objectives.

Tactics

Tactics are the tangible aspects of the strategy. There are various methods to reach a target audience, such as face-to-face interactions and media outreach through paid, earned, shared, and owned channels. Face-to-face tactics might include special events such as annual meetings, open houses, grand openings, recognition events, group

> ## *PRo Tip*
>
> ### KEEP TACTICS TOP OF MIND
>
> Review tactics regularly. While an organization's mission and goals should be relatively stable over time, and many components of a public relations plan can be considered fixed elements, tactics require constant review. Unexpected external developments, a change in the business atmosphere, emerging media channels, or the actions of competitors can require a fresh perspective and second look.

meetings, town halls, round tables, and meetups. Owned media tactics are comprised of any material that is managed and owned by the company, such as a company blog, annual report, blogs, case studies, books, infographics, mobile apps, logos, letters, brochures, websites, podcasts, webinars, videos, photographs, and newsletters. Earned media is one of the most powerful vehicles for getting messages out to the masses. Earned media refers to publicity gained through promotional efforts rather than publicity gained through paid messaging like in advertising. When a practitioner's pitch to a journalist or blogger results in some type of media placement, this is considered earned media. Social and digital media channels with opportunities for interactivity constitute the space for shared media. **Mediated** and **nonmediated** approaches should work together to create effective campaigns.

Let us examine the combination of a strategy and tactic collectively at work. Consumers often prefer products that are all natural, healthier options to those that may be less environmentally friendly or less wholesome. Coffee creamer is probably not the first product that jumps to mind when considering natural, healthy, and organic options. As a way to differentiate themselves from the competition, Nestlé Coffee-mate set out to change opinions with its line of all-natural coffee creamers, Natural Bliss. Its strategy was developed to turn heads and garner attention. Nestlé Coffee-mate surprised consumers with an all-natural coffee experience where they least expected it—at their local coffee shop. Nestlé Coffee-mate staffed a New York City coffee shop, temporarily renaming the establishment "Natural Bliss Café." Actors who looked the part of baristas, wearing little more than body paint, served coffee with Natural Bliss creamer. This strategy was successful in large part because the target audience, Millennials, were not only shocked but also had the opportunity to sample free coffee and Natural Bliss.

The strategy can be considered as the idea (a direct consumer experience of the product in a surprising setting), and the tactic is the method through which that idea is carried out (the uniquely revealing pop-up coffee shop, actors, and free products to sample). In the above example, the intent behind the strategy was to introduce the shock factor to the targeted audience, and the tactic was the unexpected pop-up coffee shop

Nestlé emphasized the *natural* in its Natural Bliss Café coffee shop takeover.

managed by scantily clad, painted baristas. This strategy also relies in part on shared social media and traditional earned media to spread the story, ensuring coverage and awareness beyond those who entered the shop itself. In this way, smart strategies and tactics can impact multiple audiences through multiple channels.

Implementation

Determining the right timing to implement a campaign and identifying who is responsible for executing the campaign is the next step in the planning process. Factors such as the complexity, duration, steps, and intricacy of the campaign play a key role during the **implementation** phase. A calendar or timeline should be developed to help guide practitioners through the implementation process. Some campaigns may only last a month while others may be staggered over several months or longer. Appropriate timing of the campaign, scheduling of the correct sequence of tactics, and building a calendar can help contribute to the development of a seamless implementation schedule and workflow.[15]

Reporting/Evaluation

The process of reporting and **evaluation** relates the results of the campaign directly back to the stated objectives. Public relations practitioners must put measures in place to track the results of each public relations campaign, then contextualize and communicate those results to key stakeholders. Reporting and evaluation should not only take place at the end of a campaign. In fact, quite the opposite is true. Savvy practitioners continually evaluate the metrics throughout the process. In doing so, a practitioner will know whether or not the stated objectives, strategies, and tactics are resonating with the intended audiences. It is appropriate to measure objectives at multiple points during the implementation phase through the conclusion of the public relations campaign. If strategies and tactics are not working as expected, this process provides the opportunity to revise them before the end of the campaign. Experienced practitioners know that flexibility is a key part of successful campaigns.

As previously noted, objectives must be measurable; therefore, it is vital to understand the appropriate metrics that will be used in order to properly evaluate if the objectives have been achieved. Reporting should reiterate the specific objectives and how each was measured. Informational objectives might include metrics such as surveys of awareness among key publics, media content analysis, number of fliers distributed, or number of hits to a website. Motivational objectives, on the other hand, are more easily evaluated using metrics evaluating the number of attendees at a specific event, direct increase in sales, or surveys that benchmark consumer's beliefs before and after using a product.

Budget

When evaluating the previous steps, it is important to not forget about the all-important **budget** that has been reserved for the campaign. At the initiation of any project, the public relations manager should sit with both the internal and external teams to establish the program costs and expectations. Budgets are generally divided into two basic categories: staff time and out-of-pocket expenses (also known as OOP expenses).

Staff expenses include the time required by the practitioners to create and execute the plan. This varies widely, but can often account for 70 percent or more of the overall budget.[16] Media kits, collateral material, website development, video production, transportation, staging, and even media costs such as radio advertising or paid social media are some examples of out-of-pocket expenditures.

PUTTING IT ALL TOGETHER

This chapter began by highlighting the importance of the 2015 Syrian refugee crisis. Global outcries for support did not go unnoticed. At the time of the crisis, President Obama's administration launched its first-ever **crowdfunding** campaign to raise money for Syria's refugee crisis and to draw the American public into helping replenish the United Nations' (U.N.) refugee agency's strained budget.[17] The White House Office of Digital Strategy led the effort. At the close of the second full day of the campaign, donors had contributed over $800,000 for the U.N. refugee agency UNHCR. This initial funding was enough to provide "immediate necessities and a place to sleep for 3,000 people in need," UNHCR reported.[18]

In this example, the White House solicited support from the American people using the Twitter hashtag #AidRefugees. A blog post from a White House staff member, Joshua Miller, explained that the Obama administration, along with other large corporations, had donated more than $5 billion to the Syrian crisis. The president called for action from all Americans.[19] Collectively, the White House asked American citizens to help in any way they could, and the response was immediate.

This Syrian child was one of 3,000 refugees that benefited from UNHCR assistance thanks to the Obama administration's crowdfunding campaign.

By creating and promoting the hashtag #AidRefugees, the White House Office of Digital Strategy was able to unite a country around a serious cause, while at the same time delivering significant funding for direct support. At the time of publication, this initiative had raised $1,777,007.[20]

For PR practitioners, this campaign represents a clear example and opportunity for identifying the objectives, strategies, and tactics behind the campaign. Taking a closer look, in the simplest form, the *objective* of this campaign was to raise funds for Syrian refugees, the *strategy* was to formulate a far-reaching, widespread social media outreach approach, and the *tactic* was to implement the hashtag #AidRefugees, calling for citizens to unite, act, and donate.

CONCLUSION

Planning is critical to effective campaigns. There are many approaches to strategic planning, but the most useful follow the practices of management by objectives: setting clearly defined targets and building out a plan of action to implement them. This allows for work to be broken down into digestible pieces and to empower every individual involved with the responsibility for their piece of the larger plan. The ROSTIR model is one approach particularly well suited to public relations campaign planning in that it emphasizes the research necessary throughout the process, as well as a clear separation of the objectives, strategies, and tactics that provide a playbook for implementation.

THINK CRITICALLY

1. What are the differences between goals and objectives?

2. What qualities go into well-written objectives?

3. How do strategies and tactics relate? Identify the best way to distinguish the two by giving examples.

4. Why are measurable objectives important during the evaluation phase? What are some advantages and disadvantages to incorporating measurable objectives into a strategic campaign?

5. Consider the role the Obama Administration played in the first ever White House-sponsored crowdfunding campaign to help Syrian refugees. Do you think it was a well-designed campaign? Support your response with evidence found in the chapter.

KEY TERMS

Budget 33
Crowdfunding 33
Diagnose 29
Evaluation 32
Hashtag 25
Implementation 32
Management by objectives (MBO) 27

Mediated communication 31
Media uses and gratification theory 39
Nonmediated communication 31
Objectives 29
R.A.C.E. 27
Research 29

R.O.P.E. 27
Social Sphere 25
Strategic communication 27
Strategies 30
Tactics 30

CONCEPT CASE: MISSION-DRIVEN PLANNING FOR EQUALITY TODAY

The mission for Equality Today is as follows:

Equality Today works to promote respect and justice for people of all sexual orientations, genders, gender expressions, and gender identities; particularly gay, lesbian, bisexual, queer, and transgender persons.

Through education, advocacy, and support, we allocate our resources across three areas:

- *Educational programs*
- *Direct services and resources*
- *Advocacy*

Extended: Programs, services, and advocacy efforts are guided by an intersectional social justice perspective. Equality Today recognizes that people experience the world through diverse approaches depending on the constellation of identities they hold and the ways that those identities are privileged and/or marginalized by existing institutional structures and societal norms.

Your task is to build out a brief strategic public relations plan sketch for Equality Today using the ROSTIR framework. Begin by using these four areas to guide your research, planning, and development:

- **Identify Publics**: Identifying publics is one of the first steps in planning a public relations program. Identify groups or subgroups with which Equality Today needs to communicate, talk, and listen. Through research identify and prioritize publics and segments of those publics. Consider the following:

- Who needs to know or understand?
- Who needs to be involved?
- Whose advice or support do you need?
- Who will be affected?
- Who has something to gain or lose?

- **Value-driven goals**: Based on the research conducted in identifying publics, create a set of value-driven goals by identifying key publics that Equality Today could target for future campaigns. Goals should be grounded in the organization's mission. Use the mission provided to help develop overarching goals.

- **Three key messages**: Identify and create at least three messages Equality Today could use to advocate for their cause. Develop messages that will motivate publics to take action.

- **Evaluation**: Evaluation of success is only as good as the quality of the objectives. Evaluation helps practitioners in at least three ways. It
  1. verifies that public relations efforts were effective because they met objectives,
  2. demonstrates return on public relations investment, and
  3. provides information for refining future public relations strategies.

Measurement should be considered when crafting the objectives, otherwise assessments cannot be completed properly.

CASE STUDY: OSCAR MAYER'S WAKEY, WAKEY, EGGS AND BAKEY!

From 360i and Oscar Mayer
Campaign Focus: Product Marketing

A collaboration between Oscar Mayer and 360i resulted in the launch of a technology-rich campaign to bring the sounds and smells of bacon to an interactive alarm clock. Capitalizing on the popularity of bacon, this campaign targeted a particular public that was fiercely passionate about bacon.

Research/Diagnosis

We have probably all heard the phase, "Everything tastes better with bacon." Well, we cannot deny that the popularity of bacon has, for many, grown to the level of a collective obsession. Bacon has seemingly exerted its influence on everything from bacon ice cream, bacon topped cupcakes, bacon-infused vodka, bacon soap, bacon lip gloss, and even the outrageous Luther Burger, which is a hamburger/cheeseburger, topped with bacon and using glazed doughnuts for buns.[21] The public relations team at Oscar Mayer had one question to answer: Americans have been waking up to the scent and sizzle of Oscar Mayer bacon for years, so how can Oscar Mayer bacon stand out to bacon-lovin' people?[22] To address this question, the team at 360i and Oscar Mayer embarked upon a research-driven campaign that breathed new life into a 100-year-old brand.

As the prepackaged, sliced meat category was shrinking, largely in part to changing consumer tastes and preferences, Oscar Mayer sought to build brand engagement and affection for a younger generation.[23] According to the 360i website, Oscar Mayer and the creative team at 360i launched a series of talk-worthy campaigns that each highlighted Oscar Mayer bacon's quality attributes. By putting Oscar Mayer in the middle of the bacon conversation, they got a new generation talking about the brand—and drove a halo effect for its entire meat portfolio.[24]

Objectives

The main objective of the "Wake Up and Smell the Bacon" campaign was to promote their bacon in a way that allowed it to stand out over the competition. Since the cost of Oscar Mayer's products was a bit more than off-brand bacon, but less than the gourmet varieties, the company needed to remind the public why its bacon was the right choice.[25] Simply stated, the Oscar Mayer brand was looking to make itself relatable to customers. Promoting an item that is both trendy and fun can create great relationships with customers, who are then more likely to remain loyal when they feel that there is a deep connection to the brand.

Strategies

Target Audience

Using the momentum gained from two very successful and imaginative 360i-led initiatives, "The Great American Bacon Barter" and "Say It with Bacon," Oscar Mayer ensured its brand was up to the challenge of "bringing home the bacon" once again. By capitalizing on the popularity of bacon, the company targeted bacon lovers the world over; specifically directing their efforts toward consumers who were gadget and technology buffs and social media enthusiasts. Oscar Mayer decided to direct their efforts toward the creation of a revolutionary mobile alarm clock that would allowed bacon enthusiasts to wake up to the sound and scent of Oscar Mayer bacon.[26]

The Oscar Mayer strategy was to connect consumers to a "euphoric, multisensory experience."[27]

For nine months, Oscar Mayer conducted in-depth research to create the perfect Oscar Mayer bacon scent, accompanied by the unmistakable sounds of sizzling bacon. The result was a user-friendly alarm clock app, a custom Oscar Mayer bacon scent, and an IOS prototype device to deliver it.[28]

Leveraging their social listening prowess, Oscar Mayer and 360i learned that their target audience was regularly connected to their social communities through their phone, but more importantly, that these individuals also slept with their phone next to their nightstand every night; even relying on it as their alarm clock in the morning.[29] Armed with these insights, Oscar Mayer realized that they could capture the attention of their consumers when they awoke each morning.

Tactics

In order to promote their new product, Oscar Mayer developed a series of tactics directly targeting bacon enthusiasts:[30]

Owned

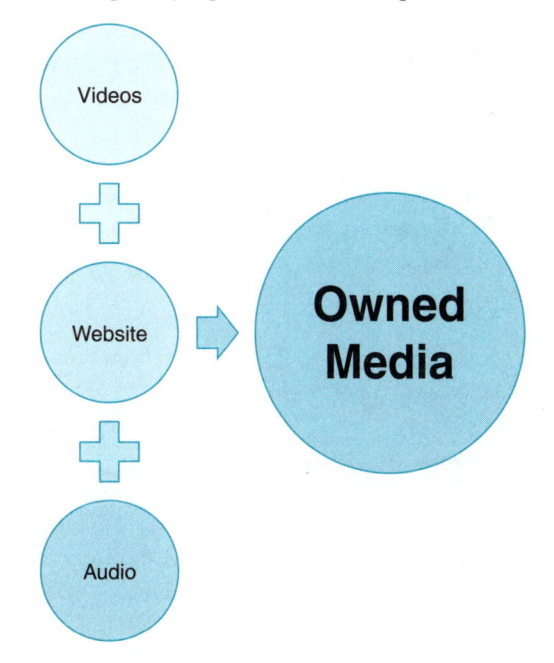

Videos: 360i and Oscar Mayer developed web video's parodying the over-the-top, whimsical tone of contemporary fragrance ads. (https://www.youtube.com/watch?v=PiWdF3u9C0w)

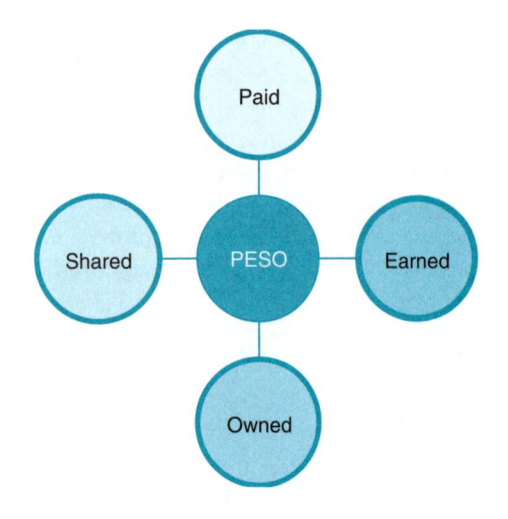

Website: Oscar Mayer launched an accompanying website, WakeUpAndSmellTheBacon.com, directing visitors to a specific page with a daily bacon quiz and a sweepstakes for the chance to win one of the 5,000 alarm clock devices.

iTunes: From the new website, Oscar Mayer drove entrants to the iTunes store to download a branded app that synced directly with the scent device so that they could wake up each morning to the sounds and smells of sizzling Oscar Mayer bacon.

Shared

Twitter: Consumers were rewarded with an additional entry into the contest if they tweeted the link to the specified website.

Earned

Media Relations: A handful of reporters and social media influencers were given the device to test and experience.

Implementation

Nearly as rapidly as the campaign was launched, a bacon pandemonium spread across the Internet and made the campaign a viral sensation. "Demand for the limited-edition product was explosive, as more than 307,000 people applied to win a free device, and more than 67,000 people downloaded the app."[31]

Fans responded to the campaign on social media with: "OHMYGOODNESS.WANT," "Would do anything for a piece of this earthly heaven," and, "Oscar Mayer Promises Bacon Alarm Clock, World Loses its Mind."[32]

Reporting/Evaluation

Media outlets including NBC News, The Huffington Post, Mashable, CNN, Time, Bloomberg Businessweek, ABC, Fox News, and The Guardian jumped at the chance to demo the devices on TV and provide reviews on the product in newspapers and periodicals. USA Today called the Oscar Mayer alarm clock, "The best invention since whatever came before sliced bread."[33] Garnering more than 520 million earned media impressions, the campaign propelled Oscar Mayer to be the most talked-about bacon brand in America, in large part due to a 2,700 percent lift in Oscar Mayer-branded bacon online conversations.

With the objectives of increasing brand recognition of their bacon and how well they related to customers, Oscar Mayer measured the success of the campaign by evaluating their social media based analytics. Over the course of the campaign, more than 300,000 people entered the sweepstakes in hopes of bringing home one of the "bacon-rific" devices, and 67,000 bacon enthusiasts had downloaded the accompanying app.[34] Oscar Mayer also had over 520 million media impressions for their efforts, making them the most talked about bacon brand in the country.[35] Mission accomplished.

"Wake Up and Smell the Bacon" has earned the Bronze Lion from Cannes Lions Awards—PR: Food & Nutrition; ADC Awards—Mobile: Mobile Advertising; Shorty Awards—Most Creative Use of Tech: Food/Beverage; The Webby Awards—Advertising & Media: Experience Marketing—People's Voice Winner; The One Show—Mobile Apps—Silver Pencil; Warc Prize

Awards—Social Strategy; Cannes Lions Awards—Mobile '14: Innovative Use of Tech—Silver Lion; Digiday Mobi & Sammy Awards '14—Best Mobile Platform Innovation; and the Gold IAB MIXX Awards '14—Best Mobile Innovation for their efforts.

3601i and Oscar Mayer have repeatedly succeeded within their target market of bacon-loving people—particularly millennials—by shifting away from television advertising. Year after year, 360i and Oscar Mayer continue to surprise their key publics with award winning, unique, and captivating strategic campaigns. To date they have implemented a coast-to-coast, bacon-and-social media-powered road trip, velvet, luxury bacon box set just in time for Father's Day; a dating app that connected bacon lovers far and wide; and a bacon-scented alarm clock, hailed by media as "the best thing since sliced bread."[36]

Theories

Media Uses and Gratification Theory: This theory indicates that people select media to satisfy their needs or "to be entertained." The "Wake Up and Smell the Bacon" campaign was considered entertaining to the Oscar Mayer customers, which in turn influenced the customers' desire to take part in the campaign. Oscar Mayer used millennials' love for bacon to help these customers satisfy their needs.

Agenda Setting Theory: Agenda setting theory states that the media does not tell people how to think, but it does tell people what to think about.[37] In garnering millions of earned media impressions and thousands of digital conversations, Oscar Mayer found that they had more people talking about their device and their brand, due in large part to the media and agenda setting theory.

3 Understanding PESO

THINK AHEAD

3.1 Understand the PESO model and the differences between paid, earned, shared/social, and owned media.

3.2 Recognize when companies should use paid, earned, shared/social, and owned media.

3.3 Identify how each area works together to form strategic, holistic campaigns.

3.4 Devise a strategy for when to use each approach.

"Did you see a cocktail napkin with our entire marketing campaign on it?"

WHAT IS PESO?

As you will discover, the **PESO model** is a strategy that builds upon the integration of paid, earned, shared, and owned media to deliver integrated marketing communication programs that extend reach and establish brands as leaders within their industry.[1] The PESO model takes these four media types—paid, earned, shared, and owned—and merges them together. Understanding when to use each element is paramount. Tailoring and customizing PESO campaigns to the audience and company goals is essential to successfully executing a public relations campaign today.

FIGURE 3.1
The PESO Model

Paid
- Controlled
- Timely
- Multi-channel

Earned
- Uncontrolled
- Credible
- Outlet-driven

Shared
- Uncontrolled
- Co-created
- Audience-centric

Owned
- Controlled
- Diverse
- Brand-focused

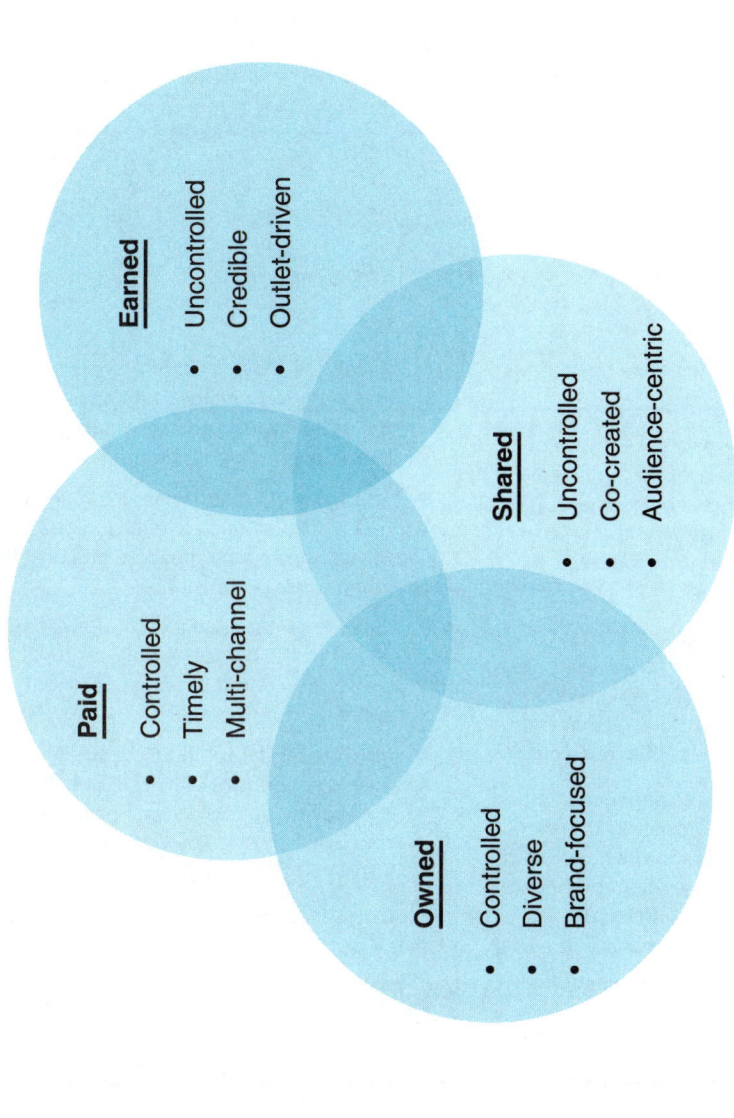

Paid, earned, shared, and owned channels allow practitioners to choose from a variety of approaches: controlled or uncontrolled, narrow or diverse media or audiences, as well as favoring a singular organizational voice or many voices (co-created).

The four areas of the model can be understood as follows.

Paid Media

Paid media (PM) is often thought of as "traditional" advertising through online channels, display ads, pay per click search ads, commercials, print ads, and sponsorships.[2] The rise in popularity of advertising on sites like Facebook, Twitter, YouTube, and LinkedIn has driven this strategic area to grow in popularity. Companies use paid media to gain a presence on channels where consumers and buyers are spending their time.[3]

PRo Tip

WANT TO MAXIMIZE SHARED MEDIA?

You'll need to follow these simple tips:

- Instagram: Post new content one or two times per day using a multitude of hashtags to capture a larger audience. Tools like hashtagify.me help organizations find the right hashtags, amplify their message, and even identify possible influencers.

- Twitter: The day you publish content, tweet the link four times, three hours apart. Day two: tweet the link twice. Day three: once. Social dashboards like Hootsuite or Cyfe can assist in scheduling when to tweet.

- Pinterest: Conservative pinners will pin five times per day. Companies that have the audience and threshold will pin up to 30 times per day. Know your audience and know company resources. But, if there is only one person managing social media, pinning 30 times per day may not be advantageous.

- Facebook: Post content at least once a day and be sure to include an image or video. Consider sponsored content as part of a larger, overarching paid media campaign.

- Snapchat: Post anywhere from one to five times daily to build a loyal audience. Use Storyheap to help measure and analyze a campaign's performance.

- LinkedIn: Post once a day to the company account, the company page, and your personal account. Encourage employees to share company posts.

- YouTube: Establishing a subscriber base is most important with YouTube. Post compelling videos at least once a week, and use targeted keywords through Google AdWords to reach your target audience.

Cross promote your content across all social channels for the most effective coverage because converging media is critical to amplifying brand messages.

Sources: Ellering, Nathan. "How Often to Post on Social Media According to 14 Studies." *CoSchedule Blog.* December 12, 2017. https://coschedule.com/blog/how-often-to-post-on-social-media/.

Roy, Tom. "Social Media Frequency 2016: How Often Should You Post." LinkedIn, 18 Apr. 2016, www.linkedin.com/pulse/social-media-frequency-2016-how-often-should-you-post-tom-roy.

Ahmad, Irfan. "How Often and When to Post on Social Media [Infographic]." *Social Media Today.* November 10, 2017. https://www.socialmediatoday.com/news/how-often-and-when-to-post-on-social-media-infographic/510206/.

Earned Media

Earned media (EM) is commonly referred to as either publicity or media relations. Examples include having a newspaper or trade publication write about you, your company, or its offerings.[4] Earned media is often associated with public relations professionals and the industry as a whole. This could be because it is one of the tangible tactics unique to public relations initiatives.

Shared Media

Shared media (SM) is also known as social media and is the result of a brand and followers, customers, or fans interacting and mutually creating content. Customers many times feel empowered to publish and create content on the brand's behalf inspiring buzz and word of mouth.[5] Shared media uses **influencer** relations. Influencers can be bloggers, journalists, celebrities, or people who are held in high regard within varied social circles, marketplaces, or industries. Influencers know their audiences. They have a keen awareness of what their audience likes and have built a following by consistently posting high quality content that resonates with their audience who, in turn, may become loyal advocates.[6] In order for shared media principles to be effective, brands must relinquish control and grant a level of editorial and creative freedom to their influencers. In this way, they feel empowered to produce authentic content, benefitting both the brand and their fans.[7]

Owned Media

Content and assets that the brand controls, like websites, blogs, newsletters, brochures, and social media accounts are all considered **owned media** (OM).[8] Brands are increasingly behaving like publishers by employing editorial staff that manage content creation steams.[9] Content is written with the idea that it will engage its customers and help foster relationships throughout the customer lifecycle.

> We live in a time of profound disruption and accelerating change. As leaders, we must shift our thinking and update our mental maps to navigate this new and unfamiliar landscape.
>
> — Mark Bonchek, CEO of Shift Thinking

WHEN SHOULD EACH OF THE PESO CHANNELS BE USED?

By using the PESO model, organizations are employing the all-channel, all-inclusive approach to strategic planning. In the PESO model, each channel delivers unique importance. Look at it this way: paid media are the channels public relations practitioners use in which money is paid to place the message and control its distribution; earned media assists practitioners with creating the opportunity to have the company story told by credible, objective, third-party influencers such as journalists, bloggers, trade analysts, and industry leaders;[10] shared media allows a company's community of users to pass along messages through various social networking sites while at the same time commenting on the messages; and owned media are the editorial messages written, published, and controlled by a company-owned blog, website, or other channel.[11]

> ## *PRo Tip*
>
> ### UNIFIED EMPLOYEE ENGAGEMENT
>
> When creating content for the company's social channels, encourage employees to retweet, share, and pin the content to their personal social networking sites.

Campaigns in Action

The following examples highlight each function of the model being used in individual campaigns. The final campaign uses all four areas of the PESO model.

Paid Media

American sporting brand Under Armour launched a groundbreaking advertising campaign targeted toward women using a strategic "take-no-prisoners approach" to capturing the attention of this untapped market. They worked with advertising agency

Renowned ballet dancer Misty Copeland lent the strength and power of her personal brand to Under Armour's "I will what I want" campaign.
#IWILLWHATIWANT Watch the video: http://bit.ly/CopelandUA

Copeland joined other "women of will" in Under Armour's empowering campaign.

Droga5 to create the company's most expansive women's campaign to date: "The 'I will what I want' campaign focuses on empowering women and creating a space for the Under Armour Women's brand to grow. The campaign aims to encourage women to go after what they want and not be held back, wait for affirmation, acceptance, or permission from others."[12] Leanne Fremar, senior VP and creative director for women's business, calls the campaign strategy a "woman-a-festo," noting that through this campaign Under Armour is looking to break through the "sea of sameness" in the category. In an interview, Fremar said that the insight behind "I Will What I Want" was not "you go, girl." The goal was to celebrate women "who had the physical and mental strength to tune out the external pressures and turn inward and chart their own course."[13]

The campaign features the stories of Misty Copeland, ballerina for the American Ballet Theatre; Lindsey Vonn, U.S. Down Hills Skier; Gisele Bundchen, model; Brianna Cope, pro surfer; and Kelley O'Hara, U.S. Soccer Women's National Team.

The campaign was received with overwhelming success. The videos have been viewed more than 2.8 million times on YouTube, there was a 293 percent lift in brand conversation, and, most importantly, traffic to underarmour.com increased by 42 percent.[14] The campaign proved that women's marketing is no longer an afterthought. Sales in Under Armour's North American women's apparel division are on pace to reach $1.8 billion by 2019.[15] The paid media campaign won the Cyber Category Grand Prix award at Cannes Lions Festival. According to the Cannes judging panel, the video was an obvious choice for the top prize as it used technology to deliver an empowering message, "this is the entry that demonstrates how a well-crafted digital experience creates an uplifting impact to bring a brand closer to people, from the point of engagement to the point of transaction."[16]

Earned Media

Baskin-Robins was eager to drive consumers to make in-store purchases of their delectable ice cream throughout the summer months. With the help of Schneider and Associates, their goal was to secure broadcast, print, and online coverage for Baskin-Robbins's summer flavors.

Schneider and Associates began their strategic earned media campaign by researching the competition, exploring the trend in "wacky" summer flavors, and leveraged existing relationships with reporters and producers to ensure Baskin-Robbins's inclusion in wacky summer ice cream flavor stories. Part of the strategy was to identify and develop "truths" around each crazy flavor to increase media interest. For example, "French Toast began dazzling the taste buds of King Henry V in the 15th Century when bread that might have otherwise been thrown away was used to create a sweet treat for the King. Now at Baskin-Robbins you can enjoy the same great French Toast taste for dessert."[17] The communications agency pitched reporter Bruce Horovitz from USA Today by developing several unique newsworthy angles such as "flavorology" and innovative leadership in all ice cream trends.

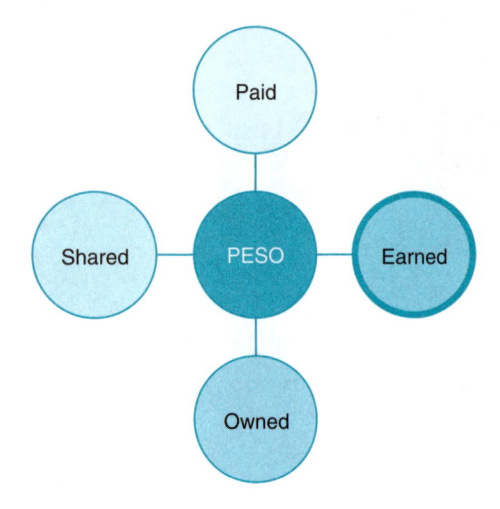

The hard work paid off. The campaign generated significant national and local media coverage. Between the summer months of May and July, the media campaign reached almost 68 million people, garnering more than 133 million impressions. The campaign led to an increase in sales for Firehouse #31 and created such a demand for French Toast that, after its September launch, many stores sold out in only a few weeks. The campaign was covered in *USA Today*, *Newsweek*, MSN.com, *Parade*, on the Today Show, Katie Brown Workshop, and *People Magazine*.

Baskin-Robbins went "wacky" to stand out from the crowd in its 2011 campaign.

Shared Media

When brands use shared media initiatives they usually evolve around content such as word of mouth, referrals, community-driven content, and cocreation. This is an area of the PESO model where content marketing and social media marketing work together.

By partnering with the National College Athletic Association (NCAA), Reese's became the official sponsor of #MarchMadness for the fourth consecutive year. According to the public relations team, the brand celebrated the passion and roller coaster of emotions that the NCAA tournament evokes in college basketball fans through a variety of creative advertising, social media content, and in-store promotions.[18] Content strategy was clearly a strength for Reese's as they curated incredible pieces with beautiful visuals that celebrated both March Madness and the Reese's brand. Moreover, the copywriting for these posts was engaging and sharable.[19]

In their joint press release, Walt Disney Parks and Resorts and the Make-A-Wish foundation announced that in honor of the 100,000th Disney wish granted globally, and in celebration of Disneyland Resort's 60th Anniversary, fans were invited to share images of Mickey Mouse ears, or any creative ears at all, to help grant wishes. By using the Share Your Ears photo frame on Facebook and sharing photos with the hashtag #ShareYourEars on Twitter and Instagram, community users unlocked a $5 donation from Walt Disney Parks and Resorts, up to $1 million.[20] The campaign used the social media entries on their websites to drive audience engagement and boost campaign awareness. The #ShareYourEars campaign became a trending topic on Facebook, and Disney Parks doubled their original pledge, donating $2 million to the Make-A-Wish Foundation.[21]

Movie releases must generate enormous amounts of buzz in order to hit sales numbers at the box office. Developing a successful strategy takes careful planning and execution. Dior, a luxury brand that is known to millions of people across the world, was particularly successful in leveraging digital conversations to get fans into theaters for the final installment of The Hunger Games series. The French fashion giant used Instagram to publish several shots of Jennifer Lawrence, the actress playing the central character Katniss Everdeen, sporting beautiful Dior dresses at movie premieres all over the world.[22]

In just a few short days, the brand's Instagram account gained hundreds of thousands of new followers. Dior's Instagram post of Lawrence at The Hunger Games world premiere remains one of its most popular posts with over 131,000 likes and more than 1,100 comments, well above the volume of engagement generated by other prestigious ambassadors of the brand such as Benedict Cumberbatch or Rihanna.[23]

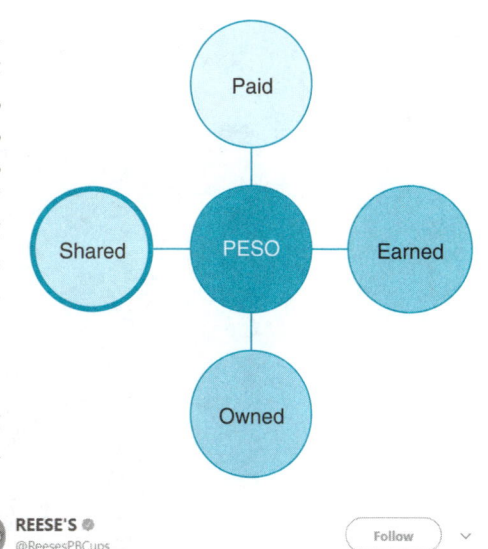

Owned Media

Owned media expresses brand portability by extending a company's presence both within and beyond its website through social media sites and unique communities. Proponents of capitalizing on owned media strategy believe that content should live

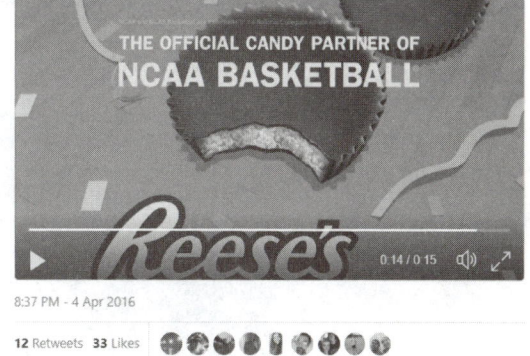

A sweet partnership between the NCAA and Reese's has embraced energetic content to capture the spirit of March Madness.

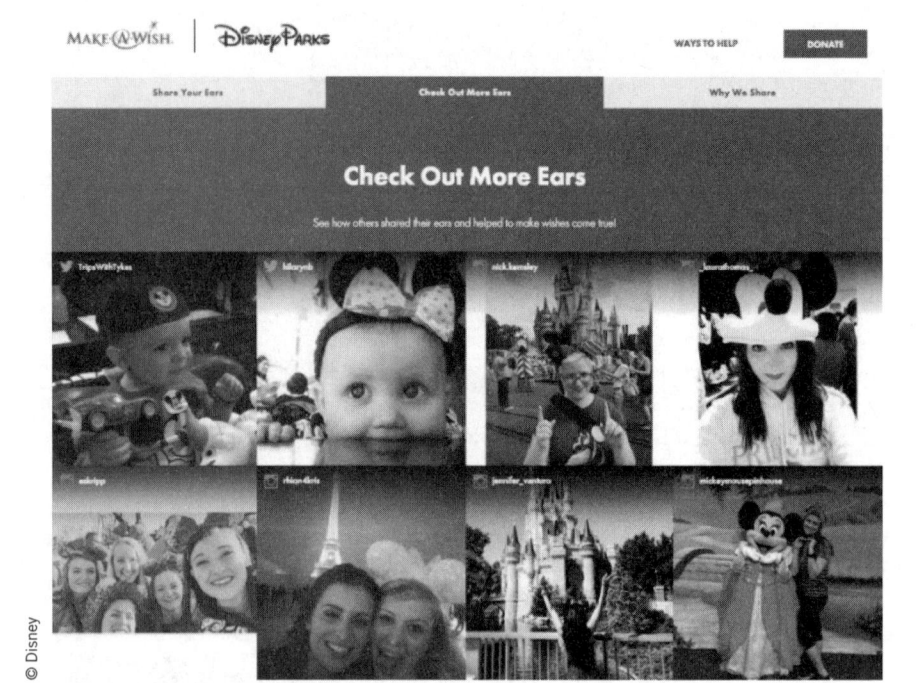

User-generated content helped Disney and #shareyourears raise millions of dollars for the Make-A-Wish Foundation.

Katniss met couture in Dior's Instagram-centered Hunger Games campaign.

on organization-controlled channels that then lend pieces to outlying owned social networks, such as Twitter, Facebook, Instagram, SnapChat or other social channels.[24] Owned content is more than just a website, it includes blogs, white papers, ebooks, webinars, podcasts, video campaigns, catalogs, and e-mail marketing, as well as hosted events and other in-person opportunities. While social channels are also part of shared media, the content posted to those channels is owned by the company. Content can flow across channels and can be used in multiple ways to reach audiences and publics. Crossover between and among each area of the PESO model is common.

Sephora, Nike, Kraft Foods, and McCormick are just some of the companies that understand the complexities of owned media and have created sustainable strategies that complement their goals and objectives.

Sephora developed a comprehensive owned media strategy through their loyalty program. They developed their own content specific channels to build community, capture data, and create value. By using the customized app from ColorIQ, consumers can connect with peers, discuss beauty pointers, discover make-up trends, edit their personal profile, and explore recommended products that best suit their skin tone.[25]

For organizations that want to create direct relationships with their community, owned media strategies are compelling. Nike has created the Nike+ Run Club community while UnderArmour developed a comprehensive owned media strategy around MapMyFitness.[26] Kraft Foods developed an entire community dedicated to sharing recipes and social currency through their own Kraft Recipes site, while the McCormick brand created its FlavorPrint taste profiler that allows users to discover exciting new flavors and recipes based on their flavor favorites.[27]

Mark Bonchek, founder and Chief Epiphany Officer of Shift Thinking, notes that owned media strategies share fundamental characteristics. "First, they create value for people beyond the products being sold. Second, they use data not just as a way to target a message, but as a way to create a useful service. Third, they treat people not as passive consumers, but active co-creators. Whereas most media strategies are about push, these owned strategies are about pull."[28]

CONTINUOUS INTEGRATION

All four media types—paid, earned, shared, owned—contribute to establishing a brand's reputation. They should continually overlap through a series of strategic and diverse approaches. Brands should share their content on all of their social media pages as well as owned channels in order to deliver their messages to as many users as possible in an effort to engage in meaningful conversations with them.

> ## PRo Tip
>
> ### INCORPORATING CONVERGED MEDIA
>
> Combining paid, earned, shared, and owned media is known as converged media. According to Rebecca Lieb and Jeremiah Owyang from Altimeter
>
> > converged media utilizes two or more channels of paid, earned, shared, and owned media. It is characterized by a consistent storyline, look, and feel. All channels work in concert, enabling brands to reach customers exactly where, how, and when they want, regardless of channel, medium, or device, online or offline. With the customer journey between devices, channels, and media becoming increasingly complex, and new forms of technology only making it more so, this strategy of paid/owned/earned/shared confluence makes marketers impervious to the disruption caused by emerging technologies.[29]
>
> *Source:* Rebecca Lieb and Jeremiah Owyang, "The Converged Media Imperative. Report," Altimeter Group, July 19, 2012, https://www.slideshare.net/Altimeter/ the-converged-media-imperative

CONCLUSION

All organizations use a mix of outreach approaches and channels to share information with their stakeholders. The PESO model helps practitioners to consider channel selection holistically and strategically: by regularly asking ourselves what the best mix of channels might be for a specific campaign, project, or program, we give organizations the greatest chance of success in execution. If we consider this in the early stages of planning, we're better able to craft content that can be repurposed across channels, to consider the needs of organizational stakeholders and publics, and to use integrated campaigns to build relationships, not just achieve short-term objectives.

THINK CRITICALLY

1. What is PESO, and how is it applied to public relations?
2. How does the PESO model differ from R.O.P.E. and R.A.C.E.?
3. Conduct a search of a small business using social media. Analyze its paid, earned, shared, and owned channels. What role does the PESO model play in the success or failure for the organization?
4. It has been said that today's public relations practitioner must embrace the PESO model in order for a strategic campaign to be effective. Do you agree or disagree?

KEY TERMS

Converged media 50
Earned media 43
Influencer 43
Owned media 43
Paid media 42
PESO model 40
Shared media 43
Situational theory of publics 53

CONCEPT CASE: EQUALITY TODAY'S CHANNEL, PARTNER, AND MEASUREMENT BRAINSTORMING

Equality Today is looking to create a year-round program of social promotion and curation campaigns in order to cultivate engagement with its audiences. Organizations similar to Equality Today have used a myriad of social channels to bring about greater awareness to their causes while cultivating global communities. Legalizing same-sex marriage is only one issue they support. They also advocate for equal rights across the continuums of gender and sexual orientation in their family, professional, and civic lives.

- Using the PESO model, create an awareness campaign to educate the public about the mission behind Equality Today. You can either choose to develop an overall awareness campaign or hone in on one specific platform.

- How might Equality Today partner with influencers to advance their awareness campaign?

- Construct a strategy for measurement. Think about how Equality Today will evaluate what constitutes success for its campaign.

CASE STUDY: THE PROUD WHOPPER—BE YOUR WAY CAMPAIGN

Campaign Focus: Community Relations

When unveiling its new "Be Your Way" tagline, Burger King leveraged a fully integrated campaign and the prevailing social issues of the day to help reposition its brand.[30] Moving from the 40-year-old "Have It Your Way" tagline to its updated language, the company sought to align with younger audiences and changing societal values. Momentum to legalize same-sex marriage nationwide had been building when Burger King decided to use the owned media of its product packaging to take a public stand on this issue. It supported these efforts with paid, earned, and shared media outreach, as well as fund-raising support for LGBTQ youth, creating a fully integrated campaign.[31] Taking place during Pride Week in San Francisco, California, in 2014, the Proud Whopper and the "Be Your Way" campaign was Burger King's way to show support for same-sex couples.[32] Through this campaign, Burger King strengthened its progressive identity as a brand, while connecting on a personal and supportive level with those who identified as or supported same-sex couples. Beyond the immediate local audience and owned-media approaches, Burger King used social media (shared) and media relations (earned) efforts to connect with others across the country and around the world.

PESO Model

Owned

Multiple tactics were used as part of the "Be Your Way" campaign. The first was the use of owned media in The Proud Whopper design. A standard Whopper hamburger was wrapped in

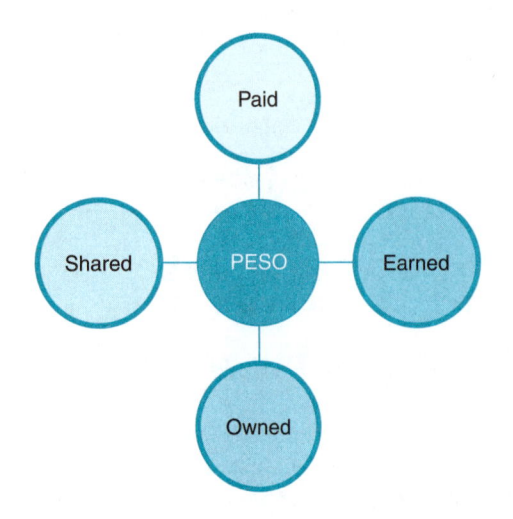

The Proud Whopper.

colorful paper reflecting the rainbow symbol of gay pride. As customers unwrapped their meal, the powerful campaign message was delivered: "we are all the same inside." This item was only sold at Burger King locations in the San Francisco area during Pride Week, but this seemingly geographically narrow audience included tens of thousands of visitors from across the country as well as the significant local and national media presence for Pride events.[33] In another owned media tactic, Burger King also used their signature paper crowns to encourage others to show support, handing out more than 100,000 rainbow paper crowns for the crowd at pride parades in New York and San Francisco, where the brand was a major sponsor.[34]

Shared

To leverage the campaign online, Burger King released a video that featured the reactions of consumers when the Proud Whopper was unveiled. Shared across all company social media platforms, the video generated conversation both with those participating in the San Francisco Pride Week events as well as those tuning in from farther away. Burger King capitalized on social media to spread the news about their Pride Week endeavors and to continue to support the cause of equality even online. Social media gave audiences an outlet to share the campaign, comment on the Proud Whopper and paper crown designs, and showcase the campaign with those not in the San Francisco area. By interacting with consumers on their pages, Burger King encouraged stakeholders to create conversation about the campaign, thus perpetuating a successful use of social media during and after the ten days that the Proud Whopper was available. Expanding the reach of the campaign outside of the city limits of San Francisco was crucial in both promoting the Burger King brand and the cause being support. Across all social media platforms, the video that Burger King released of the reactions to the Proud Whopper has gathered more than 7 million views, with 5.3 million of those views being on YouTube alone.[35]

Earned

The "Be Your Way" campaign, along with the Proud Whopper that played a large role in the campaign, had a vast reach and produced commendable results despite its very focused target group in the San Francisco area. Major media helped to spread the story nationally and internationally, with coverage from dozens of significant outlets including the *L.A. Times*,[36] MSNBC,[37] *Time*,[38] *USA Today*,[39] and *The Washington Post*.[40]

Paid

The advertisement reached more than 20 percent of the United States' population, and all of the profits made from sales of the Proud Whopper benefitted the Burger King McLamore Foundation, an organization that provides scholarships to LGBTQ+ identifying high school teenagers.[41]

Additionally, Burger King executives made internal changes to improve the company's policies toward LGBTQ employees and, importantly, to credit the campaign as a significant part of driving U.S. sales and revenue higher after several years of brand stagnation.[42] The Proud Whopper campaign demonstrates the power of integrated approaches to strengthen and unify brands to connect with consumers and make an impact on the business as a whole.

Theories

Situational Theory of Publics: Through recognizing the challenge and opportunity of the same-sex marriage debate, acknowledging the effect that this issue had on people's lives, and creating a campaign to address and intervene in the situation, Burger King's "Be Your Way" campaign exemplified the **situational theory of publics**, as defined by Patricia Swann.[43] By centering the campaign in San Francisco during Pride events, Burger King targeted a specific audience they knew would be highly involved and invested in the issues at hand.[44] These three components of the campaign process demonstrated Burger King's ability to use its platform to take a stance on issues that greatly affect the lives of their stakeholders.

Agenda Building Theory: During this campaign, Burger King zeroed in on an issue on which they could take a stand and used their platform as a global organization to draw attention to the issue through their actions and public relations tactics. This demonstrates the agenda building theory, as the organization was able to catch the attention of the media and of the publics and work toward getting same sex-marriage accepted and legalized.[45]

4 Research, Part 1

DIAGNOSIS AND DEVELOPMENTAL RESEARCH

THINK AHEAD

4.1 Describe the importance of research in understanding an organization and its environment.

4.2 Connect research to building knowledge around organizational challenges and opportunities.

4.3 Define different types and stages of research (primary/secondary, quantitative/qualitative, formal/informal, developmental/refinement/evaluation).

4.4 Consider the use of different research tools (interviews, content analysis, experiments, and so on) to help answer different research questions.

The creation of any successful public relations campaign begins with recognition of a specific situation: the challenges or opportunities the organization faces. This chapter and the following chapter provide an outline to investigate and clarify your approach before planning a campaign. Research allows practitioners to diagnose an organization's aspirations and needs—the challenges and opportunities within its environment—then craft communication goals to address them. Research involves a **methodology** (a framework for systematically processing understanding information) for analyzing **data** (such as survey results, a sample of written content, or the conversations of a focus group).[1] Research should be seen as important to inform individual campaigns as well as ongoing strategic decisions for the organization.

Public relations (PR) professionals can use both **secondary** and **primary** research techniques to develop a clearer

Developmental PR research should involve learning about an organization and its goals as well as understanding its environment and publics using tools like surveys and focus groups.

understanding of a situation. In *Advertising and Public Relations Research*, authors Jugenheimer, Kelley, Hudson, and Bradley argue that proper research positions organizations to save money, gain on competitors, adapt to change, and improve internal operations.[2] Research enables public relations campaigns to provide strategic insight and support to the organizations that they serve.

Yet, it is easy to make assumptions and begin tactical work without initially understanding the **audiences** and **publics**, challenges, competitors, and risks in the environment. Even seasoned PR professionals are guilty of this mistake from time to time. It is always more efficient in the long-run to invest time and effort at the onset of campaign development, to properly inform the goals, objectives, strategies, and tactics that will follow.

DEVELOPMENTAL RESEARCH: DIAGNOSING THE PROBLEM AND/OR OPPORTUNITY

Research comes into play throughout a public relations program or campaign cycle. Eminent public relations researcher Dr. Don W. Stacks explains research as "a continuous process that continually assesses an organization's position among its publics on a variety of outcome measures."[3] He groups these into three categories: developmental, refinement, and evaluation.[4] **Developmental research** helps practitioners to understand the environment and current situation. **Refinement research**, undertaken while the campaign is underway, assists in the regular adjustment and optimization of messages, as well as the clarification of audience needs and perspectives. Finally, **evaluative research** looks back on a campaign to understand areas of success, methods for improvement, and lessons learned. As noted, developmental research is a critical and often overlooked stage of the public relations planning process, which allows practitioners to understand the organization and the communication environment, define publics, clarify problems or opportunities, and set baselines from which to measure improvement.

As the link between the organization and its societal and industry environment, PR practitioners may be asked to create a public relations campaign with limited or incomplete knowledge of the situation at hand. Even organizational leaders who value the work of public relations teams may unwittingly withhold information or have an unclear vantage point to fully understand and diagnose potential communication challenges. It is often valuable for public relations teams to lead an internal discussion that can help create distance from the most pressing issues at hand and considers the larger perspective of the company as situated in its industry at a specific point in time.

- In your industry, how is today different than yesterday?
- How will tomorrow be different from today?
- What are competitors doing differently?
- How is the industry changing?

Research can deepen the understanding of external and internal organization publics, informing campaign goals, objectives, strategies, tactics, and messaging. These publics may include local families, businesses, employees, or other members of your community.

PRo Tip

RESEARCHING YOUR BRAND

Review the organizational mission statement: The majority of organizations have a mission statement that defines their purpose for doing business.

- Evaluate its clarity, simplicity, and trajectory as a statement of purpose.

- Review the organizational website and other owned media, social media channels, and additional external facing materials such as collateral to determine whether actions and messages support the mission statement.

- Look at discrepancies as areas where improved communication can positively impact the organization:

  ○ For example, a manufacturing organization details in its mission statement that "the customer always comes first" but rarely references its customers in any public-facing language or materials.

  ○ **Desired outcome:** The public relations team diagnoses the disconnect and recommends, as its goal, closing this identified gap by revising specific materials and updating content standards, trade media outreach topics, and internal-facing language to support the shift in focus.

Look for the "uniqueness": Every business or nonprofit should have a clear understanding of what differentiates them from their competitors, but many have difficulty articulating the specifics.

- PR professionals can evaluate a company relative to its competitors to establish, from their strategic vantage point, what the public-facing content says about each organization. This content may or may not align with leaders' perceptions.

- By examining the gaps between internal and external messaging, as well as identifying any unused communication "real estate" in the industry of interest, strategies and tactics can be further refined to help a company stand out relative to its competitors.

  ○ For example, three local theater companies are competing for the attention and financial resources of the same audiences, supporters, and reporters; often repeating the same messages with similar "calls to action."

  ○ **Desired outcome:** A PR practitioner identifies and advises one of the nonprofits to differentiate itself in the region by targeting a specific audience within the broader spectrum (perhaps students and recent graduates). By developing and promoting unique incentives, opportunities, and rewards specific to this audience, the theater creates messaging that resonates with its targeted demographic, driving media interest providing a differentiator among its competitors.

Talk to individuals on the front lines: Speaking with customer service representatives, salespeople, fund-raisers, and others who have regular interaction with an organization's most critical external publics can provide an excellent perspective on how the organization is perceived.[5] Several research techniques can gather and synthesize the insights from these critical internal stakeholders.

- Informal interviews and conversations with key informants can point toward potential areas of strength and weakness—both can be valuable for additional in-depth or formal research.
- **Focus groups** provide a structure for efficiently gathering the insights from many individuals with a shared perspective (hence the term *focus*), which can be useful for understanding a group's perspective, as well as—by carefully watching the interactions among the individuals as part of the discussion—additional pain points, fears, challenges, and, through what is not discussed, taboos.
- **Desired Outcome:** Surveys of relevant teams or departments within the organization allow practitioners to formalize and support the findings from earlier qualitative or informal research. Additionally, they can provide a relatively efficient and wholly anonymous way to gather information—particularly for teams or organizations that are rarely in the same geographic location. Digital tools such as Survey Monkey make these simple for respondents.

Source: Dennis Wilcox and Bryan H. Reber, *Public Relations Writing and Media Techniques*, (Boston, MA: Pearson, 2016), 322.

Asking some of these broad questions provides an organization with competitive, as well as historical context. Initiating this type of conversation can also help prioritize and create a framework for initiating a situational investigation to develop detailed strategic insights about the role of public relations and the best approaches to position an organization for long-term success. This inspection is considered a form of primary research (discussed in more detail later in the chapter) that informs subsequent investigative work and can provide an initial hypothesis regarding the challenge or opportunity at hand. It also begins the process of understanding the organization's goals and aspirations as defined by leadership.

RESEARCHING AND MEASURING THE PROBLEM/OPPORTUNITY

After completing the initial audience identification analysis, public relations professionals then rely on a variety of research techniques to develop the objectives and strategies that will contribute to the development of a campaign. In *Using Research in Public Relations*, Glen M. Broom and David M. Dozier describe a *communication problem* as the gap between what a group of people perceive and what is actually desired.[6] This approach recommends drafting a problem statement as the first step of the research process, summarizing the issue at hand.

All formal research (qualitative and quantitative, secondary, and primary) begins with a clear statement of the research problem at hand. The problem statement should be concise and strive to meet the following criteria: written in the present tense, specific, measurable, and blame free.[7] Examples of statements adhering to this methodology include the following:

- Company X's product market share has declined by 20 percent over the past two years, resulting in lost revenue and overproduction.

- A nonprofit organization is hiring for various positions but has struggled to attract qualified applicants over the past two months.

- The State Department of Transportation has seen a 7 percent increase in traffic deaths over the past three years (the period over which it has also been running a similar public safety outreach campaign).

Although these challenges are not entirely within the realm of communication, as strategic leaders, PR practitioners can and should serve a role in prioritizing the areas where improved communication can have the greatest impact.

Problem statements lead to a variety of potential questions, which can be answered with both formal and informal techniques. Using **formal research** techniques can help define an organization's challenges, identify audiences, select strategies, refine tactics, and evaluate success. That said, practitioners should not overlook the value of **informal research**, particularly in the early stages of the diagnosis process. Informal research can help form a general understanding of an organization and its environment, including work to read and understand organizational documents and language (as well as competitors'); building relationships and asking for the perspective of management; and gathering external viewpoints from external experts, media, and other audiences and publics. This research does not need to be done using a scientific process to be valuable, but it can still be thoughtful and thorough. The main distinction from more formal approaches is that such methods are not **generalizable** to larger groups.[8] Informal research can be extremely valuable, but it represents educated guesses in relation to formal systematic research.

Research on the same set of data can be performed in formal and informal ways. For example, a public relations practitioner may be interested in the coverage of a specific issue or organization by a certain media outlet. An informal approach could involve reading a small sample of articles to understand recent coverage in terms of structure, tone, or content, producing qualitative findings. This could end up as a report or client presentation informing future strategies, tactics, and messaging. Alternatively, a formal approach could use a quantitative method such as content analysis. This might involve selecting a time window (past five years), collecting all articles or a large, representative sample, and analyzing each using a systematic process with a group of trained researchers. Analyzing all or a representative proportion of the sample would reinforce generalizability—the idea that findings would be reflected in a wider sample than the one chosen—as well as the validity of the results themselves. Note that the two approaches do ask and answer different questions: rather than being right or wrong, better or worse, they may both be valuable in discerning a complete picture of the situation. **For more on matching the research question with specific research methods, see the Appendix, page 226.**

Data can come from many different sources, including secondary research, interviews, and content analysis.

RESEARCH TERMINOLOGY AND TECHNIQUES

Data

As mentioned at the beginning of this chapter, research involves the analysis of data. Such data includes both numeric and qualitative (written words, interview transcripts, images, and so on.) and can come from a wide variety of sources, from national databases to experiments to individual observations. Public relations practitioners should be aware of all of the communication data they collect or have access to about their organizations, including media coverage (qualitative and quantitative), social media analytics (quantitative), and customer service information (often qualitative and quantitative).

Qualitative and Quantitative Research

Both qualitative and quantitative research methods can be applied in valuable ways to answer public relations-related questions. While quantitative approaches dominate the business world, practitioners often underestimate the importance and the degree to which they already use qualitative research methods to analyze difficult-to-quantify concepts like tone and brand voice in writing, media coverage, and social media content. Quantitative methods reflect a scientific method approach to research: reducing phenomena to their component parts, measuring them, and using the results to make predictions about future events. It narrows the field of vision, which can be useful for efficiency and planning purposes, if the right factors are part of the focus. By contrast, qualitative research often starts with a wider lens, taking into account holistic situations.

Selecting the correct balance of methods should be based on the questions at hand as well as the available resources and expertise for analysis. For example, a content analysis project using quantitative methods could preselect the most important words and count them to see how often they occurred. This would be useful if the research question centered on *whether* certain subjects were brought up by the authors. A qualitative analysis of the same data would most likely begin with a complete reading. This would be the better approach if the main question at hand was *how* the subjects were discussed. If the data sample is only three articles, a qualitative approach may be more effective. But if the sample is 3,000 articles, a quantitative approach might be necessary for efficiency. Additional approaches that would increase the quality of the research are clearly devising and articulating how the sample articles were selected, having multiple researchers read the articles to compare their notes and discuss/address inconsistencies, and using both qualitative and quantitative methods to triangulate results. Additionally, such research projects can have several substages, moving back and forth between different methods and research questions as initial results emerge. Often initial qualitative questions prompt quantitative investigations. The best researchers follow the questions through multiple stages of analysis to create a complete picture of the situation at hand.

Secondary and Primary Research

Just as every campaign is unique, each formal research approach must be carefully sourced, designed, and calibrated to ensure that it is gathering the desired information. Public relations practitioners should have the skills to select and develop these tools as well as (in many cases) to implement them and interpret the results. Practitioners perform secondary research constantly, such as reading existing articles, reports, and studies. They also regularly take on primary research tasks such as media coverage analysis. While some primary methods, such as large-scale surveys or big data analysis, may be beyond the capabilities of the average practitioner, we each have a responsibility to understand the tools available and be able to recommend the best research methods for a given situation—even if they require external assistance. Both primary and secondary research can be appropriate and valuable tools in diagnosing organizational challenges and orienting practitioners toward strategic solutions; however, the relative value depends on many variables including the specific situation at hand, the budget, timelines/deadlines, and the level of research experience that the team possesses.

Validity

The term *validity* refers to whether research is measuring what it is intended to measure, whether that is at the level of a specific concept, the desired subjects/data set, or the most applicable methodological choice.[9] For example, when attempting to evaluate the quality of a relationship between an organization and a public, practitioners should begin by examining existing research on the key components that make up a relationship (such as commitment, control mutuality, trust, and satisfaction) as well as the questions that have been tested to reflect each component making up the measurement.[10] In this way, practitioners begin with proven tools for their analysis. Validity is also important when considering a data set. Are you interviewing or surveying the right individuals to answer your questions? Are you analyzing media content relevant to future campaign outreach? And, finally, validity also follows from methodological choices. A small but in-depth set of qualitative interviews would certainly be a valid way to understand *why* or *how* a certain audience interacts with a product, but it would not be a valid method for understanding the socioeconomic circumstances of a wide range of potential customers, as the sample would not be representative. In quantitative research, supporting validity is demonstrated through statistical measures, while in qualitative or case study-based research, the concept of **triangulation**—using multiple sources of data and or multiple methods of analysis to increase the reliability and credibility of findings—is a key indicator.[11] Qualitative research demonstrates quality through rigor in data collection and analysis, detailed descriptions of findings, and collaboration with other researchers.[12]

CONDUCTING RESEARCH

Secondary Research

Secondary research can be defined as the selective sampling of the research of others. While it provides less specific, tailored insights for individual campaigns or publics, carefully defined secondary research has the added benefits of providing outside credibility for the goal, objective, strategy or tactic that it directs or supports. Reputable sources for secondary research include the following.

Secondary research involves sorting through the vast amount of information and data accessible to practitioners.

Case Studies

Public relations practitioners can find publicly available case studies through Public Relations Society of America (PRSA) that reference similar challenges and potential strategies and tactics. Award-winning campaigns, such as the PRSA Silver Anvil entrants, provide a best-practices approach that can serve as a checklist and idea generator for future campaigns.

Government Data

There is a wealth of information that has been compiled and made public by the U.S. Federal Government (as well as many other governments around the world). From the Census Bureau's detailed and localized demographic content, to regular reports put out by the Bureau of Labor Statistics, PR professionals have many resources to draw from when looking to investigate basic information before formalizing a campaign. Government reports tend to be free of political or industry bias and carry significant credibility with journalists and consumer audiences. Common challenges of working with government-generated data include sorting through a vast number of volumes and correctly interpreting their meaning.

Scholarly Research

Many public relations practitioners are not aware of the research created and updated by academics. Several public relations organizations and publications are working to fill this gap, including the University of Florida–based Institute for Public Relations (www.instituteforpr.org) and the open-access *Public Relations Journal*. Both focus their efforts on making applied research accessible to public relations practitioners.

Think Tank/Nonprofit Reports

Nearly every industry has multiple organizations that provide relevant, data-rich content on specific topics. They can be university-affiliated academic centers, independently funded nonprofits, or grant-driven research organizations. Oftentimes, these

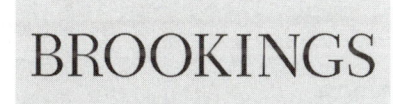

Think tanks can provide a valuable source of data and information, but practitioners should check for an organization's political bias when using this research.

reports are a source for news coverage at the time of release but can also provide strong insights for strategic communicators looking to better understand a specific issue or industry. With this in mind, while many organizations are ideologically neutral, these types of reports may be cause driven or carry an inherent bias and should not be taken as the sole source of authority on specific content.

Trade Association Research

For industry-specific data, research generated from a trade association may provide a valuable starting point for practitioners to pursue. Are you wondering how many manufacturing jobs there are in the United States today? It's more than 12 million, according to the National Association of Manufacturers (NAM).[13] Are you interested in the impact of health care industry consolidation? The American Medical Association (AMA) is, too.[14] Trade associations compile and share significant amounts of useful data with the public at large. However, strategic communicators should be wary, as these associations are generally advocacy-based organizations. This means that the data that they make available are often built to support a specific organizational or industry purpose, as opposed to government data or scholarly research. Of course, the vast majority of trade associations act and communicate ethically in the content that they share. PR practitioners simply need to be aware that there may be a perspective in these numbers and findings for which they need to account.

It is important to remember that all available information can be used to support a specific element of a project or campaign, or it may be general demographic or geographic data that can generate useful assumptions about the audience at hand. With that being said, the data alone are not inherently useful. The real value of data analysis is to create the appropriate context so that it can be properly understood by a larger audience.

Primary Research

Primary research is loosely defined as devising and executing original research. This could include a systematic round of informal interviews with internal and external stakeholders; creating and executing a survey of a relevant constituency to gauge interest in a new product; or performing textual media analysis on geographically specific coverage for a specific topic over a particular time frame. By researching these topics directly, a project can yield highly specific insights into the challenges that organizations may face or work to overcome.

However, as with any research methodology, primary research does require investment, whether financial in nature, resource based, or simply a timing commitment. Many informal approaches (including information gathering via conversations with internal stakeholders) are common, efficient, and inexpensive. Often, outside research firms are brought in to conduct large-scale, quantitative research. The following list includes a variety of commonly used public relations research approaches.

Polling and Surveys: Opinion and Awareness

Surveys are one of the most widely used tools of public relations researchers. Organizational leaders and PR practitioners regularly lack detailed insights into their key strategic publics. Practitioners can better understand an audience or public's perspective by asking them questions directly. Both internal groups (employees, volunteers, board members, or shareholders) and external groups (current customers, potential customers, community members, or social media followers) can offer valuable and often unexpected insights. Surveys, when planned well, make participation relatively quick and easy, can maintain anonymity for participants, can be analyzed in a variety of ways (including across demographic groups), and can be given in multiple forms. **See the Appendix (page 232) for more information on constructing and conducting effective surveys**.

While a larger, scientifically validated poll or survey intended to reach a significant population (such as opinion polling on a statewide ballot initiative) is both time

---

PRo Tip

SURVEY DETAILS AND TERMINOLOGY

Survey Questions: Depending on the information desired, potential questions can range from a series of open-ended qualitative prompts to **Likert-type scales** (a series of statement followed by an odd-numbered range of answers such as "Strongly Agree" to "Strongly Disagree"). For example, a multiple-choice approach would help a practitioner determine which parts of a nonprofit's mission statement were most valuable to donors. A Likert-type scale would allow a practitioner to measure the opinions of external or internal publics regarding trust or other relationship factors. An open-ended approach (either done with a questionnaire or through in-person interviews) could provide a holistic perspective on consumer complaints or challenges to catch organizational blind spots.

- Types of Survey Data Collection
  - Digital survey: Qualtrics, SurveyMonkey
  - Mail surveys: Practitioner or direct mail vendor
  - Intercept interviews: Hired or trained on-site interviewers
  - Telephone survey: Professional call center
- Sampling versus Census Data
  - Sampling: Selecting some members of a group to represent the whole
  - Representative sample: A sample that represents the makeup of the group as a whole in regard to relevant factors such as age, socioeconomic status, race, gender, or sexual orientation
  - Purposive sample: A nonrepresentative sample, where the researcher selects individuals to participate because they have certain, specific characteristics or shared experiences
  - Census: Gathering information from every member of a specific audience or public

See the Appendix (page 232) for more details on survey research.

consuming and expensive, the following strategies outline a number of techniques and processes that can easily fit within the budget of many organizations. Additional challenges include incomplete answers or inattentive respondents, gathering information from incorrect respondents (those outside the prescribed sample), or, particularly if the survey is too long or poorly constructed, the potential for confusion and fatigue.

Content Analysis

PR practitioners often need to make sense of vast numbers of words and images. They could come in the form of media coverage, social media conversations, books and reports, advertisements, or speeches. Practitioners often want to understand what is being said about an organization: is it positive or negative? What issues are being discussed? What words and phrases are used to describe an organization? In these cases, the content itself becomes the data for **content analysis**. The methodology can take several forms, from a qualitative approach to read, understand, and interpret, to a heavily quantitative approach measuring the frequency or words or phrases, the use of specific images, the tone, or the structure.[15] With the widespread availability of both traditional and social media-based research tools, an organization should have a clear and detailed picture of relevant data prior to initiating any campaign.

Most forms of content analysis use a process called **coding**, where researchers select the relevant units of analysis—such as specific words or symbols, themes, and stories; organizational identification or messaging; or tones and perspectives—and collect that

The coding process involves multiple individuals tracking a variety of themes including tone, key messages, or client/organization inclusion.

information while reviewing each article. Ideally, a team of researchers develops the criteria for what constitutes each unit and category (commonly called a **codebook**) and divides the data for analysis so that multiple individuals examine each individual piece. Often, the process also includes the gathering of metadata: data about the data itself. This would include identifying information such as the media outlet, date, author, and media type for collected coverage. For social media, it may include the platform, author, format, and length.

In her book *Measure What Matters*, K. D. Paine approaches content analysis by separating automated or computerized and manual forms. While automated analyses have evolved over time and provide unparalleled speed and efficiency, they also have significant drawbacks in their inability to distinguish quality, tone, messaging, subtext, and perspective. Conversely, manual content analysis traditionally takes far more time to complete, depending on the approach, but can yield much more detailed, tailored insights.[16] In many cases, the most effective and efficient approach tends to be a combination of both automated and manual approaches. By implementing an iterative approach to conducting an automated analysis, additional clarity can be realized that often helps define the most critical points, questions, or insights.

PRo Tip

MEDIA COVERAGE ANALYSIS

Media coverage is one type of data often examined by practitioners through the lens of content analysis.

- **Data set:** Select relevant publications and a timeframe, then keywords or authors to narrow the set. Best practice is to include all articles based on these search categories.
- **What to look for:** Practitioners should examine prominence, tone, sources, key messages, and competitors when analyzing media coverage.
- **Methodology:** Content analysis can be qualitative or quantitative.
    - **Qualitative**: Reading and interpreting key themes and messages
    - **Quantitative**: Counting the specific words, themes, or codes
- **Case:** A local financial institution is interested in raising its profile among community members. This organization can begin by conducting qualitative research on community events and media outlets for a specific geographic area (most likely based on a media market breakdown) and using financially relevant terminology as part of their search (such as "personal finance," "mortgages," "auto loans," and "savings rates" in conjunction with location-specific terms). The results of this exercise provide a number of media outlets that cover those key terms that can then serve as a starting point for conducting a deeper level of media research.

See the Appendix (page 231) for more details on content analysis.

Competitor Analysis

There are numerous approaches that a practitioner can use to uncover valuable insights about an organization's market competitors or peers. By examining the tools, tactics, strategies, and results of competitors, public relations teams gain perspective on historical successes and failures, approaches that may be less common, and what brand space or positioning may be advantageous in a particular market.

Output-based. What are your competitors saying? By researching the media output of select competitors (press releases, company website news, social media channels, and so on), PR practitioners can begin to understand the objectives and messaging existing within the market. These insights can lead to differentiation from competitors (such as choosing distinctive tactics or easily distinguishable key messages) or even lead an organization to focus on an entirely different (potentially untapped) audience. It may also encourage organizations to join and become a part of specific conversations, by incorporating or diverting resources toward specific channels, in order to balance a competitive environment.

Competitive media coverage analysis. What is the media saying about your competitors? From a competitive perspective, the same media analysis lens employed above can be aimed at key competitors in a specific market. Although the range or depth of analysis is often reduced based on the availability of resources, selecting multiple, specific variables for analysis can create an enlightening portrait of the larger competitive landscape and highlight areas for improvement or unidentified competitive advantages.

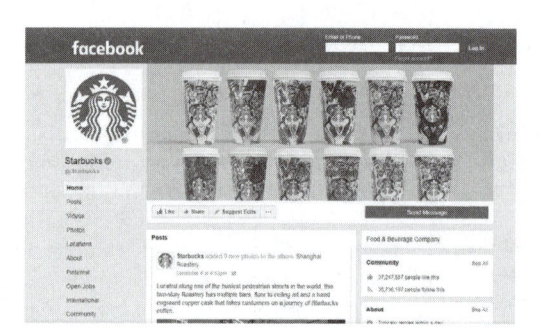

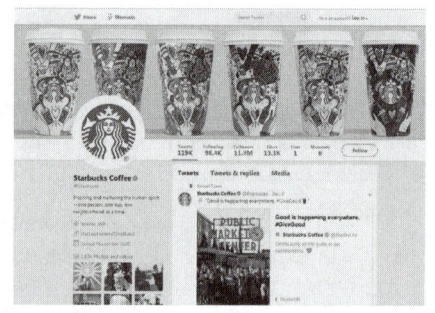

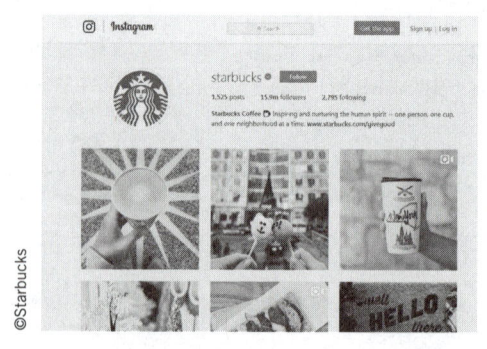

Competitive research should examine multiple facets of an organization's communication channels, including earned media, owned media, and a variety of social (or shared) media.

Experimental Research

While we don't often think about public relations professionals conducting social scientific experiments, there are several areas where they can be practical. **Experimental research** techniques test whether one factor (the independent variable) causes a change in a second variable (the dependent variable).[17] Experiments are controlled, meaning that different subjects or participants will go through distinct experiences in order to understand whether the variables in question have an impact on their awareness, beliefs, or behaviors. For example, public relations practitioners could use the marketing/advertising technique of message testing prior to implementation of specific campaigns. A robust experimental design could use multiple groups, composed of either randomly selected or representatively selected individuals, who view different messages and are asked relevant organizational questions before and after the presentation of these messages. Experiments should only change one variable at a time. Therefore, such an experiment could be constructed with similarly composed groups, the same initial information and initial questions (pretest), then a separate campaign message and relevant questions to gain insights into any changes in awareness, belief, or potential behavior (posttest) depending on the nature of the campaign. In this way, an organization can relatively easily gather feedback as to how potential messages may impact audiences.

There are some potential challenges to conducting effective experiments. The most common is establishing causation: Did the single change made to the situation truly cause any differences between the groups? Or were any changes based on the groups themselves or other external variables? For this reason, it is always valuable to carefully consider what else could have caused changes. If possible, additional experiments can be set up to examine additional variables. To anticipate such challenges, experiments must consciously eliminate potential third variables.[18] In the aforementioned experiment, participants were drawn from a similarly random or representative pool, provided with the same introductory information, and the same posttest (albeit based on different content).

Interviews

Interviews can be used to produce large amounts of extremely useful qualitative data. They are particularly well suited to helping practitioners uncover complicated situations and to better understand how publics or audiences perceive a particular event, challenge, or opportunity. In contrast to an informal conversation, research interviews start with the researcher defining the goals and purpose; finding the best willing candidates; carefully drafting questions; and investing the time to schedule, complete, and analyze each interview.[19] They can range from in-depth informant interviews—planned, long-form sessions where the interviewee is a clear representative of a specific group—to intercept interviews, where the researcher tracks down individuals on the street for quick engagement.

While interviews are more open ended than surveys, experiments, or content analysis, they still have a variety of best practices to ensure validity in execution and analysis. Research interviews are generally conducted one-on-one or in pairs (either two interviewers or two interviewees). Any larger and the interview begins to lose both intimacy and depth of conversation. Questions should be ordered to ensure that interviewees are comfortable, that the most important information is covered, and that there is time for flexibility and follow-up when interesting or unexpected answers arise. When research teams conduct multiple interviews with multiple interviewers, regular collaboration and discussion before and after each interview are crucial to ensure that similar processes are in place and common challenges are addressed with similar revisions. Interviews should be audio recorded, allowing researchers to review the content, create transcripts, and verify quotes. Transcripts and audio can be analyzed using a process not unlike content analysis, looking for commonalities and differences among the responses to similar questions from the participants. Analysis of interviews done by a team should include multiple individuals listening and providing perspective on each interview, which can help to speed the development and accuracy of themes and topics for further investigation.

Focus Groups

The term *focus* implies similarity and narrowing: The purpose of a focus group is to bring together individuals with similar perspectives to hear their conversations and

---

PRo Tip

INTERVIEWING TIPS

- It is helpful for the researcher to take notes and record the interview audio for future reference.
- The order of questions factors into any interview's success.
    - Warm-up questions: Interviews often begin with closed-ended, easy-to-answer background questions. This establishes rapport and makes the interviewee feel comfortable before asking more difficult questions.
    - Open-ended questions: The most important interview questions should be both open-ended and unbiased in their framing. In response, the interviewer should appear interested but not overly encouraging in their facial expressions and body language.
    - Probing questions: More details can be obtained related to key open-ended questions using more specific probes to gather more detail on particular aspects of the question or the response. This allows for a more conversational, back-and-forth flow to the interview.
- Be flexible: The pre-arranged order of questions should be thought out and logical but should always be flexible to reflect the natural flow of the conversation, the interests and perspective of the interviewee, as well as the time available.

Source: Sarah J. Tracy, *Qualitative Research Methods*, (Malden, MA: Wiley Blackwell, 2013), 138–152.

PRo Tip

SWOT[20]

A business management tool that is widely used in public relations campaign development consists of a strengths, weaknesses, opportunities, and threats analysis, or **SWOT**. This type of analysis can highlight many important elements of an organization's internal and external environment and is often developed through brainstorming exercises at different levels of an organization. According to Broom and Sha, this approach is important in identifying both internal strengths (to take advantage of opportunities) and minimizing weaknesses (to combat challenges).[21]

- Strengths: Organizational attributes helpful to achieving the goal
- Weaknesses: Organization attributes harmful to achieving the goal
- Opportunities: External conditions helpful to achieving the goal
- Threats: External conditions harmful to achieving the goal

Often, SWOT analyses are done by bringing together multiple organizational leaders or teams to provide a variety of perspectives. For example, front-line staff might see different external challenges than management based on their daily customer interaction. Both of these perspectives are critical for a complete picture of an organization's strategic environment. This could be done in a series of small group meetings, potentially carried out by department, and including both individual brainstorming of ideas for each of the four boxes as well as group discussion. Practitioners would benefit from comparing the results across departments to more deeply understand the similarities and differences in perception across the organization. Compiling results in this manner produces an informed SWOT analysis to drive strategic discussions and planning.

Sources: APR Study Guide, University Accreditation Board (2017), 76.
Glen Broom and Bey-Ling Sha, *Cutlip & Center's Effective Public Relations* (11th ed.), (Boston, MA: Pearson, 2013), 244–245.

---

interactions around a specific topic. Focus groups have the benefit of being more efficient than traditional interviews, in that they can gather the sentiments of more participants quickly. They are excellent venues for soliciting opinion on a concrete product, new design or brand, or a specific message. Additionally, focus groups allow researchers a unique perspective into how groups navigate the social challenges of talking about certain issues—in this way, they can be informative when observing discussion of delicate or taboo topics.

Even with these benefits, focus groups must be managed and constructed carefully. It is easy for one or several individuals to dominate and drive conversation, essentially shutting out the rest of the group. A strong moderator can help to refocus discussion on the content at hand, ensure everyone has the opportunity to participate. **See the Appendix (page 229) for additional moderator tips.**

CONCLUSION

Research plays a critical role in understanding an organization and its environment. Before any campaign begins, practitioners should engage in developmental research, driven by the questions at hand. Crafting research questions, selecting methods, and executing research are all critical skills for success in crafting effective public relations campaigns. While not every organization may have the expertise and resources to implement statewide public opinion surveys or conduct big data analysis, every practitioner can develop research skills to better analyze content, gather information from a variety of key individuals, and to measure what is genuinely important for the success of the organization.

THINK CRITICALLY

1. What is the goal of developmental research? How is it different than other types of research?
2. How can practitioners demonstrate validity in their research to others inside their organization?
3. Why should practitioners conduct research inside their organization as well as outside?
4. What are key benefits of qualitative research? Quantitative research?
5. When would you use secondary research versus primary research techniques?
6. What should drive the choice of a specific research method or approach over another?

KEY TERMS

Audience 55
Codebook 67
Coding 66
Content analysis 66
Data 54
Generalizable 59
Likert-type scale 65
Methodology 54

Publics 55
Research, Developmental 55
Research, Evaluative 55
Research, Experimental 69
Research, Formal 59
Research, Informal 59
Research, Primary 54
Research, Qualitative 67

Research, Quantitative 67
Research, Refinement 55
Research, Secondary 54
SWOT analysis 71
Triangulation 62
Validity 61

CONCEPT CASE: RESEARCH FOR ISSUE PRIORITIZATION AT EQUALITY TODAY

Before defining goals, objectives, and strategies for its upcoming campaign, Equality Today's public relations team decides to step back and perform a bit of additional research to better understand the situation at hand. ET has a $10,000 budget toward research, allowing some flexibility to work with outside vendors. Organizational leadership has established that they see opportunity in looking to new issues that would be of interest in energizing and mobilizing staff, donors, members, and supporters. They have asked you to help in the process of identifying and prioritizing national, state, or local LGBTQ issues for advocacy engagement.

- Perform a quick SWOT analysis given the information presented in this and prior chapters about Equality Today.

- How would you craft three research questions that explore (1) the organization itself, (2) key donors and fund-raisers, and (3) external audiences and publics?

- What is one formal and one informal research technique that could be used based on these questions?

- What questions may be able to be answered through secondary research?

- Given the available budget, develop an initial research step based on the recommendation to select issues that would be energizing both inside and outside the organization.

CASE STUDY: HALLMARK ITTY BITTYS STEAL THE SPOTLIGHT

Hallmark Cards with FleishmanHillard
Based on PRSA Silver Anvil Award Winner
Campaign Focus: Media Relations, Product Marketing

To compete in an expanding miniature plush toy market and build momentum for the critical holiday season, Hallmark needed to shine a spotlight on its plush toy product, itty bittys™. In less than a week, FleishmanHillard created a quick-to-market campaign that landed itty bittys on the A-list for moms and kids alike. Through impactful celebrity and media partnerships, the campaign generated nearly 400 million impressions in one month, and the campaign period was the highest grossing month of itty bitty sales since the product's launch two years earlier.

Research/Diagnosis

Hallmark's internal Consumer Understanding and Insights team continually conducts primary, proprietary research with consumers to pinpoint issues and highlight opportunities for growth. The Hallmark team provided the deep understanding of target consumers and what motivates them to purchase itty bittys. FleishmanHillard researched how to generate mass awareness in a short timeframe and drive purchases.

Primary Research: Getting to Know the Consumer

Hallmark needed to know what motivates the target consumers—millennial moms with young kids—to notice Hallmark and be motivated to purchase itty bittys. The following research, which came from Hallmark Consumer Insights and Research, provided the "why" for their behavior:

- Itty bittys are most often given to others as a gift. Kids, especially those five years and younger, are key recipients; however, adults also receive them.

- Heavy and light purchasers have similar attitudes in terms of it making a great gift and being fun for children, but heavy buyers tend to have more of a collector mindset (e.g., want the entire set, can't have too many, fun to collect).

In an effort to learn how to reach mass awareness, a cash register survey was conducted through FleishmanHillard True Survey. These were the results:[22]

- 46 percent pay attention to the products celebrities use (phones, clothing, beauty products, and so on.)
- 55 percent replied that a celebrity increases awareness of a brand
- 31 percent say a celebrity increases purchase consideration

FleishmanHillard needed to find the most effective, fast-acting tactics to support a large-scale, mass awareness campaign to counter a new competitor who was gaining market share. The research quickly led to a focus on securing celebrity partnerships in combination with consumer media outlets. The following considerations had to be taken into account:

- Make a splash, NOW!
- Focus on paid and earned media and some social media as extensions
- Reach a new audience in addition to Hallmark Gold Crown loyalists (Hallmark Gold Crown members)
- Prioritize national consumer media
- Showcase entire itty bittys collection, not just one licensing partner

Objectives

- **Business**: Achieve itty bittys' sales goal (sales information is proprietary since Hallmark is privately held)
- **Communication**: Reach large-scale awareness in one month through social and traditional media placements and generate at least 250 million impressions (based on previous similar campaigns)
- Target Audiences
  - **Primary**: Millennial moms with kids ages 3–8
  - **Secondary**: Females 18+ buying for themselves or as gifts

Strategy

- **Fuel the Craze**: Itty bittys have hit, and everyone loves them. And wants more. Now.

A budget of $500,000 supported key celebrity spokespeople, strategic partnerships with entertainment outlets, social media, and traditional earned and paid media outreach.

Implementation

Aligning with the objectives above, Hallmark implemented the following paid, earned, and owned media tactics to garner social and traditional media placements.

Tactics

A partnership with the Hallmark social media, public relations, and marketing teams was necessary to secure owned channel support. Specifically, content provided direction to Hallmark teams for social media posts (Twitter, Facebook), including photos of Katie Holmes and Jennifer Garner shopping at Hallmark Gold Crown.

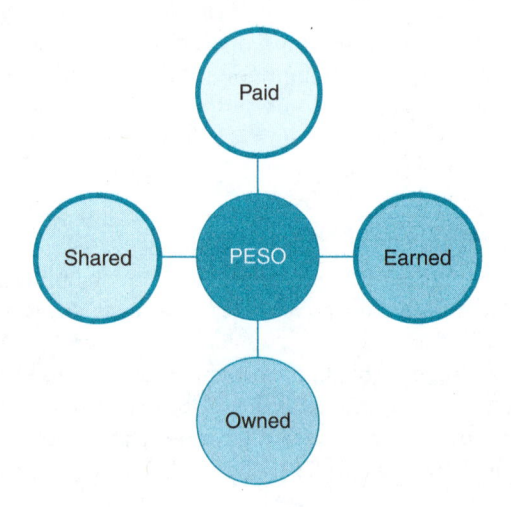

Paid

- Paid social media: Developed Facebook website click ads featuring several different licensed products to drive consumers back to the itty bittys' shop page on Hallmark.com
- Content Amplification: Extended the reach of media placements with a third-party online content amplification partner, Sharethrough, using native advertising
- Print advertising *InTouch* and *OK! Magazine* 1/2-page ads

Earned

Guerilla Outreach: Matched popular celebrities with their itty bittys celebrity twin to spark earned placements

- Created a custom mailing to fifteen celebrities that included a hand-drawn sketch of the celebrity as an itty bittys and the itty bittys twin (e.g., Robert Downey, Jr. and Iron Man)
- Tweeted at celebrities connected to itty bittys characters

Media Partnerships: Provided unique content and giveaways with large-scale consumer media outlets

- Partnered with *InTouch* and *Ok!* to feature itty bittys and celebrity photos
- Partnered with "Entertainment Tonight" to be included in a Jennifer Garner feature story and host an online giveaway

Press Release: Distributed a business-focused release via the wire

Shared

Celebrity Partnerships: Identified celebrities that resonated with key audience and had an established social media footprint

- Secured celeb moms Katie Holmes and Jennifer Garner to participate in photo shoots, then distributed photos of them shopping at a Hallmark Gold Crown store for itty bittys to entertainment media and showcase in Hallmark-owned channels
- Partnered with Tori Spelling, Soleil Moon Frye, Mario Lopez, and Dean Cain to tweet photos of their kids with their favorite itty bittys

Hallmark Social: Conducted giveaways in "Love, Hallmark," a private Facebook community for 500 volunteer mom bloggers

Reporting/Evaluation

Some challenges surrounding timing and licensing arose during the implementation. FleishmanHillard received less than a week to research, plan, develop, and implement tactics to meet deadlines and face the competitive threat in the marketplace. Additionally, tasked with showcasing the entire line of itty bittys proved challenging with the coordination of legal and creative approvals, which typically requires at least two weeks. The FleishmanHillard team revamped the creative several times to reflect licensing requirements. In evaluating the campaign FleishmanHillard and Hallmark based metrics on awareness (impressions) and sales; relying upon internal and external systems to quantify the reach. Hallmark provided the sales report.

Sales: Achieve itty bittys' sales goal *(Sales information is proprietary since Hallmark is privately held)*

- Exceeded sales goal by 159 percent
- Several weeks of campaign sales exceeded prior seasonal sales peaks
- September (the campaign period) was the largest month of sales EVER for itty bittys since the 2012 launch

Awareness: Reach large-scale awareness in one month through social and traditional media placements, and generate at least 250 million impressions

- Exceeded awareness goal by 54 percent in one month (384,104,481 impressions vs. 250,000,000 impressions)
- Celebrity partnerships accounted for more than 77 percent of overall impressions
- Secured nearly 40 major consumer media hits, including "ABC News," Huffington Post Parents, and Star Magazine

Theories

Excellence theory specifies how public relations makes organizations more effective, how it is organized and managed when it contributes most to organizational effectiveness, the conditions in organizations and their environments that make organizations more effective, and how the monetary value of public relations can be determined. This theory supports symmetrical two-way communication between organizations and publics. In this case study, Hallmark conducted significant research to understand their publics and their needs. They then reached their audience through a large-scale awareness campaign over a one-month period through social and traditional media placements and celebrity endorsements.

Research, Part 2

GOALS

5

THINK AHEAD

5.1 Understand the difference between organization-wide goals and communication or PR goals.

5.2 Connect developmental research findings to the goal-setting process.

5.3 Examine the different types of goals applicable to diverse organizations and situations.

5.4 Anticipate the potential challenges of setting public relations goals within an organization.

Creating effective and actionable communication and public relations goals balances the need for practitioners to understand the organization with the imperative to carve out the appropriate role for communication. Does no one in your community know who you are? Do your customers have an outdated image of what your products can accomplish? A nonprofit organization expanding its services must let the community know. Stockholders may need their profit expectations reset in light of new competition. A company's employees may not be taking advantage of all of the benefits offered to them. Whatever the situation, once you understand the challenge at hand, the next step is aligning communication goals with the organization's goals to best position public relations programs to make an impact.

Public relations works with the management team to connect organization-wide goals to specific public relations campaign goals.

    To begin the process, it is important to understand the distinction between **organization-wide goals** and communication or **public relations goals**. Broom and Sha explain that "an organization's vision, its mission, and its operational goals serve as the framework for public relations goals, which in turn address the problems and opportunities facing the organization."[1] In this way, practitioners must start with a thorough understanding of the organizational goals, followed by a research-based application of knowledge about the internal and external environments. From there, they can generate more specific campaign-related communication goals.

    According to Stacks, a communication goal is the overarching, long-term achievement a particular communication campaign or program attempts to accomplish.[2] Goals should be informed by research on the organization and its environment. Finally, goals are crafted to start the process of defining or narrowing audiences/publics for communication, to focus the campaign's efforts, and to apply the tools of public relations in useful, appropriate ways. Goals act as a compass for a public relations campaign, pointing practitioners toward the objectives, strategies, and tactics that best fit the organization's needs. They also help to prioritize efforts. It can be easy for public relations campaigns to attempt too much: to take on so many strategies and tactics that resources are stretched thin and completing objectives becomes difficult. Effective communication goals allow practitioners to judge potential objectives, strategies, and tactics by the degree to which they will contribute. Such a rationale for activities makes the processes of budgeting and coordinating with management significantly easier. Clearly aligned goals demonstrate a thoughtful practice and process for communication: they put public relations in the driver's seat.

Another way to begin to conceive of goals, building on Wilson and Ogden's writing about an organization's situation and environment, is as a "a positive restatement of the core problem."[3] From this perspective, part of the process of researching and developing communication goals—in conjunction with organizational goals—is to understand and reframe problems as opportunities. Practitioners can consider the problem (such as growing competition, loss of government funding, or a restrictive regulatory action) and reconceptualize it as an opportunity:

- Problem: Competition; Goal: Differentiate a brand in a crowded marketplace
- Problem: Funding; Goal: Expand fund-raising efforts
- Problem: Regulatory action; Goal: Increase public awareness of the positive impact of a particular industry, product, or process or (if it's not a particularly media-friendly or consumer-friendly issue); Goal: Inform key decision makers about the positive impact of a particular industry, product, or process

UNDERSTANDING YOUR ORGANIZATION AND ITS GOALS

When defining opportunities for any public relations campaign, it is important to focus initially on two key factors: understanding both the organization as a whole and the business model that it is built upon. All organizations, including for-profits and nonprofits, have structures that support their work. Considerations such as size, shape, vision, and history are all key elements to take into account when working to understand the company. How does it generate revenue? What are its expenses? Who are the major stakeholders it serves?

The larger the organization, the more variety it often has in its operations. Large organizations tend to be more complex due to their wider variety of product and service offerings; additional geographic, demographic, and industry-based audiences; and the volume of internal stakeholders. Such additional organizational details complicate the goal-setting process for PR practitioners but also multiply the opportunities for success. There are more stakeholders and constituencies to manage, generating more challenges, but also greater resources to address them.

Organizational structure also plays a role in the goal-setting process. Some organizations are top heavy, with more highly skilled employees. A law firm, for example, may have twenty attorneys, ten paralegals, and a support staff, while a manufacturing company is more likely to have a small executive team with a much larger number of skilled workers. The structure of a business can influence different dynamics and present various internal and external communication challenges. These situational factors may point toward very different challenges and goals for each organization. The law firm may struggle to retain top talent, while the manufacturing company

> ## PRo Tip
>
> ### ISSUE PRIORITIZATION
>
> When setting goals, how do practitioners know which issues, challenges, or opportunities to tackle first? Otto Lerbinger[4] presents three criteria to help narrow a long list of potential organizational issues down to those most important for setting communication goals:
>
> 1. **Imminence of action**: How quickly will the environment change? Concentrate on issues or opportunities that will arise more quickly.
>
> 2. **Impact on the organization**: How much will the issue or opportunity affect the organization? Prioritize those that have the largest potential impact.
>
> 3. **Actionability**: How much impact will public relations and communication have? Focus on issues and opportunities where communication can make a significant positive impact.
>
> *Source:* Otto Lerbinger, *Corporate Public Affairs: Interacting with Interest Groups, Media, and Government*, (Mawah, NJ: Lawrence Erlbaum, 2006).

may need to balance the internal and external issues of unionization, outsourcing, and cost controls.

Keep in mind that improved communication is never a silver bullet or an end in itself. Communication is a means to an end, and identifying the best-possible "end" or "ends" is the clearest path to a measurably successful campaign. Strategic public relations professionals constantly relate their actions at the planning and implementation stages to organizational goals. Creating effective communication goals helps to point a campaign in the right direction to support broader organizational goals.

THE GOAL-SETTING PROCESS

When developing a campaign's goals, research should inform the focus, priorities, and audience selection. The most important points to establish are (1) the impact role for communication and (2) the scope of the campaign, including initial decisions about the target audience(s) and publics, as well as the program's size, budget, and duration.

Seeking the Impact Role for Communication

Public relations evaluation leader K. D. Paine urges practitioners to "measure what matters": to set goals and track efforts in areas where communication can make a clear, definable impact for organizations. Public relations goals should be clearly relevant to the organization as a whole but also focus on areas where communication itself can make a difference. In practicing the insights highlighted by Paine, it is critical to set goals (and subsequently define objectives and measurement techniques) that accurately reflect the work done by communication programs.[5] It is somewhat easy to define, for example, increasing product sales as the top organizational goal and divert budget to a marketing program dedicated to supporting this task. However, when the goal is not achieved, communication may easily be viewed as the reason for failure; even when there are many additional factors in play (economic environment, sales team, competition, product quality, and so on). It points practitioners toward two key questions before setting public relations goals: What can we control? Where can we have the greatest impact?

To improve goals, one approach would be to begin by taking a holistic look at multiple parts of an executable and measurable process. For example, consider the general consumer purchasing cycle to identify the communication's impact role: If the sales team is struggling to get in the door of retail stores because the potential customer bases have not yet heard of the product or organization that offers the product, awareness may be the most important component to consider as impactful for communication when considering the components of a campaign. Conversely, if potential customers are already

---

PRo Tip

THE POWER OF "YES AND . . ."

Inherently, the process of planning a PR campaign will unearth many challenges that cannot be addressed through communication alone. In this way, it is critical to set goals based on those perceived areas wherein improved communication will have the greatest impact:

- Question: Can improved internal communication raise awareness for new employee incentives?
- Answer: Yes, with the cooperation of internal stakeholders.
- Question: Can improved media relations exposure increase sales?
- Answer: Yes, if the sales team is working in tandem with media outreach to capture, share, and integrate positive coverage into the sales process.
- Question: Can improved marketing communication increase awareness of a new product or service?
- Answer: Yes, with the appropriate budget and audience targeting.

Whether tackling these challenges from an internal viewpoint or as an outside agency professional, understand the limits of what public relations can do on its own.

The "Yes and . . ." or "qualified yes" approach allows public relations experts to underline the potential impact of a campaign while providing context for limitations based on process, budget, approvals, and timeline. "Yes and . . ." encourages practitioners to present themselves as problem solvers, rather than obstacles, and to frame campaigns realistically, rather than simply agreeing to the terms proposed.

Source: Regina M. Luttrell and Luke W. Capizzo, *The PR Agency Handbook*, (Thousand Oaks, CA: SAGE Publications, 2018).

aware of a specific product, but may have misconceptions about its use or potential, measuring specific content and defining an improved brand position in the marketplace may be a more valuable strategy.

Defining the Scope

Realistic goals must be set with an awareness of the available resources, preferred timeline, necessary expertise, and desired impact of the campaign. Combined, these comprise a campaign's **scope**. Public relations practitioners cannot accomplish everything. First, communication itself has its limits. Second, the resources available for a particular campaign bound the available toolbox of strategies and tactics for outreach. Program goals should be crafted with this concept of the appropriate scope of outreach. Four key areas for addressing this issue of scope are the budget, timeline, the desired change, and the expertise of the team. Considering these factors holistically informs realistic goal setting.

The budget provides one way to examine how much of an impact a potential campaign can achieve. From this perspective, practitioners can make judgments of priority and scope based on what resources are available to them. Campaigns may be planned with a predefined budget, where practitioners are given freedom to spend a set amount strategically. In other scenarios, the public relations function may need to make the case for their budget for a particular campaign or communicate to leadership that an initial budget is not sufficient to accomplish the desired goals. Budget may also impact factors such as the choice of media and outreach techniques (earned vs. paid media within the PESO model, for example), which can bring additional constraints (such as the potentially slower pace and lack of timing control of earned media).

At each step of diagnosing challenges, defining audiences, and planning a campaign, PR practitioners must make strategic decisions about the best uses for organization time, human resources, materials, media costs, equipment and facilities, and administrative items.[6] Before defining objectives, it is essential to conduct budgetary planning and the associated fiscal processes and research. Based on Broom and Sha's three guidelines of budgetary planning, the following are useful considerations:[7]

1. Identify all costs to the organization and resources allocated to the campaign.
2. Define the cost necessary to achieve specific results.
3. A budget is an estimate—manage and track it at each step in the process.

Selecting Audiences for Outreach

Identification of key audiences and publics should be among the first steps that a PR practitioner considers when diagnosing an organizational problem or opportunity. A more detailed and informed stakeholder research initiative can help form decisions about campaign prioritization and how best to connect with the identified public or audience.

Publics (internal and external) should be top-of-mind for practitioners from the first stages of research and planning a campaign.

Approaches for audience outreach should be based on the importance of the specific audience, organizational priorities, and the potential impact of communication. Beginning with the initial research (primary or secondary), the challenge that many PR practitioners face is evaluating each audience based on the probability of achieving the campaign objective using strategic communication. Some audience groups will inherently have a greater potential to take action: to buy a product, attend an event, or donate to a nonprofit organization. With that being said, these groups may not always be the highest priority audience at a given moment. Strategic communicators should look at the specific goal of interest (what type of product? when is the event? how is the fund-raising drive being positioned?), in conjunction with initial audience-focused research, to begin to define the best targets.

For example, an organization's goal may be to increase sales of a product. If this particular product has significant market penetration among one group, but limited penetration among another, the second group could represent an opportunity for growth. Initial research can help to identify the specific demographic, ideological, or interest-based difference between various audience groups, the results can create a strong rationale for a more tailored campaign. It may also indicate that certain media channels are less valuable because their distribution may be considerably broader and less defined. Striking the right balance is key.

Defining the Desired Change

While goals do not need the specificity of objectives as to narrowness and focus, they still must clearly identify the desired overall change. Is the highest priority financial (such as increasing revenue, market share, or fund-raising)? Reputational (such as crisis communication)? Relational (such as improving trust with employees, stockholders, or lawmakers)? Communication can drive change in multiple areas, and setting goals is where the focus and direction are set. The magnitude and measurement of this change should be developed and included as part of the objectives.

Prioritizing Budgets and Resources

While budgets should inform public relations goals, such goals also point toward the most effective use of budgets. An important point to consider is that organizations

Different teams across the organization should collaborate to craft communication and campaign goals.

and campaigns always have limited budgets and resources. Certainly, not all costs can be estimated at the goal-setting stage, but knowing general budgetary limitations for the organization or campaign, understanding the priority of the project, and considering anchor strategies or tactics (and their costs) can contribute to smart planning. For example, a campaign with a very short timeline, a narrow audience, and a clear direction (such as driving attendance) might require a significant investment in paid advertising to meet organizational goals. Media relations may not be able to reach publics quickly enough, organic social media may not be a feasible approach if the publics are not already connected with the organization, and owned media may not be impactful enough if publics do not already visit the organization's website. If the budget is not available for the paid outreach needed to reach the desired publics, different goals may have to be set or additional resources redirected.

WRITING GOALS

Crafting communication goals continues the process of understanding the similarities and distinctions between organizational goals and communication goals. It also reflects the necessary balance between a long-term and short-term focus. Finally, goals must reflect a visionary perspective, distinguishing them form concrete, measurable, time-bound objectives.

Types of Goals

Different organizations with different purposes can have very different organization-wide goals, which in turn create a variety of distinct communication goals. At a certain level, every organization has a "business model" and an activity focus: a major source of revenue for its operations as well as a functional purpose. In the case of a for-profit business, these are generally the same. The products or services are the company's purpose. In the case of nonprofits and public sector organizations, their purpose can either be the same as their source of revenue (such as a hospital) or radically different (such as a homeless shelter). Practitioners must understand both components of the organizations they work with in order to develop beneficial communication goals.

Despite these differences, all organizations have stakeholders on whom their success depends. Most communication goals, in one way or another, explicitly work to inform, persuade, or build relationships with these stakeholders. Campaign goals help to bridge the gap between what the organization should accomplish and the individuals or groups that enable such achievements or stand in their way.

Context: Mission versus Situation

In the creation of communication goals, public relations practitioners must balance an organization's long-term mission and direction with the immediate challenges and opportunities of its current environment. While both organizational and communication goals should be connected to an organization's mission,[8] they also must reflect

TABLE 5.1

Examples of Typical Organizational Goals and Relevant Communication Goals

	Organizational Goal	Potential Communication Goals
Business Sector	Maintain profitability Gradually improve stock rating Achieve a positive trust ranking Minimize governmental regulatory interference	Maintain external awareness/exposure Improve trust perception among key publics Change opinion of regulators/stakeholders toward reducing interference
Public Sector	Increase use of funded social programs Increase efficiency Decrease fraudulent use of social programs Improve citizen access to and use of information Increase government funding	Raise awareness of funded social programs Lower perceived barriers to access funded social programs Improve citizen access to and use of information Advocate for increased funding
Nonprofit Sector	Expand research efforts Expand program reach Secure private financial support of programs	Raise awareness of organizational success and growth Improve perceived reputation and trust among key publics Increase private financial support of programs

Source: Adapted from Wilson & Ogden, 2008.

the circumstances at hand. At times, unusual opportunities or challenges may arise and become more pressing. Public relations planning should be continually responsive to changes inside and outside of the organization.[9] This begins with setting goals that are in line with current circumstances as well as the organization's history, mission, and overall strategic direction.

When setting communication goals, practitioners should ask themselves the following questions:

- In what ways does this goal reflect the organization's long-term mission and vision?

- In what ways does this goal reflect the organization's short- to medium-term circumstances and opportunities?

- Do circumstances justify a temporary reprioritization of communication activities?

- What opportunities might be missed (or challenges prevented) by not prioritizing this goal? Are they more or less important than other opportunities or challenges?

Visionary Goals, Concrete Objectives

As mentioned at the beginning of the chapter, goals should be—as Wilson and Ogden explain in *Strategic Communications Planning*—"broader and more generic than the objectives that follow."[10] To use a travel metaphor, goals provide direction, while objectives describe the destination.[11] Goals need not be specifically measurable but should be attained when several underlying (and measurable) objectives are completed. Hallahan distinguishes goals that "center on organizational activities" from behavior-based objectives, which focus on knowledge, attitude, and awareness.[12] Therefore, communication goals should be the visionary statements that connect the organizational mission with the impact focus for communication. Goals may include how an organization is uniquely distinguished in the minds of its key publics. For example, *to become the recognized leader in our industry that provides patients and physicians with convenient, complementary, and cost-effective medicine.* Objectives represent the concrete steps to achieve this.

GOAL-SETTING CHALLENGES

Working with Organizational Decision Makers

Within an organization, the functional area of public relations cannot exist in a vacuum, as the success of campaigns depends on many internal stakeholders in various departments. As part of early-stage campaign planning, being able to properly understand the individual challenges faced by key internal decision makers in relation to the current challenge, including integrating their insights into the campaign, is vitally important.

The PR team may receive push-back when presenting campaign goals. It is important to make a strong case for why they represent the best approach for the organization.

Not only does a collaborative approach lead to the development of a more comprehensive plan, but a more inclusive process promotes an increased sense of buy-in from the stakeholders involved. Such insights can be gained through formal research but also through informal conversations and relationship building with individuals from across the organization. Simply getting to know a variety of individuals at different departments and different levels can make a world of difference in providing a more informed perspective when setting communication goals.

Prompting More Research

Research is an ongoing process. It's difficult to craft goals that do not prompt additional questions, which can be addressed by various types of research. At the beginning of the planning process, practitioners cannot know all of the questions they'll need answered. Initial developmental research may not address an important issue that arises while drafting goals. For example, initial research and direction from leadership may point out that a new product has not been adopted as often as has been expected, based on similar launches in the past using similar tactics and resources. Additional research into the situational differences from past campaigns (such as changes in the product, changes in the environment/economy, or changes in communication) may uncover a more specific area to focus the goal and future planning efforts. With a second look it may be a question of *who* rather than *why* that must be investigated.

Often this creates an **iterative planning** cycle: drafting goals leads to additional research, which leads to revision of the goals, which prompts additional researchable questions. Actionable and impactful goals are not easily clarified and defined. They should take multiple drafts and be informed by several stages of research. Again, this research can help to understand the true problem or opportunity the organization faces; where its competitors match up; and what broader environmental, economic, or social factors may come into play.

This iterative process of research and goal setting as part of diagnosis should not be intimidating. "Stages" of research may be as simple as a quick investigation or competitor products or a review of secondary research on a particular audience demographic. More fully and accurately developed goals will yield more focused, effective, and achievable objectives. A clearer understanding of stakeholders, audiences, and publics will drive more appropriate strategies and tactics, as well as more resonant messages.

CONCLUSION

Diagnosing the problem or opportunity is an essential role public relations practitioners must play within a larger organization. Often, PR is relied upon to be the "interpreter" for management. In the long run, helping the organization see strategic challenges, and how communication can address them, strengthens the position of the public relations team. The better the public relations team's reputation is among organizational leaders, the more likely that necessary resources and information will support future campaigns. Smart goal setting that positions communication goals within organization-wide goals provides a strong foundation to achieve and measure success.

THINK CRITICALLY

1. What are three important factors to remember for writing effective, useful campaign goals?

2. Why is it important to connect campaign goals with developmental research?

3. How can goals prompt additional research?

4. What are three issues that can arise in the goal-setting process? How would you overcome each of them?

5. How should public relations practitioners balance the organization's mission (long-term) with the current (short-term) environment, situation, or immediate communication need?

KEY TERMS

Communication/public relations goals 78
Iterative planning 88
Organizational/organization-wide goals 78
Scope 82

CONCEPT CASE: EQUALITY TODAY SETS COMMUNICATION GOALS

Armed with additional information about the beliefs and motivations of key stakeholders as well as the broader public, Equality Today's PR team looks to both inform and support the work of its leadership group. Organizational leaders are looking to move forward on several fronts: (1) to focus on state-level legislative and policy challenges to marriage equality and gay rights, (2) to maintain national momentum and engagement among members and supporters in the face of a potential post-win letdown, and (3) to secure additional and ongoing funding sources, again, knowing that major revenue sources may move on to other battles after a significant victory.

While the organization has a nationwide scope, its budget is limited. It also faces a lack of a cohesive, unifying purpose after completing a significant organizational goal. From a public relations perspective, the team must prioritize efforts, balancing the value of supporting these three goals with the need to focus on where they can have the most impact.

- How would your craft your public relations goals based on the stated organizational goals? Should you position them as challenges or opportunities?
- How would those goals point toward an impact role for communication?
- What further research would be helpful to better understand audiences or set clear baselines for improvement?

CASE STUDY: #WEIGHTHIS—REDEFINING SELF-WORTH FROM LEAN CUISINE[13]

Based on a case study by 360i
Campaign Focus: Rebranding

What happens when a company sets out to redefine an image, change perceptions, and alter the mind-set of the populace? Monumental change, that's what.

Public relations practitioners should set goals and track efforts that make a clear and definable impact for organizations. Nestlé Lean Cuisine set out to do the impossible: change the one thing they were known for most: DIET. It sounds almost unattainable when you consider that the global weight loss and weight management market is expected to reach $206.4 billion by 2019.[14]

Research/Diagnosis

Led by 360i, a global search and digital agency, research revealed that the brand's central female audience continued to face societal norms that judged women by appearance rather than by their accomplishments.

Objectives

After nearly six straight years of declining sales, the idea was to move consumers away from calorie counting and shift their outlook. The overall objective of the public relations plan was to evolve Nestlé Lean Cuisine's perception from their diet-focused heritage into a modern health and lifestyle brand.[15]

Strategy

The strategy seemed simple enough: change the conversation around health and wellness.

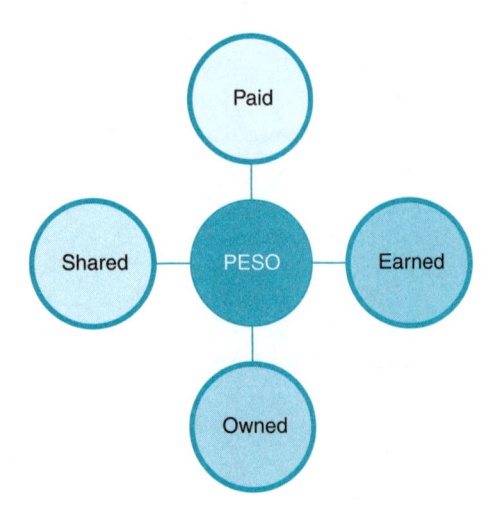

Tactics

Using a multipronged approach, Nestlé Lean Cuisine introduced a series of new advertisements and changed their packaging and frozen entrée options.

Paid

According to 360i, in a poignant and emotionally driven advertisement, Nestlé Lean Cuisine invited women to step up to the scale and weigh their proudest accomplishments, rather than their bodies.

Nestlé Lean Cuisine Weigh This http://bit.ly/LeanCuisine WeighThis

Lean Cuisine commissioned an artist to paint the women's comments on scales because the social response was so powerful. The art was installed in Grand Central Station.

Lean Cuisine Grand Central Station http://bit.ly/Lean CuisineGCS

Earned

The campaign generated 680 distinct media placements, leading to more than 211 million impressions.

Shared

To continue the momentum, at the start of a new year, when women's resolutions often center around weight loss, Nestlé Lean Cuisine and 360i gave women the power to change the conversation with digital tools that silenced everyday "diet" talk. They used the #WeighThis filter as an opportunity to encourage women to block out unproductive conversations and focus on what's really important in the New Year according to Julie Lehman, marketing director for the Lean Cuisine® brand.[16]

Owned

In addition, they created the proprietary #Weigh This Diet Filter for TV and Google Chrome™, allowing women to mute the word *diet* on their televisions and web browser. According to the company's press release, "consumers who want to focus on their best selves in the New Year—not the latest weight loss fads—can tune out these conversations by downloading the #WeighThis Diet Filter for Google Chrome™ which will block the word 'diet' from blogs, online articles and social posts. Lean Cuisine® will support the program through a one-time donation to Girls Leadership, an organization that empowers girls to create change in their world."[17]

Implementation

Over several months of research, planning, and execution, Nestlé Lean Cuisine launched a full rebrand of the company. They went from a diet focused brand to a mission driven company: "modern eating brand and ally for women's wellness, Lean Cuisine® has shifted away from a 'diet' brand and toward one that inspires overall well-being."[18]

Reporting/Evaluation

The campaign received 6.5 million views in just one week and drove a 428 percent increase in social media mentions alongside a 33 percent increase in positive brand perception. For these efforts, Ad Age rewarded the campaign with the #9 spot on its Viral Video chart.[19] #WeighThis was an integral part of Lean Cuisine's holistic turnaround in product and strategy and contributed to the brand seeing its first sales increase in nearly six years.

According to 360i, this campaign resonated emotionally with consumers. "Women everywhere were describing how they wanted to be weighed and comments flooded into #WeighThis and Lean Cuisine social channels. The responses also reduced the share of negative conversations around Lean Cuisine on social media to just 4 percent—a stark decrease from the previous year's share of 25 percent negativity."[20]

Theories and Models

This campaign utilizes **systems theory** in conjunction with the **two-way symmetrical model**. Lean Cuisine was reacting to changes in public perceptions surrounding dieting. By communicating directly with their consumers, they successfully changed opinions surrounding this issue.

6 Objectives

THINK AHEAD

6.1 Understand why objectives are crucial to the creation of successful campaigns.

6.2 Define S.M.A.R.T. objectives for public relations campaigns that contribute to organizational and communication goals.

6.3 Understand how to share and communicate objectives to build internal support and enthusiasm.

©iStockPhotos/Martin Barraud

WHAT MAKES HIGH-VALUE OBJECTIVES?

The process of setting appropriate objectives in the planning of public relations campaigns is critically important to overall success. Objectives provide public relations practitioners the opportunity to define a positive outcome. Without clear, measurable, and agreed-upon targets, the road to building momentum toward your campaign's success—both inside and outside of your team or department—is far more difficult. Objectives force clarity for yourself and others, answering the question, "what, specifically, do you want to accomplish?"

Public relations (PR) departments never work in a vacuum but constantly interact with other organizational functions and leaders. By defining objectives, practitioners support clear conversations with internal stakeholders regarding their definition of success. It is easier for leadership to provide constructive feedback for a campaign plan if the proposed results are clearly defined. Who wouldn't agree that *raising awareness of our new product* would be beneficial? But that feedback is not strategically helpful in understanding the expected *scope* of change and the resources necessary to achieve it. Alternatively, an objective of *raising awareness of our new product from 15 percent to 30 percent of current customers over the next four months* is much more clear-cut. It answers *what* as well as *who*, *when*, and *how much*.

Objectives are also about setting expectations. Particularly for leaders who may be unfamiliar with how public relations can influence opinions and behaviors, writing a clear, measurable definition of success can align expectations with reality. While there is

Major trade shows like the Consumer Eletronics Show (CES) provide opportunities for communicators to make significant progress toward objectives with a variety of paid, earned, shared, and owned media strategies and tactics.

often give and take during the process of setting objectives, the public relations function should take the lead, demonstrating a depth of understanding related to the associated challenges and how to best communication them.

So, just how reasonable is it to expect a *30 percent* increase in product awareness when we take the budget into consideration? Do the projected goals allow for the team to ask for more resources (if appropriate)? If the anticipated timeframe must be expedited, it might also require a larger investment or a change in strategy to ensure success. Alternatively, if the budget has little flexibility, the objectives may need to be modified. When these types of discussions happen in the early stages of campaign planning, they make the situation much easier to negotiate. It is only after a campaign has failed to meet expectations that public relations teams lose both budgetary support and decision-making clout for future programs.

Clarifying and specifying objectives is not possible without a well-defined audience or public. You may find it difficult to measure the objective of *raising awareness by 30 percent*; however, it may be easier to measure *raising awareness of current customers by 30 percent*. Without a defined audience, there can be no actual target. Objectives only exist relative to the audience or public for whom they are created and intended.

MANAGEMENT BY OBJECTIVES

Business scholar Peter Drucker's concept of "management by objectives," from *The Practice of Management*, outlines the structural and organizational benefits of setting clearly defined, narrow, and actionable objectives.[1] Drucker's approach allows leaders to empower employees throughout the organization by giving them clearly defined targets for success. As you may imagine, the first step toward success relies on the executive leadership setting high-level, overarching goals for the organization. These may include entering new markets, launching new products, geographic or infrastructure expansion, growing market share, or increasing revenue or profit. Executives must work with their management teams to develop actionable, measurable objectives for each department that will contribute toward achieving the larger organizational goal. Managers should collaborate with organizational leaders in the development of objectives for their teams to implement.[2] Drucker indicates that this process centralizes empowerment and accountability for large organizations.

Business performance therefore requires that each job be directed toward the objectives of the whole business, and each manager's job must be focused on the success of the whole through his or her specific objectives. Managers must know and understand what the business goals demand of their team, and their superiors must know what contributions to demand and expect of their direct reports—and must judge them accordingly. If these requirements are not met, managers are misdirected. Their efforts are wasted. Instead of teamwork, there is friction, frustration, and conflict.[3]

This description has been widely accepted as an ideal management approach for both for-profit and nonprofit organizations. Guided by clearly measurable, actionable, time-bound objectives that are coordinated with other departments, public relations practitioners are in a unique position to develop a clear understanding of what must be accomplished and how individual and departmental successes contribute to strengthening the entire organization.

The Public Relations Society of America (PRSA) strongly supports this narrow definition of objectives as the central step in communicating the business value of the public relations outreach: "Public relations programs cannot be successful without proactive, strategic planning that includes measurable objectives, grounded in research and evaluated for return on investment."[4] They are the tool through which practitioners show their strategic acumen and set the standards for their own success and value to the organization.

It should be noted that the process of setting formal objectives is not universally subscribed to within the practice of public relations. Some agencies make the reasonable case that, since awareness and opinion change are difficult to predict, these items should be tracked and measured but not used as the definition for success. Oftentimes, practitioners tend to overlook this step or set objectives that cannot be measured for the simple reason that defining success also requires defining failure. By defining failure, it makes it a potential reality. Overcoming a fear or hesitancy of setting objectives is an important step to take toward creating campaigns that clearly connect with larger organizational and communication goals. By defining objectives, an element of transparency and accountability is clear for those within the communication department and throughout the larger organization.

Types of Objectives

Objectives can be defined in a variety of ways, falling into three distinct categories based on the nature of the specific information being measured: **outputs**, **outtakes**, and **outcomes**.[5] Most campaign plans include a mix of the three in order to track efforts at several levels. Output objectives are limited in their direct connection to organizational goals. These may include metric-based targets such as the number of press releases distributed, the number of media placements secured, or the number of messages posted on a particular media channel. While output objectives are valuable to track for departmental purposes, they only provide process-related insights, rather than measuring the impact of campaigns.[6]

Outtake objectives measure whether targets "received, paid attention to, understood, and/or retained" organizational messages.[7] This information may be obtained using quantitative methods (e.g., formal surveys), qualitative methods (e.g., focus groups), or other approaches, including digital tracking of social media platforms, e-blasts, websites, or other content. These objectives provide insights with substantially more value than output objectives but are also only measuring the transactional side of outreach, rather than the impact on key audiences or the progress toward organizational goals.

Finally, outcome objectives tend to hold the most value and connection to organizational goals, measuring change in opinion and behavior. Examples of outcome objectives might include increasing event attendance, shifting public opinion on a ballot initiative, or convincing an activist group to end a boycott against your organization. Clearly, one challenge of defining outcome objectives is that communication is rarely the only factor involved. The closer an objective moves toward an organizational goal, as outcomes do, the more cooperation will be required between departments to achieve success. When possible, practitioners should aim to develop outcome and outtake objectives first to measure their own success. This is not to say that they should not track outputs; rather, that outputs alone do not equate to impact or progress toward organizational and communication goals.

Writing S.M.A.R.T. Objectives

One framework for addressing the challenges of writing objectives is outlined using the "S.M.A.R.T." framework: Ensuring they are specific, measurable, attainable, relevant, and time-bound. By using this structured approach, practitioners can develop objectives that are both actionable and valuable to organizations. The S.M.A.R.T. framework serves as a reminder that crafting objectives effectively helps to set a campaign and its expectations on the right path.[8]

Another important consideration that requires attention while developing objectives is the intended audience itself. In this way, each specific audience should be segmented and objectives developed for each.[9] By taking this approach, each objective and associated measurement is connected to a specific result that clearly demonstrates success or failure within a target population. These objectives should also serve as part of a larger communication and organizational goal. For example, an industry trade

Objectives may relate to achieving political or public policy outcomes, such as teachers unions lobbying for additional school funding.

> ## PRo Tip
>
> ### A FORMULA FOR S.M.A.R.T. OBJECTIVES
>
> Action + Context + Audience + Volume + Duration
> _____
>
> **Example:** Increase the awareness of Bill 123's potential negative industry impact among ABC Association members and key supporters (pre-determined contact list) from 25 percent to 50 percent over the next three months.

association might focus on raising awareness among its members and supporters for a new piece of legislation, connecting to a larger organizational goal of mobilizing either support or opposition. This objective focuses on one narrow aspect of the larger goal. Being able to define a timeline and specifying a measurable degree of change would complete the criteria.

Specific

As we have seen, objectives must be specific to the campaign, to a defined audience, and to the individual piece of the larger goal they reflect. *Improving awareness* is too broad. Improving awareness of a specific brand, product, event, or initiative is better. Improving awareness of a specific brand, product, event, or initiative for an important, definable audience is best.

Measurable

Once objectives are specified to the audience and an associated challenge or opportunity, their projected impact or outcome can be defined. A variety of measurement tools and tactics exist, ranging from the number of clicks on an e-newsletter link (an outtake objective) to changing the opinion or behavior of an audience (an outcome objective).

Depending on the broader goals of an organization, a number of methods exist to support the measurement of a desired objective. Measurement should connect intimately with larger, overarching goals. For example, advocacy campaigns for local ballot initiatives generally use public opinion polling of likely voters throughout an election season (as budgets allow) since their goal is, by definition, to drive a change in opinion. Efforts supporting this type of initiative would most likely include qualitative research to inform and assess message creation, as well as elements of quantitative research to define and measure progress toward an objective (awareness, attitude, intention to vote, and so on).

> ## *PRo Tip*
>
> ### COMMON ERRORS—MEASURING WITHOUT A BASELINE
>
> One common misstep that PR practitioners make is to measure an objective without having an appropriately defined baseline from which improvement can be tracked. When writing a measurable objective, it's critical to have a clear starting point. Often, this can come from data gathered during the developmental research or *diagnosis* phase of campaign planning, but the need for a baseline may also come to light as the objective is developed. Without a baseline, there is no way to demonstrate growth or success (or to see where changes need to be made). An appropriate baseline could be defined by the click rates for prior e-newsletters, RSVPs to last year's annual event, or pre-campaign public opinion surveys to quantify attitudes or awareness for the issue at hand.

Attainable

S.M.A.R.T. objectives must be realistic. Communication alone cannot transform organizations or publics overnight. Individuals will rarely change their mind after reading a single e-newsletter, viewing a promoted post, or reading one newspaper article. A functional objective hinges on the ability to appropriately set a measurable goal that is reasonably attainable with the resources and time involved. It is impossible to know what is attainable without first measuring and researching the situation.[10] This legwork establishes a baseline and provides both quantitative and qualitative insights that inform the degree of change that can be achieved.

Practitioners should also keep in mind that awareness and a change in opinion must occur before behavioral change.[11] Behavioral change, whether it is discouraging smoking or encouraging the purchase of a new consumer product, takes significant time and budget. The more specific the behavioral focus, the more effective the message can be.[12] Successful campaigns are more likely to occur when the attempted change is low cost and high reward and when budgets include sufficient resources to execute based on the size of the audience or public, the magnitude of the change, and the necessary timeline.[13]

Additionally, organizational leaders may not necessarily want to hear that the proposed objectives are unreasonable within the constraints mentioned above. Communicators must work to ensure the best-possible strategic, integrated approaches and to clarify a clear rationale for their choices in order to best position their recommended objectives and strategies for approval and success. The more that practitioners can have honest conversations with organizational leaders about attainability at the objective-setting stage, the more realistic everyone's expectations will be when reporting and evaluation occur.

Relevant

Practitioners should avoid tracking only *output* objectives that measure the number of tweets or Facebook posts, the number of press releases distributed, or the number of reporters contacted. The most useful outtake and outcome objectives measure the impact of a campaign's efforts, and generally fall into three categories: awareness, opinion change, and behavioral change. An awareness objective could involve increasing familiarity for a specific organization, event, product, or service. Opinion change might involve issue advocacy work on one end of the spectrum or sales-focused competitive product outreach on the other. Behavioral change may include efforts related to recruiting (both for employees and organizational membership), purchasing a product, **lead generation**, or **lead capture**.

While these outcome objectives tend to highlight the best-case scenario, it is not always possible to measure this way based on available expertise, resources, and timelines. Objectives that may be based wholly on output or organizational results are considered outtake objectives and include **competitive objectives.** Objectives of this nature allow organizations to measure the quality of a public relations effort in a way that can clearly connect to communication priorities, including **share of voice** or quality of media coverage determined through content analysis. Organizations can benchmark themselves against key competitors and also measure progress. While competitive objectives do not necessarily carry the same connection to organizational goals as outcome objectives, they can still add significant insights to campaign measurement.

The more relevant an objective's measurable component is to a broader organizational goal, the more valuable it becomes. This connectivity is a key component of demonstrating the success of public relations campaigns.

Time-Bound

One of the hallmarks of a good campaign objective is the inclusion of a defined timeline for its overall execution. Identifying an appropriate duration is determined by a variety of factors, including the overall campaign timeline, the scope of change desired, how the objective integrates into larger goals, and the volume of work needed by the communication team to complete the strategies and tactics involved. A larger team or a larger budget may allow for an expedited projected timeline.

Organizations should also plan to have multiple objectives running simultaneously, all following separate, overlapping timelines. Short-term objectives generally focus on knowledge and awareness, while long-term objectives can more successfully drive attitude and behavior change; as knowledge-based change necessarily comes before behavioral change.[14] Setting objectives within a time-bound campaign helps to connect projects with higher-level organizational goals. Multiple layers of objectives pointing toward tangible results demonstrate a valuable strategic understanding of the PR discipline's most valuable contribution: how public relations can improve organizations' relationships with their publics over time.

Additional Objective Frameworks

Leading public relations scholars note that various recipes exist for formulating successful objectives. Practitioners should use the framework that resonates best with them, allowing them to envision the results of their campaign.

Broom and Sha indicate that there are four elements that ultimately contribute to campaign or program objectives: a target public, outcome, measurement, and target date.[15] Identification of a target public should reflect a key constituency for the organization. The outcome should reflect a meaningful change and must be measurable using organizational resources prior to, as well as after, the communication activity. Of equal importance is the clear communication of the timelines in which the result will be achieved. If each of these elements is accounted for in the planning stage, the resulting objective will be clearly defined. As the milestone date arrives, organizational leaders should be able to clearly see whether it has been achieved or not.

Similarly, PRSA defines four components of successful objectives in the *APR Study Guide*: (1) the result or outcome, (2) the public or publics addressed, (3) the "expected level of accomplishment," and (4) the time frame.[16] While using slightly different language, it outlines the same focused four-component approach.

A complement to this formula for appropriately developing objectives, Stacks and Michaelson have defined three types of useful outcome objectives to consider: *informational objectives* measure awareness and knowledge, *motivational objectives* track

---

PRo Tip

CONSTRUCTING YOUR OBJECTIVES

Example objectives from the PRSA's *APR Study Guide*:

- To increase ridership of public transportation in the Los Angeles metropolitan area [behavioral outcome] by 8 percent [level] among workers earning less than $25,000 per year [public] within the first six months [time frame] following launch of the communication program.

- For at least 10 percent [level] of a randomly selected sample of public transportation riders in the Los Angeles metropolitan area [public] to identify as their reason for using public transportation one of the communication tactics employed in your public relations campaign [behavioral outcome] by the end of the second year of that campaign [time frame].

- To have confirmed reports that 50 percent [level] of the natives of one Asian, one African and one South American developing country [public(s)] are applying multi-yield agricultural practices [behavioral outcome] by 2020 [time frame].

Source: Universal Accreditation Board. *APR Study Guide*, 2017, 60.

information received and understood to measure opinion change, and *behavioral objectives* chart whether the audience takes an intended action.[17] If a particular message does not reach its intended audience, their opinions will remain unchanged. An opinion must change before a behavior. In this way, the three types of outcome objectives work together to drive long-term impact.

Perhaps even more important than the framework used to develop objectives is following a consistent and comprehensive approach. Each approach can act as a checklist to ensure that objectives are created with the necessary components to position a campaign for success. Practitioners can experiment to identify the approach that works most effectively for them, their organization, and the campaign at hand.

CONNECTING OBJECTIVES TO KEY INTERNAL AUDIENCES

Whether working at an agency or as a consultant, practitioners should keep in mind the internal or executive audience(s) for their objectives. During the *diagnosis* phase, formal and informal research provides insight into what leadership sees as the goal of a project as well as its communication objectives. The role of a practitioner is to gather a variety of perspectives on the challenge or opportunity, as well as to craft potential objectives. With that in mind, these may not always be the best communication objectives for that particular moment. Approved objectives also often reflect—for better or worse—the organization's internal politics, personalities, and priorities. Successful practitioners not

Objectives will not be successful if public relations team members are unable to convince organizational leaders that they are relevant and valuable to achieve.

only write objectives that are S.M.A.R.T. and focus their team's efforts on campaign elements likely to have the biggest impact but also act as counselors to provide strategic perspective with support for their positions. Communicators who have mastered the internal "client" pitch tend to get more buy-in from their organization's dominant coalition and more opportunities to put their ideas into action.[18]

Do Your Objectives Make Organizational Decision Makers Excited?

Keep in mind that the content and the objectives matter when presented to an audience comprised of internal leaders. The diagnosis phase should point not only toward organizational need and priority but also to enthusiasm. As communication teams never work in isolation, successful objectives take into account internal attitude to ensure that energies are channeled in the most useful direction.

This process does involve a degree of politicking. Practitioners must anticipate and respond to internal coalitions, key decision makers, and organizational history. Two organizations with similar goals will inherently have different objectives based on their resources and assets, as well as their structure and leadership. Goals are aspirational, but objectives must clearly reflect organizational and environmental realities. If the leadership does not agree with a campaign's direction, it will not succeed.

Proving Relevance: Will Completing Your Objectives Drive Positive Change?

If the primary goal of a campaign is to increase the number of dues-paying members for your organization, your public relations objectives should be judged by how closely they support that goal. For example, assuming final responsibility for membership growth falls within a separate member relations department, here are multiple potential communication objectives:

- Potential objective #1: Raise awareness of the organization among potential members in the community (defined demographically and geographically) from 15 percent to 20 percent over six months.

- Potential objective #2: Target the attendance of 100 potential members at organizational events as the guests of current members in the next six months.

- Potential objective #3: Identify and capture contact information for 100 potential members over the next three months.

While each of these approaches point to particular elements in the puzzle of raising membership, the second and third objectives more clearly address the problem at hand. The third objective may be the easiest to execute as only the communication department is involved. All three approaches could be implemented, but the second and third should be prioritized based on their closer relationship with the organizational priority. The final decision on which objectives to focus on may be based on the available resources as well as organizational and departmental circumstances for execution.

Event attendence may be a useful orbjective, but it may only be the first step toward attracting new customers. Ensure campaign objectives reflect the multiple stages often needed to influence the opinions and behaviors of publics.

Another item to keep in mind is that the scope of the communication department's work or an agency's agreement changes from organization to organization over time. Ideally, clear demonstration of successful and impactful communication objectives help expand the influence of top communicators and the resources and responsibilities of communication departments.[19] Overreliance on another department can doom objectives to fail if the communication team does not receive necessary information, resources, or support. The expectations for such support should be made exceedingly clear to all campaign team members when developing objectives.

Are You Connecting Short- and Long-Term Objectives?

Objectives may come in multiple simultaneous, overlapping, or separate stages, reflecting short- and long-term steps toward achieving organizational goals. For example, an internal campaign-specific objective may be to increase employees' awareness of a new health care benefits package from 0 percent (prior to launch) to 80 percent over a three-month period. The organization may have a larger, overarching goal of improving employee satisfaction and retention, which the new benefits program supports. For the public relations function, the long-term objective may be to increase employee awareness of all company benefits or (along with the human resources department) to increase employee retention by 15 percent over the course of the year. In this case, the short-term campaign objective clearly connects to the long-term organizational objective.

If the short-term objective moves out of alignment with the organizational objective or goal, practitioners should consider making an adjustment. As an example, if the top priority of the human resources function shifts to a lack of qualified job applicants in a growing division, rather than a retention problem, communications professionals should adjust or reprioritize their objectives as needed to reflect a new audience, a new message or focus, a new technique for measurement, and a new timeline. Promoting new employee benefits may still be the campaign's purpose and central message, but the most important audience could be outside the organization. This would necessitate different channels, and the measurement may be related to capturing information about incoming applicants to the organization, including whether their application had originated from the specific outreach campaign. In this way, objectives and measurement approaches should be flexible and responsive to the shifting needs of the organization as a whole.

PRo Tip

HOW *NOT* TO WRITE OBJECTIVES

- **Does the measurement matter?** Output-based rather than outcome-based objectives may mean that practitioners can easily check objectives off a list, but that they lack organizational impact. Counting Facebook "likes" and media clips or calculating ad value equivalency does not assess whether a campaign has achieved the intended result for an organization. Using awareness, attitude change, behavioral change, or content analysis metrics, for example, can more accurately measure success.

- **Is the objective primarily communication driven?** Objectives not tied directly to public relations efforts can present practitioner challenges because they are too dependent on others within organizations to complete or do not end up being a result of communication strategies and tactics.

- **How much impact will achieving the goal have?** Objectives not closely related to organizational goals will lack impact and, eventually, reduce overall organizational support for public relations efforts. Organizational goals should drive communication goals, and each goal should be represented by objectives.

- **Is it organizationally feasible?** Sometimes, there is just not enough organizational enthusiasm, time, or resources to complete the desired objective. Practitioners must be aware of such limitations when calibrating the amount of change in each objective.

For more details and to see common errors in writing objectives before and after reviewing them with the questions listed above, see the Appendix, page 233.

CONCLUSION

There are many benefits to public relations that cannot be easily measured. Community goodwill, volunteer or donor enthusiasm, and brand equity or trust do not translate smoothly to numerical data, graphs, and charts but may be clear outcomes for successful campaigns. In some cases, these can be measured using proxies (positive vs. negative media coverage or social media discussions, for example). With that being said, public relations will always be under measured. It is impossible to record each of its effects (positive and negative) on perception and behavior simultaneously. Practitioners must take on the responsibilities of understanding what is measurable with the resources at hand and developing objectives aligned with the goals that are most important to the organization. With a bit of creativity, it is possible to measure many significant components of campaigns.

By writing objectives with existing organizational structures and focuses in mind, as well as having a clear understanding of the value of each priority, practitioners can make a meaningful and sustainable impact. Organizations tend to end up stale and static. Change may be met with resistance even in situations where it is deeply needed. The public relations function within an organization can act as a "cooperative antagonist," supporting policies that encourage long-term, mutually beneficial relationships with external *and* internal publics rather than short-term advantage over them.[20] Practitioners should be able to understand and explain the organization-wide implications of their ideas and objectives. Communication cannot win every internal battle, and this will sometimes result in less-than-ideal objectives. However, over the long term, practitioners that prioritize strategy; understand their industry and competitive environment; and those that research, quantify, and justify their recommendations will make their departments and their organizations measurably better.

What word hasn't been mentioned in this chapter? You might notice we haven't often used *how*. Objectives should be written in a way that is neutral in how they are accomplished: the strategies and tactics we choose to implement.[21] In particular, thinking strategically and planning consistently successful campaigns means that we are not working backward from tactics but understanding what will be value added to our organization and public. Objectives grow from necessity and from prioritizing organizational opportunities and challenges. Strategies, covered in the next chapter, connect those objectives with the tactics, the toolbox of public relations practice.

THINK CRITICALLY

1. What is Management by Objectives, and how is the concept applied in public relations?
2. Why is it important that objectives are measurable?
3. What are some examples of potential objectives that are measurable but not relevant to organizational or communication goals?
4. What would you do if an objective you presented was met with a negative response from organizational leaders, such as "we don't have six months to wait for that change to happen"?

KEY TERMS

Competitive objectives 99
Lead capture 99
Lead generation 99

Outcome objectives 95
Output objectives 95
Outtake objectives 95

Share of voice 99

CONCEPT CASE: SETTING OBJECTIVES FOR EQUALITY TODAY

The executive director of the organization has made a decision, based in part on your research, to prioritize a new round of fund-raising to support ongoing efforts, particularly for high-dollar donors. In conjunction with the fund-raising team, you'll need to set three communication campaign objectives focusing on (1) awareness of the organization's priorities and mission, (2) regular communication and engagement with key publics, and (3) lead capture for potential donors. Based on your understanding of the organization's strengths as well as its limitations, consider the potential for S.M.A.R.T. objectives reflecting these focus points.

- Write an objective for each of these three points.
    - What audience restrictions and boundaries would be appropriate?
    - What timelines would be reasonable to complete your objectives?
    - How would you measure success? Would you need a baseline?

CASE STUDY: COOKIE CARE DELIVERS SWEET RESULTS FOR DOUBLETREE BY HILTON

Hilton Worldwide with Ketchum, Gensler, and Digital Royalty
Based on PRSA Silver Anvil Award Winner
Campaign Focus: Global Relations

For more than twenty-five years, DoubleTree by Hilton has tried to make the world a better place, one cookie at a time. The presentation of a warm, chocolate chip cookie to every guest checking in at one of its 400 properties has become an iconic symbol of the brand's care and service and a powerful, tangible emblem in an industry where it is increasingly difficult to distinguish competitors. In fact, the hotel's research reveals that the cookie is one of the top three reasons travelers stay at a DoubleTree.

For DoubleTree, 2014 was a significant year, as it launched its new "First the Cookie" ad platform. To coincide with this, and the brand's 300 millionth cookie giveaway, DoubleTree wanted a global campaign to celebrate its iconic "welcome" symbol. The company conceived "Cookie Care," a campaign to spread cookie love all year—inside and outside hotels—and to reach more travelers. DoubleTree baked up a big, but deliciously simple, idea. In honor of this sweet milestone, DoubleTree would surprise guests and consumers worldwide with two cookies rather than one. Double the cookie would generate double the smiles and satisfaction. More importantly, it would give people something they'd enjoy even more than the cookie: the chance to pay the second cookie forward. DoubleTree launched a massive consumer engagement program in priority markets internationally to unleash the simple power of two cookies, intersecting the brand with local news and cultural events for more exposure.

"Cookie Care" delighted crowds with 26 events in 23 markets globally—stretching from New York City to San Francisco, and across the ocean to London, Shanghai, Beijing, Singapore, Jakarta, Dubai, Queenstown, Auckland, and Rotorua. It surprised consumers for the 100th anniversary of Chicago's Wrigley Field, the Apple iPhone 6 launch, and Eid al Adha (Feast of the Sacrifice) in Dubai. "Cookie Care" warmed people's hearts throughout the year, generating 2.4+ billion media impressions and 4,100+ placements, as well as a 10 percent increase in brand consideration in the first two months of the campaign.

Research/Diagnosis

DoubleTree's guest survey results underscore the impact of its cookie welcome, a check-in tradition for 25+ years. Travelers overwhelmingly named the cookie as one of the top three reasons they choose DoubleTree. Therefore, the company knew the cookie was not only the essence of the hotel brand, but that it translated worldwide. Brand research revealed that the cookie is

- recognized and adored in all regions of the world;
- an iconic symbol of home, friendliness, and a welcoming attitude; and
- a positive brand differentiator.

Just as the cookie has the power to make anyone's day brighter and every moment better, it's not just special and memorable to the person receiving; it also delights the person giving the cookie. DoubleTree learned from hotel team members that handing out the cookie is one of the most rewarding parts of the job. Building on that notion, the company extended that giving experience to its valued guests and other travelers.

Objectives

DoubleTree built a creative regional activation program in the hotel's highest priority markets worldwide to achieve the following goals:

- Increase business and leisure travelers' consideration of DoubleTree by at least 2 percent
- Generate 1,500 media placements and 1 billion media impressions
- Generate 100,000 consumer sweepstakes entries
- Garner participation from 60 hotel properties to conduct their own "Cookie Care" events

Based on research defining the brand's primary consumer base and media consumption habits, as well as the brand's emphasis on team member engagement, DoubleTree identified the following three key audiences for the "Cookie Care" program:

- Primary Customer: Global business and leisure travelers (50-50 split) are the two largest parts of DoubleTree's customer base; 56 percent are female.
- Media: Local and national consumer (travel, lifestyle), business and trade, broadcast, print, and online media provide opportunities for earned coverage.
- DoubleTree by Hilton Team Members: Team members are the best ambassadors and can passionately share the brand's CARE culture beyond hotel doors. DoubleTree wanted to engage local team members to serve as volunteers for "Cookie Care" events in each market.

Strategy

Using the iconic chocolate chip cookie as the centerpiece of a year-long, integrated global marketing campaign, DoubleTree wanted to increase the brand's reputation among travelers by surprising them with two cookies in locations around the world where consumers least expected it.

Tactics

Timed with the brand's 300 millionth cookie giveaway, the company launched "Cookie Care" in New York City with a national media tour, delivering cookies to tens of thousands of unsuspecting New Yorkers. Each person received two specially packaged cookies—one to enjoy and one to share. Simultaneously, DoubleTree engaged people and businesses on the brand's social media channels, inviting them to tell the company who they would share #CookieCare with for a chance to have DoubleTree surprise others.

Since the start of the program, "Cookie Care" has made twenty-three stops throughout North America, Latin American, Europe, and Asia.

Paid

National Chocolate Chip Cooke day was celebrated with target-right segments on entertainment programs including "Jimmy Kimmel Live!" and "On Air with Ryan Seacrest," as well as other national media takeovers.

Shared

Delivering Cookies Via Social Media: #CookieCare encouraged consumers to spread "Cookie Care" on Facebook, Twitter, and Instagram for a chance to surprise colleagues, friends, and family with cookie deliveries. An online sweepstakes invited consumers to enter for a chance to win branded merchandise and two grand prize trips, one for the winner to keep and one to share.

Baking Up Excitement Where Consumers Least Expect It: "Cookie Care" encouraged people to celebrate everything from Tax Day in Los Angeles and Philadelphia (two of the country's highest-taxed cities) and the 100th anniversary of Chicago's Wrigley Field to the eagerly awaited Apple iPhone 6 launch in New York City and San Francisco, the launch of hockey season in Toronto, a long summer weekend in London, World Kindness Day in New Zealand, and more!

Owned

Promoting Do-It-Yourself "Cookie Care" Hotel Events: A PR toolkit empowered hotel teams globally to plan and host their own signature "Cookie Care" events in local markets.

Extending U.S. National Chocolate Chip Cookie Day Internationally: For the first time, DoubleTree took National Chocolate Chip Cookie Day global by inviting people into any DoubleTree property for two free cookies—with or without a reservation. The company also swarmed airports across the United States and surprised travelers with free cookies.

Reporting/Evaluation

"Cookie Care" dramatically surpassed the campaign's original targets:

Objective: Increase business and leisure travelers' consideration of DoubleTree by at least 2 percent

- In the first two months of the campaign, brand consideration among leisure travelers increased 10 percent, and overall brand consideration increased 2 percent.

Objective: Generate 1,500 media placements and 1 billion media impressions

- To date, the team generated 4,148 media stories worldwide, resulting in 2.4 billion media impressions in print, broadcast, online, and social media outlets globally. Highlights: *International*

Business Times, ABC News, CNN, *The London Daily Mail*, *Toronto Sun*, Channel Young News (Shanghai), and dozens of local broadcast affiliates in top designated market areas (DMAs).

- On average, three to five broadcast segments ran in each event market. "Good Morning America Live!" even aired a three-minute earned segment celebrating DoubleTree's National Chocolate Chip Cookie Day activities.

- Since the campaign began, Instagram followers increased by 66.7 percent, Twitter followers increased by 22.5 percent, and Facebook fans increased by 12.6 percent. The campaign generated 9,847 uses of #CookieCare with @doubletree.

- In China, DoubleTree's Sino Weibo site and social channels generated 2,678 retweets and comments.

Objective: Generate 100,000 consumer sweepstakes entries

- Nearly 150,000 consumers entered the "Cookie Care" sweepstakes, surpassing the goal by 50 percent.

Objective: Garner participation from 60 hotel properties to conduct their own "Cookie Care" events

- Teams from 110 hotels ordered "Cookie Care" DIY event kits to conduct their own events—beyond the planned event markets.

Theories

The "Cookie Care" campaign reflects **framing theory** from a brand identification perspective. DoubleTree emphasized an aspect of their brand symbolizing specific values they wanted to convey to consumers. Framing emphasizes that individuals construct their worldview through a variety of interwoven and interconnected symbols.[22] The act of focusing on cookies and aligning events and outreach with the concept of unexpected enjoyment points toward a customer experience primed for these interactions.

7 Strategies

THINK AHEAD

7.1 Understand each element of the PESO model and how these elements work together to achieve campaign objectives.

7.2 Describe the different audience segmentation techniques.

7.3 Explain how to use the organization's strengths and resources to accomplish your campaign strategies.

7.4 Summarize how to advocate for communication campaigns in competitive environments.

Strategies demonstrate synthesis in a public relations (PR) campaign. The situation has been defined, audiences have been selected, and the objectives have been developed, but it's the job of the public relations team to drive the best-possible direction for implementation. This is where strategies come into play. It is the moment when concrete objectives—crafted from research, organizational goals, communication goals, and situational realities—meet the skills, talents, and creativity of public relations professionals. Strategies are the approaches through which objectives are accomplished. They act as a compass for practitioners to navigate from written objectives to completed objectives.

Broom and Sha define strategies as "the overall concept, approach, or general plan for the program designed to achieve an objective."[1] In this way, they connect objectives to tactics, or "the events, media, and methods used to implement the strategy."[2] Strategy development involves a deep understanding of audiences and publics, of the competitive environment, and of the **channel** or medium within which the communication will take place.[3]

Strategies help practitioners consider the best-possible mix of paid, earned, shared, and owned media for a specific campaign.

CHOOSING YOUR CHANNELS: THE PESO MODEL

The PESO (paid, earned, shared, and owned) model provides a helpful checklist to ensure campaigns include strategies in multiple facets of campaign communication.[4] It serves as a framework to help communicators think systematically about the tools at their disposal for a specific campaign. Developed and championed by Gini Dietrich of Chicago-based PR firm Arment Dietrich, PESO builds on the traditional marketing duo of paid media (such as advertising) and earned media (public relations) to include shared media (social media outreach) and owned (digital properties, physical locations, events, and other wholly controlled environments). It also maps what can be referred to as converged media: additional overlaps between the four main types of communication channels.

Keep in mind that these categories work together and are not prioritized over one another. Campaigns do not force us to choose between paid and shared media or earned and owned media, rather allow us to choose from a menu based on what fits the needs of the organization and the situation. Like a painter, practitioners begin with distinct categories or colors but choose the degree to which we mix them together, place them side by side on the canvas, or leave them out of the picture entirely. These choices should not be made arbitrarily but based on the knowledge of organizational goals and audiences from the diagnosis stage in order to achieve defined campaign objectives.

FIGURE 7.1

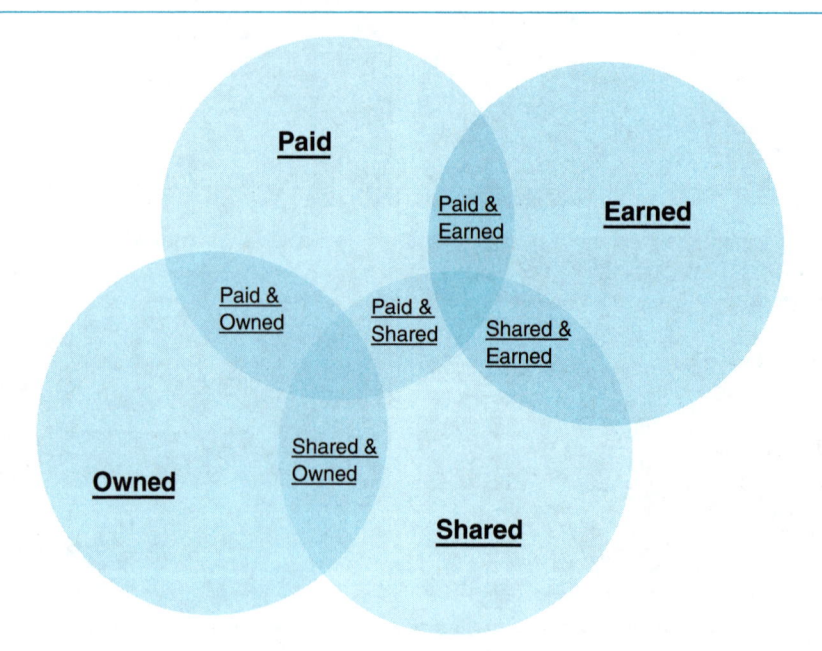

Practitioners can select from a palette of paid, earned, shared, or owned channels, as well as converged approaches that share characteristics and benefits of multiple media types.

While not every medium is a fit for every campaign, different channels are often complimentary. For example, paid media and social media allow for repetition and timeliness, but earned media's editorial processes create more credibility and trust for the messages being shared. On one hand, paid opportunities offer a clear selection of channels, choice of timing, and message control while, on the other, earned media comes with the tacit endorsement of the outlet.[5] Luckily, it does not need to be a choice. Earned and paid strategies should work together to provide both repetition and credibility. Many campaigns benefit from a mix of channels designed to reach audiences with approaches that support each other to achieve objectives.

The terms *controlled* and *uncontrolled* are applied to make the distinction between earned or shared media and paid or owned media. Broom and Sha define controlled media as "those in which practitioners have the say over what is said, how it is said, when it is said, and—to some extent—to whom it is said."[6] Conversely, they define uncontrolled media as "those over which practitioners have no direct role in decisions about media content."[7] The PESO model expands on this distinction by breaking down these categories further. In this case, the lines between categories are not absolute: there are degrees of controlled and uncontrolled within each part of the model.

The Model

Paid

Paid media includes advertising, but it is certainly not limited to this function alone. It includes the ads on television, radio, and in newspapers and magazines, as well as traditional and digital billboards and sponsored posts and tweets.[8] These are opportunities where funding is the most important factor and the major barrier to access. Generally, organizations have near-total control of the content and its timing. Some paid content has extremely high production value, meaning significant resources are spent to create a photo or video, hire talent, write a script, craft a design or logo, and so on. Alternatively, paid media can be as simple as a black-and-white print advertisement or a still digital billboard photo.

While we think of paid media as "controlled" by organizations, publics often remix many facets of brand communication.

In addition to production costs, paid media inherently includes the cost of the buy itself, based on the layout space, airtime, or page views that it will generate. The costs vary depending on the quantity and quality of the audience. For example, highly targeted trade publications with influential audiences will charge a premium per-reader cost relative to a community news outlet.

Due to the degree of content control, paid media can be a significant asset in communication related to, for example, branding or rebranding, a product launch, or event-related outreach when the specific timing of an announcement is critical. This type of media allows for an outlet to repeat the message, create a series of messages that build on each other, or present highly organization-focused messages that may not be considered newsworthy.

Earned

Earned media, the work of traditional media relations, connects organizations and reporters, providing many of the same publicity benefits as paid media, along with the added asset of the tacit endorsement of the reporting organization. Because organizations don't pay for the coverage, it carries an implication that the message has inherent news value beyond the organization promoting itself.[9] Organizations give up control of the story (making earned media *uncontrolled*) in order to reach audiences consuming news content rather than advertising content.

Newsworthy stories—those appealing to or having impact with broad audiences—can generate significant coverage. When envisioned as part of integrated campaigns, such news-friendly announcements, trends, and events can be planned to maximize earned media coverage and reinforce organizational messages. While many assume media relations strategies must appeal to a broad consumer audience, the explosion of media channels from traditional print, radio, television news, industry trade publications, and valuable digital-only channels allows for significant audience variation and nuance.

That said, earned media does not fit every campaign situation. Some organizational stories may be too complicated or narrow for audience-appropriate media outlets. They may be difficult to fit to a particular media outlet's concept of **newsworthiness**. Others might have a specific objective that requires significant repetition or personalized outreach to key audience members. They may require a very narrow time window. Earned media may not be the most effective or efficient approach in such situations, but resources could allow it to be valuable as a secondary or complimentary strategy.

Shared

Social media influencers often have very loyal followings and generate specific focused content, such as food, fashion, or parenting bloggers.

Shared media is most simply defined as social media outreach: channels where the initial message is controlled by an organization but that facilitate direct, uncontrolled conversation with individuals and other organizations without the mediation of reporters and editors.[10] Regularly updated content drives successful shared media outreach, whether campaign-related or not.[11] While the list of social media platforms changes regularly, the trinity of Facebook, Twitter, and LinkedIn account for the majority of social media use by practitioners, and all must be considered by organizations.[12] Each of the three platforms include a varying degree of largely static profile content and opportunities for microblogging: creating short posts that often include images, videos, or links to other content.[13] The expectations for the type of content and timing for each channel can vary significantly.

Organizations participate in conversations on these channels through their own branded handles or through individuals speaking for themselves or on behalf of the company. Social media conversations also reflect the impact of influencers—individuals with high credibility and visibility in specific social media communities or on specific channels that "shape audience attitudes."[14] Brands often work directly with bloggers or influencers (bloggers can also *be* influencers) using a similar framework as they would when researching, pitching, and collaborating with journalists.

Owned

Despite the importance of shared media, owned media still can, and should, act as the center of an organization's content universe. A broad definition of owned channels could include, for example, an organization's digital footprint (including, but not limited to, their website) as well as physical branded offices and the printed brochures for specific programs and projects. Owned channels provide a place for those outside an organization to gather information about it. They allow the organization to curate this path for the audience member. Wholly owned channels (such as a website) and partially owned channels (such as blogs hosted through WordPress that could allow user comments) house content that is created and controlled by an organization. Owned channels provide a central point for an organizational brand, along with content that can be shared and distributed directly to audiences or through social channels.[15]

The first, and possibly the most impactful, evolution of the digital restructuring of organizational communication occurred when companies began creating their own websites, greatly expanding the reach and scope of channels where they had complete control over the content and the environment. Not unsurprisingly, many early websites functioned much like what they replaced or were based on: the print brochure. As programming expertise has expanded and the tools for creating more elegant and functional websites have become more affordable and easier to use, owned content has become more democratic. Now, all organizations can establish a respectable digital presence, making it a near requirement for public legitimacy today.[16] Technology has also facilitated the evolution of owned channels, and brands themselves, to become more responsive to their audiences. Brand monitoring, ranging a wide variety of easily accessible free digital tools to large-scale systematic brand research, provides deep and actionable insights about how communities interact with organizations and their products and services.[17] In this way, well-designed websites and organizational blogs bridge the gap between owned and shared media, becoming interactive spaces used to listen as well as speak.

HOW THE MODEL OVERLAPS

There are areas of overlap between and among the paid, earned, shared, and owned categories. Collectively, we can refer to these as converged media although they are more accurately depicted as individual areas of convergence. Most social media channels offer a variety of paid options, which create a continuum between fully shared content and static display advertisements. For example, "boosted" posts on Facebook still reflect many qualities of shared content, with relatively inexpensive additional reach.[18] Native advertisements or "sponsored posts" on social media streams provide content that fits directly into the natural consumption of a channel but with more distinctive markers of advertisement. Native advertisements avoid ad blockers but must reflect content users want to engage with to be effective.[19] Social media channels can also have opportunities for display advertisements; the digital equivalent of a newspaper advertisement on a page, separate from the news content. All of these examples are both paid and shared media, reflecting options that may be a better fit than purely shared or paid approaches depending on the context of the campaign.

How to Build an Integrated Campaign Strategy around PESO

Strategies should be conceived to work together using multiple channels as part of the same campaign. In this way, campaigns can target multiple publics and connect with individuals through multiple channels. While it is important to identify commonalities among target audiences to reach them, there will always be significant variation within a group.[20] Employing multiple strategies using multiple channels helps bridge this gap.

The importance of integrating multiple channel approaches is also beneficial from a timing perspective. In the case of a grand opening for a new retail store, there can and should be multiple phases that draw on different parts of the PESO model. Prior to the opening, using paid, shared, and owned media channels may be the most timely and efficient ways to generate interest in the new facility. Earned media could be integrated immediately before, during, and after a grand opening event. Finally, that coverage could be used and shared with key audiences through earned and owned media channels as part of an ongoing campaign to sustain interest after the grand opening. In this way, multiple channels within the model are most appropriate at different stages in a specific campaign.

PRo Tip

CRAFTING WINNING STRATEGIES

Successful strategies combine a specific audience or public and the best channel to connect with them.[21] The following tips help to demonstrate how strategies can work together to support objectives:

- **Deepen audience segmentation:** Objectives define audiences/publics, but strategies should add a more granular level to identify the channels that can, when combined, reach the desired group.
    - **Role**: Director of public relations for a school district.
    - **Goal**: Pass a bond proposal during a local election to provide funds for

Source: Laurie J. Wilson and Joseph D. Ogden, *Strategic Communications Planning for Effective Public Relations and Marketing* (5th ed.), (Dubuque, IA: Kendall-Hunt, 2008), 102.

necessary facilities upgrades across the district.

- **Sample Objective:** Increase support for the bond proposal by 10 percent among likely voters in the community over the next three months.
  - **Strategy #1:** Share information with *parents of current students* through presentations at parent-teacher organization meetings at each school.
  - **Strategy #2:** Connect with *local seniors* through earned media outreach, starting with the monthly senior-focused community newspaper.
  - **Strategy #3:** Identify *community leaders* (political, business, religious, and so on) for personal outreach and potential public support statements.

- **Follow your publics:** Following the uses and gratifications theory, selecting the right channel to reach a specific audience begins by understanding what media and messages they already consume.
  - **Role**: Director of corporate communication for a medium-sized manufacturing company.
  - **Goal**: Increase employee use of new company-provided fitness center and equipment.
  - **Sample Objective:** Raise awareness of new fitness center from 40 percent to 80 percent over the next six months.
    - **Strategy #1:** Share consistent (monthly), image-rich updates about the fitness center through *traditional employee communication channels* (e-newsletter, departmental bulletin boards, and so on).
    - **Strategy #2:** Provide content about the fitness center *to managers to share with their employees* during staff meetings.
    - **Strategy #3:** Showcase information about the fitness center on *company social media* (knowing many employees follow these channels).

- **Let the creativity flow:** Fun, engaging and original content approaches capture each public's attention.
  - **Role**: Vice president of communication for a community bank.
  - **Goal**: Increase the share of home mortgage lending in their hometown.
  - **Sample Objective:** Increase mortgage loan market share (in the town) made to current homebuyers by 5 percent over the next year.
    - **Strategy #1:** Create *a series of humorous, but informative first-time homebuying tips*, package them in creative formats (short videos, blog posts, and so on) and share them through paid or boosted social media channels.
    - **Strategy #2:** Target real estate agents (who can point their clients toward mortgage services) through *high-visibility, memorable event sponsorships* at local professional events.

- **As long as it serves the objective:** Creativity for creativity's sake does not achieve objectives—audience reach and audience relevance should guide what strategies are selected.[22]

PRo Tip

BEYOND SEGMENTATION

Beyond Segmentation: Communicating to Publics' Multiple Identities

Public relations campaigns address varied audiences. To connect with these groups, it's as easy as slicing them into their relevant demographic parts, researching what each group needs and reads, and then crafting and distributing messages accordingly, right? *In practice, it's rarely that simple.* Publics overlap, and tactics and messages are visible far beyond their intended audiences.[23] In fact, an overly simplistic approach can easily alienate publics and reinforce stereotypes. How can practitioners with finite time and resources address all of these challenges? One place to begin is by considering publics not just as separate audience segments based on demographic factors (such as race and gender) but as groups of individuals each carrying their own layered identities.

Every individual's experiences are different, and we all share a multitude of interdependent identities that become more or less relevant or *salient* depending on the situation. Age, gender, race, and socioeconomic status (as examples) each tell part of a story about an individual or members of a community. These identities mean that organizational messages can be interpreted or experienced in very different ways by each individual. Even with the best of intentions, public relations can contribute to *othering*: reinforcing existing stereotypes and privilege structures by separating certain individuals from those with more power in a group or broader society. Here are several practical recommendations, based on the work of leading public relations scholars, to help practitioners create more inclusive and community-centered campaigns:

- **Attempt to be aware of and remove your personal biases.** We all carry subconscious biases. Rather than only seeing a campaign's goals from the organization's perspective, practitioners must place themselves squarely in the shoes of their publics.[24] This starts the processes of understanding and connecting with publics on their own terms. Targeted heath campaigns, for example, often begin with assumptions that "groups don't know what's good for them" rather than using research to understand the priorities, perspectives, and experiences of publics.[25]

- **Bring publics into the planning process early**. Research at several stages of a campaign can integrate ideas from and with (not just about) publics. From a developmental research perspective, consider asking how a public's goals are relevant to the issue at hand, rather than only focusing on organizational goals. This can help shape mutually beneficial campaigns, rather than only including publics for message testing in the later stages.

- **Consider identities together rather than separately.** Rather than isolating different publics or audiences by single demographic factors, consider how identities fit together and how they are influenced by the environments and experiences of individuals.[26]

- **Broaden your conception of diversity**. Many organizations and communication campaigns focus on racial or gender diversity, but there are many different types of diversity that should be considered, often dependent on the issue at hand. Considering sexual orientation, gender identification, religious beliefs, educational background, health status, occupation/

employment status, parental status, and many other factors can contribute to a more complete understanding of publics.

As practitioners, we should continue to challenge ourselves to avoid stereotypes and *essentialization*—singling out representative or core characteristics of groups of individuals—and instead aim to understand our publics' intersections of identities and experiences.[27] The end result should not be campaigns that avoid segmenting publics and messages entirely but rather campaigns that prioritize understanding and communicating with whole people rather than just one part of them at a time.

Sources: Dean Kruckeberg and Marina Vujnovic, "The Death of the Concept of Publics (plural) in 21st Century Public Relations," *International Journal of Strategic Communication* 4, no. 2 (2010): 117–125.

Natalie Tindall and Jennifer Vardeman-Winter, "Complications in Segmenting Campaign Publics: Women of Color Explain Their Problems, Involvement, and Constraints in Reading Heart Disease Communication," *Howard Journal of Communications* 22, no. 3 (2011): 280–301.

Jennifer Vardeman-Winter, Natalie Tindall, and Hua Jiang, "Intersectionality and Publics: How Exploring Publics' Multiple Identities Questions Basic Public Relations Concepts," *Public Relations Inquiry* 2, no. 3 (2013): 279–304.

THE RIGHT APPROACH FOR YOUR AUDIENCE(S)

Audience or publics segmentation is at the heart of successful strategic public relations and strategic campaigns. It is a simple idea with extremely complex implications: audience matters. The message, the medium, the tone, and the timing all hinge on who the intended (and unintended) recipients might be. Audiences should be defined in a campaign's early stages, and analyzing them can point toward the most effective strategies.[28]

The following list of potential factors to segment audiences moves from broad to narrow restrictions. It is just one approach to segmentation, and those interested in learning more about the process should also reference *Cutlip & Center's Effective Public Relations*, where Broom and Sha provide a list of nine approaches.[29] Narrowing down audiences or publics using these or other factors helps point practitioners toward the best strategies, channels, and messages for a given campaign. Looking for areas of overlap, practitioners should research both their intended publics as well as the audiences of a variety of existing channels that may be potential campaign strategies. Significant overlap can indicate a strong fit.

All channels have a defined audience. Media outlets are themselves particularly targeted to specific publics, so practitioners employing media relations strategies should find overlaps between their targets and a given outlet's audience. Individual channels or outlets may define their audience based on geography, demographics, psychographics, interest, or industry.

As technology and opportunity continue to shift, the field of public relations will continue to see increased diversity in the number of channels available for distribution. This serves as both an opportunity and a challenge. The increased variety allows for more

FIGURE 7.2

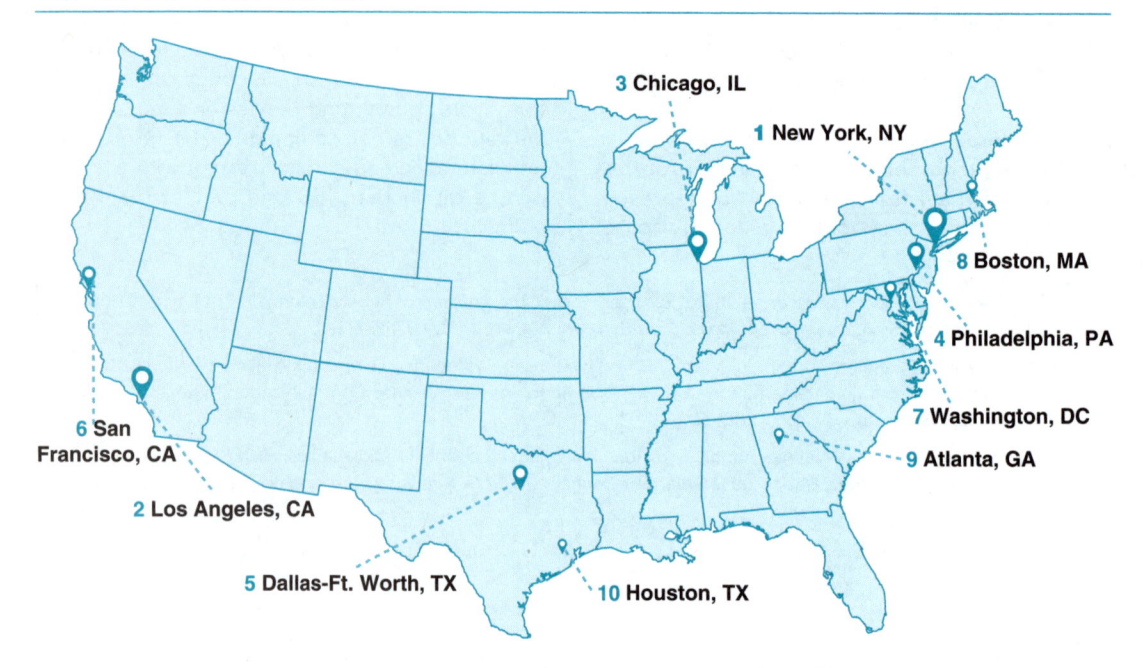

Top Ten U.S. Media Markets

1. New York, NY
2. Los Angeles, CA
3. Chicago, IL
4. Philadelphia, PA
5. Dallas-Ft. Worth, TX
6. San Francisco, CA
7. Washington, DC
8. Boston, MA
9. Atlanta, GA
10. Houston, TX

targeted, unique, and scalable strategies. It also makes it more difficult for organizations to keep pace with public expectations of increasingly instantaneous communication in a variety of formats. What will remain is the value of strategic thinking: audience-focused, objective-driven approaches will continue to pay dividends.

Demographics

Demographic factors include age, education, income, gender, and can, along with geography, narrow down a mass audience to those with the most potential interest or stake in a given product, service, or issue. For example, a campaign to support the passage of a local millage to support a new senior center may differentiate messaging based on demographics between those who would have the opportunity to use the center personally and those who would see the benefits for their parents and their community rather than in their daily lives. Additionally, both demographic and geographic data are often publicly available through the U.S. Census Bureau and other sources, making it accessible.

Geography

All organizations have geographic boundaries (zip codes, school districts, cities, regions, nations, or continents) for where their campaigns will take place. All relevant stakeholders exist within an organization's relevant geography, but many targeted publics have their own, more limited geographies. Traditional local media outlets (print, radio, television) clearly define their geographic boundaries, while national and digital outlets may take additional research to determine their impact in specific regions.

Psychographics

Characteristics related to the values and preferences of specific publics allow for psychographic analysis; another form of segmentation.[30] This approach creates a more holistic picture of audience groups that can be used to align channels with behavior. More focused than demographic or geographic approaches, psychographics analyze group audience members through their responses to a series of statements that can indicate ideological, spiritual, economic, and familial attitudes.[31] Many media outlets perform psychographic research to provide potential advertisers a clearer picture of their audience. Public relations practitioners can use such information to inform decisions about strategy and tactics (including messaging) related to audience values and perspectives.

Activity/Interest

Publics may share a profession, a passion, or a predicament. They may or may not interact with one another, and they may have an active or passive stance toward the organization or issue at hand.[32] A group of doctors, surfing enthusiasts, or those who have purchased tainted spinach at the grocery store may have nothing else in common aside from the categories above, and they often will not know each other in any meaningful sense but may constitute a critical group for the organization based on the campaign at hand. Similarly, the readers of a specific blog or magazine may have little in common outside of their passion for a specific subject. Often, the most valuable campaign channels are those with a direct interest overlap between the subject matter at hand and a channel or media outlet.

Influence

Not all members of a given public are created equal. Some individuals are decision makers within their organization, and their opinions, attitudes, or behaviors are significantly more important than others. Creative practitioners can create strategies and select channels to target these individuals as a unique audience across multiple organizations within the same campaign.

Channel Consumption

Often, practitioners can make assumptions about specific audiences based on the media they choose to consume. For example, those reading a specific industry's trade publication clearly have a stake in that industry. The majority of those reading a community weekly newspaper generally live in the community itself. In this way, channel consumption connects demographic, psychographic, and activity/interest to media outlets. To take the process one step further, targeting specific newspaper sections, local television shows, or specific bloggers marks an even narrower audience definition based on the readership/viewership/listenership of that specific show.

> ## *PRo Tip*
>
> ### DIFFERENCES IN CHANNEL CONSUMPTION
>
> - Television
>   - Passive viewership but evolving with on-demand and streaming options
>   - Local news continues to be a significant draw
> - Newspapers and magazines
>   - Mix of digital and traditional readership
>   - Deepest reporting resources lead to widely shared content
> - Radio
>   - Mix of digital and traditional listenership
>   - Drive time is prime time
> - Mobile Devices
>   - Regularly used simultaneously with other channels
>   - Accessible size and layout are critical for content
> - Desktop Computers
>   - Often used at work or while working—use peaks midday[33]
>   - Online purchases are still made predominantly on desktops[34]

Generally, such decisions are not *either/or*: multiple audiences for a campaign, as well as wide variation among members of specific publics, make it so that multiple channels should be used. That said, these questions support prioritization of strategies and channels and help decide what is necessary, what would be nice to include, and what does not need to be done. Practitioners can use audience research and understanding combined with a deep knowledge of the potential strategies and channels at hand to make a thorough case to organizational leaders in support of the recommended approach.

LEVERAGING YOUR ORGANIZATION'S STRENGTHS AND RESOURCES

In developing strategies, there is always value in identifying and leveraging the resources your organization has at its disposal to better connect with audiences and tell its story. Ragas and Culp refer to these broadly as "intangible assets," including an organization's vision and strategy, skilled management and employees, reputation, and brand value, as well as leadership in research and development.[35] From a rich history of community engagement to a new leader with a strong reputation, many organizations have people, products, policies, or successes that help them stand out from the crowd. These components of newsworthiness transcend specific or tactical opportunities and should be considered at the strategy development stage of the campaign planning process. Using PESO, practitioners can identify multiple tactics that could emanate from each asset.

Subject Matter Expertise

Issue-specific credibility, either from the organization's reputation or an individual spokesperson's reputation, can become a central element of many campaigns. For example, in a political environment where complex financial and investment regulations shift quickly, an organizational leader with a knack for explaining changes in easy-to-understand terms would add significant value to earned and shared media outreach. Armed with the right messaging, these opportunities could easily support related campaign objectives.

Imagery/Visuals

Knowing a particular campaign will generate or include strong, camera-ready visuals means strategies should maximize their use. A project with excellent photographic opportunities should absolutely be pitched to earned media (such as television and newspapers) that can take advantage, as well as shared through social media channels, such as Instagram, where they will have the most impact. Planning on-location events that make for easy media access (location, day, and time) allows journalists to capture these images, which makes content more newsworthy. Strategies could also ensure that postevent content, such as e-blasts or media relations outreach, take advantage of valuable visual elements.

Dynamic Presenters/Personalities

Having a company spokesperson with a flair for public speaking and the experience to provide quotable, media-friendly content creates a strong opportunity for multiple earned, paid, and owned media opportunities (all of which can later be shared through additional social channels). It also could open the door for more in-person or digitally mediated events and programs. Positioning an organizational leader as a speaker at local, regional, or national conferences and events can provide a compelling and highly credible platform for sharing content in the service of organizational objectives.

Data

New studies, data, and statistics can provide fuel for multiple strategic directions, including earned media outreach based on newsworthy findings or using internal design capability to create compelling and shareable infographics. Depending on budget, departmental skill sets, and the relationship to the objectives at hand, practitioners can take full advantage of the growing media appetite for accessible data.

Organizational Vision or Narrative

A powerful story could encourage practitioners to choose channels and strategic approaches that allow for the best use of such content. Depending on the resources available, that could include creating a dedicated microsite to create a complete, owned version of the narrative (as a center for content that could be shared to multiple channels) or a proactive earned media campaign focused on outlets and reporters with the interest and bandwidth to value the story. If the story is more concise or delicate, it may be a better fit for paid media channels where the organization's message can be placed front and center.

Increased access to big data is fueling the growing field of data journalism, such as the work of Nate Silver and FiveThirtyEight.com, and creating new opportunities for PR practitioners to utilize data in their campaigns.

History/Institutional Authority

An organization with deep community roots can leverage its historical impact as a campaign asset. For example, strategies can integrate current and historical content (such as classic black-and-white photographs, which can be used in all PESO media channels) as well as added clout and credibility for earned media. Both local and trade publication reporters see value in historical perspectives, particularly around milestone anniversaries and other timely events.

Of course, not all (or most) of these advantages would apply to individual objectives and individual strategies simultaneously. But organizations often underutilize and undervalue their inherently compelling resources and stories. Content generated across PESO channels should reflect a strategic approach that makes use of these potentially valuable assets.

THE COMPETITIVE LANDSCAPE

Previous chapters discussed several approaches to competitor analysis, including output-based analysis (studying an organization's messages), competitive media analysis (reviewing how media portray an organization to their audiences), and a SWOT analysis (outlining an organization's strengths, weaknesses, opportunities, and threats in a competitive context). These research processes can inform not only audience choices and creation of objectives but also the subsequent strategies and tactics.

Understand Competitors and External Challenges

Organizational competitors may be strong communicators or weak communicators across the board. More likely, they will have some areas of strength and other areas of weakness. For example, a manufacturer may have strong relationships with industry trade media, including earned and paid media, as well as a top-notch website, but lack a vibrant social media presence and relationships with local reporters. When setting strategy, a competing manufacturer may decide that it is worth the extra effort to tackle the uphill battle of gaining coverage from industry trade publications, or it may decide that the untapped opportunities through social media offer a better use of company time and resources. Either way, the strategic choice should be informed by an understanding of the competitive landscape in the industry.

Avoid What Everyone Else Is Already Doing

Organizations should seek distinctive strategies and messages to stand apart from competitors. If six companies are selling a similar product to a similar audience at the same conference, chances are that it will be difficult for customers to differentiate them from each other. If all six explain that they provide the highest quality product with the best service, built by the best team, consumers will have good reason for confusion. Particularly in a crowded market, when organizations use the same message or approach, they often cancel each other out. This rule applies as much to nonprofits angling for donors or members as for businesses seeking to grow revenue.

If a company sees that all of its competitors are on Facebook, but only one is on LinkedIn, that may signal an opportunity. Or, if Facebook is clearly the best channel to

---

PRo Tip

POSITIONING CAMPAIGNS FOR MAXIMUM IMPACT

- **Put the audience first**: Smart strategies reflect their intended audience's knowledge, needs, preferences, and experiences.
- **Play to organizational strengths**: Winning strategies put the best messages forward using the most effective channels.

- **Be memorable**: Concise, unique strategies stand out in the memories of those who hear their messages.

Get more detail on winning strategies in the Appendix, page 237.

reach the desired audience, an organization can investigate *how* their competitors are using it: shared, sponsored/boosted, or paid content? How much interactivity are they generating? These and similar questions can point practitioners toward creating a strategy that distinguishes their organizations from the competition.

CONCLUSION

Effective campaign strategies never succeed because of a single channel, tactic, or message, but they can fail because of incorrect strategy. This chapter alone cannot teach budding practitioners to develop strategies, a skill that can only truly be honed through practice, but it can provide a toolkit for thinking strategically about channels, organizations, and audiences. It should remind all public relations professionals that effective campaigns are built on research and investigation, rather than on instinct. In this way, communication departments and their leaders can enable and promote smart strategic choices in this crucial period of campaign development.

THINK CRITICALLY

1. Strategy is critical in public relations planning. Discuss how effective strategies are developed.
2. What role does PESO play in public relations?
3. How does a public relations practitioner discover the right approach to strategic planning? What tools are used to effectively promote an organization?
4. What does converged media allow public relations practitioners to do?
5. How can the history a company possesses be leveraged in a strategic campaign?

KEY TERMS

Channel 111

Newsworthiness 114

CONCEPT CASE: CHANNEL SELECTION FOR EQUALITY TODAY

Equality Today set the following objective for its upcoming campaign: capture the contact information of 2,500 new potential donors over the next year. The organization defined *potential donor* as an individual supportive of the organization's beliefs and with the means to make a recurring small-dollar donation. The organization also has several useful assets. It just released a new study about the benefits of stronger legal support for same-sex couples at the state and local levels. It has a national e-mail subscriber list of 18,000. It also has media-trained spokespersons in many media markets. What strategies and channels would be appropriate to gain exposure for the organization and collect information?

- Many organizations build specific digital landing pages for certain programs, which may provide information but also allow for lead capture. How might you build campaign strategies to make the most of this newsworthy content?

- Knowing your assets—and using PESO—what media channels would be valuable to share the report and draw publics (and potential donors) back to your website for information capture?

    o Paid?
    o Earned?
    o Shared?
    o Owned?
    o Converged?

CASE STUDY: MASTERCARD BITES INTO APPLE PAY

Based on PRSA Silver Anvil Award Winner
MasterCard with Ketchum
Campaign Focus: Product Launch

As the innovator behind the first-to-market contactless payment technology, MasterCard has been working hard to drive merchant acceptance and consumer education. With the uptake of connected devices, the real promise for widespread adoption lies in mobile payments. After a long stalemate with wireless providers and handset manufacturers, MasterCard partnered with Apple so that the new iPhone 6 and 6+ would include Near Field Communication (NFC) technology and to take advantage of "tap and go" technology with a new proprietary payment platform: Apple Pay. This platform would incorporate the most advanced payment security developed from MasterCard to deliver the most secure way to pay.

The integrated campaign included a PR "situation room;" digital press kits crafted to reaffirm leadership in the contactless technology; a select team of executives dispatched to strategic cities for Apple Pay announcements; 1,000+ "Priceless Surprises" including cupcakes delivered to iPhone buyers; the inaugural TV ad for Apple Pay; and efforts to keep MasterCard top of mind (and top of wallet) during the lag time between Apple Pay's announcement and launch.

The company dominated share of voice (SOV) by demonstrating its secure, technologically advanced payments system. During Apple Pay's announcement week, MasterCard secured 37 percent SOV globally compared to Visa's 27 percent and Amex's 21 percent. The success was repeated and used safety and security messaging in interviews and via digital content, winning millions of impressions. Within 72 hours of Apple

Pay's launch, consumers activated a million cards, creating the world's largest mobile payment system overnight.³⁶

Research/Diagnosis

For years, contactless payment was rumored to be the next big thing, but consumers were slow to adopt. Not only was there a barrier to understanding new payment technologies, MasterCard knew that one of the biggest concerns was safety. This was backed by research, which found that while 73 percent of consumers had heard of contactless payments, only 11 percent had used it. More than half (52 percent) cited fears around security. MasterCard used its proprietary social listening tool, PRIME, to understand the conversation around contactless payments; distinguished consumers' "pain points" around security; and identified keywords, themes, and appropriate angles to use to allay fears and educate about new security technologies.

Objective

MasterCard had no control over the timing of Apple Pay's announcement, learned the name of the product as the rest of the world did, and didn't know when Apple Pay would go live. The only certainty was that MasterCard knew that the technology they developed to enable Apple Pay would eclipse the security of some traditional plastic cards. The objectives were simple: cut through the chatter, lead the conversation on contactless security, and drive MasterCard sign-ups on Apple Pay.

Strategy

To convince consumers that "touch and go" payment was a viable, safe alternative to plastic, a tech leader, like Apple, could benefit by partnering with an innovative contactless payments leader. The strategy was to beat out competitors by positioning MasterCard as the leader in innovative payment solutions by reinforcing the company's development of the technology driving Apple Pay. This allowed the company to elevate their executives as thought leaders, becoming a trusted media source for contactless payments information, content, and expertise for every Apple Pay moment-in-time, from announcement day to go-live day, to reinforce MasterCard's industry leadership in safe and secure payments.

Tactics

©MasterCard

Using your TCU Debit MasterCard® with Apple Pay is easy, secure, and private.

MasterCard Pay

Using portions of the PESO model, a strategic approach was taken. Apple Pay was announced in early September but would not become commercially available until October 20, 2015, so a creative approach had to be used to engage the public during four moments-in-time.

Earned & Paid

iPhone Launch Week (9/9-12): MasterCard created a situation room of twenty from its global headquarters. As soon as Tim Cook announced Apple Pay, the room buzzed with action, reaching out to media, offering interviews, and providing comments on the safety and security of contactless payments. MasterCard distributed press kits, and in a coordinated move, became the first payments firm to run full-page contactless ads in major outlets.

Owned

iPhone Availability Day (9/19): iPhone 6 and 6+ went on sale, but Apple Pay would not launch for a month. MasterCard used this moment-in-time to sustain interest. They hand-delivered 1,000+ "Priceless Surprises" (branded cupcakes and phone chargers) to early adopters in line at Apple Stores waiting to buy the devices. They also sent Priceless Surprises to a shortlist of priority media.

Shared & Owned

Announcement of Go-Live Date (10/16): When Apple announced Apple Pay would be available in four days, MasterCard disseminated new videos, infographics, and online content addressing the shift in conversation from *What is Apple Pay?* and *How does it work?* to *Where can I use it?* and *Is it really safe?* The situation room went into overdrive, ensuring that MasterCard would be top-of-mind for experts' comments.

Paid, Earned, Shared & Owned

Launch Week (10/20-10/24): MasterCard updated digital press kits to show Apple Pay live in stores. Execs appeared on top broadcast outlets and in consumer media. MasterCard developed a video that educated consumers about the use of the technology and gave journalists an up-close look during the launch of MasterCard's new Technology Hub. This was supported by sponsored content on Mashable and promoted tweets to help educate consumers about what to expect with Apple Pay. Then, and on the 21st, MasterCard was a lead sponsor of Major League Baseball's World Series, launching Apple Pay's first TV ad. The next day, NBC Today Show tech guru, Mario Armstrong, appeared in a satellite media tour, reaching 15 million households. On the 24th, MasterCard unveiled an app, MasterCard Nearby, to help consumers find places to use contactless technology.

Implementation

As part of the one-month rollout, this offered an opportunity for MasterCard to take advantage of its leadership role in contactless innovations to generate coverage that would achieve three goals: cut through the chatter of competitors (Visa and American Express), position MasterCard as the voice of authority on contactless safety/security, and drive consumer adoption.

Reporting/Evaluation

Due in part to MasterCard's timely PR campaign and industry leadership, Apple Pay became the biggest success in mobile payments history. Evaluation and monitoring mechanisms helped chart progress, address challenges, and capitalize on success.

Cut through the Chatter

- Dominated competitors for six weeks, reaching 48 percent SOV globally twenty-four hours after the launch date of Apple Pay was revealed

- During iPhone Launch Week (9/9-9/12), secured 37 percent SOV globally compared to Visa's 27 percent and Amex's 21 percent

- During the Announcement of Apple Pay Go-Live and Go-Live Day, (10/16-10/21), repeated earlier success, proving it could sustain media interest over a six-week lag time

- Organic social engagement on Twitter resulted in 900K+ impressions, 17,026 people engaged, and 6,552 clicks

Lead the Conversation on Contactless Security

- Other payment brands were not mentioned in 73 percent of Apple Pay and MasterCard conversations.

- Nearly 100 media interviews of MasterCard execs were conducted, fifty in the first week alone, and twenty-five in the first twenty-four hours of Apple Pay's announcement.

- The digital press kits helped MasterCard frame the story it wanted to tell and reinforce its leadership in safety/security, getting 3,800 views in the first week.

- Content amplification resulted in 1.8 thousand shares of MasterCard's Mashable video (in the first twenty-four hours), 167 thousand+ impressions from Google Search, 1.6 million impressions from YouTube, two million impressions from Twitter, and 11.8 million impressions from Outbrain and Taboola.

Drive MasterCard Sign-ups on Apple Pay

- Within seventy-two hours of Apple Pay's availability, consumers activated one million cards. MasterCard had been a leading force in creating the world's largest mobile payment system.

Theories

Diffusion of Innovations: MasterCard used an approach that reflects the diffusion of innovations: engaging with consumers at differing stages of adopting technology.[37] By isolating the pain points in mobile payment adoption, the company focused its efforts directly on moving potential customers from a place of uncertainty about the technology to adopting it.

Two-way Asymmetrical Model: This campaign took a classic marketing approach, using significant research and insights from consumers to build the plan and crafting all content and outreach to fit those audiences. While consumers did not have a particularly interactive role in the campaign, MasterCard's detailed front-end approach ensured that all materials were designed with them in mind.

Tactics

8

THINK AHEAD

8.1 Apply the PESO model to selecting public relations tactics.

8.2 Understand considerations of timing, budget, messaging, and content creation for a wide variety of public relations tactics.

8.3 Connect objectives and strategies to the best-fit tactics.

After an organization agrees on the strategies to support its objectives, it is up to the public relations team to develop the required tactical approaches for implementing the overall plan. Strategies often broadly define the channel for outreach but not necessarily the specific news media outlets, social media channels, or owned-media properties to target or use. Tactics reflect the narrow audiences and focused messages that serve as the building blocks of successful campaigns. Often, practitioners and organizational leaders fall into the trap of moving straight to tactics without first establishing broader objectives and strategies. Without this framework, it is difficult to make the necessary practical and creative decisions that tactics demand or to measure their effectiveness.

PRo Tip

CRAFTING EFFECTIVE MESSAGING

Professional communicators craft campaign **messaging** based on incorporating a variety of research findings, audience knowledge, and clear focus on the campaign's most important goal.

1. **Build internal consensus for the overarching campaign message**: Campaigns should have a concise, singular message that carries through all strategies, tactics, and targeted submessages.

2. **Identify segmented publics**: Clarify and prioritize the publics with whom your campaign will communicate.

3. **Develop targeted submessages:** Effective messages should reflect the following criteria:

    Driven by organizational and communication goals: Messages must clearly support and connect to the broader goals of the campaign.

    Reflective of the overarching campaign message: Often submessages are secondary to overarching messages in specific tactics and materials for distinct audiences.

    Supported by audience research: Understanding each audience's interests, habits, channel consumption, and connection to the campaign is critical for crafting messages that resonate.

    Memorable: Messages that stick with audiences are concise, creative, and clearly relevant to their lives.

4. **Pretest overall and submessages**: As communicators, we do our best to put ourselves in the shoes of our publics, but there is no substitute for sharing these messages with publics and gathering feedback for improvement.

Tactics do not exist in isolation. They work together to support objectives and strategies, target audiences, reinforce messages, and tell stories. Regular outreach and conversation using Twitter may be a valuable part of achieving an objective related to stronger customer, donor, or member engagement for an organization, but it cannot succeed by itself. Complimentary tactics may also include earned media outreach, for reach and credibility, and owned media content on the website for deeper information and conversion. Strategies may point toward paid tactics such as building a conference presence for more one-on-one connections, earned tactics like positive media coverage in relevant publications, and owned tactics including an e-mail newsletter. The power of the PESO model comes from the perspective it provides: allowing practitioners to see the wide range of possible tactics to implement.

TACTICAL APPROACHES

Developing an understanding of multiple paid, earned, shared, and owned media approaches provides practitioners options for selecting the best set of tactics given the situation at hand. The larger your toolbox of tactical skills, the more possibilities you have on the table. That said, there is a difference between understanding the important features and benefits of a given tactic and being able to execute it. Some practitioners specialize in one area where their passion rests, while others have broader knowledge of many different approaches. Practitioners at large organizations tend to be more differentiated and specialized, while smaller organizations need more generalists who can tackle a wider variety of work.[1] All practitioners must identify the right balance between spending their time perfecting their skills for specific tactics and expanding their knowledge. Practitioners should know their comfort level with executing individual tactics and ask for support when needed.

This chapter should not be considered an in-depth overview of all public relations and marketing communication tactics. Instead, its goal is to summarize the key considerations for the core components of the PESO model. Numerous additional resources and references have also been provided in the end notes for those interested in additional details and insights related to specific tactics.

Paid Media

Communication and public relations departments often oversee paid media strategies that work to promote specific, controlled company messages that are delivered to key audiences. Paid approaches come in many shapes and sizes, as well as with wide variation in both initial and ongoing costs. This approach can be particularly useful when a message must target an audience at a specific time, when a message may not be inherently newsworthy (and thus not a good candidate for media relations outreach), or when it must be framed by exact wording or visual tone. Launching a new product, for example, often entails a timing schedule and brand (language, colors, logo, and so on) that advertising can deliver. Many paid outreach approaches require professionals who specialize in such work (advertising, digital marketing, video production, and so on), with organizations generally using agencies or other outside contracts when executing these projects.

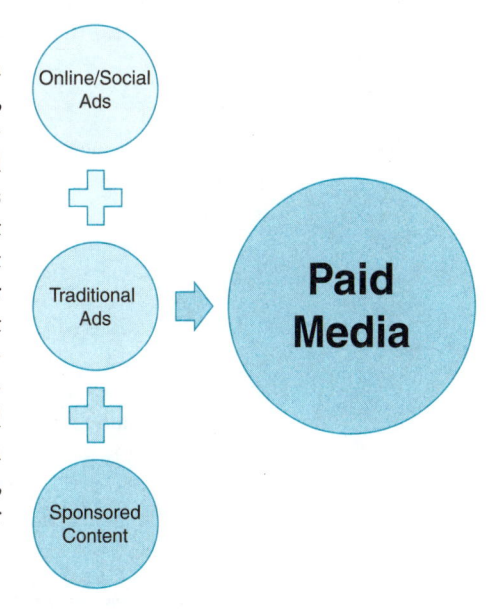

Online/Social Ads + Traditional Ads + Sponsored Content → Paid Media

Timing

Some paid media opportunities may need months of lead time in order to purchase ad space and produce content. Others, such as paid search advertising, can launch within a matter of days. Each project requires the organization to secure their *space* (such as airtime, digital real estate, or the literal space on a billboard) and to decide what type of message to place within it. The simplest digital display or print advertisements can be created in a matter of hours by expert graphic designers, while large-scale video production can easily take months. Advertisers running longer campaigns often schedule using "waves," condensing an ad spend into shorter periods with breaks to increase penetration and retention of information.[2]

Budget

Some paid mediums are more scalable than others. A national television advertisement may cost tens or hundreds of thousands of dollars to produce—not including potentially millions of dollars for national airtime—while a specifically targeted digital display or paid social media campaign could certainly be successful for less than $1,000. The cost of ads in any specific market is dependent on its population size and the viewership/readership/listenership of the individual media channel or location where the ads will be purchased.

Messaging

Paid media often contain the most organization-focused messages. Because there is no outside editorial control, the organization maintains nearly complete decision-making power over the message itself.

Content Creation

Messaging in paid media often leans toward being simple and memorable. Since the audience is not necessarily seeking out these messages, they are designed to grab attention.

Advertising

Advertising in traditional and digital forms remains a key outreach opportunity for organizations and an important revenue generator for media today.[3] The rise of digital advertising has only increased the sophistication and targeting focus available for organizations. As public relations professionals, paid advertising is generally not the center of our work, but it should not go unrecognized as a way to reach specific audiences with specific messages, particularly with time-sensitive or less-newsworthy messages.

In advertising and the subfield of media planning, each potential opportunity should be evaluated based on the target audience demographics and how well they would overlap with the advertising options available to reach them. This includes demographics, habits, and lifestyle.[4] The media options themselves differ according to cost, efficiency, reach, frequency, irritation factor, and complexity. For example, an event awareness campaign must decide whether including more details about the campaign justifies the added cost of a longer or larger advertisement, as well as whether the intended audience would pay attention long enough to digest the additional information.

PRo Tip

TYPES OF ADVERTISING

Traditional

- **Event Sponsorship**: Organizations regularly sponsor targeted industry or community events for additional visibility. The flexibility of price and variety of sponsorship opportunities makes this a popular approach.
- **Outdoor**: Billboards can be a price-friendly way to share repeated messages within a specific community or communities.
- **Print**: Newspapers, magazines, and trade publications offer a wide variety of options for selecting specific audiences that fit your campaign.
- **Radio**: Radio—national and local, for-profit, or through NPR—still maintains a strong presence in many Americans' lives, particularly during the *drive time* commuting hours. This continues to make radio a relevant option for reaching metro areas.
- **TV**: Television has higher advertising production costs but offers a wide variety of channel-specific, audience-specific, and time-specific segmentation options.

Digital

- **Digital Display**: Digital banner or billboard advertisements, generally on high-traffic websites and pages in high-visibility locations link back to relevant pages on an organization's website.
- **Digital Video**: Many popular websites, such as YouTube, offer video ads that can be targeted using a variety of content-based or geographic factors.
- **SEM**: Search-engine marketing (SEM) allows organizations to pay search engines directly so that ads pop up when specific terminology is typed in.
- **Social media**: Social media channels offer a variety of advertising options, from the strictly paid (such as sidebar display ads) to more *converged media* such as boosted posts or native advertising and other types of in-feed content.

Practitioners should also keep in mind that traditional media (newspapers, radio, and TV) have as many, if not more opportunities, for advertising as part of their digital properties as in their traditional formats.

For more information on advertising types, please see the Appendix, page 237.

In evaluating their options, practitioners often start by selecting among broadcast media (such as radio and television), print media (such as newspapers and magazines), and digital media (such as online display advertising). Keep in mind that the lines between these media types have continued to blur, as newspapers regularly produce video, digital-only media outlets generate highly credible "print" journalism, and television stations offer advertising on their websites and mobile apps. Despite that, the rules for effective advertising in each of these formats have largely endured.

Even venerable media outlets such as the *New York Times* sell digital space for sponsored content or advertorials, such as this Guiness ad, that mimic some of the design characteristics of editorial content.

Advertorial Content

Advertorial content is a growing subset of paid media, where news organizations include advertiser-supplied stories in the same form as their usual articles but mark them as *paid*, *sponsored*, or *advertiser-supplied*. These opportunities exist in print, broadcast, and digital. In most cases, the content is very clearly marked as paid. In others, the labeling is less obvious, and readers unfamiliar with such practices may not be aware that the content has been created without the usual reporting and editing process and that the content should not carry the same tacit endorsement as the media outlet's standard news product. Due to these potential grey areas, practitioners should be cautious when using advertorial tactics. From a credibility perspective, it is always preferable to leverage traditional earned media channels first before turning to paid opportunities. The worst-possible situation would be for an organization to be perceived as attempting to deceive an audience. Some media outlets' lack of clear labeling for advertorial content makes this a concern.

Earned Media

Earned media covers tactics where the public relations practitioner must assist in adding value (in the form of *information subsidies*) to a news- or story-generation process, including media relations, blogger outreach, and organic search strategies.[5] By working with journalists and bloggers, public relations professionals help their organizations participate in public conversations about issues and share content that is of interest to specific audiences. Simply improving search engine optimization (SEO) may also be considered an earned strategy. Because these tactics are **uncontrolled**, they bring significant additional credibility for organizations, but participation may also bring additional risk due to a lack of messaging control.

While different skills and customs are required to negotiate media relations, blogger relations, and SEO, they all require an understanding of multiple layers of communication: the initial audience (journalist, blogger, or algorithm) and the final audience (such as consumers, community members, or potential employees). Successful public relations professionals perfect the processes of working with earned media gatekeepers. This allows them to successfully build relationships to improve their understanding of news generation, better the organization's knowledge of the relevant media environment, and, ultimately, shape the organization's decision making to better reflect the needs of its publics.

Media Relations + Blogger Relations + SEO → Earned Media

Timing

Earned tactics lack the highly controlled timelines of many paid strategies. Successful proactive media and blogger outreach often requires weeks or months of planning, while search-related web strategies can take months to fully achieve their intent after implementation. Even then, it may be difficult or impossible to guarantee specific timing given the lack of control over, for example, media and journalistic processes or search algorithms.

Budget

By definition, earned media strategies do not require payment for the final product but certainly should include costs for the professional time required for implementation and evaluation.

Messaging

Unlike paid strategies where organizations have full control of the messaging used in each tactic, earned media outreach implies that practitioners only control what their organizations share, not the final product. To meet the needs of news organizations, there is often more variation in what's being shared with individual media outlets. For example, a practitioner can proactively secure an interview on a specific topic with their organization's CEO and an industry trade reporter. They can prepare tailored talking points for the CEO and a fact sheet for the reporter. They can manage a pre-interview run-through of the potential questions and answers with the CEO. But the final decisions about the questions and the content used in the article are made solely by the journalist and his or her editors. The CEO may provide eight answers that clearly reflect a specific organizational message and one that does not. The reporter is fully entitled to use the ninth response.

Media relations tactics may include those targeted at print, broadcast, or digital media.

PRo Tip

MEDIA RELATIONS TOOLS

- **Bylined articles/op-ed pieces**: Content written by individuals or on behalf of organizations then submitted, reviewed, and (hopefully) published by media outlets; bylined articles are "earned" because they go through an editorial approval process on the publication side

- **Media advisories/media alerts**: Event-specific, bulleted documents that provide the *who, what, when, where, why* of media-friendly activities

- **Press conferences**: Inviting multiple journalists to participate in the same conversation and ask questions together; can be held in-person or virtually

- **Press releases/news releases**: The ubiquitous, traditional document for releasing a news item in a nonsegmented manner, including key information journalists need to complete a story

For more information on media relations tactics, please see the Appendix, page 239.

Content Creation

As mentioned, the content in an earned media situation is determined by the needs of the reporter, blogger, or the key search terms that an organization is hoping to capitalize on. In earned media, the input content is never the final content. The most successful practitioners should anticipate the needs of those they are creating content for, both inside and outside the organization, and employ such tactics in a way that is mutually beneficial.

Media Relations

The traditional core of earned media is media relations. The Public Relations Society of America (PRSA) defines this function as "mutually beneficial associations between publicists or public relations professionals and members of media organizations as a condition for reaching audiences with messages of news or features of interest."[6] Media relations comes from the needs of public relations practitioners communicating on behalf of organizations and journalists' needs to share newsworthy content with audiences. While a journalist's mandate is to provide newsworthy information to a specific public (defined geographically, demographically, or by shared interest), public relations practitioners should be able to see where their organizations would be able to offer value for a journalist's audience. Is a company hiring local workers? Did a nonprofit start a new partnership to connect artists with local elementary students? These items create both compelling company news and valuable information for local consumer reporters. The former would be more valuable for media and may include detailed information

---

PRo Tip

GUIDELINES FOR MAJOR MEDIA EVENTS

In *On Deadline: Managing Media Relations*, authors Carole Howard and Wilma Mathews provide four major reminders for those planning media-focused events.[7]

1. Events should support an organization's brand and be approved by key constituencies within the organization.

2. Invite relevant community leaders: Mayors love to attend new business openings. Even if they are unable to attend, it reminds them of the positive impact on the community.

3. Spokespersons should be chosen carefully. All should be able to speak concisely, stay on message, and be available for reporter questions after their formal remarks.

4. Don't waste time on every detail. Events can become all consuming, and public relations practitioners should maintain their focus on the media-relevant portion while delegating other tasks, such as decorations, food, and other logistics.

Source: Carole Howard and Wilma Mathews, *On Deadline: Managing Media Relations*, (Long Grove, IL: Waveland Press, 2013), 129-130.

about the company's growth trajectory, revenue, and access to executives for additional comments. The latter would be more valuable if accompanied by photos and anecdotal stories about the participating students and artists.

This proactive approach can be called media relations' *publicity* function. **Publicity** is "information provided by an outside source this is used by media because the information has news value."[8] By providing useful information to journalists, media relations professionals create **information subsidies;** reducing the workload of reporters and editors by compiling data, sources, images, and video.[9] At its core, publicity allows organizations to be more visible to their publics. It supports a variety of campaigns, including sales and marketing efforts, community relations, and, when necessary, crisis communication.

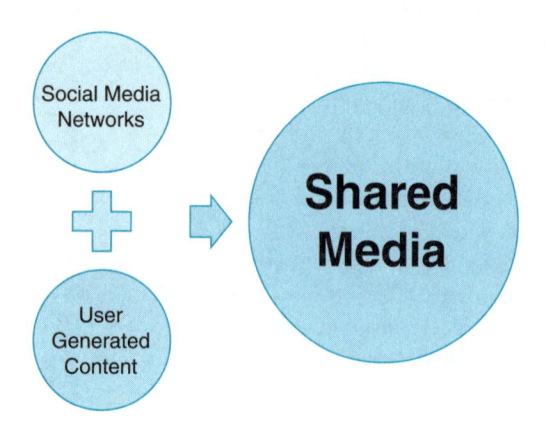

Shared Media

Social media outreach has emerged since the mid-2000s as a critical, valuable, and exciting tactic that has become a staple in the public relations toolbox. In many organizations, public relations play a leading role in social media strategy, tactics, and execution. In *The Social Media Bible*, Safko describes the "Social Media Trinity" as blogs, microblogs (such as Twitter), and social networks (such as Facebook and LinkedIn).[10] While not every campaign that integrates social media needs to use all three, the potential impact of each should be considered.

Timing

Social media can be instantaneous, making it both a useful mechanism for immediate response and a significant organizational challenge to monitor. With this in mind, each channel has its own cadence, with Twitter and Snapchat measuring time in seconds, while LinkedIn promotes content over a much longer timeline. The specific timing for any social media campaign can vary widely depending on both the channel and the audience.

Budget

While social media can include a paid component, most platforms allow for organizations to create profiles and participate in conversations for free. The challenge is typically the time required to create content, monitor channels, manage profiles, and respond, sometimes around the clock. As big brands condition consumers to treat social media profiles as customer service channels, organizations must acknowledge the commitment necessary to maintain channels, both during and after campaign-related activity. Additionally, creating a corporate blog can and should require a design and coding investment both for a professional appearance and to ensure that it has the desired functionality and smooth integration with the organization's main site.

Messaging

Social media messages are as diverse as the organizations that create them. Unlike earned media outreach, which generally stays within the messaging boundaries of the targeted media outlet, the direct-to-consumer social media environment provides more freedom to embrace a brand's voice. Its public nature means that messages may need to speak to multiple audiences simultaneously.

Content Creation

Social media channels are constantly hungry for content. Successful practitioners focus, prioritize, and plan their efforts to ensure they are not creating content ad-hoc or simply for the sake of posting. As part of a campaign, every piece of content should fit into the larger messaging picture, and efforts on multiple channels should reinforce each other. There are two schools of thought in terms of the **content creation** process, one being the "create once, publish everywhere" (C.O.P.E.) approach, popularized by National Public Radio,[11] and the other, typified in the book *Content Rules* is "reimagine, don't recycle"—stressing the importance of making the message appropriate and responsive to the needs of each channel.[12]

Owned Media

The final and most **controlled** category of content is owned media. This includes traditional marketing collateral including brochures, newsletters, and even embossed

---

PRo Tip

SOCIAL MEDIA TACTICS

As an example, LinkedIn's function will be used here to demonstrate how one network can fulfill a variety of functions or tactics in the shared media universe.

- **Blogging**: Many professionals and organizations use LinkedIn to share content from their external blogs. The blog functions as a **content hub** while the network acts to spread the content beyond those who would visit the individual blog or organizational website.

- **Community management**: Many organizations host, curate, or participate in a variety of digital communities, such as employee or alumni LinkedIn groups, which facilitate the sharing of information among those with similar interests.

- **Microblogging**: Individuals and organizations share specific timely, interesting, or valuable information in short posts to their followers, friends, or (on LinkedIn) connections.

- **Networking**: Social media can be used to build relationships at an individual level in ways that can benefit organizations, such as LinkedIn's connections, as well as for organizations to gain followers, opening the door for relationships and continued conversations.

For more information on social media tactics, please see the Appendix, page 241.

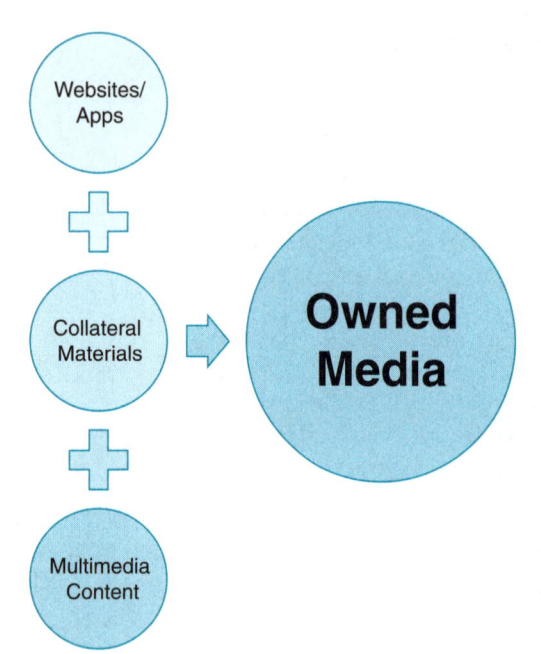

organizational logo key chains. Owned media also stretches deep into digital territory to cover organizational websites, corporate videos, many mobile apps, and e-newsletters.

Timing

Full website design and development can take many months depending on the size and functionality. However, day-to-day content updates can be made nearly instantaneously. The creation of other types of collateral materials involves a design phase and a production phase. Often, production and printing (particularly through external vendors) can be the lengthiest part of the process.

Budget

While the entry-level cost for a website is dropping, most organizations should spend a sizeable amount of their budget to create a site that will solve more problems than it causes. Additionally, ongoing website maintenance and updates are critical to include in any budget. Some organizations work with the assumption that a website has a two-year lifespan and that websites have a two-year development process, moving the website from a project to an ongoing cost of business. Collateral material production costs (and quality) vary widely based on the content.

Messaging

An organization's collateral materials must have clearly defined audiences and messages geared toward those audiences. The danger of these types of materials, as opposed to Twitter, for example, is the tendency to overload them with content and messaging. Messages must be prioritized, organized, and distilled as much as possible. Content must be scannable and navigable so that audiences can quickly find what they need.

Content Creation

For owned media, wherein a significant component of the cost supports production, the act of making a single change can lead to reprinting or redesigning. It is critical to ensure agreement on all content early in the process.

Website Content Management

Organizational websites are nonnegotiable in today's online business world. They are a foundational piece of credibility and are one of the first places any new stakeholder goes to learn about the organization, take actions such as purchasing products, download content, or renew a membership. Campaigns often seek a form of **conversion**, an action such as buying an event ticket or signing up for an e-mail list as an objective, and websites are often where such tactics occur.

Organizational websites exist prior to, during, and after campaigns, and integration should support the business's overarching purpose and message. Campaigns often need a temporary online home as part of this digital presence. This could present itself in the form of a dedicated page or section of the website or a separate microsite that integrates all campaign information and functions, often serving as a place to drive traffic from other digital and traditional channels. Organizational websites also provide opportunities for rotating, newsworthy content as part of their homepage, and campaigns should see this as one significant opportunity to draw in users who are interested in the organization but not necessarily the campaign. Similarly, they can point interested users to dedicated campaign information.

Marketing

PRSA defines marketing as "the management function that identifies human needs and wants, offers products and services to satisfy those demands, and causes transactions that deliver products and services in exchange for something of value to the provider."[13] Many public relation activities are closely connected to marketing objectives and are often underused toward marketing ends. For example, positive earned media coverage should be shared with key organizational publics. This could include integrating the media coverage into paid/**boosted content** shared via social media channels, e-newsletters, or even traditional printed brochures.

Publications

Organizations develop a wide variety of print and digital publications that serve both to distribute content and provide audiences the chance to browse a wider breadth of stories that they may otherwise not be exposed to. The bar for content creation in such outlets is high since the information must be both valuable and interesting to readers. Publications come in several varieties, including recurring *serial publications* like newsletters (print and digital), organizational magazines, and annual reports.[14] Newsletters and magazines, even in print form, are still a popular form of organizational communication and represent an accessible way to share information both within and outside of a campaign structure. While design and production costs vary greatly, particularly when printing and mailing are involved, many organizations still see the value for member/donor outreach, sales and marketing, and event promotion. Many organizations adapt the content produced for such publications for digital purposes. Digital versions of publications, often distributed via e-mail distribution services such as MailChimp, have the advantage of metrics tracking the stories and links that are most popular. Practitioners can use this information to improve story selection, multimedia content, and writing for future issues. The effectiveness of these publications is dependent on having an up-to-date mailing or e-mail distribution list.

Stand-alone (nonrecurring or nonscheduled) publications include e-blasts, reprints, reports, and whitepapers, as well as brochures and flyers. E-blasts are often used to alert specific audiences about more immediately newsworthy content and are timed around the specific event rather than on a weekly, monthly, or quarterly schedule. Reprints are designed versions of media articles that can be repurposed for print or digital use.[15]

Copyright law's fair-use provisions provide for some internal and educational use of reprints, but public dissemination generally must be approved and paid for by the media outlet itself. Reports encompass a variety of documents from public-facing research whitepapers (which can be written and disseminated on campaign-specific topics) to customer or member-focused reports on key organizational issues. Generally, the purpose of such reports is to inform the audience in detail on a specific topic or to provide

---

PRo Tip

OWNED MEDIA TACTICS

- **Apps**: Many organizations develop branded mobile applications for consumers, members, event attendees, or other audiences to create a cohesive, branded experience for them.

- **Collateral materials**: Additional materials can be developed for both digital and traditional uses, either as stand-alone pieces or as part of a broader event or campaign. These can range from a variety of branded logo items to trade show booths that represent the business focus. This can expand to a variety of posters and banners ranging from small easel-mounted foam core pieces to specialty printed banners that take up an entire side of a building.

- **Corporate video**: Video allows organizations to tell stories in a gripping and compelling way and is often used on websites and at corporate events, as well as through shared media (social media).

- **E-newsletters**: Digital tools such as Constant Contact and MailChimp have made designing and distributing e-newsletters easier than ever before. These are often image-rich, link-heavy, trackable formats that allow organizations to point readers toward a variety of compelling content and see what they respond to through analytics.

- **Events (hosted)**: By hosting events, organizations can create wholly managed experiences for publics including members, donors, and key stakeholders inside and outside the organization.

- **Infographics**: Infographics use images, icons, and colorful, easy-to-understand graphs and charts to represent data in accessible ways. Their-user friendly nature makes them a great fit to share through earned and social media.

- **Publications**: Traditional printed magazines, newsletters, and brochures are becoming more rare due to the low cost of digital editions, but this has created an opportunity. Organizations still willing to invest in the design and printing of high quality hard-copy materials may be able to stand apart from others in their industries.

- **Website**: The organizational website is the center of communication from an organization to the outside world. All content should emanate from the website and other owned channels, allowing for information, news, and multimedia to be shared (often through social channels) in a way that links publics back to owned media.

For more information on owned media tactics, please see the Appendix, page 243.

information tailored for a specific time, event, or campaign. Similarly, fewer organizations have a comprehensive brochure about their work, but many have maintained product or program specific brochures. Brochures are made up of folding panels, in contrast to flyers or sales sheets, which often accomplish the same narrowly focused purpose but on a flat piece of paper.[16] One advantage to flyers and sales sheets is that they can be printed easily in-house, although the quality, particularly with color images and photos, often suffers.

An increasingly popular format is that of the infographic, which uses a mix of symbolic imagery and language to represent specific concepts. On one end of the spectrum, infographics can be built as a more detailed version of traditional charts and graphs or process representations. In the extreme, they tend to lean more toward a heavily image-driven approach. The most effective infographics are often the product of collaboration between writers and designers, leading to an output that is both rich in information and easy to understand.

CONCLUSION

Campaign tactics should clearly support objectives and strategies. The mix of tactics should be selected and balanced based on the messages to convey and the audiences such efforts intend to reach. While no practitioners will have expertise in all of the paid, earned, shared, owned, and converged tactics described in this chapter, they can be aware of their strengths and shortcomings, budgetary and timeline implications, audience appropriateness, and message fit. Just as several objectives build toward achieving an organizational goal, several tactics can support the execution of a targeted strategy. The limit to what practitioners can achieve and execute is limited only by their creativity and resources.

THINK CRITICALLY

1. What are three characteristics of effective messages?
2. How are the limitations of earned media different than those of paid media?
3. Many organizations tend to see earned media and social media as "free" tactics. How might you address potential costs for outreach using these tactics with departmental or organizational leaders?
4. Owned tactics reach beyond our idea of *media* to include, for example, office spaces and hosted events. How do these tactics share characteristics with websites, blogs, brochures, newsletters, and other owned media tactics?

KEY TERMS

Boosted content   143
Content creation   141
Content hub   141
Controlled media   141
Conversion   142
Information subsidy   140
Messaging   132
Publicity   140
Uncontrolled media   136

CONCEPT CASE: TACTICAL CHOICES FOR EQUALITY TODAY

Equality Today has approved an objective to raise national awareness of the organization by 2 percent over the next year. While it might not sound like much, that represents a vast number of individuals, and the organization is attempting to accomplish this feat without the budget for large-scale national advertising. Strategies to achieve this broad awareness include a channel focus on social media, earned media, and events. As a public relations team, you'll need to consider particular tactics that can efficiently increase name recognition.

- What social media tactics could improve reach and awareness? Consider partnerships and potential connections with existing channels and influencers.

- How might the organization position itself as a resource to national media outlets? What preparation would need to occur?

- What types of events could capture public attention? How might they be designed in a way to make them accessible for additional coverage through traditional and social media?

CASE STUDY: CINNAMILK BY GENERAL MILLS

From General Mills
Campaign Focus: Promotional

Campaign Focus: Promotional

In the fall of 2015, General Mills embarked on a mission to solve what they described as the ultimate first world problem—the decision between eating cereal or posting on social media. This mission resulted in the creation and distribution of a new invention called the Selfie Spoon, an integral part of the Cinnamon Toast Crunch Cinnamilk campaign.

Research/Diagnosis

Prior to the development of the Selfie Spoon, General Mills identified a population of consumers who used social media to express their affection toward the cereals produced by the company. The Selfie Spoon was developed as a way to connect to those consumers and continue to encourage interaction on various social media sites.[17]

According to a blog post by General Mills, Achala Gopal, a senior marketing communications planner, said of the campaign, "Our awesome fans love to share their obsession with our cereal on social media so we wanted to show a little love back."[18] James Dawson Hollis, executive creative director at McCann, who worked on the Selfie Spoon, added "This was nearly a six-month process of prototypes, adjustments and customization. Once we settled on the design, we created an online hub where people can learn more about the product and place their order."[19]

The Selfie Spoon allowed General Mills to directly engage with its target audience on social media, as well as to reward its devoted consumers. "Selfies and selfie sticks have become such a big part of culture, we knew this would be an amusing way for Cinnamon Toast Crunch to join in the movement," said Mark Chu, associate marketing manager. "It's equal part ridiculous, awesome and strangely practical."[20]

As an established brand, General Mills campaign focused on connecting more deeply with existing customers and supporters rather than increasing awareness overall, although it accomplished this to a certain degree. Ultimately, the Selfie Spoon was designed first and foremost to increase social media engagements and connect to the target audience in a new way.[21]

The gadget was presented as an element of the Cinnamilk campaign; a campaign that used commercials and social media to engage consumers both online and offline at the breakfast table.[22] The target audience for the Selfie Spoon campaign included anyone old enough to engage online and have a use for the Selfie Spoon but still be young enough to eat Cinnamon Toast Crunch. The age of this audience essentially targeted consumers, male or female, between the ages of 12 and 25.[23]

Objective

The overarching objective of this campaign was to create an interactive and compelling activity for younger consumers, motivating them to engage with the company and continue to purchase and enjoy Cinnamon Toast Crunch cereal. By creating this content, General Mills would be able to connect more frequently with their consumers and expand upon the relationship that it already had with supporters of its product. The idea capitalized on the infamous *selfie* frenzy: "Everyone loves a bowl of Cinnamon Toast Crunch, but if you don't post it on social media, did it really happen?"[24]

Strategy

The strategy behind the Selfie Spoon and the Cinnamilk campaigns was based on three elements—social media, paid advertisements, and their website:

- Social media: The Selfie Spoon was given away to consumers, enabling them to take their own cereal selfie and share it on social media for others to see.[25]

- Commercials: In order to make the public aware of the Selfie Spoon, the company used commercials on television to show images of people eating the cereal and taking photos with the Selfie Spoons and then directed the audience members to the website to claim their own Selfie Spoons.[26]

- Website: The website created for the campaign, SelfieSpoon.com, served as the hub for the campaign and the place where stakeholders could claim their own Selfie Spoons or share their photos. The website was based on a Tumblr platform for easy user contribution, demonstrating the importance of social media in the campaign.[27]

Tactics

Paid & Owned

General Mills developed commercials to drive traffic to a specific website to learn more about the Spoon and claim one for themselves.[28]

Earned

The popularity of the campaign spread across the blogs and social media pages of its stakeholders resulting in earned support by both consumers and bloggers.[29]

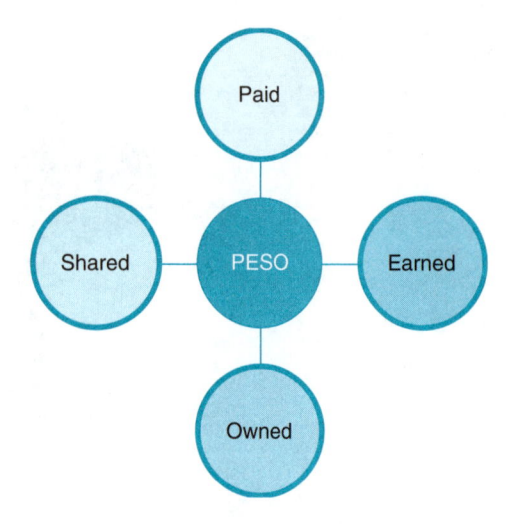

Shared

The selfie stick enabled consumers to take pictures using their very own Selfie Spoon and to share those photos across social media. This resulted in shares across the social sphere and created conversations about the thirty-inch selfie stick with a spoon on one end that helped capture and share users' passion for Cinnamon Toast Crunch.

Implementation

The Selfie Spoon debuted in September 2015 and was only available for ten days. On each of the ten days, 100 Selfie Spoons were given out on a first come, first served basis.[30]

Reporting/Evaluation

Overall, the Selfie Spoon promotion was able to drive interactions with consumers and build a personal connection with fans of the Cinnamon Toast Crunch brand. With this campaign, General Mills created an opportunity to stand out from the competition, do something that generated buzz about the product and the organization, and monopolized on a current trend in society: the selfie stick.

The limited supply of spoons generated intrigue and encouraged action. So much so, that on the first day of implementation, the Selfie Spoon was sold out within two hours of its launch.

With all of these elements combined, the campaign ended up being a success. Although short, the campaign was impactful, leaving consumers with conversations about the absurdity of it all, and for some, their very own Selfie Spoon.

Theories

On the official General Mills blog, senior marketing communications planner Achala Gopal was quoted as saying, "Our awesome fans love to share their obsession with our cereal on social media, so we wanted to show a little love back." They created a campaign focused not on short-term sales but on building long-term connections with key audience members. The campaign thus demonstrates relationship management theory (RMT) principles through the acknowledgement by General Mills that relationships with the stakeholders are crucial. The company's actions served to strategically improve those relationships.[31]

Model

During this campaign, General Mills connected with their publics via candid social media posts and goofy pictures taken with the Selfie Spoon. General Mills did not seek to use directly persuasive tactics to get its message across, rather more casual interactions. That said, the campaign and its communication all catered toward the organizational goals of building relationships with stakeholders for the purposes of the organization itself, reflecting the two-way asymmetrical model.[32] As they sent out communication about the Selfie Spoon via the Internet and television commercials, stakeholders sent information right back via social media.[33] Not only did the campaign reflect an interactive approach, it catered to what the company saw as the long-term relationships with customers, making it clearly two-way communication.

Implementation 9

THINK AHEAD

9.1 Understand which skills are crucial to the execution of successful public relations campaigns.

9.2 Prepare for the eventuality that campaigns are plans, which can often change.

9.3 Explore the role of budgeting in campaign planning and implementation.

9.4 Examine methods for improving day-to-day public relations efforts.

The execution of a public relations campaign can feel like a tightrope walk. Balancing the demands of organizations or clients with audiences and publics—particularly journalists—is both an exhilarating and humbling experience. Sometimes, everything comes together to achieve objectives and recognition from stakeholders. Often, not everything goes as planned. Veteran public relations practitioners have all experienced a moment during a campaign when the pressures of competing deadlines, managing hurried media, and frustrated clients pushes them to consider an alternate career path. However, these are likely the same moments in which practitioners learn and grow the most, witness the impact of their efforts (good and bad), and prove the value and importance of strategic communication. For Broom and Sha, this stage encompasses "putting the program into operation."[1] Implementation is where the rubber hits the road—where work is sent out into the world.

KEY SKILLS FOR IMPLEMENTING PR CAMPAIGNS

During this phase of a campaign, the distinct lines between project phases are often blurred, as they tend to happen more holistically and simultaneously. Implementation does not mean that we stop researching or planning. Rather, there are a number of new events, audiences, messages, and tasks that will emerge and require additional diligence. It is inevitable that practitioners will continue to learn as projects unfold, and each finding should be considered and implemented when appropriate. This is not to say that the effort spent on initial research, objective building, strategy creation, and tactical definitions are not important. A campaign will not succeed without these components, but changes are a required to sustain effectiveness.

Project Management Basics

Successful campaign implementation relies on a mix of preparation, expectation setting, and perseverance. It entails efficient budgeting, effective division of labor among team members, and clear identification and scheduling of tasks. Such tasks are often rooted more in project management than public relations. Morris and Pinto's introduction to *The Wiley Guide to Project Organization and Project Management Competencies* highlights that project management must first "deliver projects on time, on budget, and on scope" and then "see the project within its environment" to understand how it supports and interacts with the organization as a whole.[2] Executing this effectively involves a deep understanding of all of the steps in a process, managing timelines, motivating team members, and adjusting to changing circumstances or unforeseen obstacles.[3]

Additionally, there are numerous tasks that must occur prior to beginning work that will set the stage for a successful campaign. These include organizing and managing budgets, assigning tasks, generating timelines, and communicating effectively to all team members and stakeholders.

Budgeting

Budgeting involves estimating planned or projected costs, rather than focusing on a rigid insistence on fixed spending. Therefore, practitioners must research the costs of particular items, work with vendors to quote prices for specific tactics, and communicate with organizational leaders as numbers become solidified and choices are made. The skills of estimation are developed both through experience and effort. The closer a practitioner works with vendors, advertising representatives, and digital advertising channels, the easier it is to estimate costs, ask clarifying questions, and determine which expenditures are necessary for a given situation.

The budgets supporting public relations campaigns can generally be broken down into five categories: **personnel**, **materials**, **media costs**, **infrastructure**, and **administration**.[4]

Personnel costs cover the professional time spent researching, analyzing, writing, editing, designing, developing, executing, and evaluating campaign work. Items "associated with the tactics" constitute materials, including printing fliers, website hosting costs, video production location fees, and press release wire distribution.[5] Media costs refer to print, broadcast, and digital ad buys and advertorial content. Purchasing a video camera, upgrading editing software, adding a social media monitoring service, or expanding physical space of an organization should be considered infrastructure expenditures, which may be included as part of campaign budgets but are more often spread over multiple projects due to their value beyond a specific campaign. Finally, administrative costs include office activities, travel, and other incidental expenditures for campaign-related work. Such categories are not necessarily the only structure for organizing budgets, but they provide a framework and checklist to ensure that all potential costs are considered during the planning process.

It is also valuable to understand that there are further classifications of each cost associated with a campaign. Some budget items are fixed, known as **hard costs**, while others, **soft costs**, may be more flexible in nature. Hard costs can include vendor payments, event costs, production costs, and infrastructure expansion. Soft costs may include flexible ad buys, in-house production, as well as personnel and other discretionary spending. In many cases, the nature of an individual expenditure allows some degree of flexibility; for example, digital ad buys can be changed on a weekly or daily basis, while print or broadcast advertising is generally locked in. Organizations tend to have fixed personnel costs, while agencies have more flexibility in moving team members from project to project if additional bandwidth is needed. The art of effective budgeting examines the ratio of hard and soft costs to allow some flexibility and reactivity during campaign implementation activity. If certain advertising channels prove to be particularly effective, it is useful to allow for budget flexibility in order to adjust the resources allocated for those tactics. Building in some flexibility allows practitioners to capitalize on opportunities that arise during campaign execution, while feedback provides valuable knowledge and direction.

Of particular importance for agency work, budgets also must reflect the anticipated amount of time that will be spent on the project by agency personnel. Not only should the tasks and tactics be feasible to complete within the timeline, but they must also be possible to complete within the agency's retainer structure. If an agency allocates fifteen hours a month to a specific client, a project requiring an estimated twenty to twenty-five hours of work during a single month would cover the expense of all other efforts and move beyond retainer time (and cost). For some public relations (PR) firms, this would mean an additional project contract, while others might see the additional time as an important contributor to forming a strong relationship over the long term. Firms have built relationships with both approaches. Many public relations agencies bill by the hour or track staff time toward retainer to establish and reinforce project scope. For both in-house and agency staff, tracking time is an extremely valuable tool to understand the duration of specific tasks, creating a clearer picture of personnel time allocation. It also significantly improves the ability of campaign leadership to identify points of efficiency and inefficiency for process improvement at both individual and team levels.

Dividing Tasks among a Team

Accomplishing public relations work efficiently and effectively as a team is often harder than it sounds. Assessing the skills and abilities of team members to identify the project elements best suited to them is critical.[6] With that in mind, implementing process improvements during campaign execution will always be a work in progress. Consider these modifications less like an assembly line and more like the daily modifications required of a high-end restaurant. In a classical French kitchen, each area or station is headed by a *chef*, who oversees the work of his team or *partie*. Meat, fish, sauces, produce, and desserts all entail their own stations and teams, working together to produce a dish. This approach was popularized and perfected by legendary French chef Auguste Escoffier in the late 19th and early 20th centuries. It created a highly organized environment where everyone understood their individual role in a process and, through this efficiency, trimmed the time it took for customers waiting for his dishes at London's Savoy Hotel by up to two-thirds.[7] It is a particularly apt comparison to public relations, because the work is never a true assembly line: two press releases will never be identical in the same way that two cuts of meat will always need to be seasoned differently based on their size, shape, and fat content. The practitioner will need to use his or her full expertise to make important decisions at each stage in the research, planning, writing, editing, distribution, and evaluation processes.

Public relations project or campaign teams should also be designed based on the size, scope, and urgency of the task at hand, as well as the skills of those participating. A large team may be broken into media relations, social media, and creative production, with the leaders of each group acting as the station chefs in charge of their team's execution. Practitioners should leverage the expertise they have developed in each of these areas. Additionally, like a restaurant kitchen, each step in the campaign has a distinct timeline for planning, development, and production, wherein each group must ensure that their piece of the campaign is timed to meet deadlines and work in tandem with the other pieces. A media announcement, like entrées for a table of diners, must have all components ready to serve at the appropriate time, whether they took three months or fifteen minutes to prepare.

Creating Timelines and Deadlines

Building functional timelines, or schedules of implementation, begins by working backward. What are the main deliverable due dates? Are these "hard" (immobile) deadlines?[8] If so, it allows practitioners to plan by marking off the time for concept development and approval, content creation and approval, production and approval, as well as final delivery of the items at hand. In the case of a press release, these steps are relatively straightforward, and the timing is more flexible. For example, a project might be set up using the following estimates for writing and distribution:

- Research and information gathering (two hours to one week)
- Initial ideas and approval from staff (two days)
- Drafting (one day)

- Approval and revisions (two days to two weeks)
- Setup and distribution (one to two days)
- Follow up (one week)

In this case, practitioners would know that the process would need to begin, if possible, one month before the distribution date. However, these timelines might be overly cautious for a small, fast-moving organization or too optimistic for a complex campaign announcement that includes multiple organizations (and thus multiple public relations teams and multiple levels of approval). With experience and conscious practice, practitioners can improve their ability to estimate the length of time necessary to complete specific tasks within their own organizations or for individual clients.

Additionally, timelines for creative production can further complicate things, particularly when much of the process takes place outside the control of practitioners. In most cases, public relations professionals should schedule recurring meetings with the creative team to discuss timelines and ensure that the larger team understands what the creative team (or outside vendor) expects of them regarding turnaround times. For example, a practitioner might know that the company's executive team takes one to two weeks to approve many of their ideas. This knowledge should be communicated to the creative team to build in this approval time appropriately. The larger the project, the greater the potential exists to run into roadblocks and challenges. Some timeline padding should be built into major creative projects when possible, and public relations leaders can take the lead in holding groups involved to agreed-upon internal deadlines.

It is easy to imagine how concurrent timelines supporting various components of a single campaign can easily become confusing and difficult to manage. One tool available for organizing multiple deadlines and projects is called a **Gantt chart**, which provides a clear visual representation of the timeline for multiple campaign components at a glance. Gantt charts are useful to include in full plans because they provide those beyond the public relations department a method for understanding the time needed to complete each tactic and task. This can be particularly valuable, as it can be difficult for organizational leaders without a PR background to understand why planning and implementing a campaign may take months of effort.

Setting Clear Expectations and Ensuring Clear Communication

Conveying a clear project vision is the responsibility of the project manager.[9] Those working together on a project should understand how tasks will be divided and what the expectations are related to timelines, quality, and communication. Clarity, in this case, comes in part from defined, measurable objectives connected to the strategies, tactics, and tasks that each team member will perform. This includes processes, results, and direction from appropriate organization and conciseness of communication itself. The more complicated that a message becomes, the less clearly it will convey the point. Using a clear information hierarchy and creating scannable, reference-focused language is paramount. Don't expect project directions to be read in full or in order.

Gantt charts allow practitioners to quickly visualize the multiple timelines that are part of the preparation and implementation process of integrated campaigns.

Another important facet of team leadership is motivation. Generating enthusiasm for a project is just as important as developing and communicating an effective plan. In doing so effectively, practitioners must sometimes step out of their comfort zones. They should respond to the informational and emotional needs of their team members and provide them with the necessary support to succeed, even if it means a detour from the plan or from their usual day-to-day approach.[10] This can be particularly difficult as public relations practitioners are creative and objective driven, potentially making them less tolerant of inflexible rules and management styles.[11] Balancing the needs of deadlines and efficiency with creativity and innovation can only be done with a deep knowledge of each team member and a constant focus on keeping projects interesting and exciting for those involved.

Working with Non-PR People

Oftentimes, those outside of the marketing team become critical pieces in the function of a campaign. They may be sources of information, providers of approvals, or strategic sounding boards. In all cases, public relations professionals should take extra care in working with individuals who are outside of their day-to-day function, in part because of the different expectations for timeliness, communication, and approvals. Particularly in working with journalists in need of information or interviews on deadline, practitioners must educate those inside the organization about the need for responsiveness.

Working with journalists can be intimidating, but media relations strategies and tactics are still are cornerstones of successful integrated campaigns.

Like professionals in any industry, those in integrated marketing communications tend to use industry jargon when communicating. This can ultimately isolate them from others within organizations and undercut their credibility with executive leadership. When working with those outside of the PR field, it is critical to adjust language for easy comprehension. Practitioners should take the opportunity to educate others within their organization regarding the strategies, concepts, and research that go into planning a PR campaign. The more knowledge that others have of the strategic, integrated communication processes, the more accurately they will be able to understand recommendations and perspectives from the public relations function. Additionally, they will be better equipped to share their own perspectives and insights with the PR team in both constructive and productive ways.

In an agency setting, clients should be regarded as the experts on their industry and their business; keeping them included in discussions and decisions about messaging, strategy, and execution in regard to their products, trends, or competitors.[12] The same approach can be taken by in-house practitioners, who can defer to relevant executive team members or other subject matter experts in order to ensure their expertise is used. In both cases, the public relations team should maintain ownership of the objectives, strategy, writing, distribution, and measurement.

Working with the Media

Executing media relations not only requires knowledge of the appropriate public relations practitioner duties but also the needs of journalists. Ultimately, media outlets have a responsibility to provide a product to their specific audience. Public relations practitioners must respect this responsibility and act within its limitations. It should govern not only the way information is crafted but also its distribution method and timing.

When executing media relations, it is critical to remember that journalists, editors, and producers are beholden to daily deadline and editorial pressures. The most valuable pitches are those that are clearly framed for a media outlet's audience and an individual journalist's beat. They should choose topics and use language appropriate and understandable for the outlet's audience. Ease of translation also means that practitioners should always follow *Associated Press Stylebook* guidelines and clearly identify and showcase the facets of newsworthiness that a particular pitch or story requires.

PRo Tip

DEFINING NEWSWORTHINESS

There are six components of newsworthiness by which journalists (and, by extension, public relations practitioners) should use to identify the value of their stories and pitches.[14] Of course, no story is considered newsworthy in every category, but news items that rank strongly in multiple categories and are clearly articulated in a pitch will be of greatest interest to journalists.

1. Audience impact: Will the information have significant relevance in the lives of a majority of the media outlet's audience? Is the story about a widely attended free community festival (highly relevant) or a high-dollar, black-tie fund-raiser (less relevant)?

2. Proximity: How much geographical overlap is there between the information conveyed and the audience? Is it happening in the media outlet's coverage area or in a different state?

3. Timeliness: Would the information still be of interest to readers at the time it is published or shared? Did the event happen today or three weeks ago?

4. Prominence: Is the information about a well-known company CEO or an unknown front-line employee? Is the charitable contribution $200 or $200,000? Did the company hire 3 new employees or 300?

5. Novelty or oddity: Is the information unique and unexpected or something that happens regularly? Is a local business celebrating its 100th anniversary or announcing quarterly sales figures?

6. Conflict, drama, or excitement: Does the information generate interest because of its potentially negative or dramatic consequences? Is the organization responding to a genuine crisis or releasing a minor update to an established product?

Source: Glen M. Broom and Bey-Ling Sha, *Cutlip and Center's Effective Public Relations*, (11th ed.), (Boston, MA: Pearson, 2013), p. 293.

Additionally, practitioners should be aware of editorial processes of specific publications, particularly with respect to deadlines. While there is increasing pressure for many media outlets to provide near-constant updates as news breaks, each media type still possesses a distinct rhythm; whether it's the morning newsgathering, editing at the daily newspaper or local evening TV news, weekly deliverables for regional business weeklies, or the months-long production time for many national magazines.[13] Because of these constraints, the timing of media announcements can be critical to their success. For example, an announcement about an organization that is opening a new location in a new city and hiring several hundred new employees would be largely directed at local media (print, radio, and television) and therefore most effectively released on a weekday morning (not Friday) to maximize quick uptake. If a similar announcement was more important for trade media, it may have a very different timeline for distribution. Content distributed through earned media channels should always be simultaneously posted on logical, easy-to-find owned channels, such as a website's press room, so that other interested journalists can easily access the information.[15]

Self-awareness and Self-evaluation

Every practitioner contributes a specific skillset to a project, but practitioners should not be considered experts at every task or tactic. With this in mind, having a clear idea of where your personal strengths and weaknesses are is critical. Howard and Mathews provide particularly pointed and useful questions that communicators should ask themselves:[16]

- **"Am I doing everything I can to stay current on company activities and industry trends?"** Knowing your own organization allows practitioners to see potentially newsworthy stories as they develop. Being on top of industry trends provides significant credibility as well as a wealth of ideas for stories and pitches.

- **"Am I anticipating news and activities in my organization that would cause or generate media interest?"** If not, it might be helpful to follow internal events and news more carefully, build more relationships across departments, and always consider the potential news value for those outside of the organization.

- **"Am I, or is my boss, included in planning meetings and in the decision-making process?"** If the public relations function is not included in strategic meetings, it may be worthwhile to ask leadership for the opportunity to participate in, or at least observe, relevant discussions.

Additionally, the following questions relate to individual skill development:

- **"Am I making progressively fewer writing errors and typos?"** If not, consider changing your processes to ensure you have the time and focused energy to proofread your own work. In the meantime, ask a colleague to provide another set of eyes on your writing before sending it to leadership or journalists.

- **"Am I seeing unexpected pushback or disagreement about my best ideas or pitches from coworkers, leadership, clients, or journalists?"** If your sense of what makes an effective pitch or strategy seems not to align with others in your organization, ask for feedback whenever possible. Challenges can arise when junior practitioners are less aware of an organization's history, goals, or internal politics. Having deeper insights into these issues can help improve strategic recommendations. Working with journalists and understanding what is newsworthy often comes from additional reading and research on specific reporters, media outlets, and industries.

- **"Am I spending more time than others writing, making media follow-up calls, or tracking media coverage for similar projects?"** Efficiency, while not as important as overall quality of work, is still an area that can greatly increase a practitioner's ability to make an impact on their organization or client. Speed at particular tasks can increase with time and conscious practice, but the baseline comes from watching the clock to see how long it takes to complete certain tasks and then attempting to gradually improve efficiency over time.

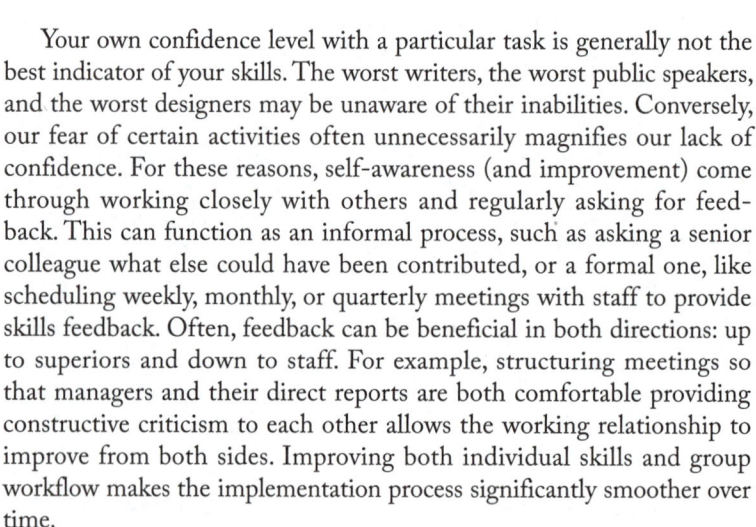

Your own confidence level with a particular task is generally not the best indicator of your skills. The worst writers, the worst public speakers, and the worst designers may be unaware of their inabilities. Conversely, our fear of certain activities often unnecessarily magnifies our lack of confidence. For these reasons, self-awareness (and improvement) come through working closely with others and regularly asking for feedback. This can function as an informal process, such as asking a senior colleague what else could have been contributed, or a formal one, like scheduling weekly, monthly, or quarterly meetings with staff to provide skills feedback. Often, feedback can be beneficial in both directions: up to superiors and down to staff. For example, structuring meetings so that managers and their direct reports are both comfortable providing constructive criticism to each other allows the working relationship to improve from both sides. Improving both individual skills and group workflow makes the implementation process significantly smoother over time.

Persistence and Perseverance

Successful public relations practitioners represent a very diverse cross section of the workforce, but they have one key trait in common: persistence. When they see an obstacle, they understand that those who break through are the most motivated, hardest working, and most resilient. Young professionals should strive to demonstrate persistence by not giving up in difficult circumstances and practice the perseverance and tenacity

Follow-up calls support proactive media pitching efforts and serve a critical role in building relationships between practitioners and journalists.

to work through and overcome obstacles. Of course, this is easier said than done. When discussing the challenges facing new practitioners, "do not expect immediate results."[17]

In media relations, for example, the vast majority of media pitches are not actually used. Failure with one, two, or three reporters does not necessarily mean an idea or a pitch does not have merit.[18] As in Major League Baseball, 30 hits in 100 attempts may be a very good stretch at the plate. For practitioners, this means keeping the energy, enthusiasm, and optimism up, even if seven pitches or follow-up calls in a row don't go your way. Maintaining a balanced, paced approach to the results of this outreach is key to long-term emotional stability and success. No individual pitch, placement, Instagram photo, or advertising tactic should make or break a campaign. Similarly, no individual setback for a practitioner should break his or her spirit. Resilience, or the ability to bounce back from adversity, comes from knowing that you have the right processes, tools, safeguards, and strategies in place; an understanding that your team has thoroughly researched a problem and identified its cause. It originates from a deep knowledge of the industries, journalists, and organizations that practitioners interact with. All of these small steps build confidence in individual areas, which translates into a broader belief that a campaign can and will succeed with enough effort and resources. Thoroughness, preparedness, and persistence breed excellence and resilience, which is a critical part of perseverance. Long-term campaign success cannot happen without it.

PRo Tip

SCRUM—A STRUCTURE FOR MANAGING CHANGE

Public relations campaigns take place in dynamic environments. The pace of technological innovation and increasing speed of multidirectional communication mean that today, more than ever before, the world surrounding organizations is in constant change—including while campaigns are taking place.

In response to these challenges, eminent public relations scholar Betteke van Ruler has adapted a scrum approach to public relations planning and implementation. Originally created for software design and development, the scrum model encourages "permanent monitoring of change"[19]:

- **Sprints:** Members execute the plan and maintain focus and direction during short, timed cycles.
- **Team reflections:** Each member is responsible for evaluating their own actions and seeking improvement—concise, regular (often daily or every-other-day) meetings, where team members discuss challenges and issues in their campaign implementation.
- **Interventions:** The team leader has final say in making changes to be implemented during the next sprint cycle.
- **Team responsibility:** Teams are largely autonomous and empowered to achieve their own objectives.

While not all public relations practitioners need to become *scrum masters*, they should have regular processes for understanding, reflecting, communicating, and integrating change into the implementation process.

Based on Betteke van Ruler's "Agile Public Relations Planning" article from *Public Relations Review* and her book *Reflective Communication Scrum*.

Crisis may strike an organization when it is least expected, making flexibility and change management a critical part of campaign implementation.

PREPARING FOR CHANGE

No plan is executed exactly as written. Even the most brilliant campaign plans may not work in the real world. From shoestring small businesses to Public Relations Society of America Silver Anvil-winners working with global PR firms, everyone revisits, rethinks, and revises their approach. Circumstances may occur that are beyond the control of the organization or reflect changes in the competitive, regulatory, technical, or local environments. *Plans* are just that: potential approaches that must be flexible and responsive.

Campaigns may also encounter circumstances that could have been anticipated but were not. Actual audience behavior may differ from survey responses. Technological progression occurs in every industry. Practitioners should adjust to the circumstances and recalibrate strategies and tactics. In this way, each new plan and its implementation incorporates the lessons learned from previous campaigns.

When campaigns do not progress completely as planned, flexibility in implementation allows practitioners to make the most of continued learning from the environment. Feedback from audience interaction, in-campaign analytics, and, potentially, structured surveys and outreach can all support the continued focusing (or refocusing) of messages, content, and channels.

One framework for understanding such changes is known as systems theory, which sees organizations as part of a complex, interdependent system within their environment.[20] When one element changes, the organizations within the environment each must respond. Such systems tend to return to a balanced state. This environment includes the company, industry (competitors, vendors, and customers), and communities (local, regional, national, and international), as well as broader political and economic factors. From this perspective, an organization's survival over the long term is tied largely to its ability to adapt to these environmental factors and pressures.

An alternate approach for understanding change has been put forth by Pang, Jin, and Cameron. Their **contingency theory** places an organization's attempts to respond to external change as a balance between "advocacy" (fighting to position the organization in a certain way relative to such forces) and "accommodation" (aligning the organization with the environmental change).[21] This approach asks practitioners to consider constant evaluation of external challenges and opportunities before and during campaigns and to see their work as "dynamic" or constantly evolving.[22] These factors include both internal and external considerations ranging from corporate culture and public relations staff experience to customer credibility and the regulatory environment. Changes to any of these factors must be monitored throughout campaigns and, if necessary, reflected by changes in priorities, objectives, strategies, and tactics.

While not all circumstances can be anticipated, there are recurring themes every practitioner can learn from both in their past experience and from the experiences of others. The public relations function cannot always predict the results of an upcoming election, but it can prepare and take into account multiple approaches to planning based on hypothetical results. This may be the most important takeaway from contingency theory: it is impossible to predict the future, but our approaches should be flexible enough to succeed when some environmental factors change.

CONCLUSION

In the end, balance is critical. Campaigns must employ both strategically planned and reactive approaches. Leaning too much in one direction or the other often has negative consequences. Being overly rigid in execution avoids using the natural and important learning that takes place in the implementation of any plan. Practitioners can make use of the insights that come from the initial stages of implementation. They should budget so that some resources can shift as individual tactics prove more effective than others. The best campaign plans are maps rather than linear directions; showing that there are several paths to successfully meeting objectives. Finally, the best practitioners are adept both at writing and reading their campaign plans for these realities.

THINK CRITICALLY

1. In what ways do public relations practitioners act as project managers?
2. Why is it important to be flexible and plan for change?
3. How might you anticipate some of the challenges of ongoing projects or campaigns with non-PR colleagues?
4. What are three areas of improvement you'd like to focus on based on the implementation recommendations in this chapter?

KEY TERMS

Budget, Administration 150
Budget, Infrastructure 150
Budget, Materials 150
Budget, Media 150
Budget, Personnel 150
Contingency theory 161
Gantt chart 153
Hard costs 151
Soft costs 151

CONCEPT CASE: EQUALITY TODAY MEETS UNEXPECTED OBSTACLES

Equality Today's campaign to increase awareness and fund-raising is underway, but several state-level legislative and judicial events have put the organization on the defensive. In a number of states, legislatures have passed legislation limiting the rights of same-sex couples. Additionally, legal decisions upheld several unexpectedly negative court rulings on the workplace rights of LGBTQ Americans. These events, particularly their occurrence in quick succession, changed the mood at the office and of the organization from one of optimism to defensiveness. As a public relations team, it is important to consider the potential impact of changes to the external environment but also to ensure campaign goals and objective are still at the center of daily efforts.

- Based on your understanding of the campaign goals and the situation, how would you recommend the organization respond in the following contexts, and why (there is no right or wrong answer)?

    o Your CEO recommends that public relations and fund-raising messages should stay optimistic despite the less-than-ideal circumstances.

- Several other similar advocacy groups take strong public stands against the state-level situations and dedicate resources to help.
  - Groups supportive of these events single out Equality Today as a leading negative force and publicly attack the organization.
- With each of the scenarios above, would they force your team to adjust tactics? Strategies? Objectives? All of the above?

CASE STUDY: MISSING TYPE—U.K.'S NATIONAL HEALTH SERVICE

Campaign Focus: Public Health, Crisis Communication, Community Engagement

Over the past ten years, there has been a 40 percent decrease in the amount of blood donors in the United Kingdom. While a variety of factors play into this number—not being able to donate after getting a tattoo, traveling to an exotic place, or simply being too busy to donate—the National Health Service Blood and Transplant set out to reverse that statistic in order to save lives and improve the quality of living for those who need blood transfusions to survive.[23]

The act of donating blood takes time, and you have to be healthy, free of numerous ailments, and meet stringent stipulations in order to give. These factors contributed to a 40 percent decrease of eligible donors over the course of the decade between 2005 and 2015. This decrease caused a shortage of a vital resource needed by patients across the United Kingdom.[24]

The Missing Type campaign began ahead of National Blood Week, which was scheduled for June 8–14, 2015.[25] Leading up to the week, representatives from NHS Blood and Transplant reached out to several high profile organizations and asked them for one simple favor—to drop the Os, As and Bs from their signage, representing the missing blood donations.[26]

Research and Diagnosis

The decrease in blood donations caused a significant problem for hospitals and patients who rely on the generosity of donors over the course of treatment or after an accident. With the decline in donors, NHS Blood and Transplant recognized that without an effort to reverse the habits of donors the problem would only continue to deepen. Jon Latham, the assistant director for Donor Services and Marketing for NHS Blood and Transplant, noted that the decline has been part due to changes in public behavior: the increased popularity of tattoos, the uptick of travel to new, exotic destinations, and the expansion of medical treatments that cause deferrals, such as endoscopies. Collectively, these seemingly small and unrelated changes were significant contributors to the drop in donations.

This campaign targeted eligible blood donors in London. In order to be eligible for donating blood in the United Kingdom, you must be between the ages of 17 and 70, and weigh more than 50 kilograms (110 pounds). In addition, NHS Blood and Transplant restricts donors based on their travel history, piercings and tattoos, sexual habits, and medications.[27]

Objectives

The Missing Type campaign was focused on shedding light on the decrease in blood donations plaguing the NHS Blood and Transplant's effort to assist patients. NHS Blood and Transplant also set out to inform individuals on the consequences of decreased donations in coming years, and breakdown the common myths associated with donating blood.[28]

Strategy

As fewer potential donors have been able to give, the strategy aimed to clearly articulate the growing gap between donated blood and the needs of hospitals and patients beginning through paid and owned channels and cascading to earned and shared channels.

Tactics

The tactics leveraged throughout the campaign included the removal of the letters O, A, and B from signage and headlines during the National Blood Week. This effort attempted to send the message that if the amount of blood donations does not increase, there will not be enough available blood that patients across the United Kingdom rely on. NHS Blood and Transplant partnered with media organizations, such as *The Daily Mirror* and Odeon, to remove the necessary letters from their signs and headlines. The city of London also got involved with the campaign by removing letters from some of their more popular street signs, such as Downing Street in Westminster, the home of the Prime Minister.[29]

More than 1,000 brands participated in the campaign, including Cadbury, McDonalds, Coca-Cola, Google, and Walkers. These major brands used their platforms to engage with potential blood donors and promote the need for blood donations for the residents of London.[30] These partnerships were a valuable asset to the NHS Blood and Transplant, and without them, the campaign may not have had as far of a reach as it did.

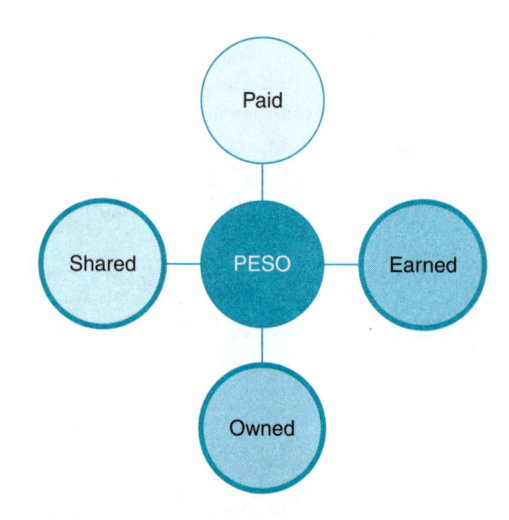

The movement to showcase the missing letters was also supplemented by press releases sent to television stations, radio stations and print and digital media that shared information about donating blood. These releases outlined the steps necessary to become a blood donor, and broke down the myths that people often assume as true in regards to blood donation.[31]

Earned

The missing letters from the street signs, and the press releases sent to various organizations caught the attention of the media and allowed the campaign to gain attention from numerous sources; helping to promote the cause of recruiting blood donors for NHS Blood and Transplant.[32] Earned media helped the campaign to connect the dots for audience members who may have been unclear of the message of the missing letters. A Buzzfeed story highlighting the campaign became the number one trending topic on the website, demonstrating the campaign's reach and appeal.[33]

Activity took place in national print, online and broadcast media:[34]

- Total pieces of coverage: 689
- Total reach: 347,619,784

Shared

Social media was a vital element in the Missing Type campaign as well. Users shared pictures of the letters missing from their daily lives, which resulted in reaching a social media audience of more than 178 billion.[35] Through these social media shares, the campaign was able to reach potential blood donors who were geographically located outside of London, enabling NHS Blood and Transplant to recruit additional donors.

Some of the largest illustrations of results included:[36]

- 60 influencers showed their support on Twitter
- 1,000 brands showed support on Twitter
- 26,121 uses of #NationalBloodWeek and #MissingType across Twitter
- 66 percent increase in Instagram fans in less than a week
- 1,700 image likes on the Instagram profile
- 478,480 people engaged with the campaign on Facebook

Owned

One goal of the campaign was to drive stakeholders to the NHS Blood and Transplant website where they could locate more information about becoming a blood donor and the importance of donating blood. By the second day of the campaign, the visits to the NHS Blood and Transplant website increased by 100 percent.[37]

Implementation

Planning for the Missing Type campaign occurred ahead of the launch of National Blood Week. The implementation of the campaign took place during the week of June 8–14, 2015.[38]

Reporting/Evaluation

At the conclusion of the Missing Type campaign, NHS Blood and Transplant reported that the campaign had reached over 2 billion individuals through the missing letters and earned media efforts. From those two billion hits, NHS Blood and Transplant received 30,000 signups for new, eligible blood donors; resulting in more than 100,000 additional lives to be saved or improved by blood donations.[39]

Theories

Situational Theory of Publics states that there are four types of publics: non-public, latent public, aware public, and active public. The factors that determine the type of public include problem recognition, constraint (obstacle) recognition and level of involvement in the situation. Communication strategies depend on the type of public involved. Throughout this campaign, NHS Blood and Transplant was able to create awareness about the need for blood donations and donors. They also shared how the downturn in donations affected people's lives and stressed the importance of donating blood. These actions exemplify the Situational Theory of Publics.[40]

Model

In the press agentry model, public information flows one way from the organization to its publics and stakeholders. It uses persuasion to achieve its organizational goals. This campaign successfully utilized the missing letters around London and media outlets in order to push out the message that blood donors are an important and necessary resource for NHS Blood and Transplant. They use persuasive tactics in order to convince eligible adults to sign up to donate blood and create the change they were pushing for.

10 Reporting and Evaluation

THINK AHEAD

10.1 Examine the variety of techniques and frameworks available for campaign evaluation.

10.2 Produce reporting strategies that meet organizational and stakeholder needs.

10.3 Understand the special reporting considerations for each of the PESO channels.

©iStockPhotos/diane39

The day following a major fund-raising event, the CEO of a local nonprofit arrives at the office a bit later than usual. The staff is understandably exhilarated but winded. The director of communication is beginning to sort through the media coverage of the event itself. The CEO asks her, "How do you think the campaign turned out?" Before responding, she pauses. The event nearly met the intended fund-raising goals. Its outreach created several new journalist relationships, including one that resulted in an unexpected radio interview the previous afternoon. It certainly energized the organization's volunteer base. Targeted social media ads leveraged the event to broaden the organization's Facebook and Instagram following. A local TV crew covered the event and crafted a highly positive feature story. That said, an influential blogger who was expected to live tweet the event came down with the flu, and one major donor felt the need to share loudly that his contributions the past year had been underappreciated. She replied, almost phrased as a question, "I think it went well," the pitch rising as she spoke.

Evaluating public relations campaigns is rarely clear-cut. Campaign work takes unexpected twists and turns, making the process of evaluation and reporting outcomes challenging; like taking aim at a moving target. Corporate and organizational leaders, understandably, prefer clear, concise, black-and-white reporting; however, the results of integrated campaigns rarely fit into tidy boxes. Successes may be wholly unexpected, while anticipated opportunities may not materialize. The value practitioners provide comes from the rich knowledge gained in the process of executing and tracking paid, earned, shared, and owned outreach to inform future campaigns and organizational actions. By listening to all audiences, practitioners gain an enviable grasp on the perspectives of many critical organizational publics. Understanding how to capture, organize, and synthesize this data allows the public relations function to provide valuable insights for all organizational leaders and departments.

Public relations practitioners have two distinct tasks at the end of a campaign: (1) cataloguing, evaluating, and learning from their own successes, challenges, and missteps, and (2) reporting those results to their peers, organizational leaders, and/or clients. Seasoned practitioners understand the importance of both stages of this process and develop a sense for what information is useful to inform future campaigns, as well as what strategic information is valuable for those outside the communication team. Often, mistakes, external pressures, or unanticipated successes lead to the most valuable insights.

Before deciding what evaluative information to share, campaigns must be examined at several distinct levels: foremost, according to their original objectives. Did they succeed in creating the proposed action or change? Were objectives met for the right audiences and within the designated timeframe? Next, they should be analyzed from a more granular perspective focused on lessons learned. Did messages resonate with the community? Were journalists interested in the campaign's biggest news hooks? Did internal audiences participate with enthusiasm or with a shrug? Did relevant content drive interaction on social media channels? Once findings have been collected, they should be analyzed, synthesized, and shared with key stakeholders within the organization. The first section of this chapter addresses the evaluative process itself, while the second portion addresses the work of developing reporting vehicles to fit the needs of an organization and the project at hand.

EVALUATING YOUR CAMPAIGN

As discussed in the research section of the text, campaign evaluation should be tied to valuable, organizationally centered objectives. As Watson and Noble explain in *Evaluating Public Relations*, a campaign's "intended communication and behavioral effects serve as the basis from which all other planning decisions can be made."[1] The same sentiment applies to evaluation. Evaluation is an opportunity to look both backward and forward at what areas succeeded and what could be improved for the future.

The primary task should be to define and understand the results using qualitative and quantitative methods. This involves examining the execution of objectives as well as their inherent usefulness. For example, if the objective of a campaign was to raise awareness of an event among potential attendees by 20 percent over a three-month timeframe, and it was surpassed, but fewer attendees than expected actually showed up, it does not necessarily make the campaign a success. Narrowly, the objective was achieved, but, in this case, it may have been the incorrect item to measure. Sometimes, seemingly valuable objectives appear less central once the campaign is complete. Such feedback and subsequent adjustment leads to continuous refinement of campaign planning and execution that progressively increases impact and relevance to organizational goals over time.

The process of evaluation allows the team to work together to examine and assess the effectiveness of planning, strategies, and implementation processes. Particularly for elements that had unexpected results, this review becomes an invaluable exercise to understand. Was the strategy or message mismatched with the audience? Was the paid media spend more effective than anticipated? Was the paper that the brochure was printed on too low grade for it to have the desired impact? Did event attendance exceed expectations? Were the wrong reporters pitched? Were the right reporters pitched but at the wrong time? Both big-picture decisions and minute details matter.

One approach is to evaluate the campaign in stages. Examining the public relations team's success in the preparation of the campaign, during implementation, and based on its impact.[2] This means examining the quality and thoroughness of preparation and implementation activities, as well as whether their consequences and results were met for each objective. This step-by-step breakdown allows practitioners to understand whether challenges occurred because a particular program did not have time to be executed properly (preparation issue), because an idea did not resonate with reporters to generate coverage (implementation issue), or because, despite a paid media spend, a new website did not receive the anticipated traffic (impact issue).

Public relations campaigns are difficult to evaluate in part because they never operate in isolation.[3] A continually changing environment and a variety of moving parts mean that each component cannot be tested independently to define exactly which features or actions affect the outcome. This is compounded by the inherent uniqueness of campaigns, numerous environmental and situational factors, and lack of **control groups**. In scientific experiments, a control group remains unchanged to demonstrate that the variable or factor being tested creates the expected impact. Real-world campaigns are rarely able to recreate the circumstances of a lab. Multiple factors often work together to influence success in ways that are complex and impossible to separate. The easier areas to evaluate (Facebook "likes," media clips, ad viewership, or website visitors) are, on their own, often the least consequential for campaign success. To this end, Watson and Noble warn against spending too much time and effort evaluating the *process* phase, and instead focusing on impact.[4]

Despite these challenges, evaluation research need not require "wide-ranging, expensive and highly technical exercises."[5] Many evaluative tools can be executed simply if built in to the campaign from the beginning. They may require an investment of time and focus, but many organizations overestimate the resources needed to glean valuable information.

Evaluating media relations is about more than counting the number of media placements earned, it's about measuring their impact toward organizational objectives.

Media Evaluation

A first step in the process of media evaluation includes media monitoring and media analysis. According to Watson and Noble, measuring media coverage should be "systemic, continuous, part of an overall evaluation process, and related to objectives."[6] Today's media monitoring uses a variety of tools; from technology-driven methods such as free Google News Alerts, to paid services like Cision. That said, the exercise still relies on many low-tech approaches, such as reading hard copy newspapers and magazines, watching television interviews, and checking media websites for updates. Not all relevant media coverage appears online in a searchable form, particularly radio and television content. Digital tools are not perfect, and many practitioners use several at any given time to attempt to fill such holes. The role of individuals tracking down specific pieces of coverage will never fully be absent from the process.

Once media coverage has been identified, the process of content analysis (as described in Chapter 5) can begin. Some professionals use the mnemonic **I.M.P. A.C.T.** to identify potential criteria for evaluation: *Influence* or tone, *Message* communicated, *Prominence*, *Audience* reached, *Consultant/spokesman* quoted, and *Type* of article.[7] Not all of these criteria are relevant in all media coverage analyses, so practitioners can focus on what is most pertinent to their goals and objectives.

> ## *PRo Tip*
>
> ### FOUR QUESTIONS FOR ANALYZING MEDIA COVERAGE
>
> 1. How much coverage was received on a specific topic and for what audiences?
> 2. How often and how prominently were the campaign's messages, spokespersons, and organizations included in this coverage?
> 3. How did the type of coverage affect audience perception?
> 4. How positively or negatively were the messages presented or framed in the coverage?

Media evaluation should include both qualitative and quantitative analysis. Some facets are easy to quantify (How many articles were run? How often were key messages included?), while others such as prominence and tone are more subjective. While prominence, for example, can be graded on a 0 to 10 scale from lowest to highest prominence, such systems implemented by public relations teams have the disadvantage of **observer bias**, where those performing the analysis have a predisposition to favor certain results.[8]

This initial analysis of campaign coverage often leads to broader questions for a wider evaluation of the campaign's results toward objectives. To demonstrate additional nuance, beyond simply reporting the **raw volume** of clips, organizations can share the **relative volume** of coverage.[9] This may be done using time benchmarks (comparing the three months of a campaign to the same three months from the prior year) or competitor benchmarks (comparing three months of an organization's media coverage to the same three months of a competitor's media coverage). Context is added through comparison. Reporting can also be completed using **weighted volume**, based on a scoring system adjusted for the campaign including factors such as organizational prominence, message inclusion, and outlet quality. This approach allows practitioners to quantify the value of media coverage in relation to other coverage and can provide valuable insights related to a campaign's effectiveness, particularly to improve the work of the public relations team over the long term. That said, such metrics alone rarely connect directly to organizational objectives and therefore should not serve as the only method of evaluation. They are first steps toward following K.D. Paine's advice: a focus on measuring "what matters" rather than on vanity metrics.[10]

Digital Evaluation Metrics and Approaches

The abundance of social media channels and owned media, including websites and blogs, has created a niche evaluation realm in the digital space. A significant amount of data is easily accessible, with major social media channels and Google Analytics providing straightforward quantitative data and, often, a variety of easy-to-share charts and tables. On one hand, the digital world is ready made for reporting campaign results

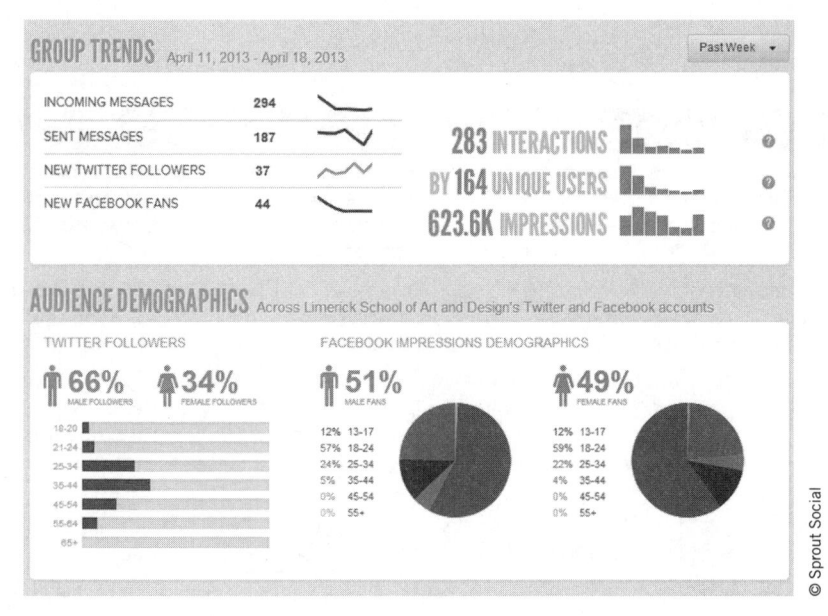

A variety of digital tools help practitioners track the impact of their campaigns, which often involves analyzing data gathered before, during, and after implementation.

to a dashboard-driven C-suite. Yet, such metrics often do not tell the whole story. They may not answer questions of awareness, opinion change, or behavior change and do not necessarily address a campaign's objectives. Gaining 200 new Twitter followers may be a valuable step for a campaign but only if they are the right audience members and actively engage with the organization. They may also be of no additional value. It is in the evaluation process where public relations practitioners must dig deeper into both qualitative and quantitative data in order to understand what is important and what is not.

As with media relations, managing digital channels includes both a monitoring/measurement and evaluation component. The four stages of digital audience outreach can be assessed as exposure (reach and impressions), engagement ("likes" and shares, as well as the sentiment and tone of interactions), influence (respect and relevance), and action (behavior change, impact, and value).[11] These stages are progressive and build on each other. Depending on their goals and objectives, individual campaigns may value specific stages more than others, but action cannot take place without exposure, engagement, and influence.

The process of selecting the appropriate metrics presents an additional challenge, particularly as *reach* and *impressions* may be calculated very differently based on the channel. These can add to the evaluation only within historical content: did a specific campaign attract more attention on Facebook this year over last year? Often, this is based on more mechanical factors such as the types of posts shared (text, links, images, or video, for example) and their priorities within ever-shifting algorithms. It may be useful for communicators to track and optimize their content and posting approaches, but it is less indicative of true impact, making it less valuable from a reporting perspective.

FIGURE 10.1

Exposure, Engagement, Influence, Action

	EXPOSURE	ENGAGEMENT	INFLUENCE	ACTION
Paid	• OTS • Click-throughs • Cost per thousand	• Duration • Branded research • Cost per click	• Purchase consideration • Change in opinion or attitude	• Visit website • Attend event • Download coupons
Earned	• Message inclusion • Impressions • Net positive impressions	• Readership • Awareness • URL visits	• Purchase consideration • Change in opinion or attitude	• Visit the store • Vote for/against • Make a donation
Shared	• OTS • Comment sentiment • Number of followers	• Number of links • Number of retweets • Subscribers	• Tell a friend • Ratings • Reviews	• Redeem coupon • Buy the product • Visit the website
Owned	• Unique visitors • Page views • Search rank	• Return visits • Durations • Subscriptions	• Tell a friend • Change in opinion or attitude	• Download white paper • Request more info

Source: Adapted from Bagnall, Richard. (2014). *Metrics That Matter: Making Sense of Social Media Measurement*. Presented at Public Relations and Corporate Communications Summit, Agra, India.

Developing reporting documents in this way, and explaining the choices to organizational leaders, helps to steer them away from vanity metrics and see social media (and public relations more broadly) as integral to success and deeply connected to organization-wide goals and objectives.

Turning Evaluation into Improvement

Initially, evaluation should take place within the communication department as an opportunity to assess the team's actions. Much of the work performed and lessons learned at this stage may not be entirely useful beyond the department itself. For example, tweaks to pitching and reporter outreach for a media relations campaign, budgetary adjustments to optimize Facebook advertising spends or deciding to change vendors for the next video production project may/may not be relevant to organizational leadership. Evaluating your campaign means understanding what worked and what could have been more effective. Moving from evaluation to reporting becomes the process of selecting the most important and beneficial information to drive improvement for those outside the department or the agency public relations team.

REPORTING ON YOUR CAMPAIGN

Public relations reporting is the process of organizing and sharing the results of campaign evaluation. It should take into account a broad perspective of a campaign's success or failure, convey lessons learned, and reflect the strategic choices of the campaign's execution. Reporting should clearly explain whether objectives have been achieved. While components should be reported in an integrated fashion, paid, earned, shared, and owned tactics often have distinct considerations for accuracy and clarity.

Ideally, campaign reports are presented in-person to key organizational stakeholders. This allows for more detailed explanation and emphasis of major points and the ability to read audience reactions to understand where more explanation may be necessary. Interactivity drives increasingly efficient and effective explanations, as well as a richer discussion regarding how campaign objectives, strategies, and tactics may be improved in the future. Written reporting documents often serve as a more detailed reference and takeaway from such meetings.

The presentation of campaign reports should be selective in content and developed specifically for the audiences at hand. Will leadership be familiar with marketing language? What information does the full group need to know, as opposed to specific departments? While reporting documents are often based on templates, they should allow enough flexibility to highlight different metrics or data based on the campaign and audience. Efforts to get to know executives personally allow for reporting documents to better reflect their priorities, as well as their preferences for receiving information.[12] Such information might drive the decision between bullet points and bar charts or between e-mailed reports and hard-copies presented during a formal meeting.

Objective-driven Reporting

Objectives can serve as an organizing tool for a campaign's results. While not all evaluation results from objectives, they should always be the center of reporting. As strategies and tactics flow from objectives, results can be framed based on whether the individual objectives were achieved. Eisenmann recommends practitioners "link achievements directly to business goals so that C-suite executives will see what PR results mean to them."[13]

Measurable objectives require a particular level of quantitative analysis, but qualitative approaches may also add significant value and insight. For example, a report describing the achievement of a narrow objective related to lead capture at a conference may describe several strategies and tactics used to build relationships and gather contact information for sales leads, including a trade booth, conference-specific social media outreach, expert presentations, earned trade media coverage, as well as advertisements and sponsorships of conference events. Quantitative analysis may show that two-thirds of the leads captured resulted from the trade booth, but qualitative analysis, which could be based on quick debriefing interviews with the on-site sales team after the conference, may show that the most valuable and promising leads came from the expert presentation. Combined, these two levels of evaluation can provide a much more complete picture of the campaign.

Practitioners should also keep in mind that it is possible for objectives to not add up to a campaign's goal. It is worth stepping back to see whether the objectives, however thoughtfully crafted, S.M.A.R.T., and well executed, may not have adequately captured what the organization needed to achieve its goal. This may be an important point to convey during the reporting stage as well as to inform future campaigns.

PRo Tip

REPORTING BEST PRACTICES

- Provide an executive summary of key takeaways.
- Be blunt: Did you reach each objective or not?
- Organize by objectives rather than by channels.
- Always report on what worked . . . and what didn't.
  - Consider what strategies, tactics, and channels made the campaign successful or where they could have been more successful.
  - What internal organizational structures, people, or resources made the campaign successful? Where could priority or emphasis shift next time? In retrospect, were the budget and objectives appropriate?
  - Who from outside your team or department should be thanked or congratulated for their support or efforts toward the campaign?
- Use language accessible to all participants: Be aware of the level of knowledge and expertise of your participants.
  - Choose the report's depth and language accordingly.
  - Explain critical concepts when necessary.
- Include visuals where possible.
  - Graphics can demonstrate success related to output, outtake, and outcome objectives.
  - Visuals should deepen the amount of information included concisely. They should shorten, not lengthen, the overall report.
- Assume the report will not be read in full. Make the contents scannable and reiterate key findings.
- Tie campaign results to broader organizational and competitive goals, objectives, and strategies.
- Move beyond findings: Include recommendations and lessons learned for future campaigns.
  - What was learned about the target public?
  - How should future objectives be structured differently to better reflect organizational goals?
  - What tactics worked particularly well? Why?
    - How can they inform the choice of future tactics?
  - What messages were most effective? Why?
    - What made these messages better vehicles for the campaign?
    - How can this improve the crafting of future messages?

Prioritization: What Information Is Most Important for the Reader?

Initially, practitioners must be able to make a judgment call on what information is the most valuable for the intended audience. This begins with an appropriate understanding of the objectives and the core evaluation questions related to the campaign. The highest priority information should describe how and why a campaign has met or not met its objectives. Which strategies and tactics were most instrumental? What external factors contributed to or hindered execution? What unexpected challenges arose? Weaving this information into a coherent, concise narrative creates an executive summary that should be reinforced throughout the report itself.

Beyond the central storyline of the objectives, the next factor to consider should be the takeaways: What information can contribute the most to inform future projects? This may include insights about how key stakeholders react to certain strategies, how competitors take advantage of an organization's lack of resources dedicated to a specific channel, or even information regarding the timing and scheduling of events. Small details can make a difference and often speak to larger issues. Positioning such recommendations early on in reporting allows the audience to glean immediate value from the necessary quantitative and qualitative research that occurs as campaigns are executed.

Additional areas that are valuable to include in the reporting structure include any challenges, surprises, and/or outright failures. By directly addressing any unexpected events resulting from a campaign, practitioners highlight additional areas of learning and improvement. Each begs the question, why did this catch us by surprise? The process of answering such questions provides a unique opportunity to demonstrate continuous improvement for the public relations team. Sharing such insights with the broader organization can also help other areas anticipate the same challenges and identify the same blind spots related to knowledge of audiences, markets, and the competitive environment.

Format: How Should Your Information Be Best Presented to Your Audience?

Reporting for a specific audience requires appropriate document development to facilitate the delivery of relevant information. Practitioners should ask themselves several questions: What background does the audience have on the campaign and on integrated communication? What organizational conventions exist? How much information are they used to receiving? Understanding their background might, for example, point toward employing more/fewer visuals, a sense of the most valuable overall length and depth, and how communication-centric the content should be.

Expectations play a key role, but practitioners should also consider timing to be an important factor. In some cases, a quick preliminary report may be what leadership requires in order to support key decisions on a pressing strategic challenge. In other instances, they may prefer the accessible depth of a well-constructed, detailed summary with appendices for more information. An extra week or two to complete a full report may matter to the audience, or the circumstance may not necessarily be urgent in nature.

PESO: SPECIAL REPORTING CONSIDERATIONS

Paid Media

An advantage of paid media, particularly within digital opportunities, is the variety and depth of available metrics to track and evaluate success. The danger for practitioners comes when there is an overwhelming volume of data. Determining the value and relevance of tracking and reporting tools, and the subsequent approach, is often half the battle. Working with vendors, whether they are advertising agencies, media outlets, or event planners, should mean having access to the metrics they compile on your campaigns—and they should do their best to present that information in a useful format for your reporting efforts.

Reporting for paid media should have an explicit focus on the budget. Was the spend sufficient? Did the content run for the most effective length of time? Was it allocated to the most effective mix channels in the right proportions? Did the dollar spend have the desired audience impact? As there is more control with the placement and messages for paid media, these factors can be more heavily scrutinized. Recommendations based on how to better scale and optimize the spend for future campaigns are always valuable.

Additionally, as there tends to be more data to share, organization and presentation becomes more critical. Tables, charts, and graphs should be scannable, contextualized, and only contain as much information as needed. Practitioners should only include relevant data, and its purpose within the overall report must be clear.[14]

Earned Media

Evaluation and reporting of media relations should reflect the motivation or purpose for the campaign itself. As described in the evaluation section, it is important to

Practitioners should work with vendors and media outlets to capture data about the impact and influence of paid media outreach.

showcase the impact of media relations, not just the coverage itself. Media relations evaluation should also include qualitative and quantitative components (for example, the value of building a new relationship with a key media contact, as well as the share-of-voice percentage in key publications). It should also, whenever possible, reinforce the impact of media coverage on audiences, including actions such as sending traffic back to organizational websites (look for spikes in visitors on days with significant media coverage) or awareness changes (measured in a pretest/posttest survey of publics). Research tools such as content analysis can play a significant role in demonstrating value, as well as understanding potential areas for improvement in future campaigns.

Organizational leaders also should be reminded of the value of earned-media coverage toward credibility. When distinguishing between paid and earned coverage, for example, it is valuable to bring up the increased credibility that publics see when organizational messages are conveyed through a trusted, appropriate media outlet, rather than coming directly from the organization.

Shared Media

As described earlier in this chapter, social media reporting provides a wide range of easily accessible data for reporting. The downside to this data-rich environment is that practitioners must wade through many irrelevant metrics to find those that connect with campaign objectives and organizational goals. Is raising awareness important? Impressions, page visits, or the right clicks or downloads may be valuable. Surveying retention of the message, event, brand, or product at hand would be best. Building relationships? Engagement through social channels can demonstrate useful activity, and analysis of tone or message content can unpack its types and qualities. Don't simply measure the size of a community, but determine the number of active members who meet a campaign's target audience. See if the number of active members is larger than in your competitors' communities. Aiming for online sales or fund-raising goals? Connect social media outreach (along with owned media channels) to Google Analytics to track buyers or donors to determine what directed them to your site. Knowledge from any of these areas can help move beyond speaking only to existing digital communities and counting Facebook "likes."

Social media can also be analyzed qualitatively as well. When reviewing engagement, for example, it's important to select key conversation themes and examples to share. Such insights can often help explain or expand on quantitative findings. A brand's tone, voice, and character cannot be fully captured in quantitative data, and reporting on the reactions and interactions among digital communities based on these factors yields valuable information for how organizations are perceived.

Owned Media

Like social media, organizational websites, e-mail newsletters, and other digital owned media provide a variety of metrics through the use of Google Analytics, MailChimp distribution data, and other various reporting tools. They can connect particular drivers (such as an e-mail newsletter) to users who take action on the website by filling out a form, purchasing a product, or making a donation. The more insights

Google Analytics provides critical insights into web traffic that practitioners should use to evaluate campaigns.

the public relations team has about the types of audience members most likely to take action, the better. Additionally, these tools can help identify issues and challenges that may arise during campaign implementation. Are digital forms too complicated for the average user? Many will begin but not complete the form. Is the form too hard to find on the page? Many will go to the page and not click on the form. From a reporting perspective, these findings allow a practitioner to explain the minutia of a campaign when needed but also defend the decisions made throughout. Not all measurement details are relevant to an executive or client audience, but those relating to specific objectives can easily become valuable insights organization wide.

Other types of owned media, from a refurbished office space to event-based outreach, can be more difficult to measure in detail, but these challenges can be overcome with a bit of planning. For example, putting processes in place to ask (both digitally and in-person) how new customers found out about your business can identify how different channels, such as the website, are informing users. Digital tracking can also support traditional owned-media efforts. A print magazine can still reference a distinct website landing page, allowing organizations to see which of their tactics sent more visitors. Tracking event attendance is relatively straightforward, but developing a brief qualitative survey can help to provide even more useful insights about publics, successes, and improvements for future outreach.

Integrated Reporting

While various channels require distinct reporting tools and approaches, strategic communication campaigns often are best served by integrated reporting. It is "highly desirable" to combine media coverage from different channels into the same evaluation and reporting documents and formats.[15] Not only does this represent the convergence of media outlets, it reinforces for leadership and clients that the content of the coverage is ultimately as important as the source. As objectives should ideally reflect behavioral and opinion-based change rather than process, reporting can be organized around strategies and tactics contributing to specific objectives. One objective may necessitate paid, shared, and owned approaches, while a second may have focused on earned and shared strategies and tactics. Organizing and connecting the reporting around objectives rather than specific channels reinforces strategic integration. It frames public relations as a solution focused rather than as fragmented and isolated. It positions organizational goals above the vanity metrics of Twitter followers and website hits. Fully integrated reporting best supports the counselor role of public relations as a conduit, a bridge, and a sounding board between and among organizations and their publics.

Integrated reporting may necessitate additional context to ensure clarity for readers. Practitioners should interpret results and connect strategies to impact in order to ensure which findings resonate. What campaign elements were successful across channels? How and why did particular tactics work well together (or not work well together)? What do integrated findings say about specific audiences? Integration should seem natural and obvious to executives or clients, but that often only happens when it is presented in a way that highlights the connections behind such choices.

CONCLUSION

Evaluation and reporting are critical steps to understanding what happened during any campaign, but they also serve as excellent examples of the larger strategic role public relations plays in helping organizations succeed. They demonstrate outreach into the environment and generate direct feedback as to what approach, messages, strategies, and tactics succeed or fail. Evaluative research provides rich insights about stakeholders and publics that are often insightful for organizational leaders beyond the realm of communication. Reporting processes give practitioners the opportunity to make the case that their work matters relative to organizational goals. Together, this understanding of a campaign's impact and the ability to effectively and efficiently share the insights gleaned during and after execution allow public relations practitioners to show their full value.

THINK CRITICALLY

1. Why is it important to evaluate objectives in terms of both achievement and relevance to the campaign?

2. What information is critical for the communication team, and what should be reported to leadership?

3. How might the specific internal audience impact the reporting choices for campaign results?

4. How does evaluation contribute to improving future campaigns?

KEY TERMS

Control group 168
I.M.P.A.C.T. (mnemonic) 169
Observer bias 170
Raw volume 170
Relative volume 170
Weighted volume 170

CONCEPT CASE: REPORTING RESULTS—EQUALITY TODAY'S ANNUAL MEETING

You've been asked to prepare a five-minute presentation for the annual meeting of Equality Today's board of directors and major donors. It is a short window to convince these elite stakeholders and supporters of the strategic value provided by public relations. The campaign is still in progress (final results are not in), but you'll need to begin organizing, creating, and formatting your presentation. The immediate audience will not be well versed in public relations and marketing language; will not have been involved in prior discussions about goals, objectives, strategies, and tactics; and is lacking the internal perspective on the challenges to the campaign's success. What reporting approaches can help you win over this potentially tough crowd?

- What elements could you use to set the scene? How might you use developmental research as part of the presentation?
- Knowing the organization's national reach, what would be the most critical social media metrics to include?
- With fund-raising as a goal, how might an integrated reporting approach connect paid, earned, shared, and owned media to support this objective?

CASE STUDY: CANS GET YOU COOKING

Can Manufacturers with Hunter Public Relations
Based on PRSA Silver Anvil Winner
Campaign Focus: Consumer Products

Research/Diagnosis

Recognizing that the canned food industry has seen a gradual and steady decline in sales over the last decade, the Can Manufacturers Institute tasked Hunter PR with developing a national consumer-facing marketing campaign to help drive increased canned food usage—purchase *and* consumption—over time. The campaign, its strategy, and messaging built on new comprehensive values-based consumer research, which identified the core target publics and the insights into consumer attitudes toward canned foods.

Developmental Research and Insights

- *Primary*: Proprietary quantitative and qualitative research revealed that while canned foods are known to deliver long shelf life, convenience, and taste, the lesser-known benefits of canned foods would have the greatest potential to encourage publics to feel confident about using canned foods more often in day-to-day meal planning, increasing the potential for usage and sales.
- *Secondary*: According to Simmons data, rather than trying to convert light canned

food users (who are less likely to be swayed) or speaking to heavy canned food users (who are already maxing out usage), the medium canned food user* was identified as the primary target. Media consumption habits of these consumers were analyzed from which a detailed media channel plan was developed and applied.

- *Primary Target:* Medium canned food user*, women 25–54, household income <$75k, main decision maker in household purchases, with one or more children.
- *Secondary Target:* Broader audience of medium canned food users* including men with children in the household.
(*Two to eight meals every two weeks that include canned foods)

Objectives

1. Create positive conversation among influencers/consumers around the lesser-known benefits of canned foods.
2. Develop an informative consumer-facing campaign inspiring and empowering the target to create more meals—more often—with canned foods.
3. Generate widespread and high impact, yearlong media coverage communicating campaign key messages.
4. Engage canned food brands and retailers in the campaign and encourage them to carry campaign messages forward to their consumer audiences, amplifying efforts.

Strategies

- Develop compelling messaging strategy to help shift the perception of canned foods from simply convenient and inexpensive to delivering (1) sealed in nutrition, freshness, and flavor; (2) high-quality, easy homemade meals; (3) locked-in nutrients, picked at the peak of ripeness; and (4) a means of wasting less food and saving money.
- Create content to disseminate across paid, earned, and owned media channels that is compelling to retailers and consumer packaged goods (CPG) canned food brands. Recurring messages include key canned food health benefits and contributions to success in daily meal planning.

Tactics
Paid

- A multiplatform, integrated media partnership with the Scripps Networks and Cooking Channel star Kelsey Nixon was executed for two key seasonal promotions; National Canned Food Month (February) and Back-to-School (September).

  ○ Campaign messaging was delivered to a broad audience in a credible editorial environment, demonstrating the benefits of canned foods.
  ○ Rich long- and short-form content was created, including a custom thirty-minute special, *Cans Make the Meal with Kelsey Nixon*, and a series of four thirty-second "pro-mercials" that aired in commercial time on Cooking Channel and Food Network TV.
  ○ The content, which was also available online and on-demand, plus a customized

digital ad campaign with robust flighting across all Scripps online food sites, helped make *Cans Make the Meal with Kelsey Nixon* the #1 most viewed content on cookingChannelTV.com.

- A partnership was facilitated with Parade Media Group, which included advertorial and editorial features in two print issues of *dash* and two Parade.com e-newsletters, as well as a five-week digital and online presence on Parade.com. The partnership offered a unique opportunity to zero in on the target demographic and deliver campaign messages directly to them via canned food-inspired meal solutions shared online and in print.

- A four-week mobile game integration with Zynga's Farmville 2: Country Escape was spearheaded. Customized in-game features allowed players to harvest produce from their virtual farms and to can their harvest to lock in nutrition, freshness, and flavor. As players engaged with the game, they came into contact with campaign messages and interacted with game characters to learn more about Cans Get You Cooking and the benefits of canned foods.

- The campaign's search engine marketing (SEM) initiative was implemented, targeting consumers on Google already searching for "what to make for dinner" or "easy recipes," among hundreds of other key word/phrase triggers, driving them to CansGetYouCooking.com, where they were exposed to campaign messages, the thirty-minute special with Kelsey Nixon, canned foods recipes, and much more.

Earned

- Proactive and reactive outreach was conducted to print and online editors, TV producers, and food/lifestyle experts, maintaining a regular stream of news and information about the benefits of cooking with canned foods.

- Fifty-six Cans Get You Cooking Canbassadors were enlisted to promote the benefits of canned foods on their blogs and social media channels, including Eighty MPH Mom (https://eightymphmom.com/2013/07/cans-get-you-cooking-easy-meals-using-canned-foods-cansgetyoucooking.html), Dough Mess Tic (https://doughmesstic.com/2014/12/23/cans-get-you-cooking), and Cupcake Diaries (https://www.cupcakediariesblog.com/2015/02/cans-get-cooking.html). Blogger influence among the target consumer continues to gain traction and be a strategic and successful way to deliver campaign messages and content.

Shared

- A Facebook community of target consumers was built to educate and engage with campaign messages. Bloggers and food influencers were engaged on Twitter, and campaign messaging was inserted into existing conversations about cooking with canned foods. Also, four highly engaging, well-attended Twitter parties were hosted throughout the year, helping increase levels of engagement. Home cooks were inspired with recipes, DIY craft ideas, and surprising facts about the sustainability of canned foods on Pinterest.

Owned

- The online hub, CansGetYouCooking.com, was created and launched, bringing canned foods into the contemporary culinary conversation via recipes, recipe videos, nutrition news, information about sustainability, and more.

- Point-of-sale (POS) and digital assets were developed and designed, carrying campaign messages for local and national retailers across the country for in-store and online promotions.

Implementation

Paying close attention to the research, Hunter PR saw an opportunity to elevate and change the conversation around canned foods and the ability to offer wholesome, home cooked meals. Thus, Hunter PR launched *Cans Get You Cooking*, an insight-driven campaign to promote the benefits of cooking with canned foods through a strategic mix of traditional, social, and integrated media tactics.

Reporting/Evaluation

- According to a study on canned food attitudes and usage conducted by Radius in 2014, there was a measurable increase in positive associations with canned foods, as well as consumption, with 28 percent of consumers reporting increased positive feelings about canned foods and 26 percent of consumers reporting they were using canned foods more often. Importantly, change in the reported use of canned foods increased in direct correlation to exposure to the campaign through key media partnerships.
- There was an 11 percent increase in volume of conversation around the benefits of canned foods on social media (Twitter and Facebook); moving from net neutral to net positive conversation.
- A 17.1 percent ACV (All-Commodity Volume) was achieved at retail as of February 2015.
- The campaign garnered more than 724 million media impressions and 19,000 placements, 57 percent over the goal. Key message pull-through averaged 93.5 percent, with the majority of placements including two or more key messages:
  - The Scripps partnership delivered more than 165.6 million TV and online impressions.
  - The Parade Media Group integration reached more than 64 million consumers.
  - The partnership with Zynga delivered more than 164 million message impressions—players entered the game twice as many times as usual. A Vizu study confirmed that players' purchase consideration of canned foods increased as a result of the integration and gameplay during the event.
  - Noteworthy national earned print, online, and TV media placements included *O, The Oprah Magazine*, *Every Day with Rachael Ray*, *Huffington Post*, *Today Show*, and *Fox & Friends*.
  - Canbassadors' unique branded blog and social media posts reached more than 17.6 million readers.
  - Since February 2013, the campaign attracted more than 122,000 Facebook, 73,000 Twitter, and 2,670 Pinterest followers.
  - The SEM initiative drove more than 6 million impressions and a 0.94 click-through rate (CTR).
  - There were more than 114,000 visits to the Cans Get You Cooking hub, which amounts to roughly 846 visits per day.

Theories

Diffusion theory asserts that people make decisions or accept ideas following ordered steps: awareness, interest, trial, evaluation, and adoption.[16] The Can Manufacturers Institute public relations campaign used multiple steps to accomplish goal. They were able to raise awareness and prompt interest from their target audience to incorporate canned food into their daily lives.

Using **Maslow's hierarchy of needs**, practitioners can predict that people listen to messages based on their personal needs. These needs have been arranged in a pyramid from the most basic physiological needs for survival to the most complex ones dealing with self-fulfillment. The Can Manufacturer's Institute conducted research to find out more about its target audience, including key consumer preferences, lifestyles, and attitudes. Their research helped inform behavioral attitudes. Messages were crafted that resonated with their target audience's needs.

11 Formulating an Integrated Campaign—Case Studies

> Even award-winning campaigns can be improved. Throughout the case studies in this chapter, you'll find question boxes asking you to apply the approaches presented earlier in the book including S.M.A.R.T. objectives, channel-focused strategies, and reporting with the audience in mind.

There are a variety of campaign types with which all public relations professionals should be familiar and comfortable. This final chapter provides campaigns that cover the areas of product marketing, activism, community and consumer engagement, crisis communication, global and multicultural outreach, and internal communication.

PRODUCT MARKETING

Integrated public relations campaigns continue to be an effective approach for product marketing, particularly in the context of newsworthy opportunities such as product launches, technological innovation, or creative customer engagement.

Particularly as consumers become less likely to consume media through traditional television broadcasts (still the largest portion of the advertising industry by revenue), earned media has become an increasingly vital part of the marketing mix for a wide variety of for-profit and nonprofit organizations.[1] When public relations is deeply integrated with marketing efforts, it has the potential to strengthen the discipline's position within organizations and bring additional perspective and insights.[2]

BREWING INSPIRATION TO ENGAGE COFFEE FANS

Caribou Coffee with Exponent PR and Colle+McVoy
Based on PRSA Silver Anvil Winner
Campaign Focus: Consumer Products

Caribou Coffee is a regional specialty coffee and espresso retailer competing against both national ubiquitous Goliaths and local trendy third-wave Davids. At the end of 2013, packaged coffee sales were at an all-time low, and Caribou had closed roughly eighty stores across the nation. Caribou needed to refocus and shift priority to its core regions.

The consumer coffee market is competitive and saturated. Coffee beans, new drinks, and bakery items are launched constantly to woo customers and capture additional share of wallet. A complex mix of brand identification, new products, and pricing drives this fragmented and difficult-to-navigate marketplace.

Research/Diagnosis

Exponent's secondary research into key industry data from the quick service restaurant industry, which follows coffeehouse trends, showed consumers favor brands that invite them to interact. Through primary research conducted with customers, Exponent identified the core consumer insight: "Coffee is more than something I drink, it's a personal experience that brightens my day." Social listening also revealed that, relative to other competitive brands, Caribou customers are creators, people with wide-ranging interests, and a desire to do, not just experience.

Armed with this consumer insight, Exponent crafted a year-long campaign focused on capturing the imagination of and sparking inspiration within this passionate group. Exponent's consumer segmentation research revealed the audiences with the biggest potential to engage with the campaign. Caribou charged Exponent PR with finding a bold new approach to marketing for the 23-year-old brand, one that deepened relationships with existing fans and attracted attention for its creative tactics. Audience mapping helped to further flesh out a profile of key target audiences.

- *Quality conscious*: Women age 25 to 44 who are married and may have children at home. They spend more than $58 each month at coffee shops.

- *Morning commuter*: Women and men ages 25 to 34 and 45 to 54 who are married and may have children at home. They spend more than $45 each month at coffee shops.

- *Treat seeker*: Primarily women ages 25 to 44, often with children at home. They spend at least $40 per month on coffee. This audience is tapped in, extremely social online and offline, and already spends a lot of quality time with brands, whether in retail locations or at home.

Objectives

There were two overarching objectives Caribou coffee was looking to achieve.
Business objective: Drive traffic and sales in retail stores.
Communications objective: Build sustained awareness of and engagement with the Caribou brand, leveraging media relations and social media channels.

> How might you rewrite these objectives with the S.M.A.R.T. framework in mind?

Strategies

To achieve their goals, the following strategies were established:

- Engage consumers in product development.
- Leverage seasonal topics to further engagement.
- Create content that reaches beyond the category itself.
- Refresh a cause-marketing program through integrated events and social media engagement.

> How could you integrate channel selection into these strategies?

Tactics

By developing and implementing a complex, multitiered, multilayered paid, earned, shared, and owned campaign, Exponent and Caribou executed a number of tactics through the year. Consumer engagement was supported on social media encouraging fans to interact and share content.

Shared

In early 2014, when packaged coffee sales were at an all-time low across the category, Caribou was—for the first time—simultaneously launching a new coffee product called Real Inspiration Blend at coffee houses and through retail distribution channels. Using the insight that Caribou's fans are makers and creators, as well as above-average Pinterest users, Exponent turned to fans to co-create the new blend. To engage consumers in the product development process, they asked fans to share what motivated them by pining images with the hashtag #InspireCaribou. Caribou's roastmasters used these images to create the recipe card for a truly one-of-a-kind coffee, Real Inspiration Blend. Playing off the images, the new flavor is "bright like a sunrise and bold like a lion, with a hint of sweetness."

In addition, the team leveraged seasonal topics to further deepen engagement. All good pranks take careful planning, and an April Fools' gag is no exception. With Exponent, Caribou drove awareness and showcased the playful nature of the brand by telling fans the company had developed a solution for coffee stains: Clear Coffee. Clear Coffee would eliminate coffee-stained teeth and mug rings while retaining full flavor. Key visuals (including faux Clear Coffee packaging and an infographic) earned extensive media attention and social engagement, thanks to help from Colle+McVoy. Most importantly, this regional brand shared a national laugh with its fans and followers.

Paid + Shared

To unveil the newly co-created coffee, Exponent and its advertising partner, Colle+McVoy, built a five-story Living Pinterest Board spanning the full height of the Mall of America Rotunda. The installation set the stage for engagement through events, mini-inspiration sessions, and plenty of coffee sampling. The Living Pinterest Board didn't just drive social content and engagement. It also provided a powerful platform for media relations and story sharing with key brand messages: its new product, the brand's playfulness, and an openness to co-creation.

Owned

Summer in the Midwest, Caribou's primary geographic focus, is fleeting. Caribou encouraged fans to "Stay Awake for It," and enjoy every moment of summer, surprising and delighting fans all season long. Exponent worked with Caribou to celebrate June 21, the summer solstice and longest day of the year, with caffeinated messaging and plenty of samples and branded swag to help consumers make the most of the day. In addition, the team created a "Barista Barge" that cruised Minnesota lakes during busy summer weekends, offering iced coffee samples. Local media and Caribou's social fans engaged with the brand's great summer surprises.

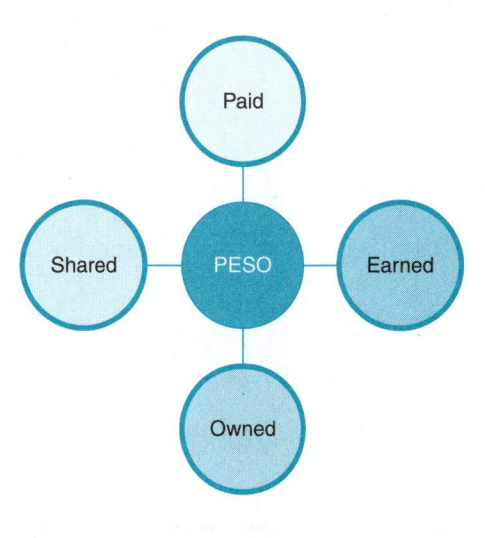

Paid + Owned + Shared

Every fall, in coffee shops around the country, each brand features its unique take on pumpkin beverages. Exponent knew that Caribou's audience would seek outdoor photo opportunities during this picturesque time of year and created an engaging tactic to differentiate themselves from competitors. The team developed a scavenger hunt for twelve painted, golden pumpkins, called "Yummmkins." Clues on hiding places were shared via Twitter, and photos of the winners (who won coffee for a year and other prizes) were shared via Instagram and Facebook. Guests sought the Yummmkins and engaged online during September, and partnerships with local bloggers helped engage a broader audience. Social media shares and sales of fall beverages soared.

Earned + Shared

With declining Black Friday sales and aggressive competitive expansion and promotion, Caribou knew that one-time seasonal outreach would not be enough. Exponent created a six-week plan to maintain a steady drumbeat of outreach and engagement throughout the holiday season. Exponent worked with prominent regional baking bloggers I AM BAKER, Ambitious Kitchen, and Satisfy My Sweet Tooth to create cookie recipes using coffee and ginger, a key ingredient in one of Caribou's new beverages. The recipes were shared across social media and the winning recipe was featured by BuzzFeed. The blogger program made a relevant, compelling vehicle for pitching traditional broadcast media, resulting in live baking demonstrations with Caribou's culinary experts. Exponent also identified a growing interest in specialized flavors that captured the spirit of holidays, such as the Midnight Mocha available only on Black Friday weekend. Capitalizing on these special occasions and inventing popular limited-time-only drinks were integral parts of the campaign and resulting coverage.

Owned + Shared

Amy's Blend is a long-standing fund-raising tradition honoring Caribou's first roastmaster, who lost her life to breast cancer in 1995. To reinvigorate the annual tradition, Exponent and Colle+McVoy tapped Eric Rieger, aka HOTTEA, an internationally acclaimed yarn artist. Exponent commissioned him to create the Arch of Hope, a colorful 60-by-40-foot installation made from more than four miles of yarn. HOTTEA creates installations to give audiences a sense of warmth and comfort, precisely the feeling Caribou wanted to exude during National Breast Cancer Awareness Month, to uplift those affected by the disease. Knowing Caribou's Arch of Hope would make for a stunning photo, Exponent partnered with prominent Instagrammer and photographer Eric Mueller to host an event on Worldwide InstaMeet Day that drew the region's top Instagrammers. They shared their experience with the Arch of Hope in real life and through photos, generating millions of impressions.

Implementation

In order to succeed, Exponent knew Caribou needed to go beyond typical product launch and digital content tactics to leverage a deeper engagement strategy. Standout events, creative executions, unique sampling experiences, digital activations, and co-creation with guests helped Caribou enjoy an outstanding year.

Reporting/Evaluation

Business objective: Drive traffic and sales in retail stores.

Traffic and sales in 2014 were strong, despite competitors' aggressive promotions and discounting. Monthly year-over-year store sales (a critical indicator in the retail industry) steadily exceeded previous year sales, highlighted by key seasonal wins:

- A year of strong sales kicked off with a 7 percent increase in in-store traffic during the first quarter promotions.
- The summer was one of Caribou's best ever in terms of traffic and sales. Caribou was able to reduce discounts and still improve in-store visits and overall sales.

Communications objective: Build sustained awareness of and engagement with the Caribou brand, leveraging media relations and social media channels.

The best year to-date for Caribou Coffee in terms of social media engagement and media relations results was 2014. Most importantly, the brand's fans interacted and engaged—whether at live events or online. Caribou reached new levels of participation for its core campaigns and exceeded expectations for new programs.

Earned

The quality and careful targeting of media placements drove engagement in key markets and among core audiences, generating nearly 500 placements and more than 350 million impressions.

- The year was such a success that national media covered the brand a number of times, including *Mashable, Digiday, USA Today, Fast Company, Huffington Post,* and *Bloomberg Businessweek.*

- Coverage in Minneapolis, Caribou's hometown market, outpaced previous years, with multiple local TV segments, feature placements on drive-time radio stations, and newspaper and magazine coverage.

- Trade placements helped elevate the brand among influential industry media such as Fast Casual, Nation's Restaurant News, QSR, Eater, The Daily Meal, Specialty Coffee Retailer, and Foodservice Monthly.

> How might Caribou have used content analysis techniques to deepen their measurement and understanding of media coverage? How, if at all, would competitive coverage analysis be useful in this situation?

Shared

In 2014, Caribou experienced a 19 percent year-over-year increase in social media engagement across channels.

Organic mentions increased by an average of 7 percent across all channels, and impressions increased by 64 percent year-over-year.

Multiple subcampaigns were executed on behalf of Caribou in 2014, all of which included specific hashtags. The combined reach of all campaign hashtags generated more than 24.4 million organic impressions.

Instagram

- Caribou's Instagram following increased by 176 percent over the course of the year.

- The average likes per post on Instagram increased by 195 percent year-over-year.

- Organic Instagram posts including the hashtag #cariboucoffee grew by 33 percent compared to 2014.

Facebook, Twitter, and Pinterest

- Caribou's Facebook following grew by 12 percent year-over-year.

- Caribou's Pinterest following grew by 57 percent year-over-year.

- Caribou's Twitter following grew by 52 percent year-over-year.

Theories

This campaign clearly reflects a two-step flow approach to public communication with its use of opinion leaders at multiple stages. Throughout the campaign, Caribou leveraged relationships with bloggers, reporters, and social media influencers in order to improve its credibility and stay top of mind with current and potential customers.

Model

With significant communication and collaboration between Caribou, its agency partners, and customers, the campaign used a symmetrical model. Opening contests and opportunities for consumers to share their creativity became a point of pride for the campaign and the brand as a whole.

ACTIVISM

Through grassroots movements and community support, organizations, people, and corporations use media to advocate for a variety of social justice issues. Scholars offer several definitions of *activism*. Some believe that it is "an attempt to change the behavior of another party through the application of concerted power,"[3] while others state that activism is a "group of two or more individuals who organize in order to influence another public or publics through action."[4] Activists seek to influence organizational actions, public policy, and social norms and values. Activists can be community members, individuals, or groups of people, customers or potential customers, investors or potential investors, and also employees or potential employees.

ONE FOR ALL: MISSISSIPPIANS' FIGHT FOR A NEW FLAG

Case Study by Melody Fisher, PhD, from Mississippi State University and Leslie Rasmussen, PhD, from Xavier University of Ohio
Campaign Focus: Advocacy, Awareness, Public Policy

The 2015 mass killing of nine African Americans attending a church prayer service in Charleston, South Carolina, reignited the issue of the confederate symbol's placement on the Mississippi state flag. The shooter, Dylann Roof, collected confederate paraphernalia in his home and cited racism as his motivation to kill the parishioners.[5] The Flag for All Mississippians Coalition used this event as the impetus to publicize concerns with the state flag and propose a change.

Research/Diagnosis

The Flag for All Mississippians Coalition conducted secondary research to gather background information about the Mississippi state flag. The organization found that the flag was redesigned in 1894 to incorporate the Confederate battle flag, and that Mississippi is the only state that still incorporates the Confederate emblem in its flag.

© Flag for All Mississippian Coalition

In 2001, state residents voted to select an official state flag. An earlier court case determined that the flag design was a "political decision," so the Mississippi State Legislature decided to schedule a special election for voters to select an official Mississippi flag.[6] More than 65 percent of Mississippi voters elected to keep the state flag including its Confederate battle cross instead of a newly designed flag.

After the mass shooting in South Carolina, coalition members conducted informal interviews with approximately 100 Mississippians, the majority of whom found the current state flag to be

- Harmful to economic progress, including tourism and investment ventures
- A symbol of racism and oppression
- A symbol of southern heritage

Objectives

The goal of the coalition campaign was to support the creation of a state flag that represented all Mississippians regardless of their race, religion, education, or socioeconomic status. The coalition's major objectives were to

- Develop the Flag for All Mississippians Act
- Collect over 100,000 valid signatures for petition to put the issue on election ballot for statewide vote
- Advocate for public opinion change to move in the direction of a new flag—a shift from the 2001 referendum

> What changes could make these objectives fit with the S.M.A.R.T. guidelines?

Strategy

The strategy used within this campaign was a grassroots approach to mobilize supporters and confront any opposition. Mississippi has a long history of galvanizing support from underrepresented groups dating back to the Civil Rights Movement. The concept of amassing individuals without political power attracts media and opposition attention, while also educating and creating awareness about the issues.

Tactics

A series of integrated communication strategies were planned which included the following:

- Website
- Rallies

- Earned media/media relations
- Social media pages
- Endorsements by local opinion leaders

Earned + Owned

The Flag for All Mississippians organized two rallies to create awareness about their campaign. During an October 2015 rally, more than 300 people marched, sang, chanted, and displayed signs supporting change to the flag.[7] Additionally, in February 2016, the coalition chartered buses from different regions of the state to the Capitol so that more Mississippians could attend. More than 200 rally participants were given the opportunity to sign a petition and listen to several guest speakers, including local civil rights attorneys, activists, political candidates, and religious leaders. The success of the Jackson, Mississippi-based rallies prompted local activists to invite the coalition to headline rallies in the towns of Natchez, Webb, and the Mississippi Gulf Coast.

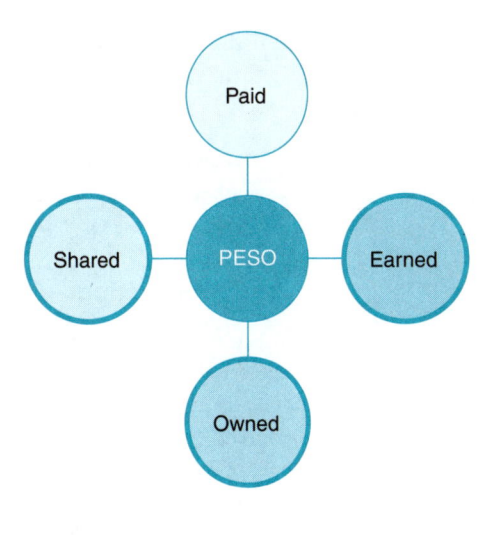

The rallies garnered the attention of several local media outlets. Numerous stories and articles were written in the state daily *The Clarion Ledger*; regional paper, the *Natchez Democrat*; and alternative paper *The Jackson Free Press*.[8,9] Stories were aired on Jackson's CBS and NBC affiliate stations. National media outlets also took notice after the coalition partnered with several organizations and held a rally on the steps of the United States Capitol in June 2016. Fifty Mississippians took the 18-hour bus trip on National Flag Day to generate support from lawmakers to change the flag. In addition to local outlets, the story was covered in several national media channels, including *USA Today*, *Washington Post*, *The Times Picayune*, and *Rollingout* magazines, CNN, and was written about in dozens of blogs.

Shared

The majority of the coalition's communications were transmitted using social media. Its Facebook page featured events, news clips, photos, and videos to keep more than 400 followers abreast of daily activities and progress. This platform allowed followers access to post-related news clips and updates; however, the coalition did not engage in two-way communication by responding to comments or posts.

Owned

The coalition's owned media served as a way for audiences to learn its background, purpose, and objectives. The website, newmsflag.org, provided background information about the coalition's members and purpose. The site included endorsements by religious leaders of various denominations across the state, adding credibility to the organization's mission. The site also provided visitors the opportunity to join the cause. For journalists, a form was included for inquiries and interview requests.

> How might the coalition have used additional integrated tactics or otherwise changed its tactical approach to increase connection with publics?

Implementation

On August 28, 2015, the coalition initiated its campaign by filing the "Flag for all Mississippians Act" with the Secretary of State.[10] Upon filing, signatures needed to be collected to send to the state legislature. The coalition's many rallies educated the public on the current flag's symbolism while it also created awareness about the campaign to change the flag.

Local opinion leaders served as spokespersons for the campaign. From the pulpit, several area pastors encouraged their congregants to sign the petition and join the campaign. These leaders were also publicized on the coalition's website. Its website and social media pages gave external audiences the opportunity to join the campaign and stay abreast of coalition events and activities.

Reporting

The campaign was suspended on April 21, 2016, the last day of the 2016 regular legislative session. At the end of the eight-month period, the coalition did not gather enough signatures, nor receive majority support from lawmakers in either the State House or Senate. At the time, the coalition planned to continue campaigning for a new state flag. Its June 2016 trip to Washington, D.C., illuminated the organization's ongoing mission and placed its fight on a national stage, expanding awareness.

As with many grassroots campaigns, this effort was championed without a formal budget. The coalition received charter bus transportation and funding from private donors and absorbed other costs through the coalition.

Theories

Framing Theory: The coalition was tasked with reframing the state flag as a symbol of racism and oppression when challenging opponents who believed the flag represented southern heritage. At its root, framing involves placing topics in a context that provides meaning and pointing an audience toward which parts and pieces of a specific image, narrative, or issue are most important.[11] The coalition had to move people from viewing the Confederacy battle cross in the flag as part of Mississippi's history and refocus on its meaning for many residents past and present: the Confederate battle cross is a symbol of racism and oppression. While the coalition was unsuccessful in obtaining the necessary 100,000 signatures to bring the issue to a statewide ballot, the group was able to gain media coverage and mobilize publics based on its framing of the flag. It was able to draw attention to a serious and culturally significant issue.

Contingency Theory: Used in public relations to focus on the unique and complex understanding of a situation needed as part of the research and planning process, contingency theory is relevant in understanding the coalition's stance, especially when considering the strong ideological roots tied to the issue.[12] Many factors influence an organization's decision to act at a particular level of engagement along the theory's continuum of advocacy to accommodation, including the degree of political and social support. In this case, the coalition faced minimal political and social support, thus it was necessary to take a strong advocacy stance—one centered on reframing the flag's meaning.

Model

This campaign employed the **two-way asymmetrical model** of public relations. While the campaign addressed residents' long-standing perspectives and opinions, organizers were not interested in gaining feedback from opponents in a way that shifted the coalition's position. The two-way asymmetrical model generally focuses on short-term attitude change and often takes a strong advocacy position. It is difficult to change long-held ideological attitudes, values, or beliefs. Unfortunately, the campaign was unsuccessful in its initial attempt to rally political and social support to the degree necessary for the state requirements. In one sense, the redesign of the flag requires more than short-term attitude change. Short-term change might persuade citizens to sign the petition and force a statewide vote, but it would not be enough to secure the needed long-term support.

ENGAGEMENT

Organizations use a variety of integrated campaign strategies and tactics to engage with audiences from customers to community members. Whether it's a nonprofit bringing new supporters to their cause or a company rewarding its best customers, genuine engagement with important publics sits at the heart of many successful campaigns. The PESO model reflects the wide variety of outreach approaches available to organizations looking to reach out, with shared and owned tactics often taking center stage. Social media has opened many new doors for engagement, breaking down time and geographic barriers to help many organizations expand. That said, both physical and digital events (owned-media tactics), provide an immediacy and connectivity that continues to provide results.

Events have been seen as an engagement and publicity generation tool for longer than public relations have been formally practiced. Today's practitioners see events not solely as publicity stunts to generate media coverage but as ways to build relationships with diverse audiences through a variety of media channels. Some events may be designed for an audience on YouTube, a very narrow stakeholder group, or an internal organizational audience. That said, integrated marketing communication campaigns that align with consumer values will never go out of style. This campaign is a tribute by American Greetings to mothers across the world for taking on the toughest job—being Mom.

APPRECIATING MOM; WORLD'S TOUGHEST JOB

American Greetings
Based on PRSA Silver Anvil Winner
Campaign Focus: Special Events & Consumer Engagement

Leading up to Mother's Day in 2014, American Greetings at Cardstore.com demonstrated their understanding of the pressures faced by mom's everywhere with the World's Toughest Job campaign.

Research/Diagnosis

At the time of the World's Toughest Job campaign, roughly half of all people in the United States were purchasing a card for their mother for Mother's Day.[13] The primary goal of the campaign was to persuade the target audience members to acknowledge their mothers with a card, more specifically a card created on American Greetings' Cardstore.

Objectives

The objectives of this campaign were straightforward—the company wanted to persuade their audience to purchase cards for Mother's Day, as well as increase awareness of the role that mom's play in the lives of both children and adults. The Boston agency behind the creative concept, MullenLowe, along with American Greetings' Cardstore, aimed to highlight the tough job that mothers have in raising children and taking care of their families. By highlighting this role, they wanted to increase the awareness of the job that is filled by moms while simultaneously persuading the audience into purchasing a Mother's Day card.[14] By focusing on working adults through targeted messaging, they reached beyond the stereotypical images of moms and young children, to emphasize the ongoing love and support mothers provide.

American Greetings targeted young professionals, those less likely to buy a card and more receptive to a nontraditional, genuinely emotional campaign. Rather than more traditional advertising campaigns, which blanket certain audiences with ads, American Greetings initiated the campaign through a fake job posting and scored a viral sensation.

> What aspects of S.M.A.R.T. objectives could be integrated into this campaign plan?
>
> How might American Greetings have tested some of their assumptions about young professionals through primary research?

After the release of a video that showcased the real-life interviews with the individuals who applied for the "World's Toughest Job," the audience grew to include any individual that had a mother figure in his or her life who would be appropriate to acknowledge with a card on Mother's Day. In this way, the campaign engineered and supported the creation of compelling, viral content that captured the honest emotional reactions of the participants in a way that would resonate across the world.

Strategies

Tugging on the heartstrings of Americans, the main strategy was the emotional appeal behind real people talking about their mothers' importance in their lives. It was this connection that impacted those who applied for the "World's Toughest Job" and also connected the audience and viewers of the video with the cause. Due to this emotional connection and compelling content, shareable social media became a logical channel choice.

Tactics

Shared + Owned

To kick-off the campaign, a phony job posting was developed and published in newspapers and on online job boards that advertised a position titled "Director of Operations." Twenty-four applicants were chosen to participate in recorded Skype interviews that were later edited together to create the viral video that served as the centerpiece of the campaign.[15]

In the interviews, job duties and expectations for the position were presented to the applicants; many of which were considered unreasonable. These included a willingness to work more than 136 hours a week; degrees in medicine, finance, and culinary arts; no holidays off; and the ability to stand for hours on end.[16] When the interviewees expressed their discontent for the requirements and how unreasonable they were, the interviewer subtly pointed out that mother's work under those conditions on a daily basis. The interviews garnered genuine reactions to this assertion, some even going as far as crying. At the end of the video collection, viewers were directed to cardstore.com, where they could create a card for their own mother.[17]

The YouTube video quickly gathered millions of views. Additionally, the campaign used the hashtag #WorldsToughestJob to continue to conversations.[18] These conversations enabled the campaign to successfully shed light on the vital and difficult job that mothers have in every household and society.

Implementation

Aligning with the objective to properly honor the important role mothers play in our lives, the company implemented paid and shared tactics over several months prior to the Mother's Day holiday.

Reporting/Evaluation

The initial job posting for the "Director of Operations" position garnered 2.7 million impressions; however, despite this large amount of impressions, only 24 individuals applied for the position.[19] This is an example of how, at different stages, a campaign does not necessarily need thousands (or even hundreds) of participants to succeed. The final video showcasing the participants and their actual interviews generated more than 27 million views on YouTube since April 2014.[20]

Largely as a result of the YouTube video popularity, the campaign received more than 800 million social impressions, including a spike in visits to the website cardstore.com.[21]

Not only did the World's Toughest Job campaign start conversations about the importance of motherhood in society, but it also was able to drive up the sale of cards for the company. According to MullenLowe U.S., orders from American Greetings' Cardstore increased by 20 percent as a result of the campaign, which ultimately enabled the company to meet sales goals for the entire year during just the Mother's Day season.[22]

Earned

The video that was developed for the World's Toughest Job campaign created a buzz that reporters found hard to ignore. This video was discussed by media outlets and on a variety of platforms across the country; conversations that helped to drive the campaign and allow the campaign to reach farther[23] than it would have with paid media alone. The innovative approach captured genuine emotional responses that connected with a wide variety of audiences, including journalists. Coverage included articles and stories from CBS News,[24] CNN,[25] *Forbes*,[26] *The Globe and Mail*,[27] and the *Wall Street Journal*,[28] among hundreds of others.

Shared

The World's Toughest Job campaign relied heavily on users spreading the message. Facebook, Twitter, and YouTube allowed the video to constantly be shared and discussed online. Individuals from all walks of life shared the video as a tribute to their own mothers, but mothers also were sharing it as a testament and an acknowledgement of the sacrifices that they make on a daily basis. The 800 million impressions were supported using the hashtag #worldstoughestjob; stimulating vast conversation in conjunction with the video.[29]

Owned

American Greetings' Cardstore developed and owned the job posting for the world's toughest job as well as the video that ultimately served as the driving force behind the campaign.

Theories

Situational theory of publics: The World's Toughest Job campaign shed light on an important topic—making sure that mom's everywhere receive the recognition that they deserve on Mother's Day and every day. Throughout the campaign, American Greetings' Cardstore was able to create awareness of the importance of this topic, as well as cultivate a personal connection that prompted the audience to reflect on their own lives, and ultimately, present them with a solution that was as simple as purchasing a card from American Greetings' Cardstore for their own mothers. This three-step process exemplifies the situational theory of publics.[30]

Communication and persuasion matrix: McGuire's communication and persuasion matrix focuses on the prerequisites for a persuasive message to get individuals to act or change behavior.[31] To summarize its thirteen steps, individuals must first pay attention to an idea before they can like it, understand it, learn from it, change their attitude, and, hopefully, change behavior. This campaign followed the model by creating emotionally gripping content that maintains interest and has a significant chance of being recalled when deciding on relevant future actions (such as purchasing gifts for Mother's Day). Rather than a traditional advertising campaign that focuses on the product, this campaign ensures that it resonates with consumers at the earlier stages in the persuasion process.

Model

American Greetings' Cardstore used the video campaign and the following online conversations to promote the goals of the organization: to sell more cards and to take time to genuinely acknowledge the role that a mother plays in society. By using one-way communication to further the organizational goals of the company, they were demonstrating the **press agentry model** of integrated public relations in a marketing context.

CRISIS COMMUNICATION

Crises can happen to anyone, at any time, and without notice. Crisis planning in today's global environment has become imperative for both large and small organizations. However, many organizations are still not prepared. Crises require a considerable amount of time and resources to resolve the issue, as well as bringing significant unwanted attention. The following case featuring Harambe, the seventeen-year-old gorilla from the Cincinnati Zoo highlights the various ways in which crisis situations and their aftermath are handled using integrated public relations campaign techniques.

HARAMBE'S LAST DAY AT THE CINCINNATI ZOO AND BOTANICAL GARDEN

Case Study by Brandon Lazovic and Greta Dreyer, Eastern Michigan University
Campaign Focus: Crisis Communication, Strategic Communication

Research/Diagnosis

On May 28, 2016, a three-year-old boy climbed into an enclosure housing several gorillas at the Cincinnati Zoo and Botanical Garden and fell an estimated ten to twelve feet into a shallow moat surrounding the habitat. Harambe, a seventeen-year-old gorilla that was part of an endangered western lowland gorilla species, was witnessed grabbing and dragging the boy by his foot through the moat. The young boy's life was at stake, and the zoo keepers needed to make a quick decision in order to save the boy from possible death. The boy was tossed about for ten to fifteen minutes, when the Dangerous Animal Response team decided that a tranquilizer dart would have taken too long to go into effect.[32] After much deliberation, a specifically trained Cincinnati Zoo sharpshooter shot and killed Harambe to save the boy who had fallen into the gorilla enclosure.[33] The event catalyzed animal rights activists and sparked a negative response across the country, as well as heated debate in traditional and social media.

Objectives

In order to address the backlash that the Cincinnati Zoo faced regarding the death of the endangered gorilla, Harambe, the zoo responded almost immediately to the public and tried to remain as transparent as possible in an effort to diffuse the situation.[34] Communication focused on minimizing backlash as well as emphasizing the safety and life of the young boy as the top priority. The Cincinnati Zoo's response targeted people that were outraged by the incident as well as those who were angry at the zoo for the decision they made. Due to the incident, many individuals who otherwise would not have paid any attention to the Cincinnati Zoo became aware and emotionally involved and invested in the crisis, with little standing in the way of their speaking out about their opinions.

> Given the constantly shifting nature of the crisis response situation, how might you craft objectives that are realistic (remembering the R in S.M.A.R.T.) and still valuable for the organization over the long term?

Strategies

The Cincinnati Zoo used social media to communicate with their audiences to show remorse for having killed Harambe while reaffirming that they made the right decision. They corresponded directly with news media to issue statements and empathize with the overarching public. The zoo tried to establish credibility by highlighting its positive relationship with the Association of Zoos & Aquariums (AZA) as well as the United States Department of Agriculture (USDA).[35]

Tactics

Owned

The zoo issued a formal statements of apology on its official website. The zoo received angry tweets, harsh words, protests, and petitions, as well as jokes about Harambe's death from people around the world who were angry that the zoo shot the endangered gorilla and blamed the parents for their supposed negligence.

Earned

The zoo used news media tactics in the form of news releases and statements pertaining to the Harambe incident. The *New York Times*, *Huffington Post*, *Washington Post*, and other major news publications ran coverage on the incident and used statements from Thane Maynard, director of the Cincinnati Zoo, in their articles. Because active publics focused on the incident, it sparked media interest, which in turn influenced what topics were being talked about in its continuation of Harambe coverage after the initial incident. The zoo also used face-to-face communication tactics through special events, including a memorial for Harambe and a candlelight vigil.[36]

Shared

On May 29, one day following the incident, the Cincinnati Zoo issued an apology using Facebook, one of the social media platforms where they received the most initial backlash. The apology illustrated the zoo's remorse over killing an endangered animal, noting that this was the first such incident that has occurred in their Gorilla World exhibit since it opened in 1978, and mentioned that the exhibit is inspected regularly by the AZA as well as the USDA. Information flowed directly from the organization to its publics via social media to maintain transparency regarding the incident.

While the zoo intended to address the backlash via the social channels, it ultimately resorted to deactivating its Facebook and Twitter accounts after being bombarded by Harambe memes, negative comments, and even having its Twitter account hacked several times.[37] The Cincinnati Zoo eventually reactivated its accounts but still received a disproportionate amount of negative comments from the public on almost all of its posts.[38] The zoo engaged in these conversations for several months on its social media platforms, but because the negative backlash was so severe, the zoo no longer acknowledges Harambe-related comments on its social media platforms.

> Do you agree with the zoo's decision to temporarily deactivate its social media accounts? Are there other reasonable options for organizations when their channels are so thoroughly dominated by negative comments?

Implementation

Planning for a crisis happens *before* the crisis occurs. Unlike typical strategic public relations campaigns that can include a timeline for implementation, when a crisis hits, responsiveness is critical, and planning can happen moment to moment. For the Cincinnati Zoo, the incident became a crisis as animal rights activists and others (through traditional and social media) expressed frustration at the zoo's decision to kill an endangered animal.[39]

As spokesperson, Thane Maynard was thrust into the difficult position of defending the very actions that were under protest. According to Mark Renfree of PR News, "by recognizing the tragedy of losing a member of a highly endangered species, but also standing by the quick thinking that ultimately saved a young life, Maynard doesn't try to ignore either side of the incident, and instead puts everything on the table."[40] The zoo attempted to maintain complete transparency; first on social media, then through a press conference Maynard held two days after the incident on May 30, 2016.

Reporting/Evaluation

The zoo used the regret and apology commiseration strategies to show remorse in killing Harambe.[41] The organization justified its response by emphasizing that the life of the child took precedence over the life of an animal. The Cincinnati Zoo used several rectifying behavior strategies including the investigation of the barrier and taking corrective action to improve the barrier so a similar incident couldn't happen again.

The zoo did attack its audience for the continued use of Harambe memes and hacking social media accounts.[42] When responses from the zoo failed to quell the negative outreach from its audience, they took strategic inaction by temporarily deactivating its social media accounts and remaining silent in its future posts regarding anything related to Harambe.

After the incident, the boy was taken to Cincinnati Children's Hospital Medical Center for serious, but non-life-threatening injuries. Bystanders captured multiple video clips of the original incident at the zoo, many of which quickly went viral. Public opinion was split, as some did not directly blame the mother of the young boy and called this incident an accident, while many others were outraged at her for not being mindful of her son. The shooting of Harambe opened the floodgates of anger, blame, and mockery toward the mother of the young boy as well as the zoo.

In what is known as the "Nasty Effect," a team of researchers found that when readers were presented with an unbiased and factually written article, any negative comments in the discussion section polarized readers and colored their view of the article as biased.[43] The anonymity of the Internet also creates a "Mob Effect," where people attack one another virtually, further influencing user opinion on social media controversies. Individuals who engage in uncivil discourse don't perceive it as facilitating mob behavior but rather acting out of self-righteousness and believing that they know what's right while others do not.[44]

On the zoo's Facebook and Twitter pages as well as on the website change.org, over 185,000 people condemned the parents of the young boy for not paying attention and allowing him to crawl into the gorilla enclosure. Cincinnati Zoo had 332,000 likes on Facebook and 100,000 followers on Twitter as of April 2016.

Many people were also angry at the zoo keepers for killing the endangered gorilla and not having an appropriate barrier in place to separate visitors from the gorilla enclosure. While the enclosure barrier currently forty-two inches tall and is covered by nylon mesh, the USDA's investigation revealed that the zoo hadn't updated the barrier since it was erected in 1978.[45]

Following the incident, a *Washington Post* headline read, "Shooting an endangered species is worse than murder," one of many similar headlines posted by publications including *The Huffington Post* and the *New York Times*. For months after the incident, the parents of the boy continued to receive backlash over the events of that fateful day. The Cincinnati Zoo's social media accounts also continued to receive a disproportionate number of negative comments from Internet users.

Theories

Two theories can be applied to this case study: **excellence theory** and **situational crisis communication theory (SCCT)**.

Excellence theory calls for symmetrical two-way communication that allows for an organization to listen and engage with key publics. By holding press conferences and responding to the media, as well as attempts to connect via social media channels, the Cincinnati Zoo illustrated a willingness to listen and engage with the public. Crisis communication scholars Fearn-Banks[46] and Marra[47] concur that when organizations have well-developed relationships with stakeholders as well as the media prior to a crisis, the organization may suffer less financially, emotionally, and reputational.

SCCT states that crisis management balances organizational responses with the type and severity of the crisis.[48] This theory offers crisis response strategies, which depend heavily on the threat and the type of crisis. In order to effectively protect an organization's reputation, an assessment of the organization's crisis history is necessary. The Cincinnati Zoo had to determine what kind response it would develop to protect its reputation. After assessing the situation, it determined it would be most effective to use the power of the media relations, their website, and the zoo's social media channels.

Model

While information flows both ways between the organization and its stakeholders and publics, this model uses scientific persuasion based on research and feedback from stakeholders; its goal is to convince others to accept the organization's way of thinking.[49] The Cincinnati Zoo attempted to convince the public that the life of the child was more important than that of an animal in defense of its actions during the crisis.

GLOBAL AND MULTICULTURAL

Public relations practitioners and their campaigns rarely, if ever target one narrow demographic group. Even those campaigns that focus on one primary public are nearly always accessible to broader secondary or tertiary audiences. The advent of the Internet and organizational websites, the digitization of local media outlets and the growth of social media have both significantly expanded the ability for organizations to have their messages reach around the world. The increasingly interconnected nature of societies, economies, and cultures has made it more difficult to separate public communication from global and multicultural communication. Global public relations can be defined as cross-country public relations, involving either an organization communicating to publics in a different country from where it is based or to publics in multiple countries at the same time.[50] Global campaigns are generally, but not exclusively, multicultural as national boundaries do not always mirror cultural lines. Multicultural public relations campaigns can, of course, also take place within individual countries.

When communicating across cultures, practitioners must take a wide variety of factors and questions into account. What assumptions am I making about the culture/country? What cultural differences exist in language, media consumption habits, or business practices (among many other potentially relevant factors)? What am I communicating back to organizational leaders about culturally appropriate practices, approaches, and objectives for a campaign? Global outreach presents an entirely new set of organizational challenges, but the tools of public relations research, listening, and planning can unlock the strategies and tactics to solve them.

UNICEF: TOYS IN MOURNING

Case study by Jordan Ross and Hope Sayler, Eastern Michigan University
Campaign Focus: Public Health

Over the last twenty years, an average of four newborns have died each day in Paraguay as a result of preventable causes. In an effort to raise awareness of this devastating statistic, UNICEF stepped in to raise awareness and to combat the trend. Their campaign, Toys in Mourning, sought to initiate a change in the health policies of the country and reverse the devastating trend.[51]

Research/Diagnosis

Every year, thousands of newborn babies lose their lives due to preventable causes. The Toys in Mourning campaign, enacted by UNICEF, served as a stark reminder to the public about this important issue—and called for a much-needed change in the country of Paraguay. UNICEF believed that by incorporating the correct strategies, including a campaign raising awareness about this cause, a path toward change could be instilled within the medical and larger communities. This campaign highlighted UNICEF as compassionate, understanding, and sensitive to such a tragic epidemic.

In order for the campaign to be successful, UNICEF had to reach the authorities within the Paraguayan government who had the decision-making power on the health and educational policies of the country.[52] These individuals had the ability to facilitate change within the health practices of Paraguay and held the key to beginning to decrease the number of preventable infant deaths in the country. It sought to connect with the broader public as a secondary audience to raise awareness of the issue and encourage those in positions of authority to act.

Objectives

The issue of infant mortality could no longer be ignored, and therefore UNICEF was looking to compel the government to take action. The objective was to press the government to improve the healthcare system immediately.

> As explained in the Strategies, the campaign clearly targeted both opinion leaders and broader publics. How might you craft two separate (and S.M.A.R.T.) objectives to focus on appropriate measurements and metrics for each?

Strategies

This campaign aimed to create conversations about preventable infant deaths in such a way that the government officials would see the need for action and take steps toward supporting prevention. The intention of the campaign was to put pressure on Paraguayan authorities through other major stakeholders, including the people of Paraguay, and motivate them to take the necessary steps toward preventing the deaths of children.[53]

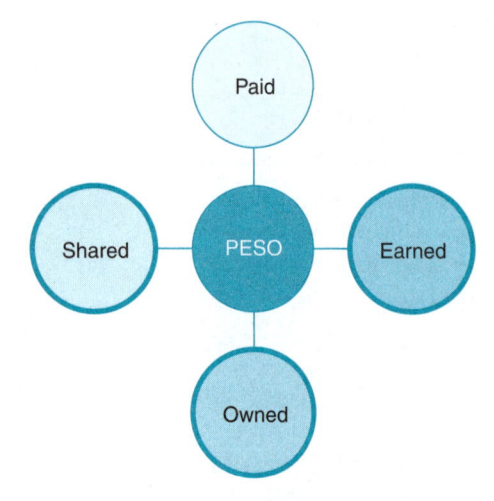

Tactics

Earned + Shared + Owned

In July, the city of Asuncion, the capital of Paraguay, awoke to find that all of the toy stores in the city were closed, and the toys in shop windows were dressed in black. The toys were mourning and included a message that read "a baby changes your life, a death also." The message was partnered with a hashtag, #ceromuertesevitables, which translates to mean #zeropreventabledeaths.[54]

By partnering with the local toy stores to begin the conversation, UNICEF also created a story ready-made for journalists to cover. Ideally, the media would deliver the message to the general public and to those with the authority and resources in government to address the problem through public policy. Without media attention, the Toys in Mourning campaign would not have been able to influence their target audiences as effectively. The earned media in this campaign resulted from journalists who were invited by UNICEF to personally witness the mourning toys as well as others who picked up on the story after the initial coverage. These journalists developed news broadcasts and published news articles about the campaign, helping to deliver UNICEF's message to the targeted stakeholders and governing officials.

Along with earned media, shared media also played a critical role. The hashtag that was developed for the campaign told the story and the purpose of the mourning toys by highlighting the preventable deaths that were happening in the country. Shared media enabled the campaign to reach beyond the city and country wherein it was taking place. Conversations on social media brought the message of the mourning toys to cities and countries all over the globe, strengthening the support for the cause being advocated for in Paraguay. Social media enabled the campaign to grow even outside of the geographic constraints of the city. As the campaign gained momentum, more and more people were able to add pressure to the primary target audience of policy makers through sharing their campaign support, outrage at the situation, and sympathy for the challenges faced by Paraguayan mothers.[55]

Implementation

The Toys in Mourning event took place on a single day during July 2015. However, conversations continued for the entire month, and UNICEF took the initiative to monitor the infant and maternal death rates for the months following the campaign to track initial impact.[56]

Reporting/Evaluation

Prior to the campaign, the issue of preventable infant deaths in Paraguay had only resulted in 27 minutes of broadcast coverage over an entire year. In the day after the Toys in Mourning campaign, news stations from around Paraguay had a combined total of 5,029 minutes of coverage about preventable infant deaths.[57] In addition to the successful earned media on broadcast news, newspapers in Paraguay were flooded with calls from people who demanded that action be taken about preventable infant deaths. Stories published about preventable infant deaths grew exponentially in the days following the campaign.[58] On social media, the hashtag garnered more than two million impressions within hours of its launch. Social media impressions, news articles, and broadcasts spanned thirteen countries.[59]

As a result, the government of Paraguay felt obligated to review the health policies and practices that were ignoring these preventable deaths. Within weeks of the campaign, the government allocated an additional $1.5 million dollars to the health budget of Paraguay.[60] This budget allowed medical facilities to hire more staff and provide additional training to staff and patients about the proper care of infants.

Over the months following the campaign, UNICEF tracked the mortality rates of infants and mothers in the county of Paraguay. Their research found that, after the campaign, the infant death rate decreased by 18 percent and the maternal death rate decreased by over 30 percent.[61]

Theories

The Toys in Mourning campaign was created by UNICEF to catch the attention of the residents of Paraguay, as well as the news media, in order to promote changes in national policy. By doing this, they were exemplifying agenda building theory, where public relations practitioners provide information subsidies to journalists in order to encourage coverage of specific issues as part of the larger agenda in public discussion.[62] UNICEF understood that their campaign was focusing on gaining media coverage in order to vie for attention from the authorities of Paraguay.[63]

Model

The Toys in Mourning campaign leverages the press agentry model of public relations, specifically because UNICEF pushed out information to the public in a one-way fashion. They did this in order to stimulate conversation and raise awareness for the cause at hand.[64]

TEENS 4 PINK: SISTERS NETWORK AND EISAI INC. WITH SHARED VOICE PUBLIC RELATIONS

Sisters Network and Eisai Inc. with Shared Voice
Based on PRSA Silver Anvil Winner
Campaign Focus: Multicultural

In 2014, the Teens 4 Pink campaign was piloted in Houston, Texas, and Memphis, Tennessee. The program, which aims to address the long-standing disparities that affect African American women with breast cancer, was created by Sisters Network, the only national African American breast cancer survivorship organization and was sponsored by Eisai, Inc. The program empowers teens with knowledge and tools to start a dialogue with their loved ones about breast cancer, emphasizing the importance of early detection and urging annual check-ups and mammograms.

While African American women have a lower risk of developing breast cancer than Caucasian women, they are more likely to die from the disease. Studies have suggested a variety of reasons for these long-standing disparities, including more advanced disease at the time of diagnosis and a longer time between diagnosis and the start of treatment. By tapping into the energy and tenacity of teens, this program seeks to create sustainable change across the African American community, one family at a time. Teens that participate in Teens 4 Pink become "Pink Ambassadors" and work to educate their family members and loved ones about breast health.

Research/Diagnosis

Despite advances in breast cancer screening and treatment, the disparity between mortality rates for African American women and Caucasian women has grown significantly since 1981. According to a 2014 Avon study on breast cancer disparities, as many as five African American breast cancer deaths per day might have been averted through earlier screening and intervention.[65] Sisters Network aimed to address these long-standing disparities as part of its mission to save lives and increase knowledge around breast cancer issues affecting the African American community.

Sisters Network piloted this initiative in Houston and Memphis, two cities identified in the 2012 Racial Disparity in Breast Cancer Mortality Study that found that twenty-one of the twenty-five largest U.S. cities have a Black/White disparity in breast cancer mortality.[66] In Memphis, 11 percent more African American women die from breast cancer than their White counterparts, according to this study. In Harris County, Texas (Houston), African American women have the highest breast cancer mortality (37.2 deaths per 100,000) compared to White (23.1 deaths per 100,000) and Hispanic (15.0 deaths per 100,000) women. The African American breast cancer mortality rate in Harris County also exceeds the African American breast cancer mortality rate in Texas (34.9 per 100,000) and the United States (33.0 per 100,000).

Objectives

The program aimed to meet the following objectives:

- Raise awareness of disparities in diagnosis and treatment of breast cancer in the African American community.

- Demonstrate Eisai and Sister Network's commitment to the breast cancer community.

- Expand reach of program messages beyond participants via local media engagement and targeted national outreach to African American outlets.

> These campaign objectives read more like communication goals—clear and relevant to organizational goals but not measurable and time bound. How might they be updated to reflect S.M.A.R.T. guidelines?

Strategy

While the breast cancer disparities affecting the African American community are well-known, Teens 4 Pink seeks to help address the issue in a new way, aiming to drive broad community change by reaching one family at a time. The program leverages a unique "teen up" approach to empower African American teens to create positive change within their own families and arming them with knowledge that will benefit them throughout their lives.

Tactics

The Teens 4 Pink pilot launched in January 2014, and teens were recruited to become Pink Ambassadors through general information sessions presented to local Girl Scouts troops, schools, and churches. Data were collected before and after each session to examine how well information is retained by teens and to track the results of family conversations. Shared Voice Public Relations supported program initiation with a variety of earned and owned media activities.

Earned

A media campaign was conducted in pilot markets at program launch by using tailored media pitches that offered a diverse range of

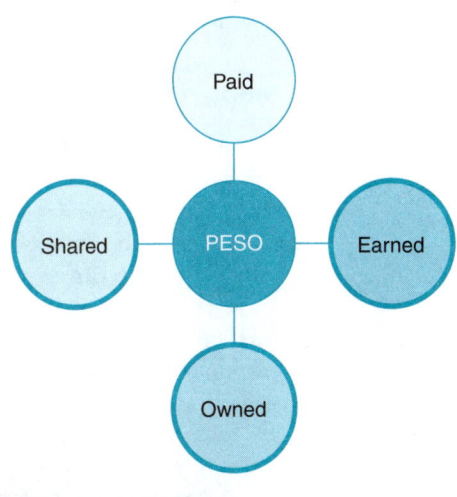

Instagram via @teens4pink

media-trained spokespeople. As the goal was to generate coverage in local media, Teens 4 Pink enlisted spokespeople who were based in each pilot market, most importantly teens who had participated in the program. These included representatives from Sisters Network, teen ambassadors and their family members, local public figures/breast cancer advocates, and representatives from Eisai.

Shared

The team seeded Facebook, Twitter, and Instagram accounts to interact with more individuals and to continue to share the message of empowerment among and beyond involved teens.

Owned

A website, www.teens4pink.org, was created as the online home for the program, providing teens access to complete their surveys and offering resources for teens nationwide to start similar dialogues about breast health with the women in their families. Local events also served as a significant catalyst for spreading the message in different communities.

Implementation

A team of teen Pink Ambassadors officially launched the campaign. Ambassadors were required to attend educational sessions, follow pre- and posttesting guidelines, conduct Family Interviews, and complete community service hours. The Family Interview is the outreach component in which teens interview the women in their families who are biological relatives.

According to its website, Teens 4 Pink empowers teens with breast health information that can equip them with the necessary facts to share with their families and communities to increase awareness. This is based on the premise that teens can have a significant impact on the dynamics of their families through the bidirectional aspect of relationships between adolescents and their family members.[67]

Reporting/Evaluation

A survey was used to measure the program's impact on behavior. Pink Ambassadors tracked and submitted data on the conversations and actions being taken within their families. Feedback from the Teen Ambassadors was extremely positive, and the results showed the program's impact as follows:

- Approximately 1,000 Teen Ambassadors (combined in Houston and Memphis) completed the Family Questionnaire, with most of the girls interviewing their mothers (35 percent) or aunts (29 percent).

- More than 25 percent of the women surveyed had never had a mammogram and, of those, almost 66 percent reported their knowledge of breast health increased significantly.

- More importantly, 85 percent reported that they would be willing to get a mammogram, 86 percent perform a breast self-exam regularly, and 82 percent said they would be more proactive about their breast health.

- Many women requested additional information from Sisters Network and approximately 30 women requested a free mammogram.

Earned Media:

- Following the program launch in March 2014, Teens 4 Pink secured media coverage and interviews with spokespeople in both pilot markets. As a result, www.teens4pink.org saw increases in web traffic following high-profile media coverage, including the Memphis NBC segment and *Houston Chronicle* piece.

- Approximately 90 percent of the resulting media coverage included key messages about the program, recognition for Sisters Network and/or Eisai, as well as the website address. Many of the key media placements included top outlets within the local markets, as well as some national coverage, as follows:

  - Sesi Magazine (African American magazine for teen girls)
  - WMC-TV (Memphis NBC affiliate)
  - WANT-TV (Memphis ABC affiliate)
  - *Houston Chronicle*
  - *Tri-State Defender*

> Teens 4 Pink used content analysis to analyze media coverage for key messages. Given a larger research/evaluation budget, what other primary research could have deepened their understanding of the campaign's impact?

Shared Media:

- Social media properties such as Instagram, Pinterest, Facebook, and Twitter created a base of loyal followers.

Theories

Diffusion theory was a key component of this program's success. For example, the presumed gaps in cancer knowledge and access to treatment within the African American community could be reduced through increased awareness of the problem and access to local resources for information and treatment. In this framework the *adoption* or behavior change comes after individuals *evaluate* and *test* the idea.[68] Using teens—who could be thought of as *early adopters*—helped to introduce new concepts and make them more socially acceptable within communities.

The campaign also used *agenda setting* approaches, through both interpersonal communication and earned media outreach. By making breast cancer in African American women a top-of-mind issue, Teens 4 Pink brought the message to the attention of both decision makers and community members who were both encouraged to take steps (personally and professionally) to improve the situation.

Model

By empowering teens in support of breast cancer awareness, this campaign not only focused on an underserved population but also gave agency to these individuals. In this way, Teens 4 Pink exemplifies a two-way symmetrical communication model, with the organization and the campaign itself shaped (and improved) by the work of many engaged participants. The campaign would have been significantly less successful without active listening and audience engagement.

INTERNAL COMMUNICATION AND EMPLOYEE RELATIONS

Internal communication and employee communication campaigns include programs targeted specifically to publics that are directly associated with an organization, such as employees, members, affiliates, board members, and franchisees. Internal audiences can be allies or activists, and practitioners may prioritize public or private channels, direct or mediated communication, and personalized or mass messages.[69] Of course, the lines between internal and external publics can be difficult to define, particularly for large organizations—such as universities—that have multiple levels of involvement and alignment with the organization. Staff and faculty would certainly be considered employees of the university and an internal public, but students and alumni could be seen as internal or external depending on their individual situation as well as the communication at hand. In this way, internal communication can be closely associated with external communication, although organizational structure and implementation varies.[70] In any case, the two should be coordinated. A strategic approach to public relations planning can also help to understand how media relations and external communication can be used effectively to improve relationships with internal publics.[71]

RESPONDING TO "FERGUSON": FROM TRAGEDY TO POSITIVE CHANGE

Washington University in St. Louis
Based on PRSA Silver Anvil Winner
Campaign Focus: Internal Communication

On August 9, 2014, a Black teenager was shot and killed in Ferguson, Missouri, in an altercation with police. It was a tragic loss of life, which, under any circumstances, would have brought an outpouring of grief. But, beyond what anyone might have imagined, the event sparked an intense community and national response in which "Ferguson" became synonymous with police brutality, social injustice, economic disparity, and political disenfranchisement. Months of simmering public unrest followed, and the St. Louis region is still healing.[72] For Washington University in St. Louis (WashU), the shooting and its aftermath cut deep. St. Louis has been home to the university for 165 years. The institution is a regional leader: when St. Louis hurts, Washington University in St. Louis hurts. Many of the faculty, students, and staff members are actively engaged in serving the extended St. Louis community to address social, economic, and educational disparities. Others, through their leading research, are experts in addressing the difficult issues that triggered public unrest.

At WashU, the shooting became a pivotal moment for the university community. Faculty, staff members, and students had been grappling with the difficult issues of diversity and inclusion. Several incidents on campus exposed serious racial divides. Students, in particular, were questioning the administration's commitment to achieving greater racial, ethnic, and socioeconomic diversity—it was even expressed as a top university priority. "Ferguson" had the potential to drive a wedge more deeply into the university community.

Research/Diagnosis

- *Campus climate*: Through surveys of the faculty, students, and staff, an assessment was conducted regarding the sentiment about diversity and inclusion and how these issues play out in everyday lives. The results helped to better understand the problem and inform planning and execution.

- *Others' experience*: Such issues are not uncommon on university campuses throughout the country. Through secondary research of universities' experiences—particularly among top tier peer institutions—WashU learned from others' best practices (and missteps).

- *Academic experts*: A relevant database was compiled for the university's academic experts on diversity issues in a variety of fields. Representing all schools—including medicine, law, social work, art and architecture, business, and arts and sciences—these experts helped to frame dialogue on campus and brought important perspective to media coverage of "Ferguson" (and adding resonance with internal audiences).

- *St. Louis Regional Disparities*: A landmark study conducted by WashU researchers and local partners detailed disparities in St. Louis, including Ferguson. "*For the Sake of All: A Report on the Health and Well-being of African Americans in St. Louis and Why It Matters for Everyone*" helped to inform a response and has become an important resource for policymakers and community leaders working to strengthen the region post Ferguson.[73]

Objectives

WashU faced a crisis and had to manage it. But, the community had the opportunity to do much more. It could turn this tragedy into a force for positive change. Through "Ferguson," the university was determined to find and amplify WashU's voice: to help this institution "do better and be better."

> How could WashU have crafted S.M.A.R.T. objectives to achieve this aim?

Strategies

In addition to relying on detailed and regularly updated crisis plans, the initiative stayed on track using the following strategies:

- *Checklists, timelines, and tactical roadmap*: Because events unfolded so quickly and the effort easily could have been overtaken by reactive crisis management needs, planning was essential. A detailed step-by-step, scenario-by-scenario roadmap guided the work and focused on core objectives.
- *Messaging*: Volatile, divisive issues had to be managed. Sensitivity and understanding had to be conveyed. Confidence had to be instilled in those worried about safety on and around campus. To strike the right balance, WashU developed a strong message matrix and pulled it through all communications. A call to action ("do better and be better") framed this experience and set the stage for a long-term effort.
- *Media targets*: The media relations team created a targeted list of traditional and nontraditional media contacts leading/influencing coverage of Ferguson and pitched academic experts as informed local sources.

Tactics and Implementation

Integrated efforts were aimed at (1) engaging the university community in open and meaningful dialogue about race and racism; (2) demonstrating WashU's leadership on important issues; and (3) when necessary, keeping the faculty, staff, and students informed and safe, without feeding into the heated rhetoric fueling public unrest. The primary tactical components included the following:

Earned + Shared

- *WashU Experts*: A diverse group of WashU thought leaders were identified with expertise in a range of related topics and they proactively pitched to local and national media covering Ferguson. From criminal justice, to the history of race relations, the social construct of race, health/educational/economic disparities, the influence of media and more—the experts contributed important context and helped frame the debate. On the WashU campus and far beyond it, their input opened minds to the complexity of the issues and potential solutions.

- *Executive communication*: Communication from university leadership had to convey empathy, challenge the community to become stronger, and maintain calm even as the region erupted with protests. It was a difficult balancing act, particularly given the range of audiences and history on the issues of race and racism. Parents wanted to know their children were safe; students wanted to know the university cared. Staff members working just blocks away from protest activity needed to be reassured; students and faculty engaged in protests wanted to feel supported. No single message, messenger, or channel would be sufficient.
- *#WashUVoices*: The use of a shared hashtag was encouraged to connect social media efforts and conversations.

Owned

- *Voices.wustl.edu*: Within days of the shooting, the university launched *WashU Voices,* an online gathering site to inspire and motivate conversation and engagement. Despite the inherent risks, *WashU Voices* became the place where differences of opinion were not only shared but also celebrated. On the WashU website (https://voices.wustl.edu/) tabs titled "Do Something," "In the News," and "Resources" were established to provide students various outlets of information. A blog "Perspectives"—to which students, faculty, and staff members submitted personal thoughts—opened hearts and minds to others' everyday realities. A social media feed provided a real-time capture of perspectives. For those who wanted to take action, "Do Something" was a clearinghouse for opportunities to engage in activities on campus and throughout the region. "In the News" captured the breadth of the thought leadership on issues underlying the public unrest. When necessary, "Resources" was used to keep the community informed of safety concerns and support services, rather than elevate fear by broadcasting via the crisis communications/emergency channels. Scheduled 7 a.m., noon, and 4 p.m. updates were particularly helpful for parents who were watching events unfold from afar.

Day of Discovery and Dialogue on Race and Ethnicity: In early February 2015, a first-ever, daylong series of conversations among students, faculty, and staff members was convened. The structure was intentionally unconventional to empower open and honest dialogue. Through small group gatherings, large forums, an online stream, social media-based conversation, and artistic expression, a comfortable way for members of the community to participate was created—knowing different people would have different needs.

"Documenting Ferguson": The WashU library created the only complete archive of the "Ferguson" experience—on and off campus—to provide historical documentation of events but also, more importantly, as an ongoing resource for those involved in finding solutions and strengthening the university and the region.

Reporting

In just a few months, WashU successfully managed a serious crisis, transformed the tone and tenor of conversation on campus, and gained momentum for a long-term effort toward a more inclusive community:

- *Voices.wustl.edu* has proven to be a powerful gathering place. In just five months, the site had 37,527 unique visitors; 143,000 page views; and 62,000 sessions. Noticeable peaks occurred during milestone events and when the site was featured through other communications.

> What other metrics (particularly integrated approaches) could WashU have used to measure the impact of its community engagement efforts?

- *#WashUVoices* was widely used with more than 26,000 social media engagements, 2,893 interactions on Twitter, and 60+ images shared on Instagram. Tweets by 380+ users generated an estimated 3.4 million impressions.

- *WashU Experts* deeply penetrated media coverage, with 330+ stories appearing with WashU commentary and representing a potential audience of 834.4 million; 74 percent of the coverage ran beyond the St. Louis market.

- *Executive communication* became an important rallying point. An end-of-year message from the university chancellor reflecting on "Ferguson" and calling for continued effort is widely recognized as groundbreaking.

- *Day of Discovery and Dialogue* drew far greater engagement than expected, with 822 faculty, staff members, and students registering for one or more live sessions; 2,141 participating remotely via live stream and 9,500 social media feed engagements. The event elicited a favorable response from all constituent groups.

- The *Documenting Ferguson archive* already has been accessed by 14,054 unique visitors from around the world as of the 2015 submission date for the PRSA Silver Anvil Awards.

Theories

WashU's campaign exemplifies two theoretical frameworks: systems theory and framing theory. Systems theory is about the organization's interactions with its environment. In this case, the university saw significant changes happening around it and chose to engage rather than simply react. This awareness and proactive approach resonated with internal and external publics. From a framing perspective, the university saw the impact of local and national media attention to Ferguson and carefully worked to present and provide information that pointed toward specific elements' importance, positioning the univsersity as a local leader willing to tackle important shared challenges. Through a variety of spokespersons, WashU continued to add its voice to the conversation within the St. Louis community, emphasizing the importance and relevance of its expertise and involvement. In this way, they pointed publics (including journalists) toward vital, engaging, and reputable information.[74]

Model

WashU engaged deeply with publics at each stage in the process and was open to criticism, reflection, and change as circumstances shifted. The open, back-and-forth approach is particularly valuable when considering internal publics whose buy-in and influence should be part of organizational decision-making processes.[75]

HP GLOBAL WELLNESS CHALLENGE

Based on PRSA Silver Anvil Winner
Campaign Focus: Employee Communication

Health and well-being are linked to employee engagement, productivity, talent retention, and creativity and innovation. Over the last two years, HP stepped up its investment in wellness programs, striving to support employees at all levels of health and fitness. HP launched its first-ever Global Wellness Challenge in April 2011 to support employee wellness and help drive wellness engagement. But how does a company of more than 300,000 get employees all over the world to sign up for a completely voluntary twelve-week activity?

Research/Diagnosis

In appealing to a large worldwide employee base, Global HR Communications worked closely with HP Global Benefits to understand the implementation of

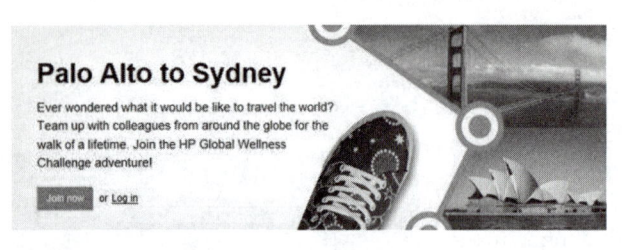

HP's "Winning with Wellness" initiative in various countries. In particular, they focused on local differences in well-being practices. To further drive planning, the team conducted primary and secondary research showing how different generations use technology and social media and have different communication preferences. Experience told the project team that incentives are popular with HP employees. The team also used survey results from the prior year's U.S. pilot of a web-based team challenge.

Objectives

The team took a multifaceted approach to reach this diverse global employee base and drive registration and participation. Communications planning supported key program objectives, including the following:

- Participation: Reach a "critical mass" of at least 50,000 employees participating from many countries; the Benefits team felt this number would be needed to make a significant impact with this first experimentation with a global wellness activity.

- Program satisfaction and continued behavior change: Achieve a surveyed rate of 80 percent or more of participants who said they were satisfied with the program, with 70 percent or more saying they plan to maintain or increase their level of physical activity in the 12 months following the event.

- Employee networking: Take advantage of how the Global Wellness Change (GWC) could provide a way for employees to actively engage with coworkers through physical activity and social media, in ways and with people they may not have otherwise encountered, as measured by anecdotal feedback and survey comments.

> HP's campaign has created objectives that meet many of the S.M.A.R.T. criteria. In what ways do these objectives support organizational goals, and what additional objectives might be valuable to add to improve the campaign's achievement?

Strategies

The approach for HP was to focus on four key audiences.

- HP Human Resources community: Ensure Human Resources representatives were aware of the program and could support it locally as needed, as well as serve as role models for participation.

- HP Communications community: Ensure HP leaders at all levels corporate-wide (and the communicators who support them) were prepared to help promote the event.

- HP "Wellness Ambassadors": Ensure that the more than 100 volunteer Global Wellness Ambassadors around the world were informed and equipped to promote the event locally.

- HP employees worldwide: Recognizing that employees are people first, HP sought to appeal to their interests in earning incentives, winning prizes, and socializing with their peers in addition to improving their health—regardless of their current state of fitness or physical activity.

Tactics

Owned & Shared

- High-impact initial e-mail to drive participation, with follow-ups: With "push" e-mail recognized as the most efficient way to reach HP's large global population and raise initial awareness, the team wanted this e-mail to stand out and be clearly recognizable as a branded HP communication. Follow-up e-mails during the registration period gave smaller-population HP countries a chance to shine by showing high participation rates during registration.

- Materials for HP leaders and HR team members: Communication toolkits were posted and publicized for leaders and their communicators to use in team meetings and in their business unit communication channels, such as newsletters and web pages.

- Materials for local use, translated if necessary.

- Web resources, including ways to share employee-generated content and a social networking platform.

- Global Wellness Challenge welcome kit was mailed to participants at home to encourage participation and add a fun element to recording personal progress with pedometers and a personal logbook.

- Weekly participant e-mails, with encouragement and reminders.

- Curated content from a variety of relevant sources, including intranet articles and flash videos.

- Invitations to participate in local wellness events such as walking tours or exercise sessions, with same graphic theme associated with the GWC was sent to all.

Implementation

Creative execution delivered a consistent look and feel online, at events, and in visual communications to sharpen the focus on wellness as a whole and give a recognizable feel to the GWC campaign. The following guidelines were used:

- Feature realistic-looking people in marketing materials rather than models and show actual employees to the extent possible.

- Deliberately tell stories through employees at all levels of the organization rather than traditional CEO/senior-executive endorsement, including testimonial videos and ongoing content. The "Winning with Wellness Heroes" stories told through multiple media exemplify this approach and really helped bring the GWC to life for everyone.

- Communicate about incentives to build excitement and anticipation. Communications about incentives and prizes (using e-mails and web postings) helped build excitement along the way by announcing new prizes for different activities and registration milestones.

- Support localized communication as much as possible. Editable poster templates and graphic e-mail headers helped maintain global consistency while supporting local flexibility with messages.

Challenges during Implementation

- Maintaining a close partnership between Global HR Communications and the Global Benefits team and vendor partners was crucial in a rapidly changing environment in which new needs/issues arose almost daily.

- Certain countries had stringent data-privacy laws that required three different versions of the launch and two follow-up e-mail messages, potentially complicating distribution.

- The period of mourning in Japan following the devastating earthquake and subsequent tsunami that occurred in March 2011 affected communications to employees in that country. Delayed delivery of welcome kits to certain countries forced some reorganization and required the start date to be moved out and recommunicated to HP Wellness Ambassadors and employees.

Reporting/Evaluation

The outcomes of the initiative met and in some cases far exceeded the objectives set by the Global Benefits team. In what is believed to be the largest corporate event of its kind, more than 50,000 employees in nearly 90 countries signed up to focus on their wellness and network with their peers.

Goal	Target	Result
Employee participation	50,000 or more	Approx. 54,000
Satisfaction with the event	80 percent	94 percent
Continued behavior change	70 percent	99 percent*
Cost of communications	Stay within budget, save money	Target met
Networking	In survey responses, many employees referenced the networking aspect of the GWC as an important benefit of participating.	

* Maintain current activity level = 30 percent; significantly increase activity = 19 percent; some increase in activity = 50 percent

Additionally, 84 percent of participants completing the survey said they plan to continue to use the HP Shape Up Central website to track their wellness progress and share stories, photos, and videos.

Theories

By providing a consistent flow of materials explaining the benefits of the wellness program, particularly the variety of relatable success stories and group nature, the campaign reflects the work of **social cognitive theory** (SCT).[76] SCT emphasizes the role of several key factors in changing behaviors and is particularly well tested in health and wellness contexts: the importance of modeling behaviors and giving individuals a sense of agency or *self-efficacy* to believe that they can succeed in making the desired change.[77]

Model

As a persuasion-based campaign, this approach successfully engaged more than 50,000 employees to participate in HP's program through a carefully planned and coordinated communication program.[78] Its objective was specific behavioral change rather than being flexible and audience-conscious in its implementation.

Appendix

TOPICS

1. Research
   a. Sample Likert Scale Items
   b. Method for Conducting Surveys
   c. Matching the Question with the Method
   d. Example Methods and Research Questions
   e. Focus Group Moderator Tips
   f. Defining Key Audiences, Stakeholders, and Publics
   g. Content Analysis
      i. Media Coverage Analysis
   h. Survey Development
      i. Survey Questions
      ii. Types of Survey Data Collection
      iii. Sampling vs. Census
2. Objectives
   a. How *Not* to Write Objectives
3. Strategies
   a. When to Not Use Social Media
   b. Review: Positioning Campaigns for Maximum Impact
      i. Uniqueness
      ii. Audience Focus
      iii. Playing to Your Strengths
4. Tactics
   a. Paid Media
      i. Outdoor
      ii. Print
      iii. Radio

      iv. TV
      v. Digital Display
      vi. Search Engine Marketing (SEM)
      vii. Social Media
      viii. Event Sponsorship
  b. Earned Media
      i. Media Advisories
      ii. Press Releases/News Releases
      iii. Press Conferences and Media-friendly Events
      iv. Bylined Articles and Op-ed Pieces
  c. Shared Media
      i. Blogs: An Organization's Content Hub
      ii. Social Media Networks
      iii. Microblogging
      iv. Image, Video, and Interest Sharing
      v. Community Management
  d. Owned Media
      i. Website Content Management
      ii. Marketing Tactics
      iii. Publications
      iv. Collateral Materials

RESEARCH

Sample Likert Scale Items

Sample Likert Scale Items for Answering PR Questions

- Awareness
    - I am aware of X.
    - I have heard of X.
- Recall
    - I have seen X.
    - I recall my friends with X.
- Knowledge
    - I know about X.
    - I really don't know much about X.

- Interest
  - I am really interested in X.
  - I am not interested in X.

- Relationship
  - I can relate well to others who have X.
  - X does not really see me with X.

- Preference
  - If I were to consider it, X would be what I want.
  - I like X more than . . .

- Intent
  - I intend to purchase X.
  - X is not something that I would buy.

- Advocacy
  - X is something I will tell others to purchase.
  - I have been advocating X for quite some time.

Source: From Stacks, 2017, p. 72

Method for Conducting Surveys

1. Write a research question (establish what you need to learn).

2. Review the literature and develop a hypothesis (what you think you might find). Example: People who like us on Facebook will have the most positive opinions of our cause.

3. Select the public or sample "universe."

4. Decide on the format—online, phone, mail, in-person, and so on.

5. Plan the arrangement of question topics—nonthreatening questions, threatening questions (items about possibly embarrassing behaviors), and demographic data (age and income questions are sometimes threatening).

6. Write questions.

7. When you write questions about nonthreatening topics, remember the following:

   - Use closed-ended responses (such as Yes/No or 1, 2, or 3) for responses that tabulate quickly.

   - Use open-ended responses to get a range of data and bring up ideas you had overlooked.

- Make questions and responses specific. Avoid double-barreled answers.
- Use terms everyone can understand; avoid jargon.

8. When you write questions about threatening topics (things such as drinking, drug use, or gambling, that might embarrass respondents if they talked about them openly), remember the following:
   - Create an environment that lets people comfortably respond.
   - Prefer open-ended items that let people decide how to respond.
   - Include necessary qualifiers and context in questions.
   - Avoid technical terms.
   - Phrase your question in terms of "most people you know." People are usually more willing to talk about others than themselves.
   - Ask about past behavior before you ask about present behavior.
   - Keep questions about deviant behavior in clusters with related items about deviant behavior.
   - Put threatening questions toward the end of the questionnaire.
   - Answers to threatening questions may be lies.

9. When you write questions to test knowledge, remember the following:
   - Ease into items (e.g., do you happen to know?). Don't make the questionnaire seem like a test.
   - Simplify questions and answers.
   - Leave questions with numerical answers open-ended.
   - If you ask yes/no questions, use related questions later to double-check responses.
   - Do not use mail or online questionnaires to test for knowledge.

10. When you write opinion questions, remember the following:
    - Be very specific.
    - Use close-ended responses.
    - Keep the affective (feeling), cognitive (thinking), and action aspects in separate questions.
    - Gauge the strength of responses by providing a response scale (e.g., how important is this issue to you? Very important, somewhat important, etc.).

- Start with general questions and then move to specific questions.
- Group questions with the same underlying values.
- Start with the least popular proposal.
- Use neutral terms (e.g., the president, not President Smith).

11. Write questions so answers will be easy to tabulate.
12. Consider question order and possible order bias.
    - Keep like questions together.
    - Start with nonthreatening items.
    - Ask demographic questions last. They can be considered threatening.
    - Diagram questions in a flow chart to see the logic.
    - Don't make your questionnaire too long. (Some topics may require many questions, but dropout rates increase with questionnaire length. Therefore, you may need to ask priority questions near the beginning of a long questionnaire to increase the likelihood of getting responses to those items.)
    - Start with general questions and then go to specifics.
    - Go forward or backward in time, but don't jump around.
    - Reverse scale order in some items to eliminate habitual responses.
13. Format the questionnaire.
14. Pretest the survey with people who know about the study. Adjust questionnaire elements that don't perform the way you expected.
15. Conduct a pilot test by surveying a small number of people from the public you want to check. Adjust survey elements that don't perform the way you expected.
16. Initiate the full-scale survey.

From APR Study Guide, University Accreditation Board, (2016), 35, https://www.prsa.org/wp-content/uploads/2016/07/apr-study-guide.pdf

Matching the Question with the Method

When performing research, practitioners should follow the question at hand to help determine the best research method to apply. Methods can serve exploratory, descriptive, or explanatory purposes. Exploratory approaches often answer open-ended questions, attempting to understand fundamental elements of a particular situation. Descriptive approaches seek to provide additional detail about the factors of a more specific situation or phenomenon. By contrast, explanatory research examines causal factors to better understand what might be motivating individual or group behaviors or opinions.[1]

- **Who?** Questions about publics and audiences can take many forms, including the examination of secondary research on demographic groups or publics, primary research using social listening tools, as well as qualitative and quantitative interviews and surveys.
  - **Example**: Who are the opinion leaders in a particular community?
    - **Method**: Secondary research on community leadership, dialogue, and demographic trends
    - **Method**: Interviews with and/or surveys of community members
  - **Example:** Who has discussed our company/brand/organization on social media in the past?
    - **Method**: Primary, quantitative, and/or qualitative content analysis, social listening
- **What?** These questions can either be exploratory ("what have we learned from . . .") or more specific and enumerable (acting in place of "how much . . . ?" or "how many . . . ?").
  - **Example:** What did our organization learn from opening our new branch location?
    - **Method:** Exploratory qualitative interviews and/or surveys with multiple audiences to examine the event from multiple perspectives
    - **Method:** A case study approach (combine the interviews with analysis of internal and external documents, media coverage, and social media conversations)
  - **Example:** What impact has our product made for our customers?
    - **Method:** Interviews or surveys (ideally qualitative and quantitative) to capture the broad range of potential insights and experiences, as well as to provide quantitative data generalizable to all customers
- **Where?** Secondary methods are often the best starting point, although there are increasingly digital tools to track and identify the location of audiences.
  - **Example:** Where do our customers and potential customers live and work?
    - **Method:** Using social listening tools to track the locations of users and potential customers (when possible)
  - **Example:** Where should we focus our resources for expansion?
    - **Method:** Demographic studies can help make the case for entering a specific geographic market (for example, finding a city with similar socioeconomic makeup or similar cluster of industries to expand your organization's outreach)

- **Why and How?** Qualitative approaches are often most effective at providing the holistic, detailed answers needed to begin to answer *why* and *how* research questions. Quantitative investigation often serves as a secondary step once researchers have initial perspectives and direction.
  - **Example:** Why would community members donate to other nonprofit organizations rather than ours?
    - **Method (Step 1):** Qualitative interviews with key informants inside and outside of the organization to assess potential factors
    - **Method (Step 2):** Based on the initial findings, quantitative survey to isolate both demographic factors among these audience groups as well as to gain additional insight into their behaviors

Example Methods and Research Questions

Based on Fig. 1.2 "Case Study Methods" by Robert K. Yin.[2]

Primary Research Method	Qualitative or Quantitative?	Advantages	Disadvantages	Example Research Question
Experiments	Quantitative	- Control of the situation - Isolation of variables - Focus on causation	- Expertise needed to design, conduct, and analyze data - Expensive to run	Will our donors and volunteers respond and take action based on emotional appeals or logical appeals about the need for support?
Content Analysis	One or both	- Flexible based on the size of the data set - Customizable to a wide variety of data and questions	- Drawbacks exist for both human analysis (time consuming) and digital methods (lack of nuance)	How much has trade media coverage reflected key campaign themes and messages?
Focus Groups	Qualitative	- More efficient than indepth interviewing - Allows observation of group interaction	- Needs skilled moderation - Individuals can be left out or overshadowed (unequal participation) - Much less depth of information for individual participants	Which messages from past campaigns have resonated most with our key stakeholder groups? Why?

Primary Research Method	Qualitative or Quantitative?	Advantages	Disadvantages	Example Research Question
In-depth Interviews	Qualitative	- Volume of information collected - Broad, holistic perspective - Brings up unrealized issues/questions	- Time investment for interviewing and analysis - Flexibility in questions can bring uneven results	Why are community members upset about our new facility announcement?
Surveys	One or both	- Efficient data collection - Readily available analysis tools - Multiple data collection methods	- Expertise needed to write questions and implement - Large data collection is expensive - Short participant attention spans	What percentage of voters support the organization's position?
SWOT Analysis	Qualitative	- Relatively quick process - Group process can involve and empower team members	- Not an indepth, systematic, or formal process	

Focus Group Moderator Tips

- Warm up the conversation: A smooth, clear introduction sets a professional tone and lays out the goals for a successful session.

- Order matters: Structure the most important questions in the middle of the session, leaving less critical concepts to the end.

- Be positive but nonpartisan: An impartial, business-like approach is best.

- Get everyone involved: Don't let one or two participants dominate—call on others who look they have something to say.

- Agreement is positive, but avoid groupthink: Encourage participants to build off of each other's ideas but acknowledge outliers and encourage different perspectives.

Defining Key Audiences, Stakeholders, and Publics

Once some of the initial questions have been answered, practitioners must define who will be impacted by the situation at hand. These may be organizational audiences, stakeholders, and publics. Audiences are the direct targets of organizational outreach—individuals and groups who come into contact with organizational campaigns, messages, and spokespersons. Stakeholders can be defined as individuals who can have an impact on the ability of an organization to meet its goals or have an interest in the corporation's success.[3] Organizational audiences include internal stakeholders (such as employees, the board of directors, and stockholders) as well as external stakeholders (such as customers, potential customers, competitors, and vendors). They can also include publics (such as community members). Audiences are defined by the organization, while publics are (as explained by the *Situational Theory of Publics*) self-organizing around issues, based on their recognition of a problem, recognition of constraints to solving the problem, and their degree of involvement.[4] From a marketing or sales perspective, external communication is about targeting audiences to achieve business objectives such as sales goals. From a purely relational perspective, external communication is about strengthening the bonds with important internal and external stakeholders and publics. An integrated communication approach, led by publics relations, takes into account all of these perspectives when researching, developing, and executing campaigns.

Although the task of identifying key groups may seem daunting, this exercise is most useful with a smaller, specific group to whom specific objectives can be designed, strategies directed, tactics implemented, and messages crafted. Campaigns conducted without research and appropriate targeting may accidentally connect with important audiences and stakeholders, but they are more likely to miss the target.[5] Practitioners should remember not to overlook the importance of internal publics, audiences, and stakeholders.

In order to evaluate and pinpoint the relevant audiences or stakeholders, it is important to understand the process for developing a more granular view. The first step can be as simple as working with the leadership team in order to identify the important internal and external stakeholders. The team may then use this information to further distinguish any key characteristics; allowing a deeper profile to emerge. Completing this exercise may result in more, fewer, or the same number of audience groups; however, it does provide a starting point to the larger team for developing a better understanding of the organizational view of its position within the marketplace, as well as its internal and external communication challenges and opportunities.

More importantly, the smaller size and inherent commonality of each subgroup allows an organization to listen more closely to these publics and engage in true, two-way communication. Awareness of any issues or challenges can impact campaign and organizational strategy at the highest levels. Companies often have a strong understanding of *some* key audience groups but are not fully able to see the complete picture. The following are a few common challenges relating to properly defining key audiences, stakeholders, and publics:

- Organizations often focus obsessively on sustaining their current customers, members, or donors, at the expense of seeking and understanding opportunities for expansion and growth in new markets.

- The opposite problem is also common: organizations may direct all of their resources and attention toward acquiring new customers, members, or donors. Current customers may be left without clear, ongoing communication.

- Organizations may not be wholly aware of activist groups or other organized publics who may see the organization, its business, or its structure as a threat.

Even with these same communication strategies at their disposal, far too many PR campaigns are initiated as an attempt to address a perceived need from an organizational perspective: "Our customers are unhappy, so we must communicate with them in a different way," or "These groups don't know about our products. If they did, they would buy them!" While this approach may identify an organizational gap, it does not help to find the root of the problem. What research can provide is a roadmap to the solution; the approach to turn the problem into an opportunity.

Content Analysis

Depending on what is appropriate for the situation at hand, the necessary media materials that require review could range from a complete analysis of all media coverage pertaining to an organization over a particular time period of interest, to a much narrower slice of coverage in trade journals on a specific issue or product. Regarding social media, this could include a review of a content and commentary on a specific social medial channel such as Twitter or event-focused research covering multiple social media channels. Social and earned media can and should be reviewed together to generate a holistic picture of public conversation on a specific topic or issue.

Paine highlights multiple categories that can be valuable to track, including prominence, visibility, tone, sources mention, and messages communicated.[6] As an example, a campaign developed to raise the profile of a specific product could examine the entire portfolio of company media coverage for a specific subset of media (audience targeted) and then evaluate how prominently product-specific messaging was a focus of given articles. Based on this baseline research, the practitioner can establish a measurable objective—increasing the frequency (percentage) of inclusion or its prominence within coverage—and devise strategies to ensure that outgoing paid, earned, owned, and social media messages reflect this shift. Tailoring for specific metrics can ensure that each campaign is measuring the correct combination of channels and variables in order to both create reliable baselines and track success.

Media Coverage Analysis. One of the more valuable places to start when initiating research on a new project is to conduct media analysis on the specific organization, challenge, or industry in question. This specific type of content analysis can be conducted either quantitatively or qualitatively, formally or informally. By using digital tools to help in the analysis, it can be easy to catalogue data or trends from the time period of interest. This is important in understanding how a specific issue has been framed and reported, which journalists are interested in the topic, and how much media coverage the topic has historically received.

As an example, consider a technology company interested in launching a new application for serious at-home cooks. In order to understand the relevant opportunities for earned media, paid media, and social media, an organization could research specific recipes, ingredients, and techniques that best fit a desired demographic profile from a variety of food-related websites. They might then select the top five websites/media outlets that support the key factors that they have researched and further investigate all associated articles, authors, and topics that appear most frequently. By following this approach, an organization can compile large amounts of quantitative data that support the subsequent planning stages of objective creation, content and messaging development, and audience demographics. Additional qualitative analysis could help to determine questions of tone, article structure, newsworthiness, and target journalists for media relations outreach.

This type of analysis requires a certain degree of pretesting to develop the appropriate scope. For example, searching publications and periodicals that specifically serve the target audience using a defined set of key terms can provide valuable insights regarding an acceptable approach to outreach. Narrowing the research down to the most relevant terminology (as defined by the publications) and the most relevant publications (as defined by the terminology) ensures that deeper, more time-intensive research is time well spent.

Survey Development

Survey questions. As part of survey construction, researchers construct scales—sets of questions or *items*—that address a particular concept or attitude. Often, such questions will be constructed on a "strongly agree" to "strongly disagree" continuum known as a Likert-type scale. Likert-type scales always have an odd number of responses to allow for a "neutral" answer.

Additional options include open-ended questions, multiple-choice questions, and ranking answers.[7] Open-ended questions (often including an empty response box, for example) are not conducive to easy quantification but can add depth and nuance to understanding a particular issue. Multiple-choice questions can be valuable for illuminating the potential causes for a particular challenge, the value of certain solutions, or the resonance of particular messages. Including an "other" option is a useful way to gather information that falls outside the researcher's initial conception of the answers. Finally, ranking answers—asking respondents to order a set of answers in a particular order (best-to-worst, most likely to least likely, etc.)—can be a valuable method for understanding the relative importance or benefits of certain concepts, messages, or potential actions.

Types of survey data collection. There are several methods through which survey data can be collected, dependent on the type of respondent and type of information at hand. For example, a survey looking to capture public opinion on a statewide ballot initiative will be most generalizable, credible, and efficient using a short telephone survey and professional callers. Surveys of existing customers or donors would be least invasive (and most truthful) when done privately and confidentially through a digital survey tool such as SurveyMonkey or Qualtrics. Examinations of specific communities for nonprofit campaigns and outreach—particularly when publics may have limited access to technology—may be accomplished most effectively through personal intercept interviews, where the survey team collects responses in-person. These often work best in high-traffic public places that reflect the survey's purpose, such as malls, libraries, or community centers. Digital and telephone surveys are most effective for collecting large amounts of data quickly, but phone numbers and e-mail addresses can be difficult and expensive to collect.[8] Personal interviews can provide the greatest depth of information and access to difficult-to-reach populations but take significant resources and training to implement. Mail surveys are still used widely but are increasingly being replaced by digital alternatives with higher response rates, significantly faster data collection, and nearly instantaneous analysis tools. That said, mail still may be a reasonable choice for select publics, demographic groups, or geographic locations. With all methods, practitioners should focus on increasing response and completion rates by having concise questions and regular follow-up.

Sampling vs. census. When conducting surveys, researchers must enter the domain of sampling: gathering data from select respondents to represent the whole. By contrast, a census is a universal sample. Practitioners may also, depending on the circumstances, choose a random or probability sample of a given population, or a nonprobability sample.[9] Probability samples allow generalizations to be made about the entire population at hand, while nonprobability samples only have statistical validity within the respondents.[10] There are many advantages to a census approach when available, including procuring specific information, rather than having to extrapolate estimates from smaller sample sizes. However, a true census requires contacting each and every member of the identified group, which is often extremely difficult and a time consuming, expensive, and inefficient approach.[11] Some audiences are easily accessible and conveniently available at the same time. This might include taking advantage of a gathering of company shareholders at an annual meeting, reaching out to employees during a work retreat, or customers at the point-of-purchase.[12]

OBJECTIVES

How *Not* To Write Objectives

There are multiple approaches that we have highlighted to aid in the development of valuable objectives, but it is also valuable to examine what *not* to do through ways objectives can be poorly written.

- **Does the measurement matter? (Output-based rather than outcome-based):**
  - A variety of metrics have been used in the history of PR to keep pace with a data-driven business world and to gain leadership buy-in relative to the marketing and advertising functions. Unfortunately, many of them have been based less on impact and more on measurement methods including ad value equivalency (AVE), or counting the number of media clips rather than looking at their value.[13] The 2010 adoption and subsequent 2015 revision of the

Barcelona Principles for PR Measurement explain that AVE and clip counting are not valuable objectives as they do not directly relate to organizational goals.[14]

- Examples:
  - Original (output) objective: Place seven media stories in targeted industry publications prior to a January event.
    - This objective is easily measurable but not based on an audience outcome.
  - Revised (outcome) objective: Drive web traffic (1,500 visitors) to the registration page for a January event among key industry audiences.
    - This objective is both easily measurable *and* clearly focused toward the organizational goal of event attendance.
    - Strategies for executing this objective may include media relations outreach with stories including a link directly to the registration page.

- **Is the objective primarily communication driven? (Not tied to public relations efforts):**
  - Public relations objectives can be sidetracked with shared objectives, specifically those relying on the outputs from another department. This can happen with sales and marketing, human resources, events, membership, fundraising, and many other functions within the organization. Organizational goals and objectives at the highest level can often only be achieved when departments work together. The development of appropriate public relations objectives improves the outcome and cohesiveness.
  - Examples:
    - Original (multidepartmental) objective: Increase employee retention by 15 percent over the next year.
      - This objective relies on multiple factors outside of communication efforts. The human resources department may not be supportive of the initiative or have any resources that support or justify communication efforts on behalf of this objective.
    - Revised (communication-specific) objective: Increase employee awareness of a new benefits package from 30 percent to 60 percent over the next six months.
      - This objective focuses on awareness and information distribution within the scope of what communication can accomplish.
      - While the revised objective may not solve the entire organizational challenge, it does tackle a communication-specific piece of the retention puzzle. Continued cross-functional cooperation during the

planning, implementation, and evaluation phases of the campaign would ensure a coordinated effort toward the larger objectives.
- Additional communication objectives working toward a similar organizational objective may include those related to a change of opinion about the employer, development of new internal communication tools, or even new channels to improve the flow of information within the organization.

- **How much impact will come from achieving the objective? (Not closely related to organizational goals):**
  - Objectives can be extremely well written, clear, and measurable, but not relate closely enough to organizational priorities. This may include a media relations effort that does not result in on-message coverage, campaigns that do not adequately prioritize the audiences they target, as well as disconnections between short-term and long-term objectives.
  - Examples:
    - Original objective: Increase awareness of consulting services for existing clients from 50 percent to 75 percent over the next six months.
      - If the organizational priority is to target *new* clients with consulting services, rather than existing clients, it doesn't matter how effective they are at exposing existing clients to this information.
    - Revised objective: Capture contact information from 20 potential clients interested in consulting services over the next three months.
      - The revised objective measures an opt-in behavior on the part of the potential client, rather than awareness, as well as focusing on new clients rather than existing clients.
      - Strategies for this approach could include internal and external research as needed to define the ideal new client; targeted awareness efforts using paid, earned, shared, and owned media; as well as a lead-capture strategy such as a dedicated landing page as part of a website or blog.

- **Is it organizationally feasible? (Not enough enthusiasm, time, or resources to complete the effort):**
  - Some objectives may be ideal from the perspective of the public relations team but not the best approach for other areas of the organization. This situation can cause significant internal conflict and divert the resources and energy needed to accomplish the goal. Of course, the more organizational clout the public relations department or agency carries (usually earned through prior success), the better chance that they have of bringing other departments and executive leadership around to their position.

- Examples:
  - Original objective: Increase awareness of a new type of mortgage loan product among targeted prior customers from 15 percent to 30 percent in the next three months.
    - Unfortunately, the objective starts at the same time as a new regulatory measure comes into effect, taking up significant time for the loan officers who would have spearheaded the outreach.
  - Revised objective: Increase awareness of a new type of mortgage loan product among targeted prior customers from 15 percent to 30 percent in the next six months.
    - As the new mortgage loan product was not revolutionary, simply new to the company, communicators may recommend that the campaign could either begin later or be spaced over a longer period of time to ensure key internal stakeholders were able to fully participate.
    - The objective can also be revised to lower the measured change, assuming that loan officers would not be able to participate.

STRATEGIES

When to Not Use Social Media

While the overwhelming narrative is that organizations must use social media constantly, it is easy to find examples of when *not* to use social media as part of strategic campaigns. In 2013, communicators at JPMorgan Chase, the largest bank in the United States, used the @JPMorgan handle to tweet, "What career advice would you ask a leading exec at a Global firm? Tweet a Q using #askJPM. On 11/14 a $JPM leader takes over @JPMorgan." The strategic transparency backfired when JPMorgan Chase, a company that had been heavily implicated in the 2008 financial crisis and had recently suffered criticism for significant losses due to exceptionally risky stock market trades, received an avalanche of negative tweets from hundreds including disgruntled consumers and opportunistic reporters. A *New Yorker* article recapping the incident put it succinctly: "This is Twitter's very purpose: to allow any individual to share the same space with, for example, a hugely powerful bank. . . . Unlike at JPMorgan's Park Avenue headquarters, there are no security guards keeping undesirable elements out of Twitter."[15]

While organizations may control the initial message, any response is out of their hands. In this way, social media strategies carry inherent risk. The rewards of a successful campaign often clearly outweigh such risks, but it is a calculation that communication team members should make based on thorough analysis and understanding of the organization and the publics involved. Practitioners should ask themselves and their colleagues, "what is the worst thing that could happen?" before undertaking strategies on potentially challenging subjects.

Review: Positioning Campaigns for Maximum Impact

Uniqueness

Whether it's a channel, a message, or the strategy itself, finding a way to make it new or distinctive will always add value. A story can become more newsworthy, an event can become more attractive for potential attendees, and a member donation can be made more impactful. Uniqueness is often found when organizations act the opposite way from how their audiences expect them to.

That said, content, programming, or campaigns need not be wholly new to reap the benefits. It can be new for a region, new to an industry, or new to a company. It's the degree of difference from expectation or from competitors that defines its value for a given audience. This holds both for the impact to a reporter (news value) as well as the impact on an organizational stakeholder.

Audience Focus

If a strategy is not right for the audience, it doesn't matter how big the budget, how bold the message, or how well-timed a campaign might be.[16] At the strategic level, practitioners should consider how the audience perceives the organization or the issue at hand, how that perception must change to achieve the goal, and what the best avenue might be to facilitate that change. What does your audience need to hear to move the needle toward completing an objective? Where are they listening? When are they most likely to hear and understand your message? If a strategy clearly addresses all three of these questions, it is well on its way to being effective.

Playing to Your Strengths (and Competitor's Weaknesses)

It is a truism in advertising, marketing, and sales: trumpet your advantages over competitors. Once you have pinpointed the areas of distinction, often through SWOT analysis, it allows communicators to choose strategies and messages that effectively reinforce them. These differences could be communication-related, such as expertise and resources devoted to managing and monitoring social media channels, or it could be company-, product-, or service-related, such as having a highly regarded industry expert on staff. This knowledge could inform strategies across a variety of channels impacting the campaign, such as content creation and distribution (expert white papers or bylined articles), media relations (expert source for reporters), or events (expert speaking opportunities). Even channel-specific advantages can support multiple strategies. A superior social media team can strengthen real-time customer interactions during an event, while improving the impact of earned media placements through additional sharing and promotion.

TACTICS

Types of Advertising

Outdoor. Outdoor advertising, traditionally dominated by print billboards that are located on or near highly trafficked roads, provides cost-effective advertising options for organizations. Both standard, highway-sized billboards and smaller *junior* billboards are generally purchased for a defined period of time (by the week or month), allowing for effective audience repetition and awareness for organizations and their events, products, or announcements. As some communities see billboards as unsightly, there are many local restrictions on their size and placement, making it difficult to blanket a community in the way that broadcast advertising can. Billboards are often purchased through national firms with availability in all major markets.[17] Beyond traditional billboards, *transit advertising* (such as on buses and trains), building signage, and digital billboards can all offer additional flexibility and target different audiences.

Print. Traditional newspaper, trade publication, or magazine advertising focuses on specific audiences bound by geography, profession, or interest much more clearly than broadcast media. There are multiple types of newspaper advertisements. *Display advertising* includes large, often image-driven ads scattered throughout the publication. By contrast, *classified ads* are smaller, organized by content, text-heavy, and contained in a specific section.[18] Print ads are generally measured in inches and priced by size, color, location, and audience. As a prime location, the back cover of a magazine, for example, is often much more expensive than inside pages. Overall, rates are often driven by the type of audience as much as its size: a publication that targets high-income consumers or business executives will often charge more for the same advertisement than one that has a lower-income or less influential readership.

Radio. Similar to television, traditional broadcast radio stations often carry a mix of local and national content based on their format (news/talk, music, community/public radio, etc.). As commuters are the primary radio listeners, the most expensive periods for advertising are during *drive time*: the morning and evening commutes of local residents. Listeners often tune in daily to the same radio personality or channel, creating a more reliable audience than other media.[19] While alternative distribution channels such as satellite radio, digital live streaming, and podcasts continue to grow, the majority of advertising opportunities are still found within traditional over-the-air broadcasts.

TV. Television advertising starts with the relatively high cost of both creative production (the ads themselves) and air-time (the duration, frequency, and location where they appear). With that in mind, there is significant variance between relatively inexpensive local network affiliate advertising, regional or national cable advertising, and national network advertising. Ads within a program are called participating program announcements, or participations. Longer-form ads that resemble programming are called infomercials.[20] When purchasing TV ads, discounts are available given quantity and frequency. Airtime during primetime evening programs is the most expensive.

Digital Display. Digital display ads come in a variety of formats, from the ubiquitous pop-ups to website banners; each with continuously evolving targeting and richness. Such ads can be directed based on a combination of the context of the content, user behavior, geography, time of day, and numerous other factors.[21] Advertisers are working to balance the robust capability of these ads to include attention-grabbing animation, sound, and other features, with the potential for intrusion and annoyance of the audience.

Search Engine Marketing (SEM). Paid advertising directly to search engines, such as Google or Bing, allows organizations to have ads served to potential customers, members, donors, or supporters based on specific search terms, demographics, and geographic factors. It is the most popular form of digital advertising.[22] Distinct from organic search and search engine optimization (SEO), paid SEM results in advertisements set apart from the organic results. Tools such as Google AdWords allow organizations to create highly customized, flexible, and scalable SEM campaigns for targeting their audiences. Rather than a negotiation method to purchase ads, used in most other formats, SEM uses a bid format based on the popularity and competitiveness of the keywords.[23] Such functionality makes SEM complicated to execute effectively, which can be a barrier for many small organizations.

Social Media. Paid social media outreach or advertising is another growing area available to even the smallest organizations. The detailed information available for each individual user allows for very specific targeting and efficient paid outreach. There are a variety of paid options available on many different social media channels; ranging from boosting existing content—paying for additional reach on organizational posts or events—to display and banner advertising. While Facebook and other platforms reward conciseness and visually compelling ads (rather than text-heavy content), research has shown that "informativeness" and creativity are critical drivers of consumer action for advertising on social networking sites.[24] To be informative, ads must give audiences the relevant information they need and expect. Creativity in this context captures attention both through the approach as well as the design and structure of the advertisement itself. Tactics can range from a variety of message strategies (i.e., functional appeals, emotional appeals, or comparative appeals) to promotions (i.e., sweepstakes, discounts, and special events), and user-generated content (i.e., submission contests, engaging surveys, or other brand engagement activities).[25]

Event Sponsorship. An opportunity to connect with professional networks or large community groups fuels investment in event sponsorship. There may be large discrepancies in pricing between becoming the named sponsor for an entire regional music festival or sponsoring snacks at the mid-afternoon break of a local professional conference. Organizations should tailor event-related opportunities to their budget and, as much as possible, to the themes and messages they are trying to convey. Event coordinators often have broad flexibility to customize sponsorship opportunities based on budget and organizational needs. That said, companies can be competitive in jockeying for position at key events, so locking in sponsorships early is always recommended.

Media Relations Tools

Media Advisories. Media advisories are invitations for media to cover a specific event scheduled for a defined date, time, and location. Any advisory should include (in a list rather than paragraph format) what the event is, who will be taking part, when it will take place, where it will take place (either geographically or digitally), and why it is newsworthy. Leveraging media advisories can be particularly useful for campaign events where a broad range of journalists may be invited. They should be concise but clearly outline why a reporter would want to attend. The hook is often about the experience that can be captured as much as the news value of the information being shared.

Press Releases/News Releases. The ubiquitous press release or news release, while often considered out-of-touch in a world of increasingly customized media outreach, can still serve as a highly effective outreach tool. Howard and Matthews describe the press release as "a for-your-information memorandum to an editor."[26] Like a memo, the information contained within a press release should be concise, while also answering the major questions a journalist might have about the announcement. It should provide a basic grounding from which a reporter can further research and gather information for a story. Most importantly, such an announcement must contain genuine news. A press release without news value is as appetizing for reporters as being offered a sandwich and receiving two pieces of dry bread. Practitioners should understand the value in a release before they send it out and only share it with reporters who would appreciate that news value for their beat and their readers.

Press Conferences and Media-friendly Events. Despite the reduction in media resources to cover news stories, media-focused events can still be a useful tactic to gain coverage and support other strategic objectives. Events cultivate relationships with key audiences, provide information, and can be much more engaging and immersive than a press release. That said, the days of holding a press conference for every major corporate announcement are long gone. Practitioners should always ask themselves what an event would add to the story for a reporter. Why would it be more effective than a traditional announcement? Would the event still be a success if no reporters attended? What content (images, video social media posts, narratives, etc.) could be captured during the event for future use? Do I have the budget to achieve the event's goals?

When planning events with the media in mind, it is important to consider what would make it convenient and valuable to cover, such as timing, visuals, and community relevance. In some cases, these questions may point to a staged media event with relevant speakers. If the news value is high enough, a full-scale event may be the best fit. If not, a media conference call with key parties may be able to address the same media needs and be more efficient for everyone involved. Reporters should be sent invitations to such events well in advance, as well as reminded as the date of the event approaches.[27] A media advisory (see description above) is designed specifically for this purpose.

Bylined Articles and Op-ed Pieces. Many practitioners underestimate a media outlets' willingness to accept and publish submitted content. When organizations have something to say, be it a clear position on a topic, an insight to share, or a point to drive home, opportunities such as op-ed pieces and bylined articles become a useful tool. An op-ed, short for *opposite of the editorial page*, is a focused, single-issue perspective piece designed for a general audience.[28] Bylined articles, often accepted by industry trade publications, can provide a look inside the successful strategies, unique decisions, or innovative technologies. The most effective bylines for both journalists and a publication's audience are educational and informative rather than self-serving for the author's organization.

For example, a company opposed to a piece of state legislation may gain added publicity and credibility, as well as influencing the debate at hand, a thoughtful 500-word essay from the CEO explaining the potential challenges of such new laws. Hundreds of local and national op-eds are published in the United States every day. Alternatively, trade publications appreciate bylined articles that provide insight into processes, innovations, trends, or controversies within that industry. With a new technology, product, or process, it may make the most sense to have an article with the VP of Engineering's byline, while a story focused on the organization itself may have more value coming from the CEO. It is particularly important to find the right degree of technical language for an industry audience, particularly as an outside agency practitioner. Often, the slow process of reading multiple industry publications and asking many deliberate questions about terminology can bring communicators up to speed.

Shared Media

Blogs: An Organization's Content Hub. The center of social media outreach is the idea of blogging; individuals sharing their ideas with anyone else in the world who stumbles upon them. Organizations should consider one central point of information for their digital presence and organize around it.[29] Often, this job is done by a blog or blog-like part of the organization's website. The ability to post original or curated content and solicit public feedback through comments and discussion are the foundation of Web 2.0; or the *social web*. This major advance made interactivity accessible to those without knowledge of programming languages and made the Internet a significantly more potent force for (and sometimes against) public relations practitioners.

Many different types of blogs exist, both in form and function. The most traditional (such as many hosted on sites such as Blogger and WordPress) feature a single author or core group of authors, a key topic or theme, and a regular posting schedule. The blogger owns and controls the main content on the site, although he or she usually allows and encourages interactivity. At the other end of the spectrum are the micro blogging sites such as Twitter, where content length is limited, and the conversational space is shared among the user base. Social media sites such as Facebook and LinkedIn are found somewhere in between and include different forms of blogging within their functionality, as well as channels such as YouTube and Vimeo that allow the creation and sharing of (among other types of multimedia) video blogs or vlogs.

Organizations can use blog tactics as the centerpiece of a content creation strategy: a content hub. It could include traditional press room content (company news and press releases, executive bios, and photographs, as well as basic company background and content information) but also feature a variety of voices, such as employee and customer posts, and perspectives from different geographic or departmental areas. The audience includes both internal and external publics, including potential employees, customers, and community members.

Social Media Networks. Social networking allows organizations to connect, share information, and listen alongside potentially millions of customers, fans, or supporters. It gives organization's the privilege of speaking directly to this audience and audience-members the opportunity to speak back. Safko notes that, because of this delicate relationship, social network content should not be a place for selling but for building brand loyalty through sharing useful and interesting information.[30]

While many networks exist, two in particular have added significant value for many organizations: Facebook and LinkedIn. As the largest social network, Facebook has significant reach to both broad and highly targeted groups of individuals. Organizations can manage their *pages* to share content, create events, capture contact information, point users toward a website, and develop a base of followers resulting from *page likes*. Both organic and paid tactics are useful for increasing exposure to key audiences and drive engagement as part of campaigns. Successful outreach requires a long-term content strategy, including multimedia, and an understanding of what your organization's audience will find both readable and shareable. As Facebook is considered a personal social network, its content tends to focus less on business-to-business and more on consumer products and services.

LinkedIn, by contrast, functions for many users like a rolodex; a listing of individuals and their job histories. Many organizations have also taken advantage of the network's underutilized sharing and connectivity functions. As part of campaigns, LinkedIn can be a valuable place to share content. As a professional network, LinkedIn provides an avenue for conducting business-to-business conversations and networking, improve job skills, or career advancement. While LinkedIn may not necessarily be a fit for every campaign, many could benefit from its reach.

Microblogging. Twitter is the clear microblogging leader with more than 320 million monthly users as of March, 2016.[31] Microblogging can be particularly effective for expanding coverage, engagement, and digital participation in campaign events, as well as to connect with key influencers or constituencies. Organizations can feature a variety of relevant content, including retweeting important information, starting public conversations about issues, and linking to organizational content, including blog posts. Since Twitter is largely public and searchable, it can serve as a useful listening tool as well. One downside of engagement is that it requires organizations to post content consistently in order to be impactful. Organizations must evaluate whether the investment required to create and manage the content will be sustainable for the length of the campaign.

Hashtags allow organizations to enter or create conversations around events, campaigns, and other interest areas.[32] By considering relevant, concise hashtags, practitioners can more easily drive conversations among those interested in specific topical content.

Image, Video, and Interest Sharing. A variety of image and video-driven social networks have evolved and added unique functionality to the social sphere. YouTube and Vimeo are the largest long-form video sharing services. As the algorithms for Facebook and other channels continue to prioritize video sharing, these channels will only grow in importance. While the quality of video for shared media does not necessarily need to match broadcast media standards or budgets, practitioners should focus on the quality of their message. As Safko points out, the most important element is "quality content, not quality production."[33] If a cellphone video communicates the message to viewers and captures a shareable, authentic moment, it may be more effective than spending tens of thousands of dollars on professional video production. It is all about the context, message, and, of course, the audience at hand.

Additionally, a wide variety of niche networks have evolved for sharing specific types of content. Each has its own set of customs and should only be used organizationally when the content is a very clear fit with its functionality. For example, many fashion and lifestyle brands have embraced Instagram's and Pinterest's cultures of high-quality images, while location-driven brands can take advantage of Snapchat's geofilters. Live video streaming using Facebook Live and other apps may also be a useful way to share important campaign events with those who may not be able to attend in person. The evolving possibilities of social media mean that practitioners must constantly investigate and evaluate new channels and possible tactics relevant to their organization or clients.

With any social network, establishing an audience is a significant investment of time, effort, creativity, and oftentimes, financial resources. As campaigns are time-bound and budgeted, practitioners must prioritize the channels for interaction based on where audiences already exist. Put simply, an organization would be better served to focus additional campaign resources to support their strong, active Facebook following, rather than branching out into new networks, even if the content may be a strong fit for Instagram or Pinterest. With that being said, campaigns can also be an opportunity to expand an organization's social media presence, particularly when it is done logically and with a long-term focus.

Community Management. Social media community management should be an ongoing activity for organizational communication, but it can also be integrated into campaigns as a tactical approach. AudienceBloom founder and CEO Jayson DeMers defined community management, distinct from social media channel management, as "the process of creating or altering an existing community in an effort to make the community stronger."[34] Communities, whether based on organizations or interest, can be extremely valuable groups to tap or empower as part of campaign tactics. Such tactics must be managed carefully to ensure that information shared is valuable to the community and not just to the organization. Communities have specific rules, and campaign tactics should only include them if the organization or its members, staff, or other stakeholders are already active, contributing participants.

Whether sharing content or managing communities for a campaign, being able to listen is also of immense importance. It goes beyond simply turning on and responding to notifications about an organization's existing channels. Listening comes in the form of following both the broad trends and discussions that happen on relevant social media channels, as well as the evaluation of specific posts, content types, channels, communities, and strategies. Even if sharing content with such communities is not an appropriate step, being a part of the conversation can lead to valuable insights about their conventions, the style and tone of discussions, and the types of messages that resonate.

Owned Media

Website Content Management. Organizational websites are nonnegotiable in today's business world. They are a foundational piece of credibility and are one of the first places any new stakeholder goes to learn about the organization and to take actions, such as purchasing products, downloading content, or renewing a membership. Campaigns often seek a form of conversion, an action such as buying an event ticket or signing up for an e-mail list, as an objective, and websites are often where such tactics occur.

Organizational websites exist prior to, during, and after campaigns, and integration should support the businesses' overarching purposes and messages. Campaigns often need a temporary online home as part of this digital presence. This could present itself in the form of a dedicated page or section of the website or a separate microsite that integrates all campaign information and functions; often serving as a place to drive traffic from other digital and traditional channels. Organizational websites also provide opportunities for rotating, newsworthy content as part of their homepage, and campaigns should see this as one significant opportunity to draw in users who are interested in the organization but not necessarily the campaign. Similarly, they can point interested users to dedicated campaign information.

Marketing Tactics. PRSA defines marketing as "the management function that identifies human needs and wants, offers products and services to satisfy those demands, and causes transactions that deliver products and services in exchange for something of value to the provider."[35] Many public relation activities are closely connected to marketing activities and are often underused toward marketing ends. For example, positive earned media coverage should be shared with key organizational publics. This could include integrating the media coverage into paid/boosted content shared via social media channels, e-newsletters, or even traditional printed brochures.

Publications. Organizations develop a wide variety of print and digital publications that serve both to distribute content and provide audiences the chance to browse a wider breadth of stories that they may otherwise not be exposed to. The bar for content creation in such outlets is high since the information must be both valuable and interesting to readers. Publications come in several varieties, including recurring *serial publications* like newsletters (print and digital), organizational magazines, and annual reports.[36] Newsletters and magazines, even in print form, are still a popular form of organizational communication and represent an accessible way to share information both within and outside of a campaign structure. While design and production costs vary greatly, particularly when printing and mailing are involved, many organizations still see the value for member/donor outreach, sales and marketing, and event promotion. Many organizations adapt the content produced for such publications for digital purposes. Digital versions of publications, often distributed via e-mail distribution services such as MailChimp, have the advantage of metrics that track clicks on stories and links. Practitioners can use this information to improve story selection, multimedia content, and writing for future issues. The effectiveness of these publications is dependent on having an up-to-date mailing or e-mail distribution list.

Stand-alone (nonrecurring or nonscheduled) publications include e-blasts, reprints, reports, and whitepapers, as well as brochures and flyers. E-blasts are often used to alert specific audiences about more immediately newsworthy content and are timed around the specific event rather than on a weekly, monthly, or quarterly schedule. Reprints are designed versions of media articles that can be repurposed for print or digital use.[37] Copyright law's fair-use provisions provide for some internal and educational use of reprints, but public dissemination generally must be approved and paid for by the media outlet itself. Reports encompass a variety of documents from public-facing research whitepapers (which can be written and disseminated on campaign-specific topics) to customer or member-focused reports on key organizational issues. Generally, the purpose of such reports is to inform the audience in detail on a specific topic or provide information tailored for a specific time, event, or campaign. Similarly, fewer organizations have a comprehensive brochure about their work, but many have maintained product or program specific brochures. Brochures are made up of folding panels, in contrast to flyers or sales sheets, which often accomplish the same narrowly focused purpose but on a flat piece of paper.[38] One advantage to flyers and sales sheets is that they can be printed easily in-house, although the quality, particularly with color images and photos, often suffers.

Collateral Materials. Additional materials can be developed for both digital and traditional uses, either as stand-alone pieces or as part of a broader event or campaign. These can range from a variety of branded logo items to the trade show booths that will represent the business focus. Organizations often use their own space as a type of collateral, including decorations inside and outside of the building for special events. This can expand to a variety of posters and banners ranging from small easel-mounted foam core pieces to specialty printed banners that take up an entire side of a building. The design should reflect the scope and importance of the campaign itself, always representing the larger brand.

Glossary

Advertising. Paid communication: Controlled information placed in a channel by an identified sponsor, often for a specific time-period, in a specific physical space, or for a specific demographic group.

Agenda Building Theory. The process through which organizations and publics advocate for bringing isses to public attention, often using earned media and journalist relationships.

Agenda Setting Theory. Widely accepted view of how mass media interacts with society, positing that mass media do not tell us not what to think but what to think about. In this way media set the public agenda.

Associated Press. AP is a nonprofit news-gathering organization that provides global reporting services to many member news outlets, allowing them to pool resources and provide coverage of events and issues otherwise beyond their capability.

Audience. The immediate listeners/viewers or targets of a particular campaign or message. Audiences are distinct from publics in that they are created or made distinct by the organization, rather than being self-selecting.

Blog. Short for weblog, a blog provides a central point for organizations or individuals to create, curate, and share content they see as being potentially valuable to readers or publics. They are generally organized chronologically and reflect a narrow topical perspective or purpose.

Boosted Content. A paid social media strategy that allows organizations to expand the reach of their organically created or curated content; specifically targeting audiences by interest, geography, demographics, and other factors depending on the platform.

Brand. A distinct organizational identity represented through language and imagery as well as an organization's actions and behaviors. Brands are also constructed in part by an organization's publics and their conversations about its actions and identity.

Branding. The process of an organization actively engaged in creating, maintaining, adjusting, or sharing its public identity or brand.

Budget, Administration. Campaign expenditures for office-related needs, travel, and other incidental activities.

Budget, Infrastructure. Costs for upgraded items such as equipment, facilities, and software that are often wholly or partially integrated into campaign budgets.

Budget, Materials. Tactic-specific outlays such as printing, video production, or newswire distribution.

Budget, Media. Advertising and marketing costs such as print, broadcast, or digital ad buys.

Budget, Personnel. Professional time costs for the research, planning, development, execution, and evaluation of campaigns.

Budget. An estimate of income and expenditure for a set period of time or particular project.

C-Suite. A corporation's senior executive team. Titles include chief executive officer (CEO), chief financial officer (CFO), or chief technology officer (CTO).

Channel. The medium through which messages are sent, such as the elements within the PESO model (e.g., paid print advertising, earned trade media placements, organizational social media channels, or an organization's website).

Codebook. Used in the coding process for content analysis, a guide to the units of measurement (words, phrases, themes, symbols, etc.). Codebooks are particularly necessary when multiple individuals are coding the same set of data.

Coding. The process of identifying words, phrases, tones, themes, or other symbols in a variety of materials to look for frequency and patterns during content analysis.

Communication Audit. A full investigation of an organization's communication practices in order to evaluate whether they are meeting the needs of the organization as well as sakeholders and publics. An audit should examine the form and function of all existing (and potential) channels to look for areas of strength and improvement.

Communication Goal. See Public Relations Goal.

Communication Theory. The branch of knowledge dealing with the principles and methods by which information is conveyed.

Community Relations. The public relations responsibility for building and strengthening relationships with an organization's communities, including both the publics within close geographic proximity as well as digital and industry-specific stakeholders.

Competitive Objectives. In a given marketplace or industry, particular objectives may be based on success relative to the results of competitors. These could be share of voice objectives in social media or earned media coverage, as well as organizational fundraising or sales goals.

Content Amplification. The convergence process that brings together content (often owned and earned media) with paid tactics. Content amplification allows marketers to use paid tactics to increase the reach of messages to publics across multiple channels, including websites, and social media sites.

Content Analysis. The process of analyzing data (often narrative data such as media articles, social media posts, or web content) to look for critical themes, the frequency of particular words, phrases, or symbols, as well as collecting relevant metadata. Content analysis can be performed from a purely quantitative perspective using digital tools (such as counting the occurrence of specific words), or from a qualitative perspective (such as coding a set of articles for a negative, neutral, or positive tone).

Content Creation. The generation of a variety of different written and visual communication on behalf of an organization, which may be used in a multiple formats as part of paid, earned, shared, owned, and converged channels.

Content Hub. A centralized digital location (part of an owned media property such as an organization's website) to house differing types of written and multimedia content that can be repurposed, shared, and linked to through a variety of channels, including social media, digital newsletters, or earned media opportunities. Excellent content hub management includes tracking the popularity, reach, and effectiveness of each piece, as well as creating a browseable environment encouraging visitors to take in additional content.

Contingency Theory. Rather than falling into rigid categories, most organizations practice a variety of models of strategic communication (on a continuum from advocacy to accommodation) based on multiple internal and external factors.

Control Group. In a scientific experiment, the group that is not acted on by the variable being studied.

Controlled Media. Primarily paid and owned media channels where the organization has full control of the design, content, timing, and reach of the messages.

Converged Media. Within the PESO model, media that overlaps several categories, such as boosted posts through social media that maintain qualities of both paid and shared content.

Conversion. Often used as a metric to track campaign success: a member of a target group completing a desired action such as donating to a fundraiser, buying a product, or signing up for an e-newsletter.

Corporate Social Responsibility. Also referred to as CSR, an organizational philosophy that emphasizes an organization's obligation to society beyond profit.

Counselling. Advising management or organizational leaders concerning policies, strategy, public relations, and communication.

Crisis Communicaiton. Communicating on behalf of organizations facing a significant threat to their reputation and/or their legitimacy. It involves investigating and understanding how publics and stakeholders view the situation and devising appropriate communication approaches to rebuild relationships with these groups.

Crowdfunding. The practice of funding a project or venture by raising small donations from a large number of people, typically through digital channels.

Data. The content analyzed through research. Data can take many forms, from interview transcripts and media articles to social media posts and experiment results.

Diagnosis. The process of identifying the core problem or opportunity for communication and public relations efforts. It should be based on information gleaned from internal and external research, balancing the organization's goals, immediate environmental circumstances, and resources to identify where the greatest positive impact can be made.

Diffusion Theory. Diffusion Theory describes the process of a community or society adopting technology (including both physical devices and ideas) from early adopters through laggards. While individuals have different degrees of desire and enthusiasm for this process, they all must go through the same steps of being exposed to the technology and testing it before choosing to adopt it. Those at the front end often become trend setters or opinion leaders helping to popularize or inform others about new developments.

Diversity. Differences among individuals within a group, including both potentially visible factors (age, gender, ethnicity, disability, etc.) and potentially invisible factors (sexual orientation, gender identity, religion, health status, and socioeconomic status, etc.). Diversity is valued among public relations practitioners due to the wide variety of individuals and publics with which organizations communicate.

Earned Media. When practitioners use media relations to provide information subsidies to and build relationships with journalists, bloggers, and others, increasing the probability that they include an organization's ideas and perspective as part of media coverage.

Employee Relations. Communication between organizational leadership and employees. Effective employee relations improves employees' understanding of their role and value within the organization as well as increases management's knowledge of employee needs.

Evaluation. The analysis of completed or ongoing activities that determine or support a public relations campaign.

Excellence Theory. Specifies how excellent public relations makes organizations more effective. It presents a strategic framework for PR departments to understand their organizations' environments, make contributions to leadership and decision-making, as well as measuring the value of public relations.

Financial Communication. Public relations efforts that focus on financial issues with organizations (often public companies), such as attracting new investors, maintaining and improving relationships with current investors, and disseminating information used by those active in the financial markets. It includes the work of investor relations or shareholder relations.

Framing Theory. By focusing attention on certain events, issues, or themes a communicator places them within a field of meaning for their audience, and points them toward what information is most critical.

Gantt Chart. A campaign planning and execution tool that visually represents a variety of campaign activities and the timeline during which they will each be implemented.

Generalizability. Formal research using a comprehensive or representative sample makes the results applicable to a larger group than the study itself.

Global Public Relations. Cross-national public relations, involving either an organization communicating to publics in a different country from where it is based, or to publics in multiple countries at the same time.

Government Relations. Communication and relationship building between organizations and government officials, including elected officials and regulators. Often, it involves advocacy to influence policy and regulatory decisions that impact an organization or industry.

Hard Costs. Fixed expenditures that cannot change during the course of the campaign, such as production of collateral materials, event costs, and broadcast ad buys.

Hashtag. Originating on Twitter, a symbol (#) preceding a word or phrase to allow for its categorization or search within a social media channel or channels.

Hierarchy of Needs Theory. As human beings, we prioritize our needs from the most essential (such as air, food, water, and shelter) to self-fulfillment. PR practitioners must understand whether publics are in need of information about their basic survival (as in a natural disaster), major household or societal needs (such as hiring or layoff announcements) or personal identity (including sales of consumer products and services).

I.M.P.A.C.T. Influence or tone, Message communicated, Prominence, Audience reached, Consultant/spokesman quoted, and Type of article.

Impact Role for Communication. Communication cannot solve all problems. Like any tool, it has areas where it is more or less effective. An important facet of setting public relations or campaign goals is understanding the circumstances so that efforts are aimed at where communication engagement can make a significant, positive impact.

Implementation. The point in the campaign process where the campaign plan is put into operation.

Influencer. An expert in a specific category with a loyal and engaged following.

Information Subsidy. The value of information provided to a reporter by a source, including public relations professionals.

Integrated Marketing Communications. Coordinated communication activities developed to promote or sell products and services using a variety of paid, earned, shared, and owned channels.

Issues Management. The organizational process of monitoring, evaluating, and (when appropriate) engaging in public conversations about societal issues.

Iterative Planning. Research, goal-setting, and campaign planning are not separate, ordered steps, but part of a continuous cycle of understanding the organization and its environment. Communicating and listening to publics serve both to share information on behalf of the organization, but also to raise new questions and prompt more research.

Lead Capture. A potentially valuable marketing-based objective, gathering contact information for interested potential customers or donors can be a useful outcome of campaign communication and relate very directly to organizational goals and objectives.

Lead Generation. Broadly, public relations generates awareness for organizations, products, and services that open the door to behaviors such as buying products, attending events, or donating to nonprofits. Specifically, public relations campaigns can generate and capture sales/donor leads among specific audiences as part of their objectives.

Likert-type Scale. A popular and established measurement item construction using an odd number of points along a "strongly agree" to "strongly disagree" continuum of answers.

Management by Objectives (MBO). A widely used model developed by Peter Drucker, management by objectives (MBO) outlines a process through which organizational goals are broken down into their component parts to create measurable objectives assigned to different professional units (PR, sales, HR, accounting, etc.). This increases transparency and accountability for accomplishing objectives.

Marketing. Marketing involves the processes for developing, designing, delivering, and tracking strategies for promoting and selling items of value (products and services) to customers or members of businesses and other organizations.

Marketing Research. Research to improve understanding of the publics who may be interested in purchasing products or services, as well as to evaluate existing marketing practices.

Media Ad Value (or Ad Value Equivilency/AVE). A historically popular, but broadly discredited, practice of measuring the impact of earned media coverage by estimating its equivalent advertising value. The Barcelona Principles—the most important statement by top industry measurement experts—specifically call for practitioners to utilize more advanced and relevant metrics, including changes in the awareness, opinion, or behavior of publics.

Media Relations. The public relations function that deals with building and strengthening relationships with journalists. Media relations involves both proactive outreach, such as sending pitches and media alerts, as well as reactive outreach, including responding to reporter inquiries and coordinating media interviews.

Mediated Communication. Communication that is conducted via any information-disseminating medium (e.g., computer, telephone, letters).

Media Uses and Gratification Theory. People select particular media to satisfy their needs or to be entertained.

Messaging. The process of defining, crafting, integrating, and distributing organizational messages through a variety of communication channels.

Methodology. A framework, process, and perspective that informs the analysis of data or information, such as quantitative or qualitative approaches to research.

Microblogging. The short posts, often including links, images, and video, that characterize social media content on platforms such as Facebook, LinkedIn, and Twitter.

Native Advertising. Organization-generated content which resembles a media outlet's editorial content but is paid for by the organization and intended to promote it. To be effective, native advertising should be tailored to the media outlet and its audience, but also clearly labeled as paid content.

Newsworthiness. The qualities that make a particular story appealing for journalists to cover, including timeliness, uniqueness, breadth of impact, and relevance to the media outlet's audience.

Nonmediated Communication. Communication that is conducted face to face and not via an information-disseminating medium (e.g., computer, telephone, letters).

Objectives. Specific, measurable statement of what needs to be achieved as part of reaching a goal.

Observer Bias. Individuals are predisposed to evaluate results to confirm their own opinions and biases.

Online Community Management. Organizational engagement with digital communities, best conducted in mutually beneficial ways that include information sharing and organizational listening.

Organizational Goal. Significant, stable, long-term aspirations defined by the management and leadership of organizations.

Outcome Objectives. Measurable changes in the behavior of publics that contribute directly to organizational goals through action, such as increased website traffic, sales, event attendance, or, for advocacy campaigns, public opinion shifts.

Output Objectives. Measurable process objectives that support reaching more important outcome objectives, but do not by themselves meet organizational goals. This may include earned media outreach and media tracking or basic social media outreach.

Outtake Objectives. Measurable objectives that support reaching more important outcome objectives, but do not by themselves meet organizational goals. This may include awareness of organizational messages or social media engagement metrics.

Owned Media. The editorial and messages produced by an organization and distributed across its numerous owned, controlled communication channels.

Paid Media. The channels for which money is paid to place the message and control its distribution.

Persuasion. An attempt to influence a person's actions or beliefs. Persuasion can take many forms, including appeals to his or her self-interest; techniques such as logical, credibility-based, or emotionally-driven arguments (logos/ethos/pathos); or using power, influence, or other compliance-gaining tactics.

PESO. An acronym for paid, earned, shared, and owned media. In the PESO model, each channel delivers unique importance and can be used together in a wide variety of combinations during campaigns.

Press Agentry Model. Creating newsworthy stories and events to attract media attention and gain public notice, although not all attention may be positive. Categorized as one-way communication, this model may use persuasion, half-truths, and manipulation to influence an audience to behave as the organization desires.

Press Room. A website page or group of pages that provide reporters and other outside entities with materials necessary for research on the organization, including traditional press releases and media kit items (i.e. fact sheets, executive bios, backgrounders, and high-resolution images), as well as videos, informational links, and prior media coverage.

Proactive Public Relations. Outreach centering on content creation and distribution through PESO channels to share organizational perspectives and drive change in awareness, opinions, and behaviors of key publics.

Programmatic Media Buying (sometimes called Programmatic Buying). Traditional paid media is purchased strategically by advertising, marketing, or public relations professionals in consultation with sales specialists at media outlets or other channels, but programmatic buying uses algorithmic approaches so that ads are continually optimized toward specific goals for awareness or activation.

Promotion. Activities and tactics designed to win publicity or attention. Promotional activities often generate interest in a person, product, organization or cause, and often focus on the needs of journalists in order to make the most of potential media coverage.

Propaganda. Persuasive messages and strategies designed to be in the best interests of an organization without consideration for the needs or preferences of publics. The term carries a strong negative connotation, having been associated with harmful political messages and the use of tactics such as lying and misinformation.

Public. Any group of people tied together by some common factor or interest. Demographics, psychographics, motivating self-interests, status of current relationships with an organization, location or other characteristics define these publics.

Public Information Model. Practitioners act as journalists-in-residence, providing newsworthy information flowing one way from an organization to its stakeholders. It is factual and logical information rather than persuasive or promotional.

Publicity. In media relations, the process of sharing information with journalists with the aim of publishing it for a wider audience.

Public Relations. Public relations is a strategic communication process that builds mutually beneficial relationships between organizations and their publics.

Public Relations Campaign. A public relations campaign is a strategic approach to achieving organizational and communication goals through researching, planning, implementing, and evaluating a series of objectives, strategies, and tactics.

Public Relations Goal. Informed by organizational goals, PR/communication goals should reflect the most effective use of campaign outreach (impact role) to support the achievement of organizational goals.

R.A.C.E. A four-step communication planning model. R.A.C.E.: Research and planning, Action, Communication, Evaluation.

R.O.P.E. A four-step communication planning model. R.O.P.E.: Research, Objectives, Programming, Evaluation.

Raw Volume. Simple media evaluation and reporting based solely on the number of "clips"—organizational or campaign mentions in relevant media coverage.

Reactive Public Relations. PR practices that respond to external forces rather than strategically considering the role of organizational engagement in public discourse.

Relationship. Considered by many scholars and practitioners to be the core unit of public relations success, relationships between organizations and publics are measured by factors including trust, satisfaction, commitment, and the degree of mutual control.

Relative Volume. Comparing the amount of media coverage between, for example, different organizational messages/objectives, or among competing organizations in the same publications or channels.

Reputation Management. Strategic communication efforts designed to build or rebuild an organization's perceived legitimacy by organizational publics and stakeholders. It may involve many coordinated PESO strategies and tactics; interpersonal, traditional media and digital media channels; as well as concrete changes to organizational policies and actions.

Research, Developmental. Formative research is done as part of the campaign planning process. Often, it's done to better understand an organization's environment or audiences and publics.

Research, Evaluative. Research to understand a campaign's impact and better inform future campaigns. This should be related to objectives (did the campaign achieve what it set out to achieve?) as well as beyond them (what unexpected results occurred due to the campaign?).

Research, Experimental. Scientific research designed to establish whether one variable (independent) is influencing a second variable (dependent).

Research, Formal. Research done using standardized, systematic techniques and accepted practices for social science research, including large-scale surveys, quantitative content analysis, and experimental research.

Research, Informal. Useful knowledge-gathering practices engaged in by public relations practitioners through conversations with multiple publics (inside and outside the organization) as well as maintaining a general knowledge of key issues and trends in the media. These processes might include maintaining relationships with leadership and stakeholders, consuming mainstream and trade media, following influencers on social media, and attending relevant community events.

Research, Primary. Research of many forms conducted by practitioners to inform their understanding of the organization, external situation, or a specific campaign.

Research, Qualitative. Research utilizing primarily non-quantitative, language-based approaches, providing a holistic and broad perspective on the data or phenomena being examined.

Research, Quantitative. Research grounded in numeric approaches to understanding specific phenomena, generally focused on narrowing the scope to one or several key elements (variables) to determine their importance and impact.

Research, Refinement. Research done in the middle stages of the campaign to ensure strategies and tactics are reaching audiences, having the desired impacts, and balancing channels and resources efficiently.

Research, Secondary. Often an early step in the research process, secondary research includes the gathering of insights from research conducted by others, often involving the collection and analysis of a significant number of existing reports, studies, or other primary research sources.

Research. The systematic collection and explanation of data used to increase understanding of particular phenomena.

Scope. The boundaries of a particular project or campaign. This can be a difficult to envision, particularly in the early planning stages, but practitioners must be aware of and do their best to define them for a campaign to effectively prioritize its efforts.

Shared Media. Social media channels characterized by the opportunities for all participants to engage with content, including commenting and sharing.

Share of Voice. A useful metric or objective comparing one organization, message, or campaign with competitors in a given space. It can be used to measure success on social media, earned media, or other venues.

Situational Crisis Communication Theory (SCCT). SCCT suggests that, to best protect an organization's reputation, crisis communication managers should base crisis responses on the level of crisis responsibility publics perceive, the type of crisis, and the degree of the reputational threat.

Situational Theory of Publics. Publics can be identified and classified by problem recognition, level of involvement, and constraint recognition: the degree to which they are aware of a problem, the degree to which a problem has an impact on them, and the extent to which they feel capable of doing something about the problem.

Social Listening. Systematic approaches to monitoring digital conversations to better understand publics, communities, and an organization's environment.

Social Media. Digital communication networks that allow users (both individuals and organizations) to connect with others as well as share information, opinions, and other content (images, videos, etc.) through both both public and private channels.

Social Media Analytics. The systematic collection of data about the usage of and interaction with social media channels to improve strategic decision-making both narrowly within the channel (optimizing content) and broadly (informing understanding of customer, member, or community opinion and behavior).

Social Media Monitoring. Continuous tracking of social media activities, conversations, influencers, issues, and trends to evaluate outreach and to identify upcoming challenges and opportunities.

Social Sphere. The broad network of interactive digital and social media channels that collectively create a new form of public sphere.

Soft Costs. Flexible outlays that can be responsive to environmental changes during a campaign, including professional time and some digital ad buys.

Stakeholder. Those with a concrete interest in a particular organization, including internal groups such as employees and board members as well as external groups such as customers/donors, vendors, and community members.

Strategic Communication. The deliberate use of communication and public relations by organizations to meet their goals and objectives.

Strategies. Public-specific communication approaches (often specifying the channel) used to send a message to achieve objectives.

SWOT Analysis. A process to help organizations define their strengths, weaknesses, opportunities, and threats. Generally, SWOT analyses are considered a qualitative research method that brings together a variety of secondary research about an organization and its competitors/industry peers, combined with primary research to organize and synthesize the input and perspective of organizational leaders.

Systems Theory. Systems theory explains that any system tends toward maintaining equilibrium. For an organization, this means constant and careful management of internal and external relationships, as well as continual awareness of the economic, political, and social conditions within communities that may impact an organization's publics and stakeholders.

Tactics. Strategy-specific communication products that carry messages to key publics. Tactics are tangible items such as a press release, social media post, or a website.

Theory. Explanations of interrelated concepts to better understand and predict events and behaviors.

Triangulation. The use of multiple methods and/or data sources to reinforce the credibility of research findings.

Two-step Flow of Communication. Suggests that mass media influence society's opinion leaders, who, in turn, influence society.

Two-way Asymmetrical Model. Organizations use organizational listening, research, and scientific methods to persuade stakeholders to adopt organizational perspectives or opinions.

Two-way Symmetrical Model of Public Relations. Two-way symmetrical communication prioritizes mutually beneficial communication and decision making among organizations and their publics.

Uncontrolled Media. Refers to outreach methods (such as media relations) that are not under direct control of the company, organization, or sender of messages. These channels include newspapers and magazines, radio and television, external websites, externally produced blogs and social media commentary, and externally developed news stories. Positive media outreach cannot guarantee that the public-facing content will be favorable to the organization.

Validity. Whether a specific research program or individual question/scale is measuring what it is intended to measure.

Vlogs. Video blogs, largely YouTube-based.

Weighted Volume. Quantitative reporting of media coverage using formulas to adjust the value of individual news stories based on factors such as prominence, outlet quality, and campaign message inclusion, providing a richer reporting perspective.

References

Introduction

1. Marianne Dainton and Elaine D. Zelley, *Applying Communication Theory for Professional Life: A Practical Introduction* (Thousand Oaks, CA: SAGE, 2015).
2. Merriam-Webster Dictionary. "Theory." Retrieved from https://www.merriam-webster.com/dictionary/theory.
3. Yunna Rhee, "The Employee-Public-Organization Chain in Relationship Management: A Case Study of a Government Organization," Unpublished doctoral dissertation, University of Maryland, College Park.
4. James E. Grunig. "Excellence Theory in Public Relations." Retrieved from http://www.kdpaine.blogs.com/files/encyclopedia-of-communication-9781405131995_chapter_399.pdf.
5. James E. Grunig, and Larissa A. Grunig, "Excellence Theory in Public Relations: Past, Present, and Future," In A. Zerfass, B. V. Ruler, and K. Sriramesh (Eds.), *Public Relations Research: European and International Perspectives and Innovations*, (Wiesbaden: VS Verlag, 2008), 327–347.
6. James E. Grunig, "Excellence Theory in Public Relations," In W. Donsbach (Ed.), *The International Encyclopedia of Communication*, Volume 4, (Oxford, UK and Malden, MA: Wiley-Blackwell, 2008), 1620–1622.
7. David Dozier, Larissa A. Grunig, and James E. Grunig, *The Manager's Guide to Excellence in Public Relations and Communication Management*, (Mahwah, NJ: Lawrence Erlbaum Associates, Inc., 1995), 48.
8. Scott M. Cutlip, Allen H. Center, and Glen M. Broom, *Effective Public Relations* (9th ed.), (Upper Saddle River, NJ: Pearson Prentice Hall, 2006).
9. "Diffusion of Innovation Theory." Diffusion of Innovation Theory. January 22, 2013. Accessed September 21, 2015.
10. Herbert F. Lionberger, *Adoption of New Ideas and Practices*, (Ames: Iowa State University Press, 1960), 32.
11. Carl H. Botan and Vincent Hazleton, *Public Relations Theory II*, (Mahwah, NJ: Lawrence Erlbaum Associates, 2006).
12. Ibid.
13. "Framing Theory." *Mass Communication Theory*. March 17, 2011. Accessed September 28, 2015.
14. "Diffusion of Innovation."
15. Kirk Hallahan, "Seven Models of Framing: Implications for Public Relations," *Journal of Public Relations Research* 11, no. 3 (1999): 205–242.
16. Maxwell McCombs, "Agenda Setting Function of Mass Media." *Public Relations Review*, 3 (1977): 89–95, doi: 10.1086/267990.
17. Botan and Hazleton, *Public Relations Theory*.
18. Matthew C. Nisbet, "Agenda Building," *The International Encyclopedia of Communication*, 2008. doi:10.1111/b.9781405131995.2008.x.
19. Ron Smith "Agenda Setting, Priming & Framing," Updated summer 2011, http://faculty.buffalostate.edu/smithrd/PR/Framing.htm
20. Sun Young Lee, "Agenda-Building Theory." *The SAGE Encyclopedia of Corporate Reputation*, doi: http://dx.doi.org/10.4135/9781483376493.n16.
21. W. Timothy Coombs, *The Handbook of Crisis Communication*, (Chichester, UK: Wiley-Blackwell, 2012).
22. W. Timothy Coombs, *Crisis Communication*, (Thousand Oaks, CA: Sage, 2014).
23. Cutlip, Allen, and Broom, *Effective Public Relations*.
24. Ibid.
25. Lynn M. Zoch and Juan-Carlos Molleda, "Building a Theoretical Model of Media Relations Using Framing, Information Subsidies and Agenda Building," in *Public Relations Theory II*, ed. Carl H. Botan and Vincent Hazleton (Mahwah, NJ: Lawrence Erlbaum, 2006), 279–309.
26. James E. Grunig and Todd Hunt, *Managing Public Relations*, (Belmont, CA: Thompson Wadsworth, 1984).
27. Cutlip, Allen, and Broom, *Effective Public Relations*.
28. Dozier, Grunig, and Grunig, *The Manager's Guide*.
29. Grunig and Hunt, *Managing Public Relations*.
30. Ron Smith, "Public Relations, History," *Public Relations, History* (2011), retrieved from http://faculty.buffalostate.edu/smithrd/pr/history.htm.

31. Sheila Clough-Crifasi, "Everything's Coming Up Rosie," *Public Relations Tactics* 7, no. 9 (2000).
32. Michael Turney, "Acronyms for the Public Relations Process," On-line Readings in Public Relations by Michael Turney, (April 01, 2011), Retrieved from https://www.nku.edu/~turney/prclass/readings/process_acronyms.html.
33. Nisbet, "Agenda Building."
34. James G. Hutton, "The Definition, Dimensions, and Domain of Public Relations," *Public Relations Review* 25, no. 2 (1999): 199–214.
35. Nisbet, "Agenda Building."
36. "Gilmore Girls' Early Ratings: Revival Ranks as One of Most-Watched Netflix Originals," *Ad Age* (December 01, 2016), Retrieved from http://adage.com/article/media/gilmore-girls-ratings-revival-ranks-watched-netflix-originals/306977.

Chapter 1

1. Marlene S. Neill and Erin Schauster, "Gaps in Advertising and Public Relations Education: Perspectives of Agency Leaders," *Journal of Advertising Education* 19, no. 2 (2015).
2. Regina Luttrell, "Social Networking Sites in the Public Relations Classroom: A Mixed Methods Analysis of Undergraduate Learning Outcomes Using WordPress, Facebook, and Twitter," PhD diss., California Institute of Integral Studies (2012).
3. Darrell Etherington, "People Now Watch 1 Billion Hours of YouTube Per Day," *TechCrunch* (Feb. 28, 2017), retrieved from https://techcrunch.com/2017/02/28/people-now-watch-1-billion-hours-of-youtube-per-day.
4. Robyn Blakeman, *Integrated Marketing Communication: Creative Strategy from Idea to Implementation* (Lanham, MD: Rowman & Littlefield, 2014).
5. Case provided by 360 Public Relations. "Seize the Holidays with Krusteaz: A Virtual Baking Event," Continental Mills with 360 Public Relations (2014).
6. Kimberly Vetrano, "Join the Krusteaz Virtual Baking Event on Saturday, December 14, 2013 #KrusteazHolidays," *She Scribes!*, December 12, 2013, http://www.shescribes.com/2013/12/join-krusteaz-virtual-baking-event-saturday-december-14-2013.html.
7. 360 Publications, Seize the Holidays with Krusteaz.
8. Ibid.
9. 360 Publications, Seize the Holidays; Vetrano, "Join the Krusteaz Virtual Baking Event."

Chapter 2

1. Amira Fathalla, "Migrant Crisis: Why Syrians Do Not Flee to Gulf States—BBC News," *BBC News*, (September 2, 2015).
2. Tom Hagley, *Writing Winning Proposals: PR Cases* (Boston, MA: Pearson Allyn and Bacon, 2006).
3. James Macnamara, "Organizational Listening: Addressing a Major Gap in Public Relations Theory and Practice," *Journal of Public Relations Research* 28 (2016): 146–169.
4. "What Is Strategic Communications?" IDEA (March 16, 2011), http://www.idea.org/blog/2011/03/16/what-is-strategic-communications.
5. Linda Childers Hon, "Demonstrating Effectiveness in Public Relations: Goals, Objectives, and Evaluation," *Journal of Public Relations Research* 10, no. 2 (1998): 103–135.
6. Norman R. Nager and T. Harrell Allen, *Public Relations: Management by Objectives* (Lanham, MD: University Press of America, 1991).
7. John E. Marston, *Modern Public Relations* (New York, NY: McGraw-Hill, 1979).
8. Jerry A. Hendrix and Darrell C. Hayes, *Public Relations Cases*, 7th ed. (Belmont, CA: Thomson/Wadsworth, 2007).
9. *Dictionary.com*, "Diagnose," Accessed October 24, 2015, http://www.dictionary.com/browse/diagnose.
10. Nager and Allen, *Public Relations*.
11. John V. Pavlik, *Public Relations: What Research Tells Us* (Newbury Park, CA: Sage, 1987).
12. Glen M. Broom and Bey-Ling Sha, *Cutlip & Center's Effective Public Relations*, 11th ed. (Boston, MA: Pearson, 2013).
13. Ibid, 272.
14. Patricia Swann, *Cases in Public Relations Management*, 2nd ed. (Boston, MA: McGraw Hill, 2014).
15. Dennis L. Wilcox, *Think Public Relations*, 2nd ed. (Boston, MA: Pearson, 2013).
16. Broom and Sha, *Cutlip & Center's Effective Public Relations*.
17. Michael Pizzi, "White House Turns to Crowdfunding Campaign for Syrian Refugee Crisis," (October 7, 2015). http://america.aljazeera.com/articles/2015/10/7/white-house-launches-crowdfunding-campaign-for-syrian-crisis.html
18. "The UN Refugee Agency Is Working to Relieve a Global Crisis. You Can Help," *Kickstarter*, (October 24, 2015), https://www.theguardian.com/

world/2015/oct/06/kickstarter-pairs-with-unhcr-to-help-syrian-refugees-after-white-house-call.
19. Joshua Miller, "#AidRefugees: Heeding the President's Call to Take Action." The White House, (October 6, 2015), https://obamawhitehouse.archives.gov/blog/2015/10/06/aidrefugees-heeding-presidents-call-take-action.
20. Swann, *Cases in Public Relations Management*.
21. Aviva Shen, "Why Are We So Crazy for Bacon?" *Smithsonian*, (January 17, 2012), https://www.smithsonianmag.com/arts-culture/why-are-we-so-crazy-for-bacon-20784529/https://www.smithsonianmag.com/arts-culture/why-are-we-so-crazy-for-bacon-20784529.
22. "Wake Up & Smell the Bacon—Shorty Awards for Brands, Agencies, and Organizations," (October 1, 2015), http://shortyawards.com/7th/360i.
23. "Oscar Mayer Reviving a Bacon Brand," 360i, accessed July 24, 2017, https://360i.com/work/oscar-mayer.
24. Ibid.
25. Regina Luttrell, Derek Kerr, and Nicole Raymond, "Wake Up & Smell the Bacon," Lecture, Eastern Michigan University, Ypsilanti, October 20, 2015.
26. Shen, 'Why Are We So Crazy for Bacon?"
27. "Oscar Mayer Reviving a Bacon Brand."
28. Ibid.
29. Ibid.
30. Ibid.
31. Ibid.
32. Ibid.
33. Jennifer Jolly, "TECH NOW: Wake up with a Whiff of Bacon," *USA Today*, (March 05, 2014), https://www.usatoday.com/story/tech/columnist/2014/03/05/oscar-mayer-bacon-alarm-gadget-and-app-tech-now/6072297.
34. "Oscar Mayer Reviving a Bacon Brand."
35. Ibid.
36. Ibid.
37. Nager and Allen, *Public Relations*.

Chapter 3

1. Mark Thabit, "How PESO Makes Sense in Influencer Marketing," *PR Week*, (June 8, 2015), http://www.prweek.com/article/1350303/peso-makes-sense-influencer-marketing.
2. Gini Dietrich, "PR Pros Must Embrace the PESO Model," *Spin Sucks*, (March 23, 2015), http://spinsucks.com/communication/pr-pros-must-embrace-the-peso-model.
3. Lee Odden, "Paid, Earned, Owned & Shared Media," *TopRank Marketing*, online marketing blog (2011), accessed July 19, 2016, http://www.toprankblog.com/2011/07/online-marketing-media-mix.
4. Sabine Raabe, "AVE - Does Anyone Actually Still Use This?" prowly.com. https://prowly.com/magazine/2017/06/01/peso-instead-of_ave/
5. Odden, "Paid, Earned, Owned & Shared Media."
6. Brian Solis, *X: The Experience When Business Meets Design* (Hoboken, NJ: John Wiley & Sons, 2015).
7. Scott Guthrie, "The 7 Rs of Influencer Relations." *Ketchum* (blog), (March 16, 2016), https://www.ketchum.com/7-rs-influencer-relations.
8. Odden, "Paid, Earned, Owned & Shared Media."
9. Ibid.
10. "PR & The Social Whirl: The Peso Model," *PRA Public Relations*, 2014, http://www.prapublicrelations.com/peso-media-model.
11. Ibid.
12. John McKelvey, "DigitaCannes Lions case study: Under Armour kicks its way to the top: Digital marketing industry case study library." digitaltrainingacademy.com. http://www.digitaltrainingacademy.com/casestudies/2015/07/cannes_lions_case_study_under_armour_kicks_its_way_to_the_top.php (accessed January 5, 2018).
13. E. J. Schultz, "Ad Age's 2014 Marketer of the Year: Under Armour," *AdAge*, (December 8, 2014), http://adage.com/article/news/marketer-year-armour/296088.
14. "Cannes Lions Case Study: Under Armour Kicks Its Way to the Top." *Digital Training Academy*, accessed July 22, 2016, http://www.digitaltrainingacademy.com/casestudies/2015/07/cannes_lions_case_study_under_armour_kicks_its_way_to_the_top.php.
15. Schultz, "Ad Ages's 2014 Marketer of the Year."
16. "Cannes Lions Case Study."
17. "Media Relations Campaign for Baskin Robbins Summer Flavor Promo," Schneider Associates, accessed August 3, 2016, http://www.schneiderpr.com/case-studies/media-relations-campaign-to-promote-wacky-summer-ice-cream-flavors.
18. Anna Lingeris, Rachel Brueno, and Gail Dent, "Reese's Tips-Off NCAA® March Madness® and Continues NCAA Partnership by Celebrating College Basketball Fandom." *BusinessWire*. https://www.businesswire.com/news/home/20160314006107/en/Reese%E2%80%99s-Tips-Off-NCAA%C2%AE-March-Madness%C2%AE-Continues-NCAA

19. Jose Angelo Gallegos, "The Best Social Media Marketing Campaigns of 2016," *TINT Blog* (August 21, 2017), https://www.tintup.com/blog/best-social-media-marketing-campaigns.
20. Walt Disney Word Parks and Resorts, "Disneyland® Resort and Make-A-Wish® Celebrate the Success of Worldwide 'Share Your Ears' Campaign," News release, *CISION PR Newswire* (March 14, 2016), https://www.prnewswire.com/news-releases/disneyland-resort-and-make-a-wish-celebrate-the-success-of-worldwide-share-your-ears-campaign-300235681.html.
21. Gallegos, "The Best Social Media Marketing Campaigns of 2016."
22. Albain Flamant, "5 Great Social Media Campaigns to Inspire Your 2016 Marketing Strategy," Talkwalker, (December 22, 2015), https://www.talkwalker.com/blog/5-social-media-campaigns-inspiration-2016-strategy-social-media-analytics#.
23. Andrea Yoo, "Lionsgate and Imagine Exhibitions to Debut THE HUNGER GAMES: THE EXHIBITION World Premiere Set for July 1 at Discovery Times Square," *Thinkwell Group*, (December 06, 2016), https://thinkwellgroup.com/news/lionsgate-imagine-exhibitions-debut-hunger-games-exhibition-world-premiere-set-july-1-discovery-times-square.
24. Ann Dwyer, "Gini Dietrich: Owned vs. Earned Media—Measuring the ROI," Crain's Chicago Business, (September 30, 1011), http://www.chicagobusiness.com/article/20110930/BLOGS06/309309996/gini-dietrich-owned-vs-earned-media-measuring-the-roi.
25. Mark Bonchek, "Making Sense of Owned Media," *Harvard Business Review*, (October 10, 2014), https://hbr.org/2014/10/making-sense-of-owned-media.
26. Ibid.
27. Ibid.
28. Ibid.
29. Rebecca Lieb and Jeremiah Owyang, "The Converged Media Imperative. Report," *Altimeter Group* (July 19, 2012), https://www.slideshare.net/Altimeter/the-converged-media-imperative.
30. Maureen Morrison, "Burger King Launches New Tagline: 'Be Your Way,'" (May 19, 2014), http://adage.com/article/news/burger-king-launches-tagline/293283.
31. Erik Oster, "Ad of the Day: Burger King Makes the Most Fabulous Whopper Ever for LGBTQ Pride: Sandwich Has Limited Reach but a Big Heart," (July 2, 2014), http://www.adweek.com/news/advertising-branding/ad-day-burger-king-makes-most-fabulous-whopper-ever-lgbt-pride-158724.
32. Kathy Steinmetz, "Burger King Debuts Gay Pride Whopper," *Time,* (July 1, 2014), http://time.com/2947156/burger-king-debuts-gay-pride-whopper.
33. Bruce Horovitz, "Burger King Sells Gay Pride Whopper," *USA Today,* (July 1, 2014), http://www.usatoday.com/story/money/business/2014/07/01/burger-king-gay-pride-burger-parade-fast-food-gay-rights/11903861.
34. Steinmetz, "Burger King Debuts Gay Pride Whopper."
35. Brendan Snyder, "How Brands Are Taking a Stance (and Winning) with LGBT Advertising," *Netimperative,* (April 13, 2015), http://www.netimperative.com/2015/04/how-brands-are-taking-a-stance-and-winning-fans-with-lgbt-advertising.
36. Jenn Harris, "Burger King Selling a Proud Whopper for Gay Pride," *LA Times,* July 2, 2014. http://www.latimes.com/food/dailydish/la-dd-burger-king-sells-a-proud-whopper-for-gay-pride-20140702-story.html
37. Anna Brand, "Burger King Reveals Special Gay Pride Whopper," *MSNBC,* (July 2, 2014), http://www.msnbc.com/msnbc/burger-king-proud-whopper-gay-pride-san-francisco.
38. Steinmetz, "Burger King Debuts Gay Pride Whopper."
39. Horovitz, "Burger King Sells Gay Pride Whopper."
40. Steven Overly, "What Burger King's Proud Whopper Tells Us about Marketing to LGBT Consumers," *Washington Post,* (July 3, 2014), https://www.washingtonpost.com/news/business/wp/2014/07/03/what-burger-kings-proud-whopper-tells-us-about-marketing-to-lgbt-consumers/?utm_term=.7bcdac66fb4b.
41. Sauus. n.d. *Burger King sells "Proud Whopper" in San Francisco to change views on LGBT.* Accessed March 12, 2016. http://sauus.com/b/Burger-King-sells-Proud-Whopper-in-San-Francisco-to-change-views-on-LGBT.
42. Eleftheria Parpis, "How Fernando Machado Is Bringing Burger King 'Back to Greatness,'" (May 23, 2016), http://www.campaignlive.com/article/fernando-machado-bringing-burger-king-back-greatness/1395717.

43. Patricia Swann, *Cases in Public Relations Management* (New York, NY: Routledge, 2014).
44. James F. Grunig and Fred C. Repper, "Strategic management, publics, and issues." *Excellence in Public Relations and Communication Management* (1992): 117–157.
45. Steinmetz, "Burger King Debuts Gay Pride Whopper."

Chapter 4

1. Don W. Stacks, *Primer of Public Relations Research* (3rd edition), (New York, NY: Guildford Press, 2107), 5.
2. Donald Jugenheimer, Larry D. Kelley, Jerry Hudson, and Samuel D. Bradley, *Advertising and Public Relations Research* (2nd ed.), (London, UK: Routledge, 2014), 11.
3. Stacks, 23.
4. Ibid.
5. Dennis Wilcox and Bryan H. Reber, *Public Relations Writing and Media Techniques* (Boston, MA: Pearson, 2016), 322.
6. Glen Broom and David M. Dozer, *Using Research in Public Relations*, (Englewood Cliffs, NJ: Prentice Hall, 1990), 24.
7. Glen Broom and Bey-Ling Sha, *Cutlip & Center's Effective Public Relations* (11th ed.), (Boston, MA: Pearson, 2013), 244–245.
8. Stacks, 360.
9. Stacks, 59.
10. Linda Childers Hon and James E. Grunig, "Guidelines for Measuring Relationships in Public Relations," *Institute for Public Relations* (1999).
11. Sarah J. Tracy, *Qualitative Research Methods: Collecting Evidence, Crafting Analysis, Communicating Impact*, (Malden, MA: Wiley-Blackwell, 2013), 40.
12. Ibid., 230.
13. National Association of Manufacturers, *Top Twenty Facts about Manufacturing*, (2017), http://www.nam.org/Newsroom/Facts-About-Manufacturing.
14. American Medical Association, *AMA Releases Analyses on Potential Anthem-Cigna and Aetna-Humana Mergers*, 92015),
15. http://www.ama-assn.org/ama/pub/news/news/2015/2015-09-08-analysis-anthem-cigna-aetna-humana-mergers.page.
16. Stack, 143.
17. Katie Delahaye Paine, *Measure What Matters*, (Hoboken, N.: John Wiley & Sons, 2011), 49.
18. Stacks, 271.
19. Stacks, 275.
20. Broom and Sha, *Cutlip & Center's Effective Public Relations*.
21. Thomas R. Lindloff and Brian C. Taylor, *Qualitative Communication Research Methods* (3rd ed.), (Thousand Oaks, CA: Sage, 2011).
22. University Accreditation Board, *APR Study Guide* (2017), 76.
23. Colby Vogt and Ephraim Cohen, "Survey: What Types of Content Consumers Do Want from Brands," FleishmanHillard, (July 25, 2014), http://fleishmanhillard.com/2014/07/true/survey-what-types-of-content-consumers-do-want-from-brands.

Chapter 5

1. Glen Broom and Bey-Ling Sha, *Cutlip & Center's Effective Public Relations* (11th ed.), (Boston. MA: Pearson, 2013), 265.
2. Donald W. Stacks, *Primer of Public Relations Research* (3rd ed.), (New York, NY: Guildford Press, 2017).
3. Laurie J. Wilson and Joseph D. Ogden, *Strategic Communications Planning*, (5th ed.), (Dubuque, IA: Kendall/Hunt, 2008), 75.
4. Otto Lerbinger, *Corporate Public Affairs: Interacting with Interest Groups, Media, and Government*, (Mawah NJ: Lawrence Erlbaum, 2006).
5. Katie Delahaye Paine, *Measure What Matters*, (Hoboken, NJ: John Wiley & Sons, 2011), 34–35.
6. Ronald D. Smith, *Strategic Planning for Public Relations* (3rd ed.), (New York: Routledge, 2009), 261.
7. Broom and Sha, *Cutlip & Center's Effective Public Relations*.
8. Dan Lattimore, Otis Baskin, Suzette T. Heiman, and Elizabeth L. Toth, *Public Relations: The Profession & the Practice* (4th ed.). (New York, NY: McGraw-Hill, 2012), 122.
9. Betteke Van Ruler, "Agile Public Relations Planning: The Reflective Communication Scrum." *Public Relations Review* 41, no. 2 (2015): 187–194.
10. Wilson & Ogden, 75.
11. Norman Nager and Harrell T. Allen, *Public Relations Management by Objectives*, (Lanham, MD: University Press of America, 1984).
12. Kirk Hallahan, "Organizational Goals and Communication Objectives," in D. Holtzhausen and A. Zerfass (Eds.) *The Routledge Handbook of Strategic*

Communication, (New York, NY: Routledge, 2015) p. 2015.
13. 360i, "Lean Cuisine #WeighThis." 360i, Accessed July 18, 2017, https://360i.com/work/weighthis.
14. "Global Weight Loss and Weight Management Market 2015–2019—Fitness Equipment, Surgical, Diet & Weight Loss Services Analysis." *PR Newswire*, April 23, 2015, http://www.prnewswire.com/news-releases/global-weight-loss-and-weight-management-market-2015-2019—fitness-equipment-surgical-diet–weight-loss-services-analysis-300071062.html.
15. 360i, "Lean Cuisine #WeighThis." 360i,. Accessed July 18, 2017, https://360i.com/work/weighthis/
16. Allison Baker, "Weigh What Really Matters," January 13, 2016, http://www.nestleusa.com/media/pressreleases/lean-cuisine-weigh-this-diet-filter.
17. Ibid.
18. Ibid.
19. 360i, "Lean Cuisine #WeighThis."
20. Ibid.

Chapter 6

1. Peter F. Drucker, *The Practice of Management: A Study of the Most Important Function in America Society*, (New York, NY: Harper & Brothers, 1954)
2. Ibid, 129.
3. Ibid, 121.
4. Universal Accreditation Board, *APR Study Guide*, (2017), 37.
5. Walter K. Lindenmann, "An 'effectiveness yardstick' to measure public relations success." *Public Relations Quarterly* 38 (1993): 7.
6. Matthew W. Ragas and Ron Culp, *Business Essentials for Strategic Communicators: Creating Shared Value for the Organization and Its Stakeholders*, (New York, NY: Palgrave Macmillan, 2014), 147.
7. Ibid, 148.
8. George T. Doran, "There's a S.M.A.R.T. way to write management's goals and objectives," *Management Review* (AMA FORUM)70, 11 (1981): 35–36.
9. Ibid, 145.
10. Glen M. Broom and David M. Dozier, *Using Research in Public Relations: Applications to Program Management*, (Englewood Cliffs, NJ: Prentice Hall, 1990), 13.
11. Ronald E. Rice and Charles K. Atkin, *Public Communication Campaigns* (4th ed.), (Los Angeles, CA: Sage, 2013), 14.
12. Robert C. Hornik, "Why Can't We Sell Human Rights Like We Sell Soap?," In R. E. Rice and C. K. Atkin, (Eds.) *Public Communication Campaigns* (4th ed.), (Los Angeles, CA: Sage, 2013), 35–49.
13. Ibid, 42.
14. Drucker, *The Practice of Management*.
15. Glen M. Broom and Bey-Ling Sha, *Cutlip and Center's Effective Public Relations*, (Boston, MA: Pearson, 2013).
16. Universal Accreditation Board, *APR Study Guide*, (2010).
17. Don W. Stacks and David Michaelson, A *Practitioner's Guide to Public Relations Research, Measurement and Evaluation*, (New York, NY: Business Expert Press, 2010).
18. David M. Dozier, Larissa A. Grunig, and James E. Grunig, *Manager's Guide to Excellence in Public Relations and Communication Management*, (Mahwah, NJ: Lawrence Erlbaum, 2013), 14.
19. Ibid, 73.
20. Ibid, 50.
21. Glen M. Broom and David M. Dozier, *Using Research in Public Relations: Applications to Program Management*, (Englewood Cliffs, NJ: Prentice Hall, 1990), 43.
22. Kirk Hallahan, "Seven Models of Framing: Implications for Public Relations," *Journal of public relations research* 11, no. 3 (1999): 205–242.

Chapter 7

1. Glen M. Broom and Bey-Ling Sha, *Cutlip and Center's Effective Public Relations* (11th ed.), (Boston, MA: Pearson, 2013).
2. Ibid, 273.
3. Ibid, 170.
4. Gini Dietrich, *Spin Sucks: Communication and Reputation Management in the Digital Age*, (Indianapolis, IN: Que, 2014).
5. Andrew T. Stephen and Joseph Galak, "The Effects of Traditional and Social Earned Media on Sales: A Study of a Microlending Marketplace," *Journal of Marketing Research*, 49, 5 (2012): 624–639.
6. Broom and Sha, *Cutlip and Center's Effective Public Relations*.

7. Ibid, 209.
8. Dietrich, *Spin Sucks*.
9. Ibid, 40.
10. Dietrich, *Spin Sucks*.
11. Guy Kawasaki and Peg Fitzpatrick, *The Art of Social Media: Power Tips for Power Users*, (New York, NY: Portfolio, 2014).
12. Donald K. Wright and Michelle Drifka Hinson, "An Updated Examination of Social and Emerging Media Use in Public Relations Practice: A Longitudinal Analysis Between 2006 and 2013," *Public Relations Journal* 7, no. 3 (2013): 1–39.
13. Angelica Evans, Jane Twomey, and Scott Talan, "Twitter as a Public Relations Tool," *Public Relations Journal* 5, no. 1 (2011): 1–20.
14. Karen Freberg et al., "Who Are the Social Media Influencers? A Study of Public Perceptions of Personality," *Public Relations Review* 37, no. 1 (2011): 90–92.
15. Ibid, 44.
16. Mikal Belicove, "Five Reasons Why Websites Still Matter," *Entrepreneur*, September 13, 2011, http://www.entrepreneur.com/article/220307.
17. Charlene Li and Josh Bernoff, *Groundswell: Winning in a World Transformed by Social Technologies*, (Boston, MA: Harvard Business Press, 2008).
18. Dennis Yu, "Does Facebook's 'Boost Post' Button Work?," *Ad Week*, June 30, 2014, http://www.adweek.com/socialtimes/does-facebooks-boost-post-button-work/299859.
19. Brian Sheehan, "More Effective Native Advertising Is a Solution to Ad Blockers," *Ad Age*, (February 3, 2016), http://adage.com/article/digitalnext/effective-native-ads-a-solution-ad-blockers/302476.
20. Brenda Dervin and Lois Foreman-Wernet, "Sense-Making Methodology as an Approach to Understanding and Designing for Campaign Audiences," *Public Communication Campaigns* (2012): 147–162.
21. Laurie J. Wilson and Joseph D. Ogden, *Strategic Communications Planning for Effective Public Relations and Marketing* (5th ed.), (Dubuque, IA: Kendall-Hunt, 2008), 102.
22. Ibid, 103.
23. Dean Kruckeberg and Marina Vujnovic, "The Death of the Concept of Publics (plural) in 21st Century Public Relations," *International Journal of Strategic Communication* 4, no. 2 (2010): 117–125.
24. Natalie Tindall and Jennifer Vardeman-Winter, "Complications in Segmenting Campaign Publics: Women of Color Explain Their Problems, Involvement, and Constraints in Reading Heart Disease Communication," *Howard Journal of Communications* 22, no. 3 (2011): 280–301.
25. Ibid, 299.
26. Jennifer Vardeman-Winter, Natalie Tindall, and Hua Jiang, "Intersectionality and Publics: How Exploring Publics' Multiple Identities Questions Basic Public Relations Concepts," *Public Relations Inquiry* 2, no. 3 (2013): 279–304.
27. Jennifer Vardeman-Winter, "Confronting Whiteness in Public Relations Campaigns and Research with Women," *Journal of Public Relations Research* 23, no. 4 (2011): 412–441.
28. James E. Grunig and Fred C. Repper, "Strategic Management, Publics, and Issues," *Excellence in Public Relations and Communication Management* (1992): 117–157.
29. Broom and Sha, *Cutlip and Center's Effective Public Relations*, 269.
30. John Vernon Pavlik, *Public Relations: What Research Tells Us*, (Newbury Park, CA: Sage, 1987), 56.
31. Roger D. Wimmer and Joseph R. Dominick, *Mass Media Research: An Introduction* (9th ed.), (Boston, MA: Cengage-Wadsworth, 2011), 335–336.
32. Kirk Hallahan, "Inactive Publics: The Forgotten Publics in Public Relations," *Public Relations Review*, 26, (2001): 499–515.
33. Dave Chaffey, "Mobile Marketing Statistics Compilation," Smart Insights, March 1, 2017, http://www.smartinsights.com/mobile-marketing/mobile-marketing-analytics/mobile-marketing-statistics.
34. Greg Sterling, "Mobile Makes Up 21 pct. of Online Spending in Q4, as Digital Commerce Reaches $109 billion," *Marketing Land*, February 14, 2017, http://marketingland.com/m-commerce-21-percent-online-spending-q4-digital-commerce-reaches-109-billion-206591.
35. Matthew W. Ragas and Ron Culp, *Business Essentials for Strategic Communicators: Creating Shared Value for the Organization and Its Stakeholders*, (New York, NY: Palgrave Macmillan, 2014), 85–91.
36. Odysseas Papadimitrou, "Where Does Apple Pay Stand on Its First Birthday?" *Tech Crunch*, (Oct. 17, 2015), https://techcrunch.com/2015/10/17/where-does-apple-pay-stand-on-its-first-birthday/
37. Everett M. Rogers, *Diffusion of Innovations* (5th ed.), (New York, NY: Free Press, 2003).

Chapter 8

1. Mary Jo Hatch and Ann L. Cunliffe, *Organization Theory: Modern, Symbolic and Postmodern Perspectives* (Oxford, UK: Oxford University Press, 2013).
2. Larry Kelley, Kim Sheehan, and Donald W. Jugenheimer, *Advertising Media Planning: A Brand Management Approach* (New York, NY: Routledge, 2015), 149.
3. Andrew McStay, *Digital Advertising* (New York, NY: Palgrave Macmillan, 2009).
4. Kelley et al., *Advertising Media Planning*.
5. Lynn M. Zoch and Juan-Carlos Molleda, "Building a Theoretical Model of Media Relations Using Framing, Information Subsidies and Agenda Building," in *Public Relations Theory II*, ed. Carl H. Botan and Vincent Hazleton (Mahwah, NJ: Lawrence Erlbaum, 2006), 279–309.
6. Universal Accreditation Board, *APR Study Guide* (2010): 18.
7. Carole Howard and Wilma Mathews, *On Deadline: Managing Media Relations* (Long Grove, IL: Waveland Press, 2013), 129–130.
8. Glen M. Broom and Bey-Ling Sha, *Cutlip and Center's Effective Public Relations* (11th ed.), (Boston, MA: Pearson, 2013), 7.
9. Zoch and Molleda, "Building a Theoretical Model of Media Relations."
10. Safko, Lon. *The Social Media Bible: Tactics, Tools & Strategies for Business Success*, (3rd ed.) (Hoboken, NJ: Wiley, 2012).
11. Daniel Jacobson, "COPE: Create Once, Publish Everywhere," *ProgrammableWeb.com* (2009), retrieved from https://www.programmableweb.com/news/cope-create-once-publish-everywhere/2009/10/13.
12. Ann Handley and Charles C. Chapman, *Content Rules: How to Create Killer Blogs, Podcasts, Videos, e-books, Webinars (and more) That Engage Customers and Ignite Your Business* (Vol. 13.), (New York, NY: John Wiley & Sons, 2012).
13. Universal Accreditation Board, *APR Study Guide*.
14. Ron Smith, *Strategic Planning for Public Relations* (Mahwah, NJ: Lawrence Erlbaum, 2005), 201.
15. Ibid, 202.
16. Ibid, 201.
17. Olivia Waxman, "The Selfie Spoon Is Now a Thing That Exists," *Time*, September 18, 2015, http://time.com/4040016/cinnamon-toast-crunch-cereal-selfie-spoon.
18. Kevin Hunt, "Selfie Spoon Helps Cereal Get Social," Taste of General Mills, September 21, 2015, http://www.blog.generalmills.com/2015/09/selfie-spoon-helps-cereal-get-social.
19. Ibid.
20. Ibid.
21. Waxman, "The Selfie Spoon."
22. Lauren Johnson, "Cinnamon Toast Crunch Created a Selfie Spoon to Help You Snap the Perfect Breakfast Pic Yes, It's a Thing," *Adweek*, September 23, 2015, http://www.adweek.com/news/technology/cinnamon-toast-crunch-created-selfie-spoon-help-you-snap-perfect-breakfast-pic-167093.
23. Kelly, Sheehan, and Jugenheimer, *Advertising Media Planning*.
24. Hunt, "Selfie Spoon Helps Cereal Get Social."
25. Lydia Bryant, "Cinnamon Toast Crunch Creates the World's First Selfie Spoon," *prexamples* (September 24, 2015), http://prexamples.com/2015/09/cinnamon-toast-crunch-create-the-worlds-first-selfie-spoon.
26. General Mills, *Crunch Selfie Spoon*, n.d., http://cinnamontoastcrunch.tumblr.com/selfiespoon.
27. Zoch and Molleda, "Building a Theoretical Model of Media Relations."
28. Hunt, "Selfie Spoon Helps Cereal Get Social."
29. McStay, *Digital Advertising*.
30. Kelley et al., *Advertising Media Planning*.
31. Universal Accreditation Board, *APR Study Guide*.
32. James E. Grunig and Todd Hunt, *Managing Public Relations*, (New York, NY: Holt, Rinehart, and Winston, 1984).
33. Ibid.

Chapter 9

1. Glen M. Broom and Bey-Ling Sha, *Cutlip and Center's Effective Public Relations* (11th ed.), (Boston, MA: Pearson, 2013), 287.
2. Peter Morris and Jeffrey K. Pinto, *The Wiley Guide to Project Organization and Project Management Competencies* (Hoboken, NJ: John Wiley & Sons, 2011), x–xi.
3. Dennis P. Slevin and Jeffrey K. Pinto, "An Overview of Behavioral Issues in Project Management." In *The Wiley Guide to Project Organization & Project Management Competencies*, edited by Peter Morris and Jeffrey K. Pinto, 1–19.
4. These categories are based on those developed in the following text: Ronald Smith, *Strategic Planning for Public Relations* (3rd ed.), (London, UK: Routledge, 2009), 261.
5. Ibid, 261.

6. Connie Delisle, "Contemporary Views on Shaping, Developing, and Managing Teams." In *The Wiley Guide to Project Organization & Project Management Competencies*, edited by Peter Morris and Jeffrey K. Pinto, 36–69.
7. Ken James, *Escoffier: The King of Chefs*, (London, UK: Hambledon and London, 2002).
8. Smith, 257–259.
9. For more on project team leadership, see Thomas and Kerwin's chapter: Peg Thomas and John J. Kerwin," Leadership of Project Teams," In *The Wiley Guide to Project Organization & Project Management Competencies*, 70–88.
10. Ibid, 80.
11. Doug Newsom, Judy VanSlyke Turk, and Dean Kruckeberg, *This Is PR: The Realities of Public Relations*, (7th ed.), (Belmont, CA: Wadsworth, 2000), 329.
12. See Alvin C. Croft, *Managing a Public Relations Firm for Growth and Profit*, (New York, NY: Haworth Press, 1996), 160.
13. Carole Howard and Wilma Mathews, *On Deadline: Managing Media Relations* (Long Grove, IL: Waveland Press, 2013).
14. Broom and Sha, 293.
15. Ibid, 66.
16. Howard and Mathews, 75.
17. Ed Zitron, *This is How You Pitch*, (Muskegeon, MI: Sunflower Press, 2013), 30.
18. Ibid, 71.
19. Betteke van Ruler, "Agile Public Relations Planning: The Reflective Communication Scrum," *Public Relations Review* 41, no. 2 (2015): 187–194.
20. James E. Grunig and Fred C. Repper, Fred C. (1992). "Strategic Management, Publics, and Issues," in *Excellence in Public Relations and Communication Management*, J. E. Grunig, Ed. (Hillsdale, NJ: Lawrence Erlbaum, 1992), 118.
21. Augustine Pang, Yan Jin, and Glen T. Cameron, "Contingency Theory of Strategic Conflict Management: Directions for Practice of Crisis Communication from a Decade of Theory Development, Discovery, and Dialogue." In W. T. Coombs and S. Holladay (Eds.), *The Handbook of Crisis Communication* (Malden, MA: Wiley-Blackwell, 2010), 527–549.
22. Ibid, 27.
23. Sophie Brown, "NHS Missing Type Campaign Makes Letters Disappear in London In Drive For New Blood Donors," *HuffPost* September 6, 2015, http://www.huffingtonpost.co.uk/2015/06/09/missing-letters-blood-donation_n_7541302.html.
24. Kate Magee, "Missing Letters Revealed as Part of Blood Donation Campaign," campaign, June 5, 2015, http://www.campaignlive.co.uk/article/missing-letters-revealed-part-blood-donation-campaign/1350174.
25. NHSBT, "Missing Type Summary," 2015, https://www.blood.co.uk/news-and-campaigns/campaigns/campaign-archive/missing-type/.
26. Magee, "Missing Letters."
27. NHSBT, "Who Can Give Blood," Accessed March 19, 2016, https://www.blood.co.uk/who-can-give-blood.
28. Morris and Pinto, *The Wiley Guide*.
29. NHSBT, "Who Can Give Blood."
30. NHSCBT, "Missing Type Summary."
31. Ibid.
32. NHSBT, "Who Can Give Blood."
33. Ibid.
34. Magee, "Missing Letters."
35. Ibid.
36. Ibid.
37. NHSBT, "Who Can Give Blood."
38. Magee, "Missing Letters."
39. Campaign Big Awards, "Missing Type," Accessed March 19, 2016, http://www.campaignbigawards.com/finalists/missing-type.
40. Patricia Swann, *Cases in Public Relations Management*, (New York, NY: Routledge, 2014).

Chapter 10

1. Tom Watson and Paul Noble, *Evaluating Public Relations: A Guide to Planning, Research and Measurement* (London, UK: Kogan Page, 2014), 22.
2. Dan Lattimore, Otis Baskin, Susan T. Heiman, and Elizabeth Toth, *Public Relations: The Profession and the Practice*, (4th ed.) (New York, NY: McGraw-Hill, 2011).
3. Watson and Noble, *Evaluating Public Relations*, 17.
4. Watson and Noble, *Evaluating Public Relations*.
5. Ibid, 36.
6. Ibid, 76.
7. Ibid, 79.
8. Ibid, 76.
9. Ibid, 99.
10. Katie Delahave Paine, *Measure What Matters*, (Hoboken, NJ: John Wiley & Sons, 2011).
11. Watson and Noble, *Evaluating Public Relations*, 147.

12. Marianne Eisenmann, "Speak Their Language: Communicating Results to the C-Suite," *Public Relations Tactics*, (PRSA, 2011).
13. Ibid.
14. Larry Kelley, Kim Sheehan, and Donald W. Jugenheimer, *Advertising Media Planning: A Brand Management Approach*, (New York, NY: Routledge, 2015), 323.
15. Watson and Noble, 98
16. Everett M. Rogers, "A Prospective and Retrospective Look at the Diffusion Model," *Journal of Health Communication 9*, no. S1 (2004): 13–19.

Chapter 11

1. "Winner Takes All: A Slow-motion Revolution," *The Economist*, (Feb. 9, 2017), https://www.economist.com/news/special-report/21716459-peak-tv-its-way-slowly-traditional-tvs-surprising-staying-power.
2. Brian Smith and Katie R. Place, "Integrating Power? Evaluating Public Relations Influence in an Integrated Communication Structure," *Journal of Public Relations Research* 25, no. 2 (2013): 168–187.
3. W. Timothy Coombs and Sherry J. Holladay, *The Handbook of Crisis Communication*, (Malden, MA: Wiley-Blackwell, 2012).
4. James E. Grunig and David M. Dozier, *Excellent Public Relations and Effective Organizations: A Study of Communication Management in Three Countries*, (New York, NY: Routledge, 2003).
5. Francis Nobles, "Dylann Roof Photos and a Manifesto Are Posted on Website," *New York Times*, June 20, 2015, http://www.nytimes.com/2015/06/21/us/dylann-storm-roof-photos-website-charleston-church-shooting.html?_r=0.
6. *Mississippi Division of the United Sons of Confederate Veterans v. Mississippi State Conference of NAACP Branches* et al. 1994, 94-CA-00615-SCT, Supreme Court of Mississippi.
7. Therese Apeal, "Hundreds March for Flag Change," *Clarion Ledger* (Jackson, MS), October 12, 2015, http://www.clarionledger.com/story/news/2015/10/11/hundreds-gather-push-one-flag-all/73680070.
8. Megan Leoni, "One Flag for All Rally Set for Sunday," *Natchez Democrat* (Natchez, MS), April 1, 2016, http://www.natchezdemocrat.com/2016/04/01/one-flag-for-all-rally-set-for-sunday.
9. Maya Miller, "Big Day: Flag Rally, Mississippi Primaries and Campaign Parties," *Jackson Free Press* (Jackson, MS), March 8, 2016, http://www.jacksonfreepress.com/weblogs/jackblog/2016/mar/08/big-day-flag-rally-miss-primaries-and-campaign-par.
10. https://www.sos.ms.gov/elections/initiatives/InitiativeInfo.aspx?IId=55
11. Robert M. Entman, "Framing: Toward Clarification of a Fractured Paradigm," *Journal of Communication* 43, no. 4 (1993): 51–58.
12. Jae-Hwa Shin, Glen T. Cameron, and Fritz Cropp, "Occam's Razor in the Contingency Theory: A National Survey on 86 Contingent Variables," *Public Relations Review* 32, no. 3 (2006): 282–286.
13. Jennifer Rooney, *Here's How American Greetings Is Working To Maintain Momentum of Award-Winning "World's Toughest Job,"* July 16, 2015,. http://www.forbes.com/sites/jenniferrooney/2015/07/16/heres-how-american-greetings-is-working-to-maintain-momentum-of-award-winning-worlds-toughest-job/#67359ad1272f.
14. "Winner Takes All." [1]
15. Smith and Place, "Integrating Power?"
16. Tim Nudd, "24 People Who Applied for the World's Toughest Job Were in for Quite a Surprise," *Adweek*, April 14, 2014, http://www.adweek.com/adfreak/24-people-who-applied-worlds-toughest-job-were-quite-surprise-157028.
17. "Behind the Scenes of The World's Toughest Job," *Newscred*, (September 07, 2016), https://insights.newscred.com/worlds-toughest-job.
18. Andrew McMains, "American Greetings' Mother's Day Video Takes Top Prize at Effie Awards," *Adweek*. June 04, 2015, http://www.adweek.com/brand-marketing/american-greetings-mothers-day-video-takes-top-prize-effie-awards-165175.
19. Ibid.
20. Ibid.
21. "Winner Takes All." [1]
22. News Cred, "Behind the Scenes."
23. McMains, "American Greetings' Mother's Day Video Takes Top Prize at Effie Awards."
24. Suzanne Lucas, "Ad Calling Motherhood World's Toughest Job Goes Viral," *CBS News: Moneywatch*. April 17, 2014, http://www.cbsnews.com/news/ad-calling-motherhood-worlds-toughest-job-goes-viral.
25. Steve Almasy, "Ad for World's Toughest Job Draws Few Applicants and Many Smiles," *CNN*, April 16,

2014, http://www.cnn.com/2014/04/16/us/mothers-day-viral-video/index.html.

26. Rooney, "Here's How American Greetings Is Working to Maintain Momentum."
27. Susan Krashinsky, "Ad for 'The World's Toughest Job' Has a Twist," *The Globe and Mail*, April 15, 2014, https://www.theglobeandmail.com/report-on-business/industry-news/marketing/an-ad-campaign-for-a-job-that-leaves-you-stressed-and-guessing/article18033961.
28. Jonathon Welsh, "What's the Story Behind the 'World's Toughest Job?'"*The Wall Street Journal*, April 18, 2014, https://blogs.wsj.com/speakeasy/2014/04/18/whats-the-story-behind-the-worlds-toughest-job/.
29. Coombs and Holladay, *The Handbook of Crisis Communication*.
30. Patricia Swann, *Cases in Public Relations Management*, (New York, NY: Routledge, 2014).
31. William J. McGuire, "McGuire's Classic Input-Output Framework for Constructing Persuasive Messages," in *Public Communication Campaigns*, ed. Ronald E. Rice and Charles K. Atkin (Thousand Oaks, CA: Sage, 2013), 133–145.
32. Cameron Knight and Shauna Stiegerwald, "Family: Boy Who Fell into Gorilla Exhibit 'doing Just Fine'" Cincinnati.com, May 29, 2016, http://www.cincinnati.com/story/news/2016/05/29/boy-who-fell-into-zoo-gorilla-exhibit-out-hospital/85131108.
33. "How Zoo Emergency Response Teams Handle Dangerous Animals." *Insurance Journal*. http://www.insurancejournal.com/news/national/2016/06/10/416566.htm.
34. Mark Renfree, "Cincinnati Zoo Highlights Transparency Amidst Gorilla Crisis," *PR News*, May 31, 2016, http://www.prnewsonline.com/zoo-crisis.
35. Cincinnati Zoo, "The Cincinnati Zoo & Botanical Garden," November 17, 2016,http://cincinnatizoo.org/blog/2016/11/17/cincinnati-zoo-statement-regarding-usda-review.
36. CNN Wire Service, "Vigil Held at Cincinnati Zoo in Tribute to Slain Gorilla; Boy's Family Releases Statement," *FOX6Now*, May 30, 2016, http://fox6now.com/2016/05/30/vigil-planned-at-cincinnati-zoo-in-tribute-to-slain-gorilla.
37. Melissa Chan, "Cincinnati Zoo Returns to Twitter-But Is Greeted by More Harambe Harassment," *Time*, October 21, 2016, http://time.com/4540768/cincinnati-zoo-twitter-harambe.
38. David Williams, "Cincinnati Zoo Deletes Twitter Accounts," *CNN*, August 23, 2016, http://www.cnn.com/2016/08/23/us/cincinnati-zoo-harambe-twitter.
39. Mark, Renfree, "Cincinnati Zoo Highlights Transparency Amid Gorilla Crisis." prnewsonline.com. http://www.prnewsonline.com/zoo-crisis
40. Renfree, "Cincinnati Zoo Highlights Transparency Amidst Gorilla Crisis."
41. The Cincinnati Zoo & Botanical Garden, "Cincinnati Zoo Devastated by Death of Beloved Gorilla," May 29, 2016, http://cincinnatizoo.org/blog/2016/05/29/cincinnati-zoo-devastated-by-death-of-beloved-gorilla.
42. Mark Renfree, "Cincinnati Zoo Highlights Transparency Amid Gorilla Crisis." prnewsonline.com. http://www.prnewsonline.com/zoo-crisis
43. Natalie Trusso Cafarello, "The Anti-social Side of Social Media," *The Blade*, October 16, 2016, http://www.toledoblade.com/Living/2016/10/16/Anti-social.html.
44. Ibid.
45. Fox19 Cincinnati, "Barrier in Cincinnati Zoo's Harambe Exhibit Failed to Meet Standards, Feds Say," *Fox News*, November 17, 2016, http://www.foxnews.com/us/2016/11/17/barrier-in-cincinnati-zoos-harambe-exhibit-failed-to-meet-standards-feds-say.html
46. Kathleen Fearn-Banks, *Crisis Communications: A Casebook Approach*, (London, UK: Routledge, 2016).
47. Francis J. Marra, "Crisis Communication Plans: Poor Predictors of Excellent Crisis Public Relations," *Public Relations Review* 24, no. 4 (1998): 461–74. doi:10.1016/s0363-8111(99)80111-8.
48. W. Timothy Coombs, "Attribution Theory as a Guide for Post-Crisis Communication Research," *Public Relations Review* 33, no. 2 (2007): 135–139.
49. Swann, *Cases in Public Relations Management*.
50. Rajul Jain, Maria De Moya, and Juan-Carlos Molleda, "State of International Public Relations Research: Narrowing the Knowledge Gap about the Practice across Borders," *Public Relations Review* 40, no. 3 (2014): 595–597.
51. "*Toys in Mourning,*" Cream, (July, 2014), http://www.creamglobal.com/case-studies/latest/17798/36852/toys-in-mourning.

52. "Unicef—'Toys In Mourning,'" *AdForum*, Accessed July 26, 2017, https://www.adforum.com/creative-work/ad/player/34515857/toys-in-mourning/unicef.
53. "Toys in Mourning," *Cream*, (July, 2014, http://www.creamglobal.com/case-studies/latest/17798/36852/toys-in-mourning.
54. News, "Lograr #CeroMuertesEvitables es possible," Volver a la página de inicio, (July 2, 201), http://www.mspbs.gov.py/lograr-ceromuertesevitables-esposible.
55. Cream, "Toys in Mourning."
56. TBWA Worldwide, "How Unicef's Toys in Mourning Raised Paraguay's Healthcare Budget, LBBOnline," *Little Black Book* (2015), https://lbbonline.com/news/how-unicefs-toys-in-mourning-raised-paraguays-healthcare-budget
57. Oniria, *Unicef - "Toys In Mourning,"* Asuncion, (2015), https://lbbonline.com/news/how-unicefs-toys-in-mourning-raised-paraguays-healthcare-budget.
58. Smith and Place, "Integrating power?"
59. Oniria/TBWA, "Unicef—'Toys In Mourning,'" *AdForum*, (July 2015), https://www.adforum.com/creative-work/ad/player/34515857/toys-in-mourning/unicef
60. TBWA Worldwide, "How Unicef's Toys in Mourning Raised Paraguay's Healthcare Budget," *Little Black Book*, (2015), https://lbbonline.com/news/how-unicefs-toys-in-mourning-raised-paraguays-healthcare-budget/.
61. Oniria/TBWA, "Unicef—'Toys in Mourning.'"
62. Oscar H. Gandy, *Beyond Agenda Setting: Information Subsidies and Public Policy*, (New York, NY: Ablex, 1982).
63. Swann, *Cases in Public Relations Management*.
64. Coombs and Holladay, *The Handbook of Crisis Communication*.
65. Bijou R. Hunt, Steve Whitman, and Marc S. Hurlbert, "Increasing Black: White Disparities in Breast Cancer Mortality in the 50 Largest Cities in the United States," *Cancer Epidemiology* 38, no. 2 (2014): 118–123.
66. Steven Whitman, Jennifer Orsi, and Marc Hurlbert, "The Racial Disparity in Breast Cancer Mortality in the 25 Largest Cities in the United States," *Cancer Epidemiology* 36, no. 2 (2012): e147–e151.
67. "What is Teens 4 Pink?" Teens 4 Pink, Accessed July 26, 2017, http://teens4pink.org/about/.
68. Everett Rogers, *Diffusion of Innovations*, (New York: The Free Press, 1995).
69. Nance McCown, "The Role of Public Relations with Internal Activists," *Journal of Public Relations Research* 19, no. 1 (2007): 47–68.
70. Ana Tkalac Verčič, Dejan Verčič, and Krishnamurthy Sriramesh, "Internal Communication: Definition, Parameters, and the Future," *Public Relations Review* 38, no. 2 (2012): 223–230.
71. Brian G. Smith and Katie R. Place "Integrating Power? Evaluating Public Relations Influence in an Integrated Communication Structure," *Journal of Public Relations Research* 25, no. 2 (2013): 168–187.
72. Jack Healy, "Ferguson, Still Tense, Grows Calmer," *New York Times*, Nov. 26, 2014.
73. Jason Purnell, Gabriela Camberos, and Robert Fields, "For the Sake of All: A Report on the Health and Well-being of African Americans in St. Louis and Why It Matters for Everyone," (report, Washington University in St. Louis/Saint Louis University, 2015), http://www.forthesakeofall.org.
74. Kirk Hallahan, "Seven Models of Framing: Implications for Public Relations," *Journal of Public Relations Research* 11, no. 3 (1999): 205–242.
75. Swann, *Cases in Public Relations Management*.
76. Albert Bandura, "Social Cognitive Theory," *Handbook of Social Psychological Theories* 2012 (2011): 349–373.
77. Bandura, Albert. "Social Cognitive Theory: An Agentic Perspective," *Annual Review of Psychology* 52, no. 1 (2001): 1–26.
78. Swann, *Cases in Public Relations Management*.

Appendix

1. Robert K. Yin, *Case Study Research: Design and Methods* (5th ed.), (Thousand Oaks, CA: SAGE, 2013), pp 10–11.
2. Ibid, 9.
3. Brad L. Rawlins, *Prioritizing Stakeholders for Public Relations*, (Gainesville, FL: Institute for Public Relations, 2006), available online at http://www.instituteforpr.org/wp-content/uploads/2006_stakeholders-1.pdf.

4. Linda Aldoory and Bey-Ling Sha, "The Situational Theory of Publics: Practical Applications, Methodological Challenges, and Theoretical Horizons," In E. L. Toth (Ed.), *The Future of Excellence in Public Relations and Communication Management: Challenges for the Next Generation*, (Mahwah, NJ: Lawrence Erlbaum Associates, 2007), 339–355.
5. James E. Grunig and Fred C. Repper, "Strategic Management, Publics, and Issues," in J. E. Grunig (Ed.), *Excellence in Public Relations and Communication Management*, (Hillsdale, NJ: Lawrence Erlbaum Associates, 1992), 118.
6. Katie Delahaye Paine and William T. Paarlberg, *Measure What Matters: Online Tools for Understanding Customers, Social Media, Engagement, and Key Relationships*, (Hoboken, NJ: Wiley, 2011).
7. APR Study Guide, University Accreditation Board, (2017), 35.
8. Ibid, 35.
9. Don W. Stacks and David Michaelson, *A Practitioner's Guide to Public Relations Research, Measurement, and Evaluation*, (New York, NY: Business Expert Press, 2010), 115.
10. Glen Broom and David M. Dozer, *Using Research in Public Relations*, (Englewood Cliffs, NJ: Prentice Hall, 1990), 119.
11. Ibid, 118.
12. Broom and Dozer, 117.
13. Tom Watson, *Advertising Value Equivalence—PR's Illegitimate Offspring*, Paper presented at 15th International Public Relations Research Conference (IPRRC), Miami, FL (Marc, 2012).
14. Andre Manning and David B. Rockland, "Understanding the Barcelona Principles," *The Public Relations Strategist*, March, 2011), retrieved from http://www.prsa.org/Intelligence/TheStrategist.
15. Emily Greenhouse, "JPMorgan's Twitter Mistake," *The New Yorker*, (Nov. 16, 2013), http://www.newyorker.com/business/currency/jpmorgans-twitter-mistake.
16. Charles K. Atkin and Vicki Freimuth, "Guidelines for Formative Evaluation Research in Campaign Design," *Public Communication Campaigns* (2013): 53–68.
17. Larry D. Kelley, Donald W. Jugenheimer, and Kim Sheehan, *Advertising Media Planning : A Brand Management Approach*, 4th ed., (New York, NY: Routledge, 2015).
18. Ibid, 171.
19. Ibid, 168.
20. Ibid, 158.
21. Andrew McStay, *Digital Advertising*, (Houndmills, Basingstoke, Hampshire, U.K.: Palgrave Macmillan, 2010).
22. Ibid, 49.
23. Kelley et al., 192.
24. Jieunn Lee and Ilyoo B. Hong, "Predicting Positive User Responses to Social Media Advertising: The Roles of Emotional Appeal, Informativeness, and Creativity," *International Journal of Information Management* 36, no. 3 (2016): 360–373.
25. Christy Ashley and Tracy Tuten, "Creative Strategies in Social Media Marketing: An Exploratory Study of Branded Social Content and Consumer Engagement," *Psychology & Marketing* 32, no. 1 (2015): 15–27.
26. Carole Howard and Wilma Mathews, *On Deadline: Managing Media Relations*, (Long Grove, IL: Waveland Press, 2013), 44.
27. Ibid, 128.
28. Ibid, 52.
29. Andrew Rohm and Michael Weiss, *Herding Cats: A Strategic Approach to Social Media Marketing*, (New York, NY: Business Expert Press, 2014).
30. Lon Safko, *The Social Media Bible: Tactics, Tools, and Strategies for Business Success*, (Hoboken, NJ: John Wiley & Sons, 2012).
31. AdWeek (April 4, 2016). *Here's How Many People Are on Facebook, Instgram, Twitter and Other Big Social Networks.* Retrieved from http://www.adweek.com/digital/heres-how-many-people-are-on-facebook-instagram-twitter-other-big-social-networks/#/
32. Regina Luttrell, *Social Media: How to Engage, Share, and Connect*, (Lanham, MD: Rowman & Littlefield, 2016).
33. Safko, *The Social Media Bible*, 567.
34. Jayson DeMers, "Why Community Management Is Different than Social Media Marketing," *Forbes*, retrieved from https://www.forbes.com/sites/jaysondemers/2015/02/12/why-community-management-is-different-from-social-media-marketing/#63fe1f8567d9
35. Universal Accreditation Board, 18.
36. Ronald D. Smith, *Strategic Planning for Public Relations*, (New York, NY: Routledge, 2017).
37. Ibid, 202.
38. Ibid, 201.

Index

Acceptance of messages, 12
ACE (Assessment, Communication, and Evaluation) planning model, 10
Actionability, in issue prioritization, 80
Activism, case study of integrated campaign for, 191–195
Activity factors in segmentation, 121
Ad Age Viral Video chart, 91
Administration budget, 150–151
Ad value equivalency, 233
Advertising:
    public relations integrated with, 15
    social media and, 42
    types of, 134–136, 237–239
Advertising and Public Relations Research (Jugenheimer, Kelley, Hudson, and Bradley), 55
Advertorial content, 136
Advisories, media, 239–240
Agenda setting and agenda building theories, 6–7, 39, 53, 207, 212
#AidRefugees campaign, 33–34
Allen, T. Harrell, 12, 27
Altimeter, Inc., 50
American Ballet Theater, 44–45
American Greetings *Appreciating Mom* campaign, 196–199
American Medical Association (AMA), 64
Appreciating Mom campaign (American Greetings), 196–199
APR Study Guide (PRSA), 100
Arment Dietrich PR firm, 112
Assessment, Communication, and Evaluation (ACE) planning model, 10
Associated Press Stylebook, 156
Association of Zoos & Aquariums (AZA), 201
Attitude change, as PR goal, 12
AudienceBloom, 243
Audiences:
    goal setting and, 82–84
    impact on, 156
    key, 229–231
    objectives connected to, 101–104
    positioning campaigns to focus on, 237
    research on, 55–56
    strategy choice and, 119–122

Bagnall, Richard, 172
Barcelona Principles for PR Measurement of 2015, 234
Baskin-Robbins, Inc., 45–46
Bateson, Gregory, 4
Behavior change, as PR goal, 12
Best practices, reporting on, 174
Be Your Way campaign (Burger King), 51–53
Blogging, 241. *See also* Shared (social) media, in PESO model
Blood donation, promoting, 163–165
Bonchek, Mark, 43, 49
"Boosted posts," on social media, 135, 143
Bradley, Samuel D., 55
Brand monitoring, 115
Brand research, 57–58
Broom, Glen M., 4, 58, 78, 100, 111, 113, 119, 150
Budget:
    earned media, 137
    implementation, 150–151
    owned media, 142
    paid media, 134
    prioritizing, 84–85
    staff time and expenses, 33
Bundchen, Gisele, 45
Bureau of Labor Statistics, 63
Burger King, Inc., 51–53
Bylined articles, as tactic, 138, 240–241

Cameron, G. T., 161
Cannes Lions Festival, 45
Caribou Coffee product marketing campaign, 185–191
Case studies:
    blood donation promotion, 163–165
    Burger King *Be Your Way* campaign, 51–53
    Can Manufacturers Institute, 180–183
    Doubletree by Hilton, 106–109
    General Mills Cinnamilk, 146–148
    Hallmark Cards, 73–76
    Lean Cuisine, 89–91

Mastercard iPay, 127–130
research through, 62–63
Seize the holidays with Krusteaz, 21–24
Wakey, Wakey Eggs and Bakey!, 36–39
See also Integrated campaigns, case studies on
Census information, 65, 233
Center, Allen H., 4, 119
Change:
  attitude, 12
  behavior, 12
  implementation, 161
  scrum approach to managing, 160
Channels, 111, 121–122. See also PESO (paid, earned, shared, and owned) media
Chu, Mark, 146
Cincinnati Children's Hospital Medical Center, 203
Cincinnati Zoo and Botanical Garden, 200–204
Cinnamilk, from General Mills, 146–148
Cision Service, 169
Clough-Crifasi, Shelia, 10
Coding, in content analysis, 66–67
Collateral materials, 142, 144, 245
Colle+McVoy advertising, 185, 187
Communication campaigns. See Strategic communication campaigns
Communications, implementation need for, 153–154
Communications-driven objectives, 234–235
Community management, in shared (social) media, 243
Competition:
  analysis of, 68
  objectives related to, 99
  strategy choice and, 124–126
Concept case: Equality Today:
  channel, partner, and measurement, 51
  channel selection, 126–127
  communications goals, 89
  description of, 21
  external events impact on, 162–163
  issue prioritization research, 72–73
  mission-driven planning for, 35–36
  objective setting for, 106
  overview, 21
  reporting results, 180
  tactical choices, 146
Conflict, in newsworthiness definition, 156
Content amplification, 15
Content analysis, 66–67, 231–232

Content creation:
  earned media, 139
  overview, 43
  owned media, 142
  paid media, 134
  publications in, 143
  shared media, 141
Content hub, blogs as, 141
Content Rules (Handley and Chapman), 141
Continental Mills, Inc., 21–22
Contingency theory, 161, 195–196
Control groups, for evaluation, 168
Controlled media, 113, 141
Converged media, 50, 135
Conversion, campaigns seeking, 142
Cooking Channel, 181–182
Cope, Brianna, 45
C.O.P.E. (Create once, publish everywhere) approach to content creation, 141
Copeland, Misty, 44–45
Copyright law, 144
Corporate Public Affairs (Lerbinger), 80
Corporate video, as tactics, 144
Coverage analysis on media, 67–68, 170, 231–232
"Create once, publish everywhere" (C.O.P.E.) approach to content creation, 141
Crisis communication, 7, 199–204
Crowdfunding, 33
C-suite leadership, 18–20
Culp, Ron, 122
Cumberbatch, Benedict, 47
Cutlip, Scott M., 4, 12, 119

Dainton, Marianne, 2
Data resources, 59–60, 123
Deadlines, in implementation, 152–153
DeMers, Jayson, 243
Demographic factors in segmentation, 120
Developmental research. See Research, developmental
Dietrich, Gini, 18, 112
Diffusion theory, 4–5, 24, 130, 182, 211
Digital advertising, 135
Digital communities, 141
Digital display advertising, 238
Digital evaluation metrics, 170–172
Dior, 47–48
Dissemination of messages, 12

Dozier, David M., 58
Dreyer, Greta, 200
Droga5 advertising agency, 45
Drucker, Peter, 94–95

Earned media, in PESO model:
    American Greetings *Appreciating Mom* campaign, 198
    Burger King *Be Your Way* campaign, 52
    campaign example, 45–46
    Can Manufacturers Institute, 182
    Caribou Coffee product marketing campaign, 188–191
    description of, 18–19, 42–43, 114
    exposure, engagement, influence, and action metrics, 172
    Flag for All Mississippians Coalition campaign, 191
    General Mills, 147
    Hallmark Cards campaign, 75
    Mastercard iPay campaign, 128–129
    metrics for reporting and evaluation, 176–177
    Missing Type Campaign, of National Health Service Blood and Transplant (U.K.), 164–165
    tactics involving, 136–140
    Teens 4 Pink: Sisters Network campaign, 209–210
    UNICEF *Toys in Mourning* campaign, 206
    Washington University in St. Louis *responding to Ferguson* campaign, 214–215
Eastern Michigan University, 200, 205
Effective Public Relations (Cutlip and Center), 119
Eisai, Inc., 208
Eisenmann, Marianne, 172
Employee engagement, 44
Employee relations and internal communications integrated campaign, 212–217
E-newsletters, as tactics, 144
Engagement, case study on integrated campaign for, 195–199
Engline, Shayna, 27
Equality Today:
    channel, partner, and measurement, 51
    channel selection, 126–127
    communications goals, 89
    description of, 21
    external events impact on, 162–163
    issue prioritization research, 72–73
    mission-driven planning for, 35–36
    objective setting for, 106
    overview, 21

    reporting results, 180
    tactical choices, 146
Evaluating Public Relations (Watson and Noble), 167
Evaluating theories, 2
Evaluation, 157–158. *See also* Reporting and evaluation
Evaluative research, 55–56
Event sponsorship, as advertising, 135, 144, 239
Excellence theory, 2–3, 75–76, 203–204
Experimental research, 68–69
Exponent PR, 185

Facebook.com:
    "boosted" posts on, 115–116
    maximizing, 42
    overview, 23–24
    trending on, 47
    See also Shared (social) media, in PESO model
Fisher, Melody, 191
FiveThirtyEight.com, 124
Flag for All Mississippians Coalition, 191–192
FleishmanHilliard agency, 73, 75
Focus groups, 70–71, 228
Formal research techniques, 59
Formatting reports, 175
Framing theory, 5–6, 109, 194, 217–218
Fremar, Leanne, 45

Gantt charts, for deadline organization, 153–154
Generalization, from research, 59
General Mills Cinnamilk, 146–148
Geographical factors in segmentation, 120
Georgetown University, 27
George Washington University, 27
Global and multicultural integrated campaigns, 205–212
Goals. *See* Research, goals for
Goffman, Erving, 4
Google AdWords, 239
Google Analytics, 170–171, 177
Google News Alerts, 169
Google Trends data, 22
Gopal, Achala, 146, 148
Government data for research, 63
Gratifications theory, 39
Grunig, James E., 3, 9, 12

Hallmark Cards, 73–76
Hard costs, in budgets, 151

Hashtags, 25
Hendrix, Jerry, 27
History, as organizational resource, 124
Hollis, James Dawson, 146
Horovitz, Bruce, 46
Howard, Carole, 139, 157, 240
HP global wellness challenge, 217–221
Hudson, Jerry, 55
Hunt, Todd, 9
Hunter Public Relations, 180

IABC (International Association of Business Communicators), 3
Image, video, and interest sharing, in shared (social) media, 242–243
Imagery/visuals, as organizational resources, 123
Imminence of action, in issue prioritization, 80
I.M.P.A.C.T. (influence, message, prominence, audience, consultant, type of article), 169
Impact on organization, in issue prioritization, 80
Implementation, 149–165
    budgeting for, 150–151
    Caribou Coffee product marketing campaign, 189
    case study on, 163–165
    changes in, 161
    concept case on, 162–163
    expectations and communication for, 153–154
    media involved in, 155–157
    non-PR people involved in, 154–155
    persistence and perseverance in, 158–160
    project management in, 150
    ROSTIR planning model inclusion of, 32
    self-awareness and self-evaluation in, 157–158
    teamwork for, 152
    timelines and deadlines for, 152–153
Influence, message, prominence, audience, consultant, type of article (I.M.P.A.C.T.), 169
Influencer relations, 43, 114–115, 121
Infographics, 144–145
Informal research techniques, 59
Information subsidies, 8, 140
Infrastructure budget, 150–151
Instagram.com, 42. See also Shared (social) media, in PESO model
Institute for Public Relations, University of Florida, 63
Institutional authority, as organizational resource, 124
Integrated campaigns, 14–24
    case study on, 21–24
    concept case on, 21
    emerging models for, 15–16

    planning models, value of, 16–20
    ROSTIR six steps, 16
Integrated campaigns, case studies on, 184–221
    activism, 191–195
    crisis communication, 199–204
    engagement, 195–199
    global and multicultural, 205–212
    HP global wellness challenge, 217–221
    internal communications and employee relations, 212–217
    product marketing, 184–191
Interest factors in segmentation, 121
Internal communications and employee relations integrated campaign, 212–217
International Association of Business Communicators (IABC), 3
Interviews, 69–70
Issue prioritization, 72–73, 80
Iterative planning cycle for research, 88

Jackson, Patrick, 12
Jin, Y., 161
JPMorganChase, 236
Jugenheimer, Donald, 55

Kelley, Larry D., 55
Ketchum, Gensler, and Digital Royalty agency, 106
Ketchum Campaign Focus, 127
Kraft Foods, Inc., 49

Latham, Jon, 163
Lawrence, Jennifer, 47
Lazovic, Brandon, 200
Lead generation/lead capture, 99
Lean Cuisine, 89–91
Lerbinger, Otto, 80
Lieb, Rebecca, 50
Likert scales, 65, 222–223
LinkedIn.com, 42, 141. See also Shared (social) media, in PESO model

MailChimp distribution data, 177
Make-A-Wish Foundation, 47
Management by objectives (MBO), 94–101
    Drucker concept of, 94–95
    objective types, 95–96
    overview, 27
    S.M.A.R.T. objectives in, 96–99
    successful objectives in, 100–101

Marketing:
    owned media for, 244
    PRSA definition of, 143
    public relations integrated with, 15
Marston, John, 10, 27
Maslow's hierarchy of needs, 182
Mastercard iPay, 127–130
Materials budget, 150–151
Mathews, Wilma, 139, 157, 240
Maynard, Thane, 201–202
MBO (management by objectives). *See* Management by objectives (MBO)
McCann Advertising, 146
McCombs, Maxwell, 5
McCord, Catherine, 22–23
McCormick, Inc., 49
Measure What Matters (Paine), 67
Media:
    budget for, 150–151
    converged, 50
    evaluation of, 169–170
    events for, 139
    implementation and, 155–157
    relations with, 8, 138–139, 239–241
    See also PESO (paid, earned, shared, and owned) media
Media coverage analysis, 67–68, 170, 231–232
Mediated approaches, 31
Media uses theory, 39
Messages:
    earned media, 137
    effective, 132
    exposure of, 12
    owned media, 142
    paid media, 134
    shared media, 140–141
    strategic, 11
Methodology, research, 54
Metrics That Matter: Making Sense of Social Media Measurement (Bagnall), 172
Michaelson, 100
Microblogging, 141, 242
Miller, Joshua, 33
Missing Type Campaign, of National Health Service Blood and Transplant (U.K.), 163–165
Mission, situation *versus*, in goal-setting, 85–86
Mississippi State University, 191
"Mob Effect" on Internet, 203
Molleda, Juan-Carlos, 8
Morris, Peter, 150
Mueller, Eric, 189

MullenLowe agency, 196
Multicultural and global integrated campaigns, 205–212

Nager, Norman, 27
"Nasty Effect," 203
National Association of Manufacturers (NAM)., 64
National Canned Food Month, 181
National College Athletic Association (NCAA), 46–47
National Health Service Blood and Transplant (U.K.), 163–165
National Public Radio, 141
Native advertising, 15, 116
Nature of Public Relations, The (Marston), 10
Near Field Communication (NFC) technology, 127
Neill, Marlene, 15
Nestlé Company, 31, 89
Networking, 141
News releases, 138, 240
Newsworthiness, 156
New Yorker magazine, 236
New York Times, 124, 136
NFC (Near Field Communication) technology, 127
Nike, Inc., 49
Nixon, Kelsey, 181–182
Noble, Paul, 167–169
Nonmediated approaches, 31
Nonprofits, reports from, 63–64
Novelty, in newsworthiness definition, 156

Obama, Barack, 33
Obergefell v. Hodges (2015), 21
Objective-driven reporting, 173–174
Objectives, 92–109
    case study on, 106–109
    concept case on, 106
    high-value, 93–94
    key internal audiences connected to, 101–104
    management by, 94–101
    poorly written, 233–236
    ROSTIR planning model inclusion of, 29–30
Observer bias, in evaluation, 170
Ogden, Joseph D., 79, 86
O'Hara, Kelley, 45
On Deadline: Managing Media Relations (Howard and Mathews), 139
Online community management, 15
Op-ed articles, as tactic, 138, 240–241

Opinion leaders, 7–8
Organizations:
  decision makers in, 87–88
  goals of, public relations goals *versus*, 78–80
  owned media of, 142–143
  strengths and resources of, 122–124
Oscar Mayer, Inc., 36–39
Outcome-based objectives, 233–234
Outdoor advertising, 135, 237–238
Output-based competitor analysis, 68
Output-based objectives, 233–234
Outputs, outtakes, and outcomes of campaigns, 95–96
Owned media (content), in PESO model:
  American Greetings *Appreciating Mom* campaign, 197, 199
  Burger King *Be Your Way* campaign, 51–52
  campaign example, 47–49
  Can Manufacturers Institute, 182
  Caribou Coffee product marketing campaign, 187–189
  Cincinnati Zoo and Botanical Garden campaign, 201
  collateral materials as, 245
  description of, 18–19, 43, 115
  exposure, engagement, influence, and action metrics, 172
  Flag for All Mississippians Coalition campaign, 191
  HP global wellness challenge campaign, 219–220
  marketing tactics as, 244
  Mastercard iPay campaign, 128–129
  Missing Type Campaign, of National Health Service Blood and Transplant (U.K.), 165
  publications as, 244–245
  reporting and evaluation metrics, 177–178
  tactics involving, 141–145
  Teens 4 Pink: Sisters Network campaign, 210
  UNICEF Toys in Mourning campaign, 206
  Washington University in St. Louis *responding to Ferguson* campaign, 215
  website content management as, 243–244
Owyang, Jeremiah, 50

PACE (Planning, Action, Communication, and Evaluation) planning model, 10
Paid media, in PESO model:
  Burger King *Be Your Way* campaign, 53
  campaign example, 44–45
  Caribou Coffee product marketing campaign, 187–188
  costs included in, 113
  description of, 18–19, 42
  exposure, engagement, influence, and action metrics, 172
  General Mills, 147
  reporting and evaluation metrics, 176
  tactics involving, 133–136
Paine, K. D., 67, 80–81, 170
Pang, A., 161
Parade Media Group, 182
Personnel budget, 150–151
PESO (paid, earned, shared, and owned) media, 40–53
  campaigns in action examples, 44–49
  case study on, 51–53
  channels in, 112–115
  concept case on, 51
  continuous integration of, 49–50
  earned media, description of, 42–43
  explanation of, 18
  overlap in, 115–119
  overview, 40–41
  owned media, description of, 43
  paid media, description of, 42
  ROSTIR model, 15
  Seize the Holidays with Krusteaz campaign, 23
  shared media, description of, 43
  tactics using, 30–31
  See also Earned media, in PESO model; Owned media (content), in PESO model; Paid media, in PESO model; Shared (social) media, in PESO model
Pinterest.com, 23–24, 42. *See also* Shared (social) media, in PESO model
Pinto, Jeffrey K., 150
Planning, Action, Communication, and Evaluation (PACE) planning model, 10
Polling and surveys, 64–66
Positioning campaigns, 125, 237–238
Practice of Management, The (Drucker), 94
Press agentry model, 3, 9, 165, 199, 207
Press conferences/releases, 138, 240
Primary research, 54, 61, 64
Print advertising, 135, 238
PR News, 202
Product marketing campaigns: Caribou Coffee case study:
  implementation, 189
  objectives, 186
  reporting and evaluation, 189
  research, 185
  strategies, 186
  tactics, 186–189
  theories and models, 190–191
Programmatic buying, 15

Project management, in implementation, 150
Prominence, in newsworthiness definition, 156
PRo Tips:
   advertising types, 135
   agenda setting, 6
   best practices, reporting on, 174
   brand research, 57–58
   channel consumption differences, 121–122
   employee engagement, 44
   evaluating theories, 2
   how not to write objectives, 104
   integrating campaigns, 15
   interviewing, 70
   issue prioritization, 80
   listen first, plan second, 26
   measuring without a baseline, 98
   media coverage analysis, 67, 170
   media events, 139
   media relations, 8, 138
   message effectiveness, 132
   newsworthiness, 156
   objective construction, 100
   owned media tactics, 144
   PESO (paid, earned, shared, and owned) media, 18
   positioning campaigns, 125
   power of "yes and…," 81
   scrum approach to change management, 160
   segmentation and beyond, 118–119
   S.M.A.R.T. (specific, measurable, attainable, relevant, and time-bound) objectives, 97
   social media maximization, 42
   social media tactics, 141
   strategic messaging, 11
   strategy crafting, 116–117
   surveys, 65
   SWOT (strengths, weaknesses, opportunities, and threats) analysis, 71
   tactics, 31
Proximity, in newsworthiness definition, 156
pr reporter, 12
PRSA Silver Anvil award, 62–63, 73, 127, 185, 196, 208, 212, 217
Psychographic factors in segmentation, 121
Publications:
   organizational, 143–144
   owned media as, 244–245
Public information model, 9
Publicity, 140
Public relations, context of, 1–13
   agenda setting and agenda building theories, 6–7
   communications goals in, 11–12
   diffusion theory, 4–5
   excellence theory, 2–3
   framing theory, 5–6
   press agentry model, 9
   public information model, 9
   R.A.C.E., R.O.P.E., and R.O.S.I.E. planning models, 10–11
   ROSTIR planning model, 11
   situational crisis communication theory, 7
   systems theory, 3–4
   two-step flow model of communication, 7–8
   two-way asymmetrical model, 9
   two-way symmetrical model, 10
Public Relations Journal, 63
Public Relations Society of America (PRSA):
   APR Study Guide of, 100
   case studies from, 62
   management by objectives and, 95
   marketing described by, 143
   media relations described by, 139
   Silver Anvil Award of, 62–63, 73, 127, 185, 196, 208, 212, 217
Publics:
   goal setting and, 82–84
   identifying, 35–36
   key, 229–231
   research on, 55
   segmentation of, 118–119
   situational theory of, 53, 165
Purposive sample, for surveys, 65

Qualified "yes" approach, 81
Qualitative and quantitative research, 60–61

R.A.C.E. (Research, Action, Communication, Evaluation) planning model, 10–11, 27
Racial Disparity in Breast Cancer Mortality Study of 2012, 208
Radio advertising, 135, 238
Ragas, Matthew W., 122
Rasmussen, Leslie, 191
Raw volume of coverage, 170
Reese's candy, 46–47
Refinement research, 55
Reflective Communication Scrum (van Ruler), 160
"Reimagine, don't recycle" approach to content creation, 141

Relative volume of coverage, 170
Relevance of objectives, 102–103
Renfree, Mark, 202
Reporting and evaluation, 166–183
    Caribou Coffee product marketing campaign, 189
    case study on, 180–183
    concept case on, 180
    digital evaluation metrics, 170–172
    earned media metrics for, 176–177
    formatting, 175
    improvement from, 172
    integrated, 178–179
    media evaluation, 169–170
    objective-driven, 173–174
    overview, 166–167, 166–168
    owned media metrics for, 177–178
    paid media metrics for, 176
    prioritization in, 175
    ROSTIR planning model inclusion of, 32–33
    shared media metrics for, 177
Representative sample, for surveys, 65
Research, Action, Communication, Evaluation (R.A.C.E.) planning model, 10–11
Research, developmental, 54–76
    Caribou Coffee product marketing campaign, 185
    case studies as, 62–63
    case study on, 73–76
    competitor analysis, 68
    concept case on, 72–73
    content analysis, 66–67
    diagnosing problem or opportunity, 55–58
    experimental, 68–69
    focus groups, 70–71
    government data for, 63
    interviews, 69–70
    matching questions with methods in, 226–228
    measuring problem or opportunity, 58–59
    polling and surveys, 64–66
    primary, 64
    scholarly, 63
    secondary, 62
    terminology and techniques in, 59–62
    think tank and nonprofit reports for, 63–64
    trade association, 64
Research, diagnosis, and goal setting, in ROSTIR planning model, 29
Research, goals for, 77–91
    case study on, 89–91
    concept case on, 89
    decision makers and, 87–88
    goal-setting process, 80–85
    iterative planning cycle for, 88
    organization and, 79–80
    overview, 77–79
    writing goals, 85–87
Research, Objectives, Programming, and Evaluation (R.O.P.E.) planning model, 10–11
Research, Objectives, Strategies, Tactics, Implementation, and Reporting/Evaluation (ROSTIR) planning model:
    elements of, 28–33
    overview, 11
    six steps of, 16
Research, Objectives, Strategies and planning, Implementation, and Evaluation (R.O.S.I.E.) planning model, 10–11
Resources, prioritizing, 84–85
Rihanna, 47
Rogers, Everett, 4
Roof, Dylann, 191
R.O.P.E. (Research, Objectives, Programming, and Evaluation) planning model, 10–11, 27
R.O.S.I.E. (Research, Objectives, Strategies and planning, Implementation, and Evaluation) planning model, 10–11
Ross, Jordan, 205
ROSTIR (Research, Objectives, Strategies, Tactics, Implementation, and Reporting/Evaluation) planning model:
    elements of, 28–33
    overview, 11
    six steps of, 16
Ruler, Betteke van, 160

Safko, Lon, 140, 242
Sampling, for surveys, 65, 233
Sayler, Hope, 205
Scan, Track, Analyze, Respond, and Evaluate (STARE) planning model, 10
SCCT (situational crisis communication theory), 7, 203–204
Schauster, Erin, 15
Schneider and Associates, 45–46
Scientific persuasion, 204
Scope of campaign, 82
Scripps Networks, 181
Scrum approach to change management, 160
SCT (social cognitive theory), 221

Search engine marketing (SEM), 135, 182–183, 239
Search engine optimization (SEO), 136–137, 239
Secondary research, 54, 61–62
Segmentation of markets, 118–119
Seize the holidays with Krusteaz (case study), 21–24
Sephora, Inc., 49
Serial publications, 143
Sha, Bey-Ling, 78, 100, 111, 113, 119, 150
Shared (social) media, in PESO model:
   American Greetings *Appreciating Mom* campaign, 197–198
   blogs, 241
   Burger King *Be Your Way* campaign, 52
   campaign example, 46–47
   Can Manufacturers Institute, 182
   Caribou Coffee product marketing campaign, 185–191
   Cincinnati Zoo and Botanical Garden campaign, 202
   community management, 243
   description of, 18–19, 43, 114–115
   exposure, engagement, influence, and action metrics, 172
   Flag for All Mississippians Coalition campaign, 191
   General Mills, 147–148
   Hallmark Cards campaign, 75
   image, video, and interest sharing, 242–243
   Mastercard iPay campaign, 128–129
   microblogging, 242
   Missing Type Campaign, of National Health Service Blood and Transplant (U.K.), 165
   reporting and evaluation metrics, 177
   social media networks, 241–242
   tactics involving, 140–141
   Teens 4 Pink: Sisters Network campaign, 210, 211
   UNICEF Toys in Mourning campaign, 206
   Washington University in St. Louis *responding to Ferguson* campaign, 214–215
Shared Voice Public Relations, 208
Share of voice (SOV), 99, 127
Shaw, Donald, 5
Shift Thinking, 43, 49
Simmons data, 180
Situation, mission *versus,* in goal-setting, 85–86
Situational crisis communication theory (SCCT), 7, 203–204
Situational theory, 53, 165, 199
60 Second Marketer, 11
S.M.A.R.T. (specific, measurable, attainable, relevant, and time-bound) objectives, 96–99, 106, 173
Smith, Ron, 6

Snapchat.com, 42. *See also* Shared (social) media, in PESO model
Social cognitive theory (SCT), 221
Social listening, 15
Social media:
   advertising growth on, 42
   advertising on, 135, 239
   employee engagement and, 44
   influencers in, 114–115
   networks in, 241–242
   overview, 15
   "sponsored posts" on, 116
   tactics for, 141
   when not to use, 236
   See also Shared (social) media, in PESO model
Social Media Bible, The (Safko), 140
Social sphere, 25
Soft costs, in budgets, 151
SOV (share of voice), 99, 127
Spokespersons, as organizational resources, 123
"Sponsored posts," on social media, 116, 136
Stacks, Don W., 55, 78, 100
Stakeholders, 20, 229–231
Stand-alone publications, 143
STARE (Scan, Track, Analyze, Respond, and Evaluate) planning model, 10
State University of New York at Buffalo (SUNY), 6
Strategic communication campaigns, 25–39
   case study on, 36–39
   concept case on, 35–36
   implementing, 33–34
   plan elements, 28–33
   planning purposes, 26–28
Strategic Communications Planning (Wilson and Ogden), 86
Strategic communication targets, 20
Strategic messaging, 11
Strategies, 110–121
   audiences in choosing, 119–122
   Caribou Coffee product marketing campaign, 185
   case study on, 127–130
   competitive landscape and, 124–126
   concept case on, 126–127
   organization strengths and resources in, 122–124
   overlap in PESO model, 115–119
   PESO model of channels, 112–115
   ROSTIR planning model inclusion of, 30
   social media, when not to use, 236
   synthesis demonstrated by, 111

Strengths, weaknesses, opportunities, and threats (SWOT) analysis, 71–72, 237
Subject matter expertise, as organizational resource, 123
Surveys:
    conducting, 224–226
    developing, 232–233
    polling and, 64–66
Swann, Patricia, 53
SWOT (strengths, weaknesses, opportunities, and threats) analysis, 71–72, 237
Symmetrical model, 191
Systems theory, 3–4, 217–218

Tactics, 131–148
    Caribou Coffee product marketing campaign, 185–189
    case study on, 146–148
    concept case on, 146
    earned media, 136–140
    overview, 131–132
    owned media, 141–145
    paid media, 133–136
    ROSTIR planning model inclusion of, 30–32
    shared media, 140–141
Teams, implementation, 152
Teens 4 Pink: Sisters Network campaign, 208–212
Television advertising, 135, 238
Texas Council on Family Violence, 30
Think tanks, reports from, 63–64
360i search and digital agency, 36, 90–91
360 Public Relations, 21–23
Timeliness, in newsworthiness definition, 156
Timing:
    earned media, 137
    implementation, 152–153
    owned media, 142
    paid media, 133–134
    reporting and, 175
    shared media, 140
Trade associations, research by, 64
Triangulation, to increase research validity, 62
Turner, Jamie, 11
Twitter.com, 23–24, 42. *See also* Shared (social) media, in PESO model
Two-step flow model of communication, 7–8, 190
Two-way asymmetrical model, 9, 130
Two-way symmetrical model, 10, 24, 195, 212

Uncontrolled media, 113, 136–137
Under Armour, Inc., 44–45
UNICEF *Toys in Mourning* campaign, 205–207
Uniqueness, in positioning campaigns, 237
United Nations, 33
University of Florida, 63
USA Today, 46
U.S. Census Bureau, 63, 120
U.S. Department of Agriculture (USDA), 201
Using Research in Public Relations (Broom and Dozier), 58
U.S. Soccer Women's National Team, 45
U.S. Supreme Court, 21

Validity of research, 61–62
Vision, as organizational resource, 123–124
Vonn, Lindsey, 45

Wakey, Wakey Eggs and Bakey! case study, 36–39
Walt Disney Parks & Resorts, 47–48
Washington University in St. Louis *responding to Ferguson* campaign, 212–217
Watson, Tom, 167–169
Websites, 115, 142–144, 243–244. *See also* Owned media (content), in PESO model
Weighted volume of coverage, 170
White House Office of Digital Strategy, 33–34
Wiley Guide to Project Organization and Project Management Competencies, The (Morris and Pinto), 150
Wilson, Laurie J., 79, 86

Xavier University (Cincinnati, OH), 191

"Yes and…" approach, 81
YouTube.com, 42. *See also* Shared (social) media, in PESO model

Zelley, Elaine D., 2
Zoch, Lynn, 8
Zynga's Farmville game, 182